UNIVERSITY LIBRARY
UW-STEVENS POINT

W9-BJN-566

Political Science Research Methods

Political Science Research Methods

Janet Buttolph Johnson
University of Delaware

Richard A. Joslyn
Temple University

A division of Congressional Quarterly Inc.
1414 22nd Street N.W., Washington, D.C. 20037

Copyright © 1986 Congressional Quarterly Inc.

All rights reserved. No part of this publication may be reproduced or transmitted in any form or by any means, electronic or mechanical, including a photocopy, recording, or any information storage and retrieval system, without permission in writing from the publisher.

Printed in the United States of America

Library of Congress Cataloging in Publication Data

Johnson, Janet Buttolph, 1950-
    Political science research methods.

    Includes bibliographies and index.
    1. Political science—Research—Methodology.
I. Joslyn, Richard.   II. Title.
JA73.J64 1986   320′.072   85-30732
ISBN 0-87187-329-X

JA
71
.J55
1986

To our families

Art, Ross, and Ned,
Kathy, Erin, and Andrew

358584

335584

Preface

Fifteen years ago it was a rarity for students of political science to be encouraged, let alone required, to study the methods of empirical research and hypothesis-testing. Much has transpired in the intervening decade-and-a-half so that today it has become commonplace to include such coursework in the curriculum. While we applaud this change, we recognize that the addition of courses in social science research methods has not always been handled well by curriculum designers nor welcomed by the students themselves. This book is our attempt to provide political science students with an introduction to empirical research methods that is, in the parlance of the day, as "user-friendly" as possible.

In the pages that follow we have been guided by three main objectives. First, we have attempted to demonstrate that the research methods we describe have been used by political scientists to produce worthwhile knowledge about significant political phenomena. Several case studies of political science research illustrate important aspects of the research process. Through these and other examples of the actual research efforts of political scientists, we hope that students will see how research methods can enhance the study of almost any area of politics.

Second, we have tried to arm our readers with the tools necessary not only to conduct empirical research projects of their own but also to evaluate others' research. Of the two enterprises the latter may be more important in these days when assessments must frequently be made on research topics such as the deterrent effects of crime control procedures, the results of income maintenance and child nutrition programs, and the impact of campaign spending on elections. While most students probably will seldom be in a position to design and conduct a research project of their own from start to finish, throughout their adult lives they will be asked to respond to the measurement schemes, research designs, and causal claims of researchers.

Third, we have attempted to make the statistical procedures and calculations that are a part of social science research methods accessible to students with modest mathematical backgrounds. Consequently, the use of complicated mathematical formulas has been kept to a minimum, and the statistics we explain require a familiarity with algebra only. Thus students who are mathematically unsure of themselves should not be intimidated by the techniques covered herein and should be able to see the utility of the statistics presented.

Like any authors, we have incurred a number of debts to those who have so graciously helped us in the preparation of this book. We would like to acknowledge the contribution of several people in particular: our former instructors—David Karns, E. W. Kelley, and Douglas VanHouweling—for acquainting us with the research analysis techniques when it was less fashionable to do so; our own students who, unknown to them, allowed us to use them as a pre-test for many of the presentations that made it into the book, and an equal number that were discarded; the secretarial staff at our two universities—Gloria Basmajian at Temple University and Pamela De Mond, Ginger Carroll, and especially Pat Traynor at the University of Delaware—who patiently transformed our seemingly indecipherable scribblings into readable text far more quickly and expertly than we had any right to expect; our editors at CQ Press—Joanne Daniels, Barbara de Boinville, Carolyn Goldinger, and Nola Healy Lynch—who worked diligently to turn our manuscript into lucid prose; and our reviewers—David Nice and Robert Weissberg—who amazed us with their ability to reveal all of the weaknesses in the manuscript that we thought we had so cleverly disguised. We can only hope that they will conclude that their efforts were not in vain and that the book has benefited from their cogent and penetrating comments. Finally, we would like to acknowledge the contribution of our spouses, children, and pets, who endured our frequent threats that they would be left out of the acknowledgments and who, in fact, provided us with the encouragement, distraction, and comic relief necessary to see the project through to completion.

Contents

Tables and Figures

Tables

Figures

Political Science Research Methods

1. *Introduction*

This book is an introduction to the process and methods of using *empirical research*—research based on the actual, "objective" observation of phenomena—to achieve scientific knowledge in political science. Scientific knowledge, which will be discussed in more detail in Chapter 2, differs from other types of knowledge such as intuition, common sense, superstition, or mystical knowledge. One difference involves the way in which scientific knowledge is acquired. In conducting empirical research the researcher adheres to certain well-defined principles for collecting, analyzing, and evaluating information. *Political science,* then, is simply the application of these principles to the study of phenomena that are political in nature.

There are two major reasons for learning about how political scientists conduct empirical research. First, citizens in contemporary American society are often called upon to evaluate empirical research about political phenomena. Debates about the wisdom of the death penalty, for example, frequently hinge on whether it is an effective deterrent to crime. Similarly, policy debates about using busing to achieve racial desegregation of the nation's schools involve conclusions about the effects of segregated schools on student performance. In these and many other cases, thoughtful and concerned citizens find that they must evaluate the accuracy and adequacy of the research done by political (and other social) scientists.

A second reason for learning these research methods is that students often need to acquire scientific knowledge of their own. Whether it be a term paper for an introductory course on American government, a research project for an upper-level seminar, or a series of assignments in a course devoted to learning empirical research methods, students of political science are increasingly being asked to conduct empirical research of their own conception and design. Familiarity with empirical research methods is generally a prerequisite to making this a profitable endeavor.

The prospect of learning empirical research methods is often intimidating to students. Sometimes students dislike this type of inquiry because it involves numbers and statistics. Although a complete understanding of research does include a basic knowledge of statistics and the use of statistics in analyzing and reporting research findings, the empirical research process that we will describe here is first and foremost a way of thought and a prescription for disciplined reasoning. Statistics will be introduced only after an understanding of the thought process involved in scientific inquiry is established and then in a nontechnical way that should be understandable to any student familiar with basic algebra.

Students are also sometimes uneasy about taking a course in social science research methods because they view it as unrelated to other courses in their political science curriculum. But an understanding of the concepts normally included in a course in social science research methods is integrally related to a student's assimilation, evaluation, and production of knowledge in other courses. An important result of understanding the scientific research process is that a student may begin to think more independently about concepts and theories presented in other courses and readings. For example, a student might say, "That may be true under the given conditions, but I believe it won't remain true under the following conditions. . . ." Or, "if this theory is correct, I would expect to be able to observe the following. . . ." Or, "before I'm going to accept that interpretation, I'd like to have this additional information. . . ." Students who are able to specify the information that is needed and the relationships between phenomena that must be observed in support of an idea are more likely to develop an understanding of the subjects they study.

Researchers conduct empirical research studies for two primary reasons. One reason is to accumulate knowledge that will apply to a particular problem in need of solution or to a condition in need of improvement. Research on the causes of crime, for example, may be useful for reducing crime rates, and research on the reasons for poverty may help governments devise successful income maintenance and social welfare policies. Such research is often referred to as *applied research* because it has a fairly direct, immediate application to a real-world situation.

Researchers also may conduct empirical research to satisfy their intellectual curiosity about a subject, regardless of whether the research will lead to changes in governmental policy or private behavior. Political scientists, for example, study why Supreme Court justices reach the decisions they do, and why different states adopt different public policies, quite apart from any desire to modify or influence these practices. Such research is sometimes referred to as *pure, theoretical,* or *recreational research* to indicate that it is not concerned primarily with practical applications.[1]

In this chapter we will describe four social science research projects that were designed to produce scientific knowledge about political phenomena. These examples illustrate a variety of actual research topics and methods of investigation. They also show how decisions about various aspects of the research process affect the conclusions that may be drawn about the phenomena under study. Then, in Chapter 2, the scientific study of politics will be addressed.

Automobile Safety Inspection Policy

Suppose you are trying to decide whether to support a compulsory automobile safety inspection program.[2] Advocates of the program argue that it is an effective method of reducing traffic fatalities. Fewer deaths and injuries resulting from automobile accidents would produce many benefits, among them reductions in the loss of productivity of killed and disabled persons, lower hospital and health care costs, and lower automobile replacement and repair costs, not to mention less pain and suffering associated with death and injury.

There are also costs associated with safety inspection systems, however. These include administrative and enforcement costs and costs to the automobile owner—namely, inspection fees, loss of use of the car during examination, and inconvenience. Other potential costs may be a reduction of incentives for automobile manufacturers to build safer cars with fewer mechanical defects and more durable components as well as the political costs of adverse citizen reaction to unnecessary repairs and to increased governmental bureaucracy and coercion.

Your evaluation might be easier if you knew whether automobile safety inspection programs in other states had been effective in reducing automobile related death rates. A comparison of automobile death rates in states with inspection programs with the death rates in states without inspection programs would provide one source of information about such an effect.

In this study, which illustrates the promise and limitations of research on the impact of governmental policies, average automobile death rates were calculated for 1966, 1967, and 1968. A three-year period was used to reduce the effect of an abnormal death rate for a state in a given year (for example, due to a bus accident or to a freak ice storm during rush hour in a state with normally warm winter weather). Figure 1-1 shows that states with inspection systems had a lower average death rate (26.1 deaths per 100,000 persons per year) than those states without inspection systems (31.9 deaths per 100,000 persons per year). All but three of the inspected states had averages less than the overall average of the noninspected states. The difference of almost 6 deaths per 100,000 people between states with and without inspection systems translated into a difference of 15,000 lives per year. If this difference is due to

Figure 1-1   Average Death Rates in Inspected vs. Uninspected States

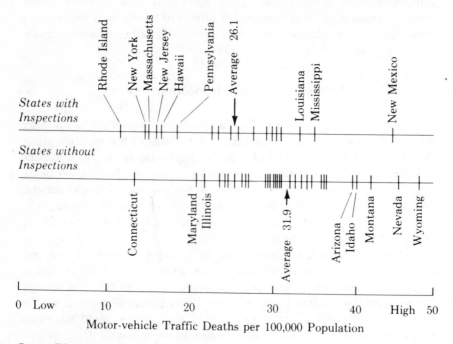

Motor-vehicle Traffic Deaths per 100,000 Population

Source: Edward R. Tufte, *Data Analysis for Politics and Policy,* © 1974, p. 13. Adapted by permission of Prentice-Hall, Inc., Englewood Cliffs, New Jersey.

inspection systems, it would be strong evidence that inspection systems are effective and beneficial.

However, the data in Figure 1-1 indicate it is likely that factors other than the existence of automobile inspections affect automobile fatality rates. For example, New Mexico, an inspected state, had a very high death rate (45.0) compared with other inspected states, while Connecticut, an uninspected state, had a very low death rate (14.7). Other methods of measuring fatality rates or inspection systems might also yield other results. Therefore, the researcher investigated other possible measures and causes of automobile fatalities to see if the benefits of automobile inspections had been accurately estimated.

First, since different states provided different types of inspection systems, the quality of the state inspections was investigated. If inspection systems really do make a difference, one would expect automobile death rates to decrease as the quality of the inspection system increases. The quality of inspections, however, was found to have only a slight impact on the fatality rate.

Second, the differences in the distances traveled by people in different states was taken into consideration by measuring the number of deaths per 100 million miles traveled. One might suspect that the automobile fatality rate depends more on the amount of automobile travel than on the existence of state inspections. However, inspected states also experienced a lower death rate per 100 million miles traveled than uninspected states, 5.48 deaths versus 5.95 deaths, respectively.

Third, the effect of population density was analyzed and was found to be strongly related to death rates. Sparsely populated states had higher fatality rates than densely populated ones. This makes sense since drivers in sparsely populated states go further at higher speeds. Yet even after taking distance into account, by measuring deaths per 100 million miles driven, death rates were higher in thinly populated states. This may have been due to the smaller likelihood of an accident victim being discovered promptly and being close to a hospital. Because of the relationship between population density and death rates, death rates were adjusted to take population density into account. The result was a finding of 2.5 fewer deaths per 100,000 people in inspected states than in uninspected states.

This study would provide useful information to a citizen faced with the decision whether to support a mandatory automobile inspection program. There is some strong evidence, after all, that states with inspections have fewer fatalities than states without inspections, even considering the amount of automobile travel and population density of a state. There would seem to be, then, some tangible benefit to having an automobile inspection policy.

But the information is not definitive. Other variables, such as the weather, could have influenced the relationship between lower death rates and inspection systems. States with hazardous weather could have higher death rates. On the other hand, states with chronic bad weather could have better road maintenance and more experienced drivers. Thus bad weather could affect death rates only in states where severe weather is relatively unusual. Also note that the study did not compare the death rates within the same state before and after inspection programs were adopted, so it is not known how quickly the benefit of having inspections is realized. Before making a decision to support a safety inspection program, a citizen might also want to consider the effectiveness and benefits of alternatives to inspection programs, such as a crackdown on drunken driving and improvements in the interior of vehicles to reduce injury in case of an accident. Nonetheless, despite the limitations of this study, it does provide useful information concerning the automobile safety inspection issue.

Money in Congressional Elections

If running for Congress is among your future plans, or if you wonder how your representative's campaign coffer affected his or her election chances, then *Money in Congressional Elections* will be of interest to you.[3] Author Gary C. Jacobson provides convincing evidence concerning the effects of campaign spending. Money in congressional elections is vitally important, says Jacobson, especially to challengers trying to unseat incumbents.

Elections to the House of Representatives have not been very competitive in recent years. A high percentage of incumbents seek and win reelection each year (the percentage of first-term House members has declined steadily since the Civil War), and incumbents are winning reelection by greater electoral margins. Jacobson discusses institutional changes in Congress and in voting behavior that explain this increase in incumbent security and that point to the importance of campaign spending by challengers.

Congressional reforms have given members opportunities to advertise their names, to take credit for desirable government decisions, and to take positions on policies favored by constituents without necessarily taking any effective action. Official perquisites—such as congressional staff, trips home to the district, franking privileges, and media access to constituents back home—have all increased. These changes help incumbents develop greater visibility and name recognition and improve their reelection chances.

In addition, voters' ties to political parties have been weakening. Party affiliation is being replaced by name recognition as a voting cue. Since voters are more likely to recognize the names of incumbents than the names of challengers, this produces a benefit for incumbents. Even though information about candidates does not always evoke a positive response by voters, name recognition itself is an important resource that incumbents usually possess in abundant supply. To make up for this advantage, challengers must try to increase their recognition during the election campaign by meeting or exceeding incumbent spending levels.

Using data for 1972, 1974, and 1976, Jacobson found that campaign expenditures were—as expected—more important to challengers than to incumbents. Challengers for U.S. House seats in 1972 and 1974 gained slightly more than 1 percent of the vote for every $10,000 dollars they spent. Among challengers for U.S. Senate seats, as spending per voter increased, a challenger's vote percentage also increased. In 1972, as spending per voter increased from nothing to 6.25 cents the Senate challenger's vote percentage increased by 11.5 percentage points; thereafter, each time spending doubled, an additional 4.4 percentage point increase was observed. (Similar calculations were made for 1974 and

1976.) The increase in vote percentages for identical increases in incumbent spending was less than that of challengers. In fact, heavy spending by incumbents was positively related in some cases to *challengers'* victories. In these cases, spending by incumbents was a reaction to the seriousness of the challenge they were facing, and even though they increased their spending, they lost the election.

Jacobson considers the possibility that votes and expenditures are related because more money is contributed to candidates who are expected to do well, and the very characteristics that help candidates attract votes help them attract money. Even after taking into account this reciprocal relationship, however, campaign spending was still shown to be more useful to challengers than to incumbents in gaining voter recall of candidates' names. In 1972, challengers who spent more than $150,000 were as likely as incumbents to be remembered by voters. Thus, the benefits of incumbency in terms of exposure were overcome in these contests, and other differences between the incumbent and challenger determined the outcomes.

Jacobson's research provides useful information for prospective congressional candidates and for citizens. It allows challengers to estimate how much money would have to be spent to overcome the prior advantage in name recognition enjoyed by incumbents. And it enables citizens to gain a clearer understanding of national policy regarding campaign finance. Jacobson concludes that subsidies to candidates would enhance electoral competition and limits on campaign expenditures would decrease it, since the limits might prevent a challenger from mounting a viable campaign.

Several precautionary notes should be sounded about Jacobson's conclusions, however. He relied on the campaign finance reports that candidates filed with the Federal Election Commission. Some doubt exists about how accurately these reports reflect the amount of money actually spent: money spent independently on behalf of candidates is not included in candidates' reports. Such independent spending—that is, spending by individuals and groups unaffiliated with a particular candidate—has increased since Jacobson conducted his research in the 1970s. Another limitation to the study is that other factors besides money may have accounted, at least in part, for the success or failure of challengers, even though Jacobson considered many factors in addition to spending in the races he studied.

Foreign Investments

Suppose you are interested in the causes of civil disorder and conflict in different countries. You may be concerned with this question simply because of your intellectual curiosity about an important political phenomenon, or you may have a professional interest in the subject. For example, you might be the person in charge of overseas investments for a large corporation. If deciding where to locate manufacturing plants in other countries is your job, then you must protect the corporation's investments and assess the chances that production will be disrupted or employees threatened by the outbreak of internal violence. Since the plant's operation will increase the supply of jobs and boost the economy of the nation in which it is located, a decision *not* to locate a plant in a nation is an important one. An error in your calculations would be extremely costly, both to your employer and to the nations involved.

With these thoughts in mind, you decide that you would like information about the incidence of internal violence abroad. Also you would like to know what factors lead to violence in nations and how to measure these factors. Thus you are seeking theories on the causes of violence as well as empirical information that will allow you to use those theories to assess the likelihood of violence in particular countries.

Why Men Rebel by Ted Robert Gurr is a source you might consult.[4] Gurr has developed the concept of relative deprivation to explain and predict political violence. The concept is based on the belief that frustration leads to aggression. Gurr states that a gap may exist between the goods and conditions to which people believe they are rightfully entitled and those that they think they are capable of attaining or maintaining. This gap, or relative deprivation, causes frustration and under the right conditions leads to political violence. Relative deprivation can result from 1) a decline in capabilities while expectations increase, 2) a decline in capabilities while expectations remain the same, or 3) an increase in expectations while capabilities of attaining these expectations are perceived to remain constant. Thus absolute deprivation in objective terms does not lead to frustration if expectations are equally low.

Gurr produced a measure of relative deprivation in 13 nations based on the responses of individuals to opinion polls administered from 1957 to 1963. The polls asked respondents how they compared their past, present, and future position with their ideal of a good life. When this measure of relative deprivation was related to the magnitude of turmoil in the countries between 1961 and 1965, a fairly strong relationship was found, supporting the theory that the greater the relative deprivation, the greater the internal violence.

Gurr suggests that relative deprivation is influenced by a number of factors, including economic well-being, power values such as physical security and ability to participate in politics, and interpersonal values such as social status, family happiness, and moral and ethical standards. Whether or not relative deprivation leads to political violence (defined by Gurr as violent political strikes, riots, coups d'état, civil wars, and revolutions) depends upon the extent and intensity of shared discontent by members of a society and the degree to which the political system and political actors are blamed. Moral and social attitudes toward violence and expression of aggression, the use of alternative methods of redress, the expected utility of violence, and the extent of coercive measures practiced by the ruling regime also affect the likelihood of political violence.

Group expectations are related to the greatest gains experienced by other groups perceived to be socioeconomically similar, Gurr suggests. For instance, wage and benefit demands by one set of municipal workers are related to the gains by similar sets of municipal workers more than they are related to similar or dissimilar groups of workers in the private sector. Gurr also takes note of the theory that exposure to Western ways of life makes non-Westerners discontented with their own way of life and that migration to urban areas raises expectations unreasonably and hence leads to violence. These possibilities might be of special interest to you if you were considering investments in non-Western nations or in nations experiencing rapid migration to urban areas.

The relationship between relative deprivation and civil unrest is a complex one, involving the measurement of phenomena that are difficult to measure and the inclusion of many other variables. Nonetheless, Gurr's research would provide you with a theoretical basis for understanding the causes of political violence and with the means necessary to predict where civil unrest would be least likely to occur.

Busing

The policy of busing children to achieve racial balance in public schools evokes strong emotions and has been hotly contested at every level of politics: local, state, and national. Across the nation, school officials and community leaders are wrestling with the task of implementing court-ordered busing plans. Citizens interested in evaluating desegregation plans as well as implementers of the law may find recent research on whites' opposition to busing useful.

In their article "Whites' Opposition to 'Busing': Self-Interest or Symbolic Politics?" David Sears, Carl Hensler, and Leslie Speer investigate the ability of two models of politics to explain opposition to busing.[5] The first is called the *self-interest model*, which claims that self-interest determines attitudes toward policy issues. In other words, individuals choose policy positions that enable them to minimize losses and maximize gains to their "tangible" private well-being. Tangible costs and benefits include economic ones as well as safety and the protection of one's children. Individuals also adopt policy attitudes that are based on their personal experience. Those who are personally harmed in a tangible way by a policy will adopt negative attitudes toward the policy; those who are not harmed will not.

According to the *symbolic politics model,* adult policy attitudes are shaped by predispositions acquired in early life. "Whether or not the issue has some tangible consequences for the adult voter's personal life is irrelevant. One's relevant personal 'stake' in the issue is an emotional, symbolic one; it triggers long-held, habitual responses." [6]

The authors argue that whites' opposition to busing could be based on self-interested concerns such as fears that their own children will be bused, reduction in property values due to the loss of neighborhood schools, and increased taxes to pay for busing. On the other hand, "symbolic politics" opposition is likely to be associated with longstanding political predispositions such as racial prejudice and political conservatism.

Using survey data from a 1972 election study, the authors measured an individual's self-interest in the busing issue, degree of racial intolerance, political conservatism, and degree of opposition to busing for racial integration. They found that the symbolic political attitudes of racial intolerance and political conservatism predicted antibusing attitudes quite well; self-interest did not. Even when looking only at individuals who lived in areas where busing was happening or was threatened, opposition to busing was related to symbolic attitudes, not to whether an individual had a child in public school or whether the neighborhood schools were white.

An article by John McConahay leads to a similar conclusion: racial attitudes, not self-interest, influence attitudes toward busing. [7] On the basis of his findings, McConahay makes several recommendations for the implementation of school busing plans:

> Obviously, one thing that will not be effective is to call busing opponents ... racist. Most do not think they are any sort of racist now, and showing them a great deal of data and the analysis of a social scientist or two will not cause them either to accept their beliefs as racist or to change their minds about busing.
>
> Much more effective would be to push ahead with busing where it is necessary and at the same time deal constructively with the symbolic needs of whites. Actions and words by court, school and public officials showing that whites' values and needs are recognized officially will symbolize to whites that they also are respected. One approach might be to institute highly visible programs designed to make the school system attractive to white parents and students. ... [T]hese programs would be open to all students, of course, and not only whites are concerned about having these programs in the schools. [8]

This suggestion for additional programs could appeal to the self-interested individual weighing costs and benefits of busing. The greater value of such programs, however, is symbolic, both to those directly affected by busing and to those opposed to busing whose self-interest is not affected.

As these few examples illustrate, empirical research in political science is useful for satisfying intellectual curiosity and for improving real-world political conditions. Conducting empirical research is not a simple process, however. The information a researcher chooses to use, the method that he or she follows to investigate a research question, and the statistics used to report research findings may affect the conclusions that are drawn. For example, several of these studies employed surveys, yet surveys are not always an accurate reflection of people's ideas, beliefs, and behavior. In addition, the manner in which a researcher measures the phenomena of interest can affect the conclusions that are reached. Tufte, for example, chose to average death rates for a three-year period rather than rely on a single year's rate. He also measured deaths per 100,000 persons and per 100 million miles. Other ways of measuring these phenomena might well have affected his conclusions. Moreover, several researchers relied on information collected by others, particularly government agencies. Can one always find readily available data to investigate a topic? If not, does one choose a different topic or collect data oneself? How does one collect data firsthand? Finally, do research findings based on the study of particular people, communities, or countries have general applications to all people, communities, or countries? Developing answers to these questions depends on an understanding of the process of scientific research, the subject of this book.

Chapter 2 examines exactly what is meant by *scientific research,* and the development of empirical political science. In Chapters 3 and 4 we introduce the building blocks of scientific research. In Chapter 3 concepts, hypotheses, variables, units of analysis, and the relationship between social theories and hypotheses are discussed. Developing good hypotheses is especially important since they are the basic statement of the problem or question that a researcher plans to investigate. Chapter 4 covers measurement, a topic that is essential in testing hypotheses. Chapter 5 addresses research design; good research is well-planned, and there are many choices to be made in designing a research project. We will try to alert the reader to some of the important decisions that should be made before a research project reaches an advanced stage. In Chapter 6 we discuss how and why to conduct background research. This part of the process entails discovering what others have said and found out about your topic. Sampling is the topic of Chapter 7. Quite often researchers study only a portion of a population but extrapolate their findings to the whole population. How one selects a sample and the limits to extrapolation are some of the issues discussed. Collecting data will be discussed in Chapters 8-10, which focus on the methods that are most frequently used by political scientists and that students are likely to find useful in conducting or evaluating empirical research. The subject of Chapters 11-13 is data analysis: how to interpret data and present it to others. In Chapter 14 we evaluate an actual research report, noting how it addresses each step of the research process.

Notes

1. *Recreational research* is a term used by Shively. See W. Phillips Shively, *The Craft of Political Research,* 2d ed. (Englewood Cliffs, N.J.: Prentice-Hall, 1980), chap. 1.
2. This example is based on the research reported in Edward R. Tufte, *Data Analysis for Politics and Policy* (Englewood Cliffs, N.J.: Prentice-Hall, 1974), 5-17.
3. Gary C. Jacobson, *Money in Congressional Elections* (New Haven, Conn.: Yale University Press, 1980).
4. Ted Robert Gurr, *Why Men Rebel* (Princeton, N.J.: Princeton University Press, 1970).
5. David O. Sears, Carl P. Hensler, and Leslie K. Speer, "Whites' Opposition to 'Busing': Self-Interest or Symbolic Politics?" *American Political Science Review* 73 (June 1979): 369-84.
6. Ibid., 371.
7. John B. McConahay, "Self-Interest versus Racial Attitudes as Correlates of Anti-Busing Attitudes in Louisville: Is it the Buses or the Blacks?" *Journal of Politics* 44 (August 1982): 692-720.
8. Ibid., 716-17.

Terms Introduced

Applied research. Research designed to produce knowledge useful in altering a real-world condition or situation.

Empirical research. Based on actual, "objective," observation of phenomena.

Political science. The application of the methods of acquiring scientific knowledge to the study of political phenomena.

Pure, theoretical, or recreational research. Research designed to satisfy one's intellectual curiosity about some phenomenon.

2. *Studying Politics Scientifically*

As Chapter 1 explained, empirical research employs scientific principles and methods of observation and results in scientific knowledge. In this chapter we shall explore the ways in which scientific knowledge is different from other types of knowledge both with respect to the kind of knowledge it is and the method by which it is acquired. Important features of the scientific research process and the scientific study of politics also will be discussed. The chapter concludes with a brief history of political science as a discipline.

Characteristics of Scientific Knowledge

In our daily lives we "know" things in many different ways. For example, we know that the bus will get us to work more quickly than the train will, and that small towns are safer than big cities. We also may "know" that blondes are more fun than brunettes, and that there is life after death. In some cases we know something because we believe what someone has told us. In other cases we know something through personal observation or because it appears to be logical or consistent with common sense.

One particular way in which knowledge is acquired is through a *scientific* process. As we noted earlier, scientific knowledge differs from knowledge derived from myth, casual observation, intuition, belief, or common sense. It has certain characteristics that these other types of knowledge do not share completely: it is empirical and subject to empirical verification, non-normative, transmissible, general, explanatory, and provisional. Each of these characteristics will be examined in turn.

When we say that scientific knowledge is *empirical* we mean that it is "grounded in observation and experience." [1] We can use our senses to observe actual occurrences of some phenomenon (such as political protests, votes cast in the U.S. Senate, invasions of the territory of one nation by another) and to record those observations as accurately as possible. In the examples in Chapter 1, for example, researchers recorded actual occurrences of traffic accidents, political disorder and violence, voting and spending in congressional campaigns, and attitudes toward busing.

By *empirical verification,* we mean that our acceptance or rejection of a statement must be influenced by observation.[2] Thus if we say that New York State has mandatory seat-belt-use legislation, we must be able to provide tangible evidence, such as a copy of the law, to verify the statement. Similarly, as Chapters 3 and 5 will make clear, proposed explanations (that is, statements that claim that the occurrence of a phenomenon is caused by another phenomenon) must be tested in a scientific and logical fashion; they cannot simply be assumed to be true.

The empirical nature of scientific knowledge distinguishes it from mystical knowledge because in the latter case only "true believers" are able to observe the phenomena that support their beliefs, and observations that would disprove their beliefs are impossible to specify. Knowledge derived from superstition and prejudice is usually not subjected to thorough empirical verification either. Superstitious or prejudiced persons are likely to note only phenomena that reinforce their beliefs, while ignoring or dismissing those that do not. Thus their knowledge is based on selective and biased experience and observation. Superstitious people are often fearful of empirically testing their superstitions and resist doing so.

Common sense knowledge as well as knowledge derived from casual observation (for example, pigeon-toed people are more athletic than those whose feet point outward—knowledge based on observation of one's friends) may be valid, yet they do not constitute scientific knowledge until they have been empirically verified in a systematic and unbiased way. Alan Isaak notes that common sense knowledge is often accepted "without question, as a matter of faith," which means that facts are accepted without being explained properly. Common sense knowledge is, therefore, limited and superficial.[3]

Sometimes scrutiny of common sense knowledge can have surprising results. In Ted Gurr's study of civil strife, for example, common sense might have led one to expect that civil violence is apt to occur whenever economic conditions are poor and/or worsen.[4] The evidence accumulated by Gurr, however, indicated that violence is apt to occur when expectations and attainment do not coincide—in other words, when *relative* deprivation (not deprivation itself) is felt. Consequently, in contrast to common sense knowledge, he concluded that conditions can be quite bad and a society relatively peaceful if poor conditions are expected and accepted.

Another good example of the limitations of common sense may be found in a study of presidential campaign rhetoric. In 1960 four televised debates took place between the Republican party's nominee, Richard M.

Nixon, and the Democrats' presidential candidate, John F. Kennedy. In the first debate Kennedy was generally considered to have given the better performance and to have benefited from his more aggressive debating style and attractive personal appearance. Common sense might lead one to expect that a significant portion of the electorate would have decided to vote for Kennedy after that first debate. Evidence collected during the 1960 campaign, however, has indicated that that one debate did not greatly influence voters' candidate preferences. Although there was a noticeable postdebate surge for Kennedy, it was neither of monumental size nor necessarily due to the debate itself. Most people retained their predebate vote intentions. What little surge there was for Kennedy came mainly from wavering Democrats who might have decided to vote for Kennedy anyway before the end of the campaign.[5] In this case, then, common sense might have led to an overestimation of the ease and rapidity with which a single campaign event could alter voters' intentions.

In the examples given in Chapter 1, each of the researchers subjected their ideas and explanations to empirical verification. They observed the phenomena they were trying to understand, recorded instances of the occurrence of these phenomena, and looked for a pattern in their observations that was consistent with their expectations. In other words, a body of empirical evidence was accumulated and presented that gave others an empirical basis for acquiring knowledge about some political phenomenon.

Scientific knowledge is also distinctive in terms of its scope and immediate purpose. The empirical research used to acquire scientific knowledge addresses what is, why, and what might be in the future. It does not typically address whether what is, is good or bad, or what ought to be, although it may be useful in making these types of determinations. Political scientists use the words *normative* and *non-normative* to express the distinction. Normative knowledge evaluates what is and prescribes what ought to be. Empirical knowledge is non-normative.

This is not to say that empirical research is conducted in a valueless vacuum. Often a researcher's values and concerns will determine the topic of research interest, and his or her beliefs will affect the focus of the research. For example, a researcher may feel that crime is a serious problem and that stiffer penalties for those who commit crimes will deter would-be criminals, thereby reducing the crime rate. But the test of the proposition that stiffer penalties will reduce the crime rate should be conducted in such a way that the values of the researcher do not bias the results of the study. It is the responsibility of the researcher to test the proposition without prejudice. It is the responsibility of others to evaluate the research to ascertain whether the conclusions drawn by the researcher are justified and based on valid information. Scientific principles and methods of observation help both the researcher and those who evaluate the researcher's conclusions to perform their tasks.

Even though political scientists may strive to minimize the impact of personal biases when making observations, it is often difficult to achieve total objectivity. A fourth characteristic of scientific knowledge, however, helps to identify and weed out biases that may enter research activities.[6] Scientific knowledge is *transmissible,* by which we mean that the method of knowing is made explicit so that it can be analyzed and replicated. It is transmissible "because science is a social activity in that it takes several scientists, analyzing and criticizing each other, to produce more reliable knowledge."[7] For knowledge to be transmissible the researcher must specify what data were collected and how they were analyzed. A clear description of research procedures allows others to independently evaluate the worth of the research. It also allows other researchers to collect the same information and test the original propositions themselves. If the original results are not replicated using the same procedures, they may be incorrect.

This does not mean that scientific knowledge is accumulated primarily through the exact repetition of research by many researchers. Often research procedures are changed intentionally to see if similar results are obtained under other conditions. Consider, for example, two studies concerning the connection between TV violence and antisocial aggressive behavior among children who view TV.[8] One study compared children in two Canadian towns, one with TV, one without. The researchers found that younger children (ages 11 and 12) from the TV town were less, not more, aggressive; for older children (ages 15 and 16) there was no difference. This research was subsequently criticized because the two towns were not matched closely enough and because other factors related to aggressiveness among children, such as differences in school discipline between the two towns, were not considered. Another study was then conducted involving children in one town, thus avoiding the problem of matching. Children were divided into "high" and "low" TV viewers, with high viewers found to be slightly more aggressive than low viewers. Yet in this study no attempt was made to assess the amount of violence seen on TV. Low viewers could have watched particularly violent programs, so that the difference between the groups would have been minimized. The method of measuring aggressiveness was also suspect.

Thus flaws in a research study often lead others to doubt the results and to design their own tests. This would not be possible, however, if the researchers did not clearly specify their research design and methods. This description of methods and results permits a better assessment of results and allows others to conduct further studies with adjustments in design and measurement. The results of these new studies can then be compared with the earlier results, and a body of evidence concerning the political phenomena in question may be accumulated. In each of the examples in Chapter 1, the researchers revealed enough information about their methods and procedure that others could evaluate the strengths and weaknesses of their research. The way of measuring certain phenomena could be questioned and improved, the range of situations studied could be broadened, and alternate explanations could be tested by other researchers. In this way evidence on a particular aspect of social and political life may be accumulated and, it is hoped, become increasingly informative.

Another important characteristic of scientific knowledge is that it is *general*. Knowledge that describes, explains, and predicts many phenomena rather than a few is more valuable. For example, the knowledge that states with easier voter registration systems have higher election turnout rates than states with more difficult systems is preferable to the knowledge that Wisconsin has a higher turnout rate than Alabama. To know that familiarity with a candidate, rather than similarity of party affiliation, increasingly influences how people vote is general knowledge. It is more useful to someone seeking to understand the outcomes of elections than is the knowledge that John Doe, a Democrat, voted for the Republican candidate for Congress and knew the name of the Republican candidate but not the Democrat's. Knowing that Pennsylvania, which has a safety inspection program, has a lower automobile fatality rate than Georgia, which does not, is less useful to the legislator debating the worth of inspection programs than knowing that inspected states in general have lower average fatality rates than uninspected states. General knowledge is preferred, then, because it accounts for a wider range of phenomena than specific knowledge and helps us understand more of the world in which we live.

Statements that communicate general knowledge are called *empirical generalizations;* they summarize relationships between individual facts.[9] For example, the statement that states with easier voter registration systems have higher turnout rates than states with more burdensome systems connects information about voter registration systems and voter turnout rates in individual states and summarizes that information for many states.

Another characteristic of scientific knowledge is that it is *explanatory*. It provides a reason for a behavior, attitude, or event; it answers a "why" question. For example, one might explain differences in voter turnout among states by differences in the difficulty of their voter registration systems.

As we have seen, scientific knowledge requires the accurate description of attributes and behaviors based on careful observation and measurement. Knowing facts is important—for example, that 45 percent of registered voters voted in a particular election, that 11.2 percent of all teenagers in a city are unemployed, or that the amount of money spent on national defense rose by 2.5 percent. But most political scientists are not content just to describe a factual situation. They are usually interested in identifying the factors that account for or explain patterns in human behavior.

For example, Gurr's theory of relative deprivation offers an explanation for why political violence occurs and why certain combinations of expectations and value attainment are associated with political violence. It is more than a description of where violence occurs. Other political scientists may try to explain why legislatures in some states adopt particular policies, why some people run for office, and why some cities are more fiscally solvent than others.

Accurate description is the basis for observing patterns and regularities in phenomena and for explaining them. One must have as accurate a picture as possible of what *is* before one can determine *why* it is so. History is replete with examples of erroneous explanations that were developed on the basis of inadequate observation. These explanations have been rejected and new ones have taken their place often as the result of technological advances. Recent space exploration, for example, has made it possible to observe many more phenomena in astronomy than ever before and has led to the reappraisal of many theories regarding Saturn's rings, Jupiter's moons, and Mars's red spot. In political science the development of sample surveys has allowed political scientists to study a wide range of human attitudes that previously had been virtually impossible to observe.

Explanatory knowledge is important because it is the basis for *prediction,* the application of explanation to events in the future. In fact, many consider the ultimate test of an explanation to be its usefulness in prediction. Prediction is an extremely valuable type of knowledge since it may be used to avoid undesirable and costly events and to achieve desired outcomes. To protect company investments, the business person in the example in Chapter 1 wanted to avoid countries where political violence was likely. Therefore, explanations of violence that accurately predict where it is likely to occur would be useful to him or her.[10]

But exactly how accurate do scientific explanations need to be? Do they have to account for or predict phenomena 100 percent of the time? Some accept the idea of probabilistic or statistical explanation in which it is not necessary to explain or predict a phenomenon with 100 percent accuracy. But others believe an explanation is acceptable only if it explains or predicts what it purports to explain or predict all the time. In political science, explanations rarely account for all of the variation observed in attributes or behavior. Probabilistic explanations are usually considered acceptable as they are in other disciplines as well.

Explanation is the primary purpose of a *theory*. A "theory's major function is ... to explain singular facts and occurrences, but perhaps more importantly to explain empirical generalizations." [11] Empirical generalizations linking phenomena are a basis for developing explanations. Theories go beyond empirical generalizations, however; they are more powerful and abstract. As Isaak states, "A theory can explain empirical generalizations because it is more general, more inclusive than they are." [12] Theories also have two other functions: "to organize, systematize, and coordinate existing knowledge in a field" and to "predict an empirical generalization—predict that a particular relationship holds." [13] For example, a theory of voting may explain voter turnout by proposing that people generally weigh the costs and benefits of voting: the higher an individual's cost of voting in comparison with the benefits, the less likely he or she is to vote. [14] The more empirical generalizations a theory systematizes and organizes, and the more of them it suggests or predicts, the stronger the theory.

Finally, scientific knowledge is *provisional*. Future research may demonstrate the inadequacy of our understanding of a phenomenon up to that point. New observations, more accurate measurements, improvements in research designs, and the testing of alternative explanations may always reveal the limitations or empirical inadequacies of a body of scientific knowledge. [15] One must always remain open to the alteration and improvement of the understanding of human phenomena. To say that scientific knowledge is provisional does not mean that the evidence accumulated to date can be safely ignored. It does mean, however, that future research could always significantly alter our present understanding. Often when people think of science and scientific knowledge they think of scientific "laws." A scientific law is a "generalization that was tested and confirmed through empirical verification." [16] Generally law refers to generalizations that have held up under repeated testing. The provisional nature of scientific knowledge alerts us to the possibility that future observations may contradict currently accepted laws.

So far we have described the characteristics of scientific knowledge. In the next section we will discuss two ways in which this knowledge is typically produced: induction and deduction. Empirical observation and theories are key elements in both of them.

Acquiring Scientific Knowledge: Induction and Deduction

Induction is the process of reasoning from specific observation to general principle or theory. In induction, observation precedes theory. The researcher objectively observes the phenomena of interest and records those observations. Upon studying them, the researcher notices a pattern or regularity in the data and develops a theory that explains why the pattern has occurred. This theory may also offer an explanation for patterns in other related observations.

For example, imagine that you have made the following three observations. First, the Bemba of South Central Africa live a life of marginal subsistence consisting of nine months of abundance and three months of hunger. Despite deplorable conditions, there is no outbreak of violence or protest among the tribe during the three-month hunger period.[17] Second, the income of American blacks compared with that of whites of equal education rose rapidly during the 1940s and early 1950s but then declined so that half the relative gains were lost by 1960. Violence broke out among blacks in the 1960s.[18] Third, political violence in Europe occurred during the growth of industrial and commercial centers, despite the fact that opportunities for alternatives to the hard life of peasants were created.[19]

In two cases the objective well-being of people declined, but in only one did violence break out. In the other there was no decline in the objective well-being of the people yet violence did occur. Let's assume that in seeking an explanation in the first case, you reason that the cycle of the seasons and its ensuing periods of feast and famine had been experienced for many years and was unlikely to change. In the second case you reason that blacks expected to maintain and continue the gains they had made in the past decade. And in the third case you reason that perhaps all people expected to improve their living conditions, yet some in society were benefiting much more from increased industry and commerce than others. Based on this reasoning, you could conclude that the two latter cases were similar because there was a discrepancy between expected and actual conditions, while in the first there was no discrepancy. From this you might develop the general theory that a discrepancy between expectations and attainable conditions causes discontent, which leads to political violence. Thus you might induce the theory of relative deprivation from a few observations of specific cases of deprivations and violence.

Generally speaking, it is difficult to point to examples of pure induction since often a researcher will start with a hunch and proceed to collect information that he or she expects to show certain patterns in line with the hunch. A hunch is not a full-blown theory, yet it is more than starting with observations alone.

In the second mode of scientific inquiry, *deduction*, theory precedes observation. Deduction is the process of proceeding from general principle or theory to specific observations. On the basis of theory certain phenomena are predicted. Then events are observed and measured to see if they occur as predicted. For example, to test the theory that the earth is flat, it should be possible to find its edge and to sail in a straight line directly away from one's starting point and encounter the edge of the earth before returning to one's starting point. Or take the theory in psychology—the theory of imitation—that new behavior is partly acquired by copying others. If this theory is correct, an increase in the portrayal of sex and violence on TV could be expected to lead to an increase in such behavior among those viewers.[20] To test this theory one might take two groups with similar sex habits or levels of aggression, and expose one group but not the other to TV programs with sex and violence. If the former group exhibits an increase in sexual activity and aggressive or violent behavior, but the latter does not, then one could conclude that TV did affect viewer behavior in accordance with the theory of imitation.

Scientific research typically involves both deduction and induction. Thus a researcher may start with a theory and deduce certain phenomena that he or she will attempt to observe. If the observations are not quite as expected, some modification of the theory will be made and the revised theory subjected to further testing. Sometimes the theory may have to be discarded, and on the basis of observations a new theory will be induced.

For example, Ptolomy's theory that the heavens revolved around the earth was initially developed two centuries before Christ.[21] It was quite successful at predicting the changing positions of planets and stars, but it was not completely successful at predicting other astronomical phenomena. There were many discrepancies between actual astronomical observations and predictions derived from Ptolomy's theory. Astronomers responded at first by making adjustments in Ptolomy's system of compounded circles. Changes in the theory to correct discrepancies in one place created discrepancies in other places, however. Over the centuries the theory became increasingly more complex yet no more accurate. Finally, by the sixteenth century, it was concluded that the Ptolemaic system was so complex and inaccurate that it couldn't be true of nature. Copernicus then suggested an alternative heliocentric theory that the planets revolved around the sun. This theory was simpler and more accurately accounted for a variety of astronomical phenomena.

A good example of social science research that involves both induction and deduction is the work of two psychologists regarding news coverage and social trust.[22] For some time they had been studying the rate at which people would return wallets dropped in the streets of New York City to the addresses of the owners identified inside. To observe this phenomenon the researchers would periodically drop a number of wallets in various locations and wait and see how many were returned. Typically, half the wallets dropped were eventually returned. However, one day something happened that had never happened before: none of the wallets was returned. This unexpected result led them to think about what a plausible explanation for the result would be. Hence, they were involved in developing an explanation based on an observation—induction.

It so happened that the day this particular wallet drop occurred was the day Robert Kennedy was assassinated in June 1968. They wondered: could the assassination have something to do with the failure to recover any of the dropped wallets? Perhaps the news coverage of the event made people upset, socially mistrustful of strangers, and unwilling to help people whom they did not know or had not seen. Hence they hypothesized that exposure to "bad" news makes people less socially trusting and cooperative.

To test this hypothesis the researchers devised a series of experiments in which people were divided into two groups and were subtly exposed to "bad" or "good" news broadcasts. Then they were asked to reveal their attitudes toward other people and to play a game with other people that allowed the observation of how cooperative they were. Thus a general theory was being tested with research designed to measure the occurrence of certain predicted observations—deduction.

The experiments demonstrated that those exposed to bad news were, indeed, less socially trusting and cooperative, confirming the researchers' expectations. Both induction and deduction had been involved in accumulating an empirical, verifiable, transmissible, explanatory, general (yet provisional) body of evidence regarding an important social phenomenon.

Applying an existing theory to new situations, deciding which phenomena to observe and how to measure them, and developing a theory that explains many more things than the specific observations that led to its discovery are all creative enterprises. Unfortunately it is difficult to teach creativity. But being aware of the processes of induction and deduction, and keeping in mind the characteristics of scientific knowledge, will make your own evaluation and conduct of research more worthwhile.

Can Politics Be Studied Scientifically?

We have implied throughout this chapter that politics can and should be studied scientifically. Some people question this assumption, however. Political science involves the study of human beings and the discovery of explanations for the political behavior that they exhibit. This discovery of regularities and patterns of behavior in politics requires that human beings act consistently or in a nonrandom, nonidiosyncratic, or discoverable manner. But if human beings do not act predictably, political scientists cannot explain and predict their political behavior.

Even if one accepts the assumption that human beings are generally predictable, some persons may deliberately act in an unpredictable or misleading manner. This problem may be encountered among subjects "cooperating" in a research project. For example, a person may figure out that he or she is part of an experiment to test a theory about how people will behave when faced with a particular situation. That person may deliberately act in a fashion not predicted by or in conflict with the theory, or that person may alter his or her behavior to conform to what the researcher is looking for. Similarly, a person may never reveal in public, or to another individual, what he or she is really thinking, or what his or her behavior in the past has been or would be in the future. In other words, our ability to observe accurately the attributes of people may be severely limited. For example, it is difficult to develop explanations for why some people use certain drugs when accurate measures of how often people use drugs (especially illegal ones) are notoriously inaccurate.

Measurement problems also arise in political science because the concepts of interest to many political scientists are value-laden. Thus it is difficult to measure objectively these concepts, and value disagreements lead to conflict over which measure to use. For example, one measure of unemployment counts persons who are out of work and actively seeking employment. Some argue that this measure underestimates unemployment because it does not include those who are so discouraged from failure to find a job that they no longer are actively seeking employment.

Political scientists must also deal with the fact that human beings and their behavior are complex, perhaps fundamentally more complex than the subject matter of other sciences (bacteria, elements, subatomic particles, insects, and so on). This complexity poses difficulties for the researcher. For example, the complexity of human behavior is an obstacle to the discovery of general theories in political science that accurately explain and predict a wide range of political behavior. A theory with broad applicability might be extremely cumbersome. Specification of many variables might well be necessary to apply the theory to a large number of situations with any acceptable degree of accuracy. On the other hand, due to the complexity of human behavior, a theory that appears to be relatively simple and elegant may be attacked on the ground that it is fairly easy to find exceptions to it. Certainly no empirically verified propositions in political science match the simplicity and explanatory power of $E = mc^2$.[23]

As in any science, political scientists must deal with obstacles to empirical observation.[24] Because political science is concerned with human behavior and its products, data needed to test theories may be extremely hard to obtain. For instance, those with necessary information (such as the rate of nuclear arms build-up or the possession of racist attitudes) may not want to release it for political or personal reasons. Moreover, because human beings are the subjects of analysis in the social sciences, researchers must contend with ethical considerations. Obtaining certain information may interfere with an individual's right to privacy, for example. In many studies, individuals are informed about the purpose of the research; consequently, some people may not answer questions honestly or may not behave naturally. Others who know the true purpose of a study may not be willing to participate at all. Similarly, some critical experiments to test a theory may manipulate human subjects. Testing the impact of incarceration on subsequent lawful behavior, for example, could conceivably involve placing innocent people in prison. Fortunately, researchers are not given the power to interfere in people's lives in this manner. Other obstacles to observation may arise from technological limitations on measurement and analysis. For example, computers have facilitated storage and analysis of large quantities of information that was not feasible previously, yet it is still difficult to measure accurately attitudes and behavior that are socially undesirable or that typically occur in private.

Despite the difficulties of studying politics scientifically, the scientific approach has had a profound effect on the discipline of political science. The differences between the scientific approach and other approaches to the study of politics are discussed in the remainder of this chapter.

Political Science as a Discipline

The study of politics is often divided into two historical periods: the period of traditional political inquiry and the period of modern or behavioral political science, which did not appear until the 1950s in the United States, although certain developments that are responsible for its appearance took place earlier.

Traditional Political Science

There were three major approaches to the study of politics during the period of traditional political inquiry: historical, legalistic, and institutional.[25] The historical approach produced detailed descriptions of the historical developments leading to political events and other phenomena. The legalistic approach involved the study of constitutions and legal codes. The institutional approach yielded descriptions of the powers and functions of political institutions (legislatures, executive branches, courts, for example). In general, traditional political science focused on formal governmental institutions and their formal powers. Legal and historical documents, such as constitutions, proclamations, and treaties, were studied to trace the development of international organizations and key concepts, such as sovereignty, the state, federalism, and imperialism. Informal political processes, the exercise of informal power, and the internal dynamics of institutions were generally ignored.

Under the traditional approach, the study of politics was usually subsumed in academia under the disciplines of history and philosophy.

Political theories concerning the nature of man and politics, the purpose and most desirable form of government, and the philosophy of law were the province of philosophy departments. When separate departments for the study of politics appeared, they were frequently called departments of government, reflecting the emphasis on governmental institutions rather than on political processes and behavior. In fact, some universities still have government departments.

Traditional political science was primarily descriptive rather than explanatory. While political theorists offered intriguing and well-reasoned theories of politics, these theories or explanations were usually not subjected to extensive empirical verification. Knowledge in political science was not acquired scientifically, nor was there a felt need to produce knowledge that had the characteristics of scientific knowledge.

Modern Political Science

The appearance of the scientific study of politics in the United States can be attributed to several developments.[26] First, numerous European social scientists and theorists came to the United States in the 1930s, many of whom were skilled in the use of new, more scientific research methods.[27] Second, war-related social research in the following decade promoted the exchange of ideas among scientifically minded persons from the disciplines of political science, sociology, psychology, and economics. This research effort was aided by a related development: the collection of large amounts of empirical data and the development of technology and practices to store and process this information. For example, Paul Lazarsfeld pioneered in the development of large-scale survey research while working for the federal government during World War II. In 1940 he conducted the first study of voting behavior based on sample surveys.[28]

Much of the new research focused on the political behavior of individuals and groups, hence the term *behavioral political science*. Unlike traditional political science, modern political science embraces the scientific method.[29] This relationship to the scientific method is illustrated by the assumptions and objectives of behavioralism, which David Easton outlined in his article entitled "The Current Meaning of 'Behavioralism.'" A few of them are listed here:

> There are discoverable uniformities in political behavior. These can be expressed in generalizations or theories with explanatory and predictive value.
> Means for acquiring and interpreting data . . . need to be examined self-consciously, refined, and validated.
> Precision in the recording of data and the statement of findings requires measurement and quantification.
> Ethical evaluation and empirical explanation involve two different kinds

of propositions that, for the sake of clarity, should be kept analytically distinct.

Research ought to be systematic.[30]

Behavioral political science assumes and advocates the search for fundamental units of analysis that can provide a common base for the investigation of man by all social scientists. For example, some political scientists suggest that groups are an important unit on which to focus, while others suggest that decision-making and decisions are.[31] There is hope that a few units of analysis will be found and focused upon much the same as physicists and chemists focus on atoms, molecules, and the like.

The reaction to behavioral and empirical political science has not been entirely positive. Critics of empirical political science point to the trivial nature of applications of scientific methods to politics. Common sense would have told the average person the same thing, they argue. As explained earlier, however, there is a difference between common sense knowledge and scientific knowledge. In order to build a solid base for further research and accumulation of scientific knowledge in politics, common sense knowledge must be empirically verified. Common sense is, after all, frequently wrong.

Some political scientists have also been concerned about the prominence of nonpolitical factors in explanations of political behavior. Psychological explanations that stress the effect of personality on political behavior or economic explanations that attempt to show how people behave in terms of costs and benefits, incentives and disincentives, offer competing ways of understanding political phenomena for those used to studying political institutions and political philosophies. To them it looks like political inquiry is being fundamentally altered by the concepts, language, and methods of other disciplines.

A more serious criticism of the scientific study of politics is that it leads to a failure to focus enough scholarly research attention on important social issues and problems. Not only is this research conducted in an objective, value-free, scientific fashion, some say, but the values, moral questions, and philosophical topics to which the research can be related are seldom considered. The implications of research findings for important public policy choices are rarely addressed. Some also argue that the quest for scientific knowledge of politics has led to a focus on topics that are quantifiable and relatively easy to verify empirically but that are not related to significant, enduring, and relevant social concerns.[32] One response to these criticisms has been renewed interest in normative political philosophy, that is, in questions of "what ought to be" rather than "what is." [33] Others have responded by turning their attention to public policy, the policymaking process, and policy analysis.[34] Many political scientists who study these topics apply scientific methods to socially relevant and important questions.

Conclusion

In this chapter we have described the characteristics of scientific knowledge and the scientific process of investigation. We have presented reasons why political scientists are attempting to become more scientific in their research and have discussed some of the difficulties associated with empirical political science. We have also touched on questions that exist about the value of the scientific approach to the study of politics. Despite these difficulties and questions, the empirical approach is widely embraced, and students of politics need to be familiar with it. In the next chapter we shall begin to examine how to take a general topic or question about some political phenomenon and develop a strategy for investigating that topic scientifically.

Notes

1. Alan C. Isaak, *Scope and Methods of Political Science,* 4th ed. (Homewood, Ill.: Dorsey Press, 1985), 106.
2. Ibid., 107.
3. Ibid., 66; see also 67.
4. Ted Robert Gurr, *Why Men Rebel* (Princeton, N.J.: Princeton University Press, 1970).
5. Kurt Lang and Gladys Engel Lang, *Politics and Television* (Chicago: Quadrangle Books, 1968), chap. 6.
6. Isaak, *Scope and Methods,* 30.
7. Ibid., 31.
8. The studies are reported in J. J. Eysenck and D. K. B. Nias, *Sex, Violence and the Media* (London: Maurice Temple Smith, 1978), 103-104.
9. Isaak, *Scope and Methods,* 103.
10. For a discussion of prediction, see Edward R. Tufte, *Data Analysis for Politics and Policy* (Englewood Cliffs, N.J.: Prentice-Hall, 1974), chap. 2, 36-40.
11. Isaak, *Scope and Methods,* 167.
12. Ibid.
13. Ibid., 167, 169.
14. See Raymond E. Wolfinger and Steven J. Rosenstone, *Who Votes?* (New Haven, Conn.: Yale University Press, 1980).
15. For discussion of the process of changing scientific knowledge, see Thomas Kuhn, *The Structure of Scientific Revolution,* 2d ed. (Chicago: University of Chicago Press, 1971).

16. Isaak, *Scope and Methods,* 297.
17. Gurr, *Why Men Rebel,* 57.
18. Ibid., 54.
19. Ibid., 51.
20. For a discussion of the theory of imitation and its role in explaining possible effects of increased sex and violence in TV, see Eysenck and Nias, *Sex, Violence and the Media,* 56-59.
21. This example is based on the discussion in Kuhn, *Scientific Revolution,* 68-69.
22. The wallet episode is described in Stephen Holloway and Harvey A. Hornstein, "How Good News Makes Us Good," *Psychology Today,* December 1976, 76-78. The results of the subsequent experiments are discussed in Stephen Holloway, Lyle Tucker, and Harvey A. Hornstein, "The Effects of Social and Nonsocial Information on Interpersonal Behavior of Males: The News Makes News," *Journal of Personality and Social Psychology* 35 (July 1977): 514-22; and in Harvey A. Hornstein, Elizabeth Lakind, Gladys Frankel, and Stella Manne, "Effects of Knowledge about Remote Social Events on Prosocial Behavior, Social Conception, and Mood," *Journal of Personality and Social Psychology* 32 (December 1975): 1038-1046.
23. For further discussion of complete and partial explanations, see Isaak, *Scope and Methods,* 143.
24. See Charles A. McCoy and John Playford, eds., *Apolitical Politics: A Critique of Behavioralism* (New York: Thomas Y. Crowell, 1967).
25. Isaak, *Scope and Methods,* 34-38.
26. Ibid., 38-39. For a history of the development of survey research, see also Earl F. Babbie, *Survey Research Methods* (Belmont, Calif.: Wadsworth, 1973), 42-45.
27. For early American sources of behavioralism, see Charles E. Merriam, *New Aspects of Politics* (Chicago: University of Chicago Press, 1924).
28. Paul F. Lazarsfeld, Bernard Berelson, and Hazel Gaudet, *The People's Choice* (New York: Duell, Sloane and Pearce, 1944).
29. David B. Easton, "The Current Meaning of 'Behavioralism,'" in James C. Charlesworth, ed., *Contemporary Political Analysis* (New York: Free Press, 1967), 11-31.
30. Easton, "Behavioralism," 16-17.
31. David B. Truman, *The Governmental Process* (New York: Knopf, 1951), and Robert A. Dahl, *Who Governs? Democracy and Power in an American City* (New Haven, Conn.: Yale University Press, 1961).
32. See McCoy and Playford, eds., *Apolitical Politics.*
33. Isaak, *Scope and Methods,* 45.
34. Ibid., 46.

Terms Introduced

Behavioralism. The study of politics that focuses on political behavior and embraces the scientific method.

Deduction. A process of reasoning from a theory to specific observations.

Empirical generalization. A statement that summarizes the relationship between individual facts and that communicates general knowledge.

Empirical verification. Demonstration by means of objective observation that a statement is true.

Explanation. A statement that provides a reason for a phenomenon.

General. Applicable to many rather than a few cases.

Induction. A process of reasoning from specific observations to general principle.

Non-normative knowledge. Concerned not with evaluation or prescription but with factual or objective determinations.

Normative knowledge. Evaluative, value-laden, concerned with prescribing what ought to be.

Prediction. The application of explanation to events in the future. The ability to correctly anticipate future events.

Probabalistic explanation. An explanation that does not explain or predict events with 100 percent accuracy.

Provisional. Subject to revision and change.

Theory. A statement or series of statements that organize, explain, and predict knowledge.

Transmissible knowledge. Knowledge for which the method of knowing is made explicit.

Suggested Readings

Isaak, Alan C. *Scope and Methods of Political Science.* 4th ed. Homewood, Ill.: Dorsey Press, 1985.

McCoy, Charles A., and John Playford, eds. *Apolitical Politics: A Critique of Behavioralism.* New York: Thomas Y. Crowell, 1967.

3. The Building Blocks of Social Scientific Research: Hypotheses, Concepts, and Variables

Chapters 1 and 2 discussed what it means to acquire scientific knowledge and presented a number of examples of political science research intended to produce this type of knowledge. In this chapter we will develop a framework for evaluating and acquiring scientific knowledge by explaining the initial steps in an empirical research project. These steps require a researcher to 1) specify the *question* or *problem* with which the research is concerned; 2) develop a suitable *explanation* for the phenomena under study; 3) define the *concepts* thought to be useful in this explanation; and 4) formulate testable *hypotheses*. Although we will discuss these steps as if they represent a logical sequence of thought, in the conduct of actual research the order may vary. They must all be accomplished eventually, however, before a research project can be completed successfully. The sooner the issues and decisions involved in each of the steps are addressed, the sooner the other portions of the research project can be completed.

Specifying the Research Question

One of the most important purposes of social scientific research is to answer questions about social phenomena. The research projects summarized in Chapter 1, for example, all attempt to answer questions about some important political behavior. Why are auto fatality rates higher in some states than in others? Why do some congressional candidates win and others lose? Why is there more political violence in some societies than in others? And why are some people more opposed to busing than others are? In every case the researchers identified some political phenomenon that interested them and tried to answer questions about that phenomenon.

The phenomena investigated by political scientists are diverse and are limited only by whether they are *significant* (that is, would advance our understanding of politics and government), *observable,* and *political.* Political scientists attempt to answer questions about the political behavior of individuals (voters, citizens, residents of a particular area, Supreme Court justices, presidents), groups (political parties, interest groups, labor unions, ethnic organizations), institutions (state legislatures, city governments, bureaucracies, district courts), and nations.

The first task of a researcher is to specify the "why" question with which the research is concerned. That will identify the phenomenon being investigated and will point the research project in the direction of providing an explanation for that phenomenon. Failure to specify the "why" question clearly can lead to confused researchers as well as confused readers.

Where do the research questions of political scientists originate? The answers are several. Some researchers become interested in a topic because of personal observation or experience. For example, a researcher who loses a political campaign may wonder what factors are responsible for electoral success. Some researchers are drawn to a topic because of the research and writing of others. A scholar familiar with studies of congressional decisionmaking may want to investigate the reasons for the success and failure of different public policy proposals. Still others select a research topic because of their interest in some broader social theory, as in the researcher whose fascination with economic theories of rational decisionmaking prompted the study of federal bureaucrats' behavior. Finally, it must be admitted, researchers sometimes select research topics for less lofty reasons: because grant money for a particular subject is available, or because demonstrating expertise in a particular area will advance one's professional career objectives. In short, reasons for selecting research topics differ widely.

The framing of an engaging and appropriate research question will get a research project off to a good start. Any of the following questions would probably lead to a politically significant and informative research project:

Why are some cities more healthy fiscally than others?
Why are some ethnic groups more cohesive than others?
Why are some U.S. senators more liberal than others?
Why do some nations spend more on weapons systems than others do?
Why do some states have more extensive welfare systems than others do?

Students sometimes have difficulty formulating interesting and appropriate research questions. Researchers also occasionally pose questions that are simplistic, trivial, or impossible to answer. A research project will get off on the wrong foot if the question that shapes it is inappropriate, unduly concerned with discrete facts, or focused on reaching normative conclusions.

Political scientists seek knowledge about political phenomena. While the definition of *political phenomena* is vague and inconclusive, it does not include the study of all human characteristics or behavior. For example, research studies guided by questions such as "Why do some people eat eggs for breakfast and others do not?" or "Why did dinosaurs become extinct?" might be interesting studies, but they would be unlikely to yield fresh insights into political phenomena. Questions such as those would be inappropriate for a study of politics and would be better asked by people in fields other than political science.

Research questions may also delimit the significance of a research project if they are unduly focused on discrete facts. Questions such as "Who is the secretary of state?" or "Which interest groups contribute the most money to political campaigns?" or "How many nuclear warheads does the Soviet Union possess?" may yield important factual knowledge, but they will not sustain a research project of the type developed in this book. Each of them asks for one discrete piece of information or fact. While facts are important, they alone will not yield *scientific knowledge*—knowledge about patterns, relationships, and explanations. Scientific knowledge should be consistent with facts, but facts are not enough to yield scientific explanations. Instead one phenomenon must be related to another phenomenon, and generalizations must be advanced and tested. In the absence of such generalizations, factual knowledge of the type called for by the preceding research questions will be fundamentally limited in scope.

Another type of question that is inconsistent with the research methods discussed in this book is a question calling for a *normative* conclusion. Questions such as "Should the United States deploy nuclear missiles in Europe?" or "Is the 'actual malice test' too stringent a guideline for the resolution of libel suits?" or "Are Ronald Reagan's budget proposals unfair to the working poor?" are important and suitable for the attention of political scientists (indeed, for any citizen), but they, too, are inappropriate as presently framed. They ask a normative question or for an indication of what should or ought to be done. Although scientific knowledge may be helpful in answering questions like these, it cannot provide the answers without regard for an individual's personal values or preferences. What someone ultimately likes or dislikes, values or rejects, are involved in the answers to these questions.

Proposing Explanations

Once a researcher has developed a suitable research question or topic, the next step is to propose an explanation for the phenomenon the researcher is interested in understanding. In the previous section we said that most political science research is concerned with answering questions about some political phenomenon. As noted earlier, questions that most political scientists ask are "why" questions in which the researcher is trying to explain the variation in political phenomena—in other words, why political characteristics and behavior occur at some times rather than others, or why they are more likely to be exhibited in some circumstances than in others.

To advance our understanding of political behavior, we propose explanations for a phenomenon and then produce evidence bearing on those explanations. Proposing an explanation involves identifying other phenomena that we think will help us account for the object of our research and then specifying how these two (or more) phenomena are related.

In the research examples described in Chapter 1 the researchers proposed explanations for the political phenomena they were studying. Edward Tufte thought that auto fatality rates might be accounted for by state auto inspection laws. Gary Jacobson thought that congressional election outcomes might be influenced by campaign spending. Ted Gurr thought that political violence might be affected by a population's sense of relative deprivation. And David Sears, Carl Hensler, and Leslie Speer thought that attitudes toward busing might be explained either by racial prejudice or by individuals' cost-benefit analysis of the impact of busing on them and their families.

Those phenomena that we think will help us explain the political characteristics or behavior that interest us are called *independent variables*. Independent variables are the measures of the phenomena that are thought to influence, affect, or cause some other phenomenon. *Dependent variables* are the phenomena that are thought to be caused, to depend upon, or to be a function of the independent variables. Thus if a researcher has hypothesized that acquiring more formal education will lead to increased income later on (in other words, that income may be explained by education), then years of formal education would be the independent variable and income would be the dependent variable.

Proposed explanations for political phenomena are often more complicated than the simple identification of one independent variable that is thought to explain a dependent variable. More than one phenomenon is usually needed to account adequately for most political behavior. For example, suppose a researcher proposes that an individual's income and an individual's attitude toward busing are related, with the higher the income (independent variable), the more liberal the attitude (dependent variable). The insightful researcher would realize the possibility that another phenomenon, such as whether the individual has school-age children, might also affect his or her attitude toward busing. The proposed explanation for attitudes toward busing, then, would involve an alternative variable in addition to the original independent variable, and the researcher would be interested in determining the relative effect of each variable on the dependent variable. This is done by "controlling for" or "holding constant" one of the independent variables so that the effect of the other may be observed. This process will be discussed in more detail in Chapter 13.

Sometimes researchers are also able to propose explanations for how the independent variables are related to each other. In particular, we might want to distinguish between which independent variables come before other independent variables and indicate which have a more direct, as opposed to indirect, effect on the phenomenon we are trying to explain (the dependent variable). Variables that occur prior to all other variables and that may affect other independent variables are called *antecedent variables.* Variables that occur closer in time to the dependent variable and are themselves affected by other independent variables are called *intervening variables.* The role of antecedent and intervening variables in the explanation of the dependent variable differs significantly. Consider these examples.

Suppose a researcher hypothesizes that a person who favors increased military spending is more likely to vote for a Republican presidential candidate than a person who does not favor military spending increases. In this case the attitude toward military spending would be the independent variable and the presidential vote the dependent variable. The researcher might wonder what causes the attitude toward military spending and might propose that those people who are paranoid are more apt to favor increased military spending. This new variable would then be an antecedent variable since it comes before and affects (we think) the independent variable. Thinking about antecedent variables pushes our explanatory scheme further back in time and, it is hoped, will lead to a more complete understanding of a particular phenomenon (in this case presidential voting). Notice how the independent variable in the original hypothesis (favoring increased defense spending) becomes the dependent variable in the hypothesis involving the antecedent variable (paranoia). Also notice that in this example paranoia is thought to exert an indirect effect on the dependent variable (presidential voting) via its impact on attitudes toward military spending.

Now let us consider a second example. Suppose a researcher hypothesizes that the number of years of formal education affects one's chances of turning out to vote. In this case education would be the independent variable and turnout the dependent variable. If the researcher then begins to think about what it is about formal education that has this effect, he or she has begun to identify the intervening variables between education and turnout. For example, the researcher might hypothesize

Figure 3-1   Arrow Diagrams of Military Spending and Voter Turnout
Examples

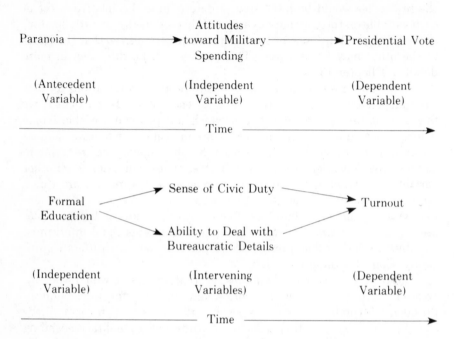

that formal education causes a sense of civic duty, which in turn causes voter turnout, or that formal education causes an ability to deal with bureaucratic detail, which in turn causes voter turnout. Intervening variables come between an independent and dependent variable and help explain the process by which one influences the other.

Explanatory schemes that involve numerous independent, alternative, antecedent, and intervening variables can become quite complex. An *arrow diagram* is a handy device for presenting and keeping track of such complicated explanations. It specifies the phenomena of interest; indicates which variables are independent, alternative, antecedent, intervening, and dependent; and shows which variables are thought to affect which other ones. Figure 3-1 presents arrow diagrams for the two examples we just considered.

In both diagrams the dependent variable is placed at the end of the time line, with the independent, alternative, intervening, and antecedent variables placed in their appropriate locations to indicate which ones come first. Arrows indicate that one variable is thought to explain or be related to another; the direction of the arrow indicates which variable is independent and which is dependent in that proposed relationship.

Figure 3-2 shows two examples of actual arrow diagrams that have been proposed and tested by political scientists. Both are thought to explain presidential voting behavior. In the first diagram the ultimate dependent variable is the "Vote," and is thought to be explained by "Candidate Evaluations" and "Party Identification." "Candidate Evaluations," in turn, is explained by "Issue Losses," "Party Identification," and "Perceived Candidate Personalities." These, in turn, are explained by other concepts in the diagram. The variables at the top of the diagram tend to be antecedent variables; the ones in the center tend to be intervening variables. Nine independent variables of one sort or another figure in the explanation of the vote.

The second diagram also has the "Vote" as the ultimate dependent variable, which is explained directly by only one independent variable, "Comparative Candidate Evaluation." The latter variable, in turn, is dependent upon six independent variables: "Personal Qualities Evaluations," "Comparative Policy Distance," "Current Party Attachment," "Region," "Religion," and "Partisan Voting History." In this diagram 16 variables figure, either indirectly or directly, in the explanation of the vote, with the antecedent variables located around the perimeter of the diagram and the intervening variables more toward the center. Both of these diagrams clearly represent complicated and extensive attempts to explain a dependent variable.

Defining Concepts

One of the primary purposes of political science research is to provide scientific explanations for political phenomena. In this section we will consider what these phenomena are and how our research can be sharpened so that the knowledge we acquire is transmissible, empirical, and general.

Political scientists are interested in why people or social groupings (organizations, political parties, legislatures, states, countries) behave in a certain way or have particular attributes or properties. The words that we choose to describe these behaviors or attributes are called *concepts*. Concepts should be accurate, precise, and informative.

In our daily life we use concepts frequently to name and describe features of our environment. For example, we describe some snakes as poisonous and others as nonpoisonous, some politicians as liberal and others as conservative, some friends as shy and others as extroverted. These attributes or concepts are useful to us because they help us observe and understand aspects of our environment, and they can help us communicate with others.

Concepts also contribute to the identification and delineation of the scientific disciplines within which research is done. In fact, to a large

Figure 3-2   Two Causal Models of Vote Choice

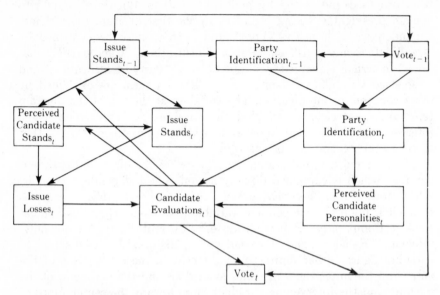

Source: Gregory B. Markus and Philip E. Converse, "A Dynamic Simultaneous Equation Model of Electoral Choice," *American Political Science Review* 73 (December 1979): 1059. Reprinted with permission.

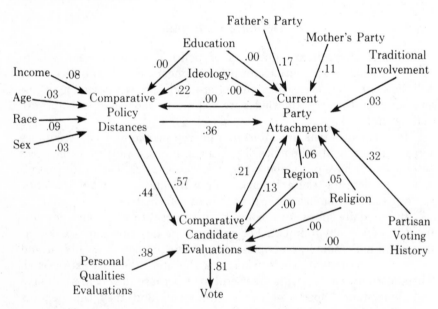

Source: Benjamin I. Page and Calvin C. Jones, "Reciprocal Effects of Policy Preferences, Party Loyalties and the Vote," *American Political Science Review* 73 (December 1979): 1083. Reprinted with permission.

extent a discipline maintains its identity because different researchers within it share a concern for the same concepts. Physics, for example, is concerned with the concepts of gravity and mass (among others); sociology with social class and social mobility; psychology with personality and deviance. By contrast, political science is concerned with concepts such as democracy, power, representation, justice, and equality. The boundaries of disciplines are not well-defined or rigid, however. Political scientists, developmental psychologists, sociologists, and anthropologists share an interest in the socialization process, for example. Nonetheless, because a particular discipline has some minimal level of shared consensus concerning its significant concepts, researchers can usually communicate more readily with other researchers in the same discipline than with researchers in other disciplines.

Concepts are developed through a process by which some human group (tribe, nation, culture, profession) agrees to give a phenomenon or property a particular name. The process is ongoing and somewhat arbitrary and does not ensure that all peoples everywere will give the same phenomena the same names. In some areas of the United States, for example, a "soda" is a carbonated beverage, while in other areas it is a drink with ice cream in it. Likewise, the English language has only one word for love, whereas the Greeks have three words to distinguish between romantic love, familial love, and generalized feelings of affection.[1] Concepts disappear from a group's language when they are no longer needed, and new ones are invented as new phenomena are noticed that require names (for example, computer "programs" and "software," "cultural imperialism," and "hyperkinetic" behavior).

Some concepts—such as "car," "chair," "vote"— are fairly precise because there is considerable agreement about their meaning. Others are more abstract and lend themselves to differing definitions—for example, "liberalism," "crime," "democracy," "equal opportunity," "human rights," "social mobility," "alienation." A similar concept is "orange." Although there is considerable agreement about it (orange is not usually confused with purple), the agreement is less than total (whether a particular object is orange or red is not always clear).

. Unfortunately, most interesting concepts that political scientists deal with lack a completely precise, shared meaning. This hinders communication concerning research and creates uncertainty regarding the measurement of a phenomenon. Consequently, a researcher must explain what is meant by the concept so that a measurement strategy may be developed and so that those reading and evaluating the research can decide if the meaning accords with their own understanding of the term. Although some concepts that political scientists use—such as "amount of formal education," "presidential vote," and "amount of foreign trade"—are not particularly abstract, other concepts—such as "partisan realignment," "political integration," and "regime support"—are far more abstract and need more careful consideration and definition.

Suppose, for example, that a researcher is interested in the kinds of political systems that different countries have and, in particular, why some countries are more democratic than others. "Democracy" is consequently a key concept and one that needs definition and measurement. The word contains meaning for most of us; that is, we have some idea what is democratic and what is not. But once we begin thinking about the concept, we quickly realize that it is not as clear as we thought originally. To some, a country is democratic if it has "competing political parties, operating in free elections, with some reasonable level of popular participation in the process." [2] To others, a country is democratic only if there are legal guarantees protecting free speech, press, religion, and the like. To others, a country is democratic if the political leaders make decisions that are acceptable to the populace. And to still others, democracy implies economic equality among the citizenry. If a country has all of these attributes, it would be called a democracy by any of the criteria and there would be no problem classifying the country. But if a country possesses only one of the above attributes, its classification would be uncertain, since by some definitions it would be democratic but by others it would not. Different definitions require different measurements and may result in different research findings. Hence defining one's concepts is important, particularly when the concept is so abstract as to make shared agreement difficult.

Concept definitions have a direct impact on the quality of knowledge produced by research studies. Suppose, for example, that a researcher is interested in the connection between economic development and democracy, the working hypothesis being that countries with a high level of economic development will be more likely to have democratic forms of government. And suppose that there are two definitions of economic development and two definitions of democracy that might be used in the research. Finally, suppose that the researcher has data on 12 countries (A-L) included in the study. (See Table 3-1.)

This table shows that the definition selected for each concept has a direct bearing on how different countries are categorized on each attribute. By definition 1, countries A, B, C, D, E, F are economically developed; while by definition 2, countries A, B, C, G, H, I are. By definition 1, countries A, B, C, D, E, F are democracies; by definition 2, countries D, E, F, J, K, L are.

This is only the beginning of our troubles, however. When we look for a pattern involving the economic development and democracy of countries, we find that our answer depends mightily on how we have defined the two concepts. If we use the first definitions of the two concepts, we find that all economically developed countries are also

Table 3-1 Concept Development: The Relation between Economic Development and Democracy

1. *Is the country economically developed?*

		By definition 1:	
		Yes	No
By definition 2:	Yes	A, B, C	G, H, I
	No	D, E, F	J, K, L

2. *Is the country a democracy?*

		By definition 1:	
		Yes	No
By definition 2:	Yes	D, E, F	J, K, L
	No	A, B, C	G, H, I

democracies (A, B, C, D, E, F), which supports our hypothesis. If we use the first definition for economic development and the second for democracy (or vice-versa), half of the economically developed nations are democracies and half are not. If we use the second definitions of both concepts, none of the economically developed countries is a democracy while all of the undeveloped countries are (D, E, F, J, K, L). In other words, because of our inability to formulate a precise definition of the two concepts, and because the two definitions of each concept yield quite different categorizations of the 12 countries, our hypothesis could be either confirmed, disconfirmed, or contradicted by the data at hand. Our conceptual confusion has put us in a difficult position.

Consider another example. Suppose a researcher is interested in why some people are liberal and some are not. In this case one needs to define what is meant by liberal so that those who are liberal can be identified. "Liberal" is a frequently used term, but it has many different meanings: one who favors change, one who favors redistributive income or social welfare policies, one who favors increased government spending and taxation, one who opposes government interference into the political activities of its citizens. If a person possessed all these attributes, there would be no problem deciding that he or she was a liberal. A problem arises, however, when a person possesses some of these attributes but not others.

The previous examples illustrate the elusive nature of concepts and the need to define them. The empirical researcher's responsibility to "define terms" is a necessary and challenging one. Unfortunately, many of the concepts used by political science researchers are fairly abstract and need careful thought and extensive elaboration.

Researchers can clarify the concept definitions they use simply by making the meanings of key concepts explicit. This requires researchers to think carefully about the concepts used in their research and to share their meanings with others. Other researchers often challenge concept definitions, requiring reseachers to elaborate upon and justify their meanings.

Another way in which researchers get help in defining concepts is by reviewing others' research and reflecting on their concepts. This is one of the reasons why researchers conduct literature reviews of pertinent research, a task we take up in detail in Chapter 6. For example, a reseacher interested in the political attitudes and behavior of the American public would find the following definitions of key concepts in the existing literature:

> *Political participation.* Those activities by private citizens that are more or less directly aimed at influencing the selection of governmental personnel and/or the actions they take.[3]
>
> *Political violence.* All collective attacks within a political community against the political regime, its actors—including competing political groups as well as incumbents—or its policies.[4]
>
> *Political efficacy.* The feeling that individual political action does have, or can have, an impact upon the political processes, i.e., that it is worthwhile to perform one's civic duties.[5]
>
> *Belief system.* A configuration of ideas and attitudes in which the elements are bound together by some form of constraint or functional interdependence.[6]

Each of these concepts is somewhat vague and lacks complete shared agreement about its meaning. Furthermore, it is possible to raise questions about each of these concept definitions. Notice, for example, that the definition of political participation excludes the possibility that government employees (presumably "nonprivate citizens") engage in political participation, and the definition of political efficacy excludes the impact of collective political action on political processes. Consequently, we may find these and other concept definitions inadequate and revise them to capture more accurately what we mean by the terms.

Over time a discipline cannot proceed very far unless there is some minimal agreement about the meanings of the concepts with which scientific research is concerned. Researchers must take care to think about the phenomena named in a research project and make explicit the meanings of any problematic concepts.

Formulating Hypotheses

Thus far we have discussed three stages in the research process: identifing the research question, proposing explanations for the phenomena of interest, and defining the concepts used to describe these phenomena. By this point, then, the researcher (or reader of social science research) is ready to state what his or her hypotheses are. *Hypotheses* are explicit statements that indicate how a researcher thinks the phenomena of interest are related. They are guesses (but of an "educated" nature) that represent the proposed explanation for some phenomena and that indicate in what way an independent variable is thought to affect, influence, or alter a dependent variable. Since hypotheses are proposed relationships, they may turn out to be incorrect. To test a hypothesis adequately and persuasively, it must be properly formulated.

Actually, our everyday language is filled with hypotheses (though they may not be properly formulated). When we wonder why a particular child is shy, for example, and we assert that it is because he is the baby of the family, we are actually proposing an explanation for a concept (shyness) that relies on another concept (birth order). When we wonder why a local public official turned down our request for a new street light, and we suspect that it's because we are from different political parties, we are suggesting a hypothesis relating partisan identification and official responsiveness. When we wonder why Iran is experiencing social turmoil, and we decide that it is because the population is illiterate, poor, and ethnically diverse, we are proposing hypotheses relating literacy, wealth, ethnic similarities, and political stability. In fact, whenever we propose an explanation for any phenomenon, we are engaging in the preliminary stages of hypothesis formulation. One of the differences between doing this in everyday conversation, and doing it as part of a scientific research project is that in research, hypothesis formulation is only the beginning of a process that will include a test of our hypotheses. In everyday life we seldom test our hypotheses systematically.

Types of Hypotheses

There are essentially four different types of hypotheses, depending upon what the researcher is willing to propose about the relationship between concepts. Hypotheses can be null, correlative, directional, and causal.

A *null hypothesis* is simply a hypothesis that states that there is no relationship between two variables. When we analyze data to test a hypothesis, we often work with the null hypothesis and attempt to disprove it. A null hypothesis posits the absence of a relationship between two or more variables and usually represents the opposite of the hypothesis we are actually trying to confirm. (Null hypotheses will be discussed more fully in Chapter 12.)

A *correlative hypothesis* states that there is a relationship between two (or among more) concepts. However, it does not specify the nature of this relationship. "There is a relationship between age and political cynicism" and "there is a relationship between cultural homogeneity and political terrorism" are two correlative hypotheses. Notice that they do not tell us whether it is the old or the young who are thought to be more cynical, nor whether terrorism is thought to be more or less likely when cultural homogeneity is present.

With the *directional hypothesis,* the researcher makes a guess about the direction of the relationship between concepts. If the researcher thinks that concepts are apt to increase in size together or decrease in size together, then there is a *direct relationship* hypothesized between them. Consider these examples:

As a person's years of formal education increases, that person's income increases.

As the percentage of a country's population that is literate increases, the country's political process becomes more democratic.

The older a person gets, the more conservative the person becomes.

The less newspaper reading a person does, the less informed about current events the person will be.

If, on the other hand, the researcher thinks that as one concept increases in size or amount another one will decrease in size or amount, then an *inverse relationship* is suggested. Here are some examples:

The older a person is, the less tolerant of social protest the person becomes.

The more income a person has, the less concerned about mass transit the person will become.

The more affluent a country becomes, the less property crime that country will have.

Both types of directional hypotheses specify the existence and the direction of the proposed relationship. Consequently, the researcher's hypothesis will be disproved if there is no relationship between the two concepts or if the relationship is in the opposite direction of that hypothesized. On the other hand, if the hypothesis is supported by the evidence, then we have learned more than simply that there is a relationship between two concepts. To know that there is a relationship between income and education does not tell us whether income goes up or down with increased education. To learn that there is a relationship between the size of a country's population and the amount of democracy that exists in the country's political process does not tell us whether large or small populations have more democratic political processes. To discover that there is a relationship between age and political participation does not tell us whether the young or the old are more apt to participate. In all three of these cases, the direction of the relationship would be illuminating.

Directional hypotheses do not necessarily specify either a simple direct or inverse linear relationship between two concepts, however. There are many other possibilities. For example, the relationship between age and political participation might be *curvilinear,* with the youngest and the oldest populations the least participatory (due to the mobility of the young and the poor health of the elderly) and with the middle-aged participating the most. Or the relationship between two concepts might be *logarithmic,* with increasing amounts of one concept having less and less effect on the other concept. An example of this is the relationship between campaign spending and votes received: the initial amount of money is the most crucial; at higher levels of spending each dollar spent has less and less impact.[7] Basically, a directional hypothesis may specify any type of mathematical function relating the independent and dependent variables. Most directional hypotheses in political science, however, are simple linear ones.

A *causal hypothesis* makes the boldest claim about the relationship between two or more variables, yet it is also the most difficult to confirm. Causal hypotheses may take a number of forms. They may simply state that one variable is a cause of another, as in "literacy, affluence, and cultural homogeneity cause democratic movements in countries." Or they may be stated in "if/then" terms, as in "if a congressional challenger spends less than $200,000, then he will lose." Finally, a causal hypothesis may be stated negatively, as in "if it were not for the large security forces maintained by modern national governments, civil strife would be much more prevalent."

What is distinctive about a causal hypothesis is not so much its form as the nature of the claim it makes. Null, correlative, and directional hypotheses are primarily concerned with relationships, correlations, or covariations between variables. They posit either the absence or presence of a connection between one phenomenon and another. Causal hypotheses, on the other hand, advance this proposition but also make two other important claims: that one phenomenon (the cause) preceded the other phenomenon (the effect) in time and that the effect was dependent upon or could not have occurred in the absence of the cause. Researchers evaluating causal hypotheses must present evidence concerning both these claims.

It is possible to confirm a relationship between two phenomena without one being the cause of the other. There is a relationship between the amount of television individuals watch, for example, and how fearful they are, but we do not know which phenomenon came first in time. There is also a relationship between the height of major-party presidential candidates and their electoral success, but we suspect that the relationship is accidental (that is, not necessary or dependent) rather than causal. And there is a relationship between income and voter turnout, but it is largely due to the impact of education on both income and turnout and hence not due to the causal influence of income.

Deciding whether an observed relationship is causal is one of the most challenging aspects of scientific research. A causal hypothesis makes a distinctive and more significant assertion than any of the other types of hypotheses do. Consequently, the evaluation of a causal hypothesis requires extraordinary research designs and data analysis. The knowledge derived from the confirmation of a causal hypothesis is so valuable that researchers are often intent on evaluating such hypotheses. For example, all of the researchers mentioned in Chapter 1 wanted to discover the causes of various phenomena although their particular research studies may not have provided evidence adequate for such a task.

Political scientists often speak about causal hypotheses, construct causal models, and perform causal analysis, but they seldom achieve causal knowledge. Either the world of politics is too complex, or we have not been lucky or insightful enough to discover the causes of political phenomena. Whatever the reason, causal knowledge remains elusive, and causal hypotheses are rare. But since a causal hypothesis posits the most informative form of scientific knowledge, it is in many respects the most desirable type of hypothesis.

Characteristics of Good Hypotheses

So far we have discussed what a hypothesis is and identified four types of hypotheses. The characteristics and wording of a good hypothesis will now be examined.

First, hypotheses should be *empirical* statements, that is, they should be educated guesses about relationships that exist in the real world, not statements about what ought to be true or about what a researcher believes should be the case. Statements such as "South Africa should respect the civil rights of its nonwhite residents" are *normative* statements, and they cannot be evaluated with the research methods discussed here. While empirical findings may be pertinent to the formulation and evaluation of a normative statement, they can never tell you for certain whether the normative statement is justified or not.

Let us return to our example of the researcher interested in the causes of democracy. By now, this researcher ought to have defined the central concept (democracy) and those concepts thought to be related to democracy (such as literacy, size of population, geographical isolation, and economic development). If the researcher then hypothesizes that "democracy is the best form of government," he or she has formulated a normative, nonempirical statement that cannot possibly be tested in its present form. The statement simply states the preference of the researcher rather than an explanation for a phenomenon. To produce an acceptable hypothesis, the researcher ought to make an educated guess about the way the real world is, for example: "democracy exists only where the population is literate and affluent." This hypothesis now proposes an explanation for a phenomenon that can be empirically observed. Whether the hypothesis is confirmed is not necessarily related to whether the researcher thinks the phenomenon (in this case democracy) is good or bad. Some proposed hypotheses need to be revised because they are nonempirical. They cannot be evaluated with empirical observations alone. Consider these two examples:

Increasing the size of the navy rather than the number of stationary antiballistic missiles would be good for the United States.

Democrats ought to reject their New Deal liberalism philosophy and develop an alternative view.

This does not mean, however, that empirical knowledge is completely irrelevant for normative inquiry. Often people have reached normative conclusions based on their evaluation of empirical relationships. Someone might reason, for example, that

1) current government welfare programs lead to family disintegration;
2) family disintegration is bad;
3) therefore, current government welfare programs are bad.

The first statement could be considered a research hypothesis and could be investigated using the techniques developed in this book. The results could then be used to evaluate the third statement. However, the second statement, which is a normative statement of preference, cannot be tested, as it stands, using these techniques.

Normative thinking is useful because it forces an individual to clarify his or her values, and it encourages research on significant empirical questions. For example, a normative distaste for crime encourages empirical research on the causes of crime. Consequently, the two modes of inquiry—normative and empirical—should be viewed as compatible rather than competitive.

A second characteristic of a good hypothesis is *generality*. It should explain a general phenomenon rather than one particular occurrence of the phenomenon. For example, one might hypothesize that the cause of World War II was economic upheaval in Germany. If the hypothesis was confirmed what would be the extent of our knowledge? We would know the cause of one war. This knowledge is valuable, but it would be more useful to know if economic upheaval *in general* caused wars. That would be knowledge pertaining to many occurrences of a phenomenon (in this case many wars), rather than knowledge about just one occurrence. A more general hypothesis, then, might be "the greater the economic upheaval experienced by a country, the more likely that country is to become involved in a war." Knowledge about the causes of particular occurrences of a phenomenon could be helpful in formulating more general guesses about the relationships between concepts, but with a general hypothesis we attempt to expand the scope of our knowledge beyond individual cases.

Below are four hypotheses that are too narrow, followed by four acceptable hypotheses that are more general:

Senator X voted for that bill because it is the president's bill and they are both Republicans.	Senators are more likely to vote for bills sponsored by the president if they belong to the same political party as the president.
The United States is a democracy because its population is affluent and literate.	Democracies exist in affluent and literate countries.
The United States has more murders than other countries because so many people own guns there.	The more guns per capita a country possesses, the more murders that country will experience.
Joe is a liberal because his mother is one too.	If a person's mother is liberal, then that person is apt to be liberal also.

A third characteristic of a good hypothesis is that it should be *plausible;* that is, there should be some logical reason for thinking that it might be confirmed. Of course, since a hypothesis is a guess about a relationship, whether it will be confirmed cannot be known for certain. There are an infinite number of hypotheses that could be thought of and tested, but many fewer plausible ones. For example, if a researcher hypothesized that "people who eat dry cereal for breakfast are more likely to be liberal than people who eat eggs," we would question his or her logic even though the form of the hypothesis might be perfectly acceptable. It is difficult to imagine why this hypothesis would be confirmed.

But how do we make sure that a hypothesis has a good chance of being confirmed? Sometimes the justification is provided by specific instances in which the hypothesis was supported (going from specific to general knowledge in the manner discussed in Chapter 2—that is, induction). For example, a researcher may have observed a particular election in which a hotly contested primary campaign damaged the eventual nominee's chances of winning the general election. The researcher may then have concluded that "the more difficult it is for candidates to secure their party's nomination, the more poorly those candidates will do in the general election." A hypothesis also may be justified through the process of deduction. A researcher may deduce from more general theories that a particular hypothesis is sensible.

Formulating plausible hypotheses is one of the reasons why researchers conduct a literature review early in their research projects. Literature reviews (discussed in more detail in Chapter 6) can acquaint researchers with both general theories and with specific hypotheses advanced by others. In either case, reading the literature on a subject can improve the chances that a hypothesis will be confirmed. There are no hard and fast rules to ensure plausibility, however. After all, we used to think that "germs cause diseases" was an implausible hypothesis and that "dirt may be turned into gold" was a plausible one.

The fourth characteristic of all good hypotheses is that they be *specific*. The concepts used in a hypothesis should be carefully defined. For example, a hypothesis that suggests that "there is a relationship between personality and political attitudes" is far too ambiguous. What is meant by personality? Which political attitudes? A more specific reformulation of this hypothesis might be "the more self-esteem a person has, the less likely a person is to be an isolationist." Now personality has been defined to mean self-esteem, and political attitudes has been defined to mean isolationism, both more precise concepts. Eventually, of course, even these two terms must be given more precise definitions when it comes to measuring them. (We will return to the problem of *measuring* concepts in Chapter 4.)

Following are four examples of ambiguous hypotheses that have been made more specific:

How a person votes for president depends on the information he or she is exposed to.	The more information favoring candidate X a person is exposed to during a political campaign, the more likely that person is to vote for candidate X.
A country's geographical location matters for the type of political system it develops.	The more borders a country shares with other countries, the more likely that country is to have a nondemocratic political process.
A person's capabilities affect his or her political attitudes.	The more intelligent a person, the more likely he or she is to support civil liberties.
Guns do not cause crime.	People who own guns are less apt to be the victims of crimes than persons who do not own guns.

Finally, a good hypothesis is *testable:* there must be some evidence that is obtainable and that will indicate whether the hypothesis is correct. For example, the hypothesis "God created the universe" is impossible to test because it is difficult to tell what sort of evidence would indicate that God did not create the universe. Hypotheses for which either confirming or nonconfirming evidence is impossible to gather are untestable.

Consider this example of a promising yet untestable hypothesis: "The more supportive of political authorities a child is, the less likely that child is to engage in political dissent as an adult." This hypothesis is general, plausible, fairly specific, and empirical, but it is currently untestable because no data exists that could be used to test the proposition. The hypothesis requires data that measure a set of attitudes for individuals when they are children and a set of behaviors when they are adults. Survey data do exist that includes the political attitudes and behavior of 17- and 18-year-olds and their parents in 1965 and many of the same people in 1973.[8] These data lack childhood measures for the parents, however, and for the others there are only late adolescent and early adulthood (25- and 26-year-olds) measures. Consequently, a frustrating practical barrier prevents the testing of an otherwise acceptable hypothesis.

Students in one-semester college research methods courses often run up against this constraint. A semester is not usually long enough to collect and analyze data, and some data may be too expensive to acquire. Many interesting hypotheses are rejected simply because researchers do not have the resources to collect the data necessary to test them.

Hypotheses stated in tautological form are also untestable. A *tautology* is a statement linking two concepts that mean essentially the same thing: for example, "the less support there is for a country's political institutions, the more tenuous the stability of that country's political system." This hypothesis is going to be difficult to disconfirm because the two concepts are so similar. To provide a fair test one would have to measure independently the support for the political institutions and the stability of the political system. Otherwise, if both are measured in a similar way (and especially if both are measured in identical ways), the hypotheses would be difficult to disconfirm.

"Conspiracy" theories often suffer from this defect of being tautological. The typical conspiracy theory states that "Group X always gets its way when political decisions are made." If a skeptic then provides a disconfirming case of a decision where Group X was apparently the loser, the conspiracy theorists typically respond, "They permitted that decision to disguise their power." If decisions on which Group X "wins" are evidence for a conspiracy theory, and decisions on which Group X "loses" are also evidence for the same conspiracy theory, then it is impossible for any evidence to disconfirm the hypothesis. A hypothesis that *cannot* be disconfirmed is not a hypothesis at all, and is not a statement suitable for empirical data analysis.

There are many hypotheses, then, that are not formulated in such a way as to permit an informative test of them with empirical research. Readers of empirical research in political science, as well as researchers themselves, should take care that research hypotheses are empirical, general, plausible, specific, and testable. Hypotheses that do not share these characteristics are likely to cause difficulty for the researcher and reader alike and to make a minimal contribution to scientific knowledge.

Unit of Analysis

In addition to proposing a relationship between two or more variables, a hypothesis also specifies the types or levels of political actor to which the hypothesis is thought to apply. This is called the *unit of analysis* of the hypothesis, and it also must be selected thoughtfully.

As noted in Chapter 2, political scientists are interested in understanding the behavior or properties of all sorts of political actors: individuals, groups, states, governmental agencies, regions, and nations. The particular type of actor whose political behavior is named in a hypothesis is the unit of analysis for the research project. For example, the individual member of the House is the unit of analysis in the following hypothesis:

> Members of the House of Representatives who belong to the same party as the president are more likely to vote for legislation desired by the president than members who belong to a different party.

In the following hypothesis the city is the unit of analysis since it is attributes of cities that are being explored:

> Northeastern cities are more likely to have mayors, while western cities have city managers.

Finally, consider this hypothesis:

> The more affluent a country the more likely that country is to have democratic political institutions.

Here the unit of analysis is the country. It is attributes of countries—affluence (the independent variable) and democratic political institutions (the dependent variable)—that will need to be empirically observed. In sum, the research hypothesis indicates what the researcher's unit of analysis is and what behavior or attributes must be measured for that unit.

A discrepancy between the unit of analysis specified in a hypothesis and the entities whose behavior is actually empirically observed can cause problems. For example, suppose a researcher wants to test the hypothesis "blacks are more likely to support female candidates than Italians are." He or she might select an election with a female candidate and obtain data on the voting returns in election precincts with varying proportions of blacks and Italians. If it is found that female candidates received more votes in precincts with high proportions of blacks than in the precincts with a high proportion of Italians, the researcher might conclude that there was evidence in support of the hypothesis.

There is a fundamental problem with this approach, however. In the original hypothesis the unit of analysis is the individual voter, yet the data apply to election precincts, a different unit of analysis. Unless a district is 100 percent black or Italian, the researcher cannot necessarily draw conclusions about the behavior of individuals from the behavior of election districts. It could be that a female candidate's support in a district with a high proportion of black voters came mostly from nonblacks, and that most of the female candidate's votes in the Italian districts came from Italians.

Let us take two hypothetical election precincts to illustrate this fallacy. Suppose we have Precinct 1, a "black" district, and Precinct 2, an "Italian" district. If the black district voted 67 percent to 33 percent in favor of the female candidate, and the Italian district voted 53 percent to 47 percent in favor of the female candidate, we might be tempted to conclude that blacks voted more for the female candidate than Italians did.

But suppose we peek inside each of the election precincts to see how individuals of different ethnicity behaved. (See Table 3-2.) In the black district, blacks split 25-25 for the woman, Italians voted 18-2 for her, and others voted 24-6 for her. This resulted in the 67-33 edge for the woman in Precinct 1. In the Italian district, blacks voted 16-24 against the woman, Italians split 30-20 for her, and others voted 7-3 in her favor. This resulted in the 53-47 margin for the woman in Precinct 2. When the individual votes are counted by ethnicity, however, we find that all the blacks in the two districts split 41-49 against the woman. Italians voted 48-22 in her favor, and others voted 31-9 for her. In other words, more Italians as individuals voted for the woman candidate than did blacks as individuals (68.6 percent to 45.6 percent, respectively), even though the precinct level data gave the opposite impression.

Whenever a researcher uses the behavior of groups to draw inferences about the behavior of individuals, the danger of just such an *ecological fallacy* exists. An ecological fallacy is when the attributes of groups lead to a misleading assessment of the attributes of individuals. Sometimes data from a group can be used as evidence regarding the characteristics of individual members of the group. Generally, however, the unit of analysis of the measures and of the hypothesis should match.

Table 3-2 Voting by Blacks, Italians, and Others
for a Female Candidate

Ethnicity	*Raw Vote by*			*Percent Vote by*	
	Number	*Male*	*Female*	*Male*	*Female*
Precinct 1					
Blacks	50	25	25	50.0	50.0
Italians	20	2	18	10.0	90.0
Other	30	6	24	20.0	80.0
Total	100	33	67	33.3	67.0
Precinct 2					
Blacks	40	24	16	60.0	40.0
Italians	50	20	30	40.0	60.0
Other	10	3	7	30.0	70.0
Total	100	47	53	47.0	53.0
Voting of Individuals					
Blacks	90	49	41	54.4	45.6
Italians	70	22	48	31.4	68.6
Other	40	9	31	22.5	77.5
Total	200	80	120	40.0	60.0

Source: Hypothetical data.

Similarly, one cannot necessarily use the characteristics of individuals as measures of the attributes of groups. Suppose a researcher is interested in how much cooperation or conflict exists in two groups (say a group of ten Democratic committeemen and a group of eight Republican committeemen). The researcher devises a questionnaire designed to measure cooperation and administers it to the 18 subjects. Individual scores on the questionnaire can vary from 1 (for a very cooperative person) to a 7 (for a very uncooperative person).
Suppose the results of the questionnaire are as follows:

Scores of 10 *Democratic Committeemen*	*Scores of 8* *Republican Committeemen*
1	3
2	4
3	3
2	2
1	5
7	4
1	3
2	4
1	**Average: 3.5**
7	
Average: 2.7	

The Democrats look more cooperative. Forty percent of them are very cooperative (score of 1), 70 percent are cooperative (scores of 1 or 2), and their average score is well to the cooperative side of the scale. The Republicans have no one who is very cooperative, only 12 percent who are cooperative, and an average score that is near the middle of the scale. When cooperation is measured for individuals, then, and aggregated to make an inference about the group, the Democrats look more cooperative.

Cooperation is not only an attribute of individuals, however. It is also an attribute of a group. It would not be difficult to imagine that when the Democrats get together they might have a difficult time cooperating. Not only is the size of their group larger, which might jeopardize cooperation, but it also includes two very uncooperative individuals (score of 7), who might make cooperation among the group impossible. In other words, the Republicans as a group might be able to cooperate more than the Democrats, even though our individual level measures indicated otherwise.

Another mistake sometimes made by researchers is to mix different units of analysis in the same hypothesis. "The more education a person has, the more democratic his country is" doesn't make much sense since it mixes the individual and country as units of analysis. However, "the smaller a government agency, the happier its workers" concerns an attribute of an agency and an attribute of individuals, but in a way that makes sense. The size of the agency in which individuals work may be an important aspect of the context or environment in which the individual phenomenon occurs and may influence the individual attribute. In this case the unit of analysis is clearly the individual, but a phenomenon that is experienced by many cases is used to explain the behavior of individuals, some of whom may well be identically "situated."

In short, a researcher must be careful about the unit of analysis specified in a hypothesis and its correspondence with the unit measured. In general, a researcher should not mix units of analysis within a hypothesis.

Conclusion

In this chapter we have discussed the beginning stages of a scientific research project. A research project must provide—to both the producer and consumer of social scientific knowledge—the answers to these important questions. What phenomenon is the researcher trying to understand and explain? What explanation has the researcher proposed for the political behavior or attributes in question? What are the meanings of the concepts used in this explanation? What specific hypotheses relating two or more variables will be tested? What is the unit of analysis for the observations? If all of these questions are answered adequately, then the research will have a firm foundation.

Notes

1. Kenneth R. Hoover, *The Elements of Social Scientific Thinking* (New York: St. Martin's Press, 1980), 18-19.
2. W. Phillips Shively, *The Craft of Political Research* (Englewood Cliffs, N.J.: Prentice-Hall, 1980), 33.
3. Sidney Verba and Norman H. Nie, *Participation in America* (New York: Harper & Row, 1972), 2.
4. Ted Robert Gurr, *Why Men Rebel* (Princeton, N.J.: Princeton University Press, 1970), 3-4.
5. Angus Campbell, Gerald Gurin, and Warren E. Miller, *The Voter Decides* (Evanston, Ill.: Row, Peterson, 1954), 187.
6. Philip E. Converse, "The Nature of Belief Systems in Mass Publics," in David E. Apter, ed., *Ideology and Discontent* (New York: Free Press, 1964), 207.
7. Gary Jacobson, *Money in Congressional Elections* (New Haven, Conn.: Yale University Press, 1980).
8. For a description of this dataset, see M. Kent Jennings and Richard G. Niemi, *Generations and Politics* (Princeton, N.J.: Princeton University Press, 1981).

Terms Introduced

Antecedent variable. An independent variable that precedes other independent variables in time.

Arrow diagram. A pictorial representation of a researcher's explanatory scheme.

Causal hypothesis. A hypothesis in which the independent variable is thought to be a cause of the dependent variable.

Concept. The definition or meaning of a phenomenon used in empirical research.

Correlative hypothesis. A hypothesis that proposes a relationship between two variables without indicating the nature of that relationship.

Curvilinear relationship. A relationship between two variables that may best be described by a curved, rather than a straight, line.

Dependent variable. The phenomenon thought to be influenced, affected, or caused by some other phenomenon.

Direct relationship. A relationship in which the values of one variable increase as the values of another variable increase.

Directional hypothesis. A hypothesis that specifies the expected relationship between two or more variables.

Ecological fallacy. When the attributes or behavior of groups is a misleading indication of the attributes or behavior of individuals.

Explanation. A systematic, empirically verified understanding of why a phenomenon occurs as it does.

Hypothesis. A statement proposing a relationship between two or more variables.

Independent variable. The phenomenon thought to influence, affect, or cause some other phenomenon.

Intervening variable. A variable coming between an independent and dependent variable in an explanatory scheme.

Inverse relationship. A relationship in which the values of one variable increase as the values of another variable decrease.

Logarithmic relationship. A mathematical relationship in which increasing amounts of one variable have less and less effect on another variable.

Null hypothesis. A hypothesis that proposes no relationship between two variables.

Relationship. The association, dependence, or covariance of the values of one variable with the values of another variable.

Tautology. A hypothesis in which the independent and dependent variables are identical, making it impossible to disconfirm.

Unit of analysis. The type of actor (individual, group, institution, nation) specified in a researcher's hypothesis.

Exercises

1. Read Ada Finifter, "Dimensions of Political Alienation," *American Political Science Review* 64 (June 1970): 389-410. What concept is she attempting to define? How many different meanings of the concept does she give? Do these definitions capture what the concept means to you?

2. Read Robert D. Putnam, Robert Leonardi, Raffaella Y. Nanetti, and Franco Pavoncello, "Explaining Institutional Success: The Case of Italian Regional Government," *American Political Science Review* 77 (March 1983): 55-74. What dependent variables are the authors attempting to explain? What independent variables do they use? What hypotheses are advanced by the researchers? Draw an arrow diagram that summarizes the explanatory scheme proposed and evaluated in this piece of research.

3. For the following hypotheses, identify the *type of hypothesis* (null, correlative, directional, or causal); *unit of analysis;* and *independent and dependent variables.* Then see if you can improve the hypotheses in any way.

a. The more education a person has, the more politically active that person is.

b. The American electorate has become more tolerant of ideological nonconformists.

c. City agencies direct more effort at neighborhoods with strong community organizations.

d. Lobbyists representing interests with noncontroversial objectives deal with staff members, while lobbyists representing positions on controversial issues contact legislators.

e. A person who is experiencing economic distress is likely to vote against candidates from the same party as the incumbent president.

f. Affluent Acres is an exclusive community because it practices exclusionary zoning.

g. When the two chambers of a legislature are controlled by different parties, more bills end up in a joint conference committee than if both chambers are controlled by the same party.

h. The longer a person has worked for an agency, the less willing the agency is to assume new tasks.

i. Joe will probably not vote in the upcoming election because he is poor.

j. City councils with a high level of conflict rarely pass legislation unanimously.

4. Read Benjamin I. Page and Robert Y. Shapiro, "Effects of Public Opinion on Policy," *American Political Science Review* 77 (March 1983): 175-190. What do the authors say about the causal hypothesis advanced in their article? Do they discuss a) the temporal sequence of their two variables, and b) whether the effect could have been caused by some other factor? What do they ultimately conclude about whether public opinion causes public policy?

5. Think of a political phenomenon that you are interested in understanding. Define the phenomenon as completely and carefully as possible. Now think about other phenomena or concepts that you think might help you explain the phenomenon you chose. Pick one of these concepts and state how it is related to the first phenomenon. Draw an arrow diagram to summarize your explanatory scheme.

Suggested Readings

Blalock, Hubert M., Jr. *Causal Inferences in Nonexperimental Research,* New York: W. W. Norton, 1964.
Hoover, Kenneth R. *The Elements of Social Scientific Thinking.* New York: St. Martin's Press, 1984.

Isaak, Alan C. *Scope and Methods of Political Science.* Homewood, Ill.: Dorsey Press, 1985.

Jacob, Herbert, and Robert Weissberg. *Elementary Political Analysis.* New York: McGraw-Hill, 1975.

Kerlinger, Fred N. *Behavioral Research.* New York: Holt, Rinehart & Winston, 1979.

Shively, W. Phillips. *The Craft of Political Research.* Englewood Cliffs, N.J.: Prentice-Hall, 1980.

Simon, Julian L., and Paul Burstein. *Basic Research Methods in Social Science.* New York: Random House, 1985.

4. The Building Blocks of Social Scientific Research: Measurement

In the previous chapter we discussed the beginning stages of political science research projects: the choice of research topics, the formulation of scientific explanations, the development of testable hypotheses, and the definition of concepts. In this chapter we show how to test empirically the hypotheses we have advanced. This entails understanding a number of issues involving the *measurement* of the variables we have decided to investigate.

In Chapter 1 we said that scientific knowledge is based upon empirical observation. In this chapter we confront the implications of this fact. If we are to test empirically the accuracy and utility of a scientific explanation for a political phenomenon, we will have to observe and measure the presence of the concepts we are using to understand that phenomenon. Furthermore, if this test is to be an adequate one, our measurements of the political phenomena must be as accurate and precise as possible. The process of measurement is important because it provides the bridge between our proposed explanations and the empirical world they are supposed to explain.

The researchers discussed in Chapter 1 measured a number of political phenomena. Edward Tufte measured state public policy toward automobile inspections and the rate of automobile fatalities in each state. Gary Jacobson measured levels of campaign spending by candidates for the U.S. Congress and the number of votes that these candidates received. Ted Gurr measured the level of relative deprivation and the frequency of political violence in different countries. And David Sears, Carl Hensler, and Leslie Speer measured people's attitudes toward busing.[1] In each case some human behavior or attribute was measured so that a scientific explanation could be tested.

Devising Measurement Strategies

As Chapter 3 pointed out, researchers must define the concepts they use in their hypotheses. Researchers also must decide how they are actually going to measure the presence, absence, or amount of these concepts in the real world. Political scientists refer to this process as providing an *operational definition* of their concepts—in other words deciding what kinds of empirical observations should be made to measure the occurrence of an attribute or behavior.

Let us return, for example, to the researcher trying to explain the existence of democracy in different nations. If the researcher were to hypothesize that higher rates of literacy make democracy more likely, then a definition of two concepts—literacy and democracy—would be necessary. The researcher could then develop a strategy, based on these two definitions, for measuring the existence and amount of both attributes in a number of nations.

Suppose literacy was defined as "the completion of six years of formal education," and democracy was defined as "a system of government in which public officials are selected in competitive elections." These definitions would then be used to develop operational definitions of the two concepts. These operational definitions would indicate what should be observed empirically to measure both literacy and democracy, and they would indicate specifically what data should be collected to test the researcher's hypothesis. In this example, the operational definition of literacy might be "those nations in which at least 50 percent of the population has had six years of formal education, as indicated in a publication of the United Nations," while the operational definition of democracy might be "those countries in which the second place finisher in elections for the chief executive office has received at least 25 percent of the vote at least once in the past eight years."

When a researcher specifies the operational definition of a concept, the precise meaning of that concept becomes clear. In this example, we now know exactly what the researcher means by literacy and democracy. Since different people often mean different things by the same concept, operational definitions are especially important. Someone might argue that defining literacy in terms of formal education ignores the possibility that people who complete six years of formal education might still be unable to read or write well. Similarly, it might be argued that defining democracy in terms of competitive elections ignores other important features of democracy such as freedom of expression and citizen involvement in government actions. In addition, the operational definition of competitive elections is clearly debatable. Is the "competitiveness" of elections based on the number of competing candidates, the size of the margin of victory, or the number of consecutive victories by a single party in a series of elections? Unfortunately, operational definitions are seldom absolutely correct or absolutely incorrect; rather they are evaluated in terms of how well they correspond to the concepts they are meant to measure.

It is useful to think of the operational definition as the last stage in the process of defining a concept precisely. We often begin with an abstract concept (such as democracy), then attempt to define it in a meaningful way, and finally decide in specific terms how we are going to measure it. At the end of this process we hope to attain a definition that is sensible, close to our meaning of the concept, and exact in what it tells us about how to go about measuring the concept.

Let us consider another example: the researcher interested in why some individuals are more liberal than others. The concept of liberalism might be defined as "believing that government ought to pursue policies that provide benefits for the less well off." The task then is to develop an operational definition that can be used to measure whether particular individuals are liberal or not. The researcher might decide that anyone is a liberal who agrees on a public opinion poll with the following statement: "The federal government should increase the amount of money spent on food stamp and free lunch programs."

An abstract concept, liberalism, has now been given an operational definition that can be used to measure the concept for individuals. This definition is also related to the original definition of the concept, and it indicates precisely what observations need to be made. It is not, however, the only operational definition. Others might suggest that questions regarding busing, the death penalty, and pornography could be used to measure liberalism. The important thing is to think carefully about the operational definition you choose and to try and ensure that it coincides closely with the meaning of the original concept.

Examples of Political Measurement

Let us take a look at the operational definitions used by the researchers mentioned in Chapter 1. Tufte wanted to know "whether compulsory automobile safety inspections help reduce traffic fatalities" so he had to measure the existence of automobile inspections and the number of traffic fatalities.[2] The existence of inspections was measured in two ways. First, states were divided into two categories: those with compulsory automobile inspections (18 states) and those without compulsory inspections (32 states). Second, states with compulsory inspections were subdivided into three categories reflecting the quality of the inspection: those with one inspection per year conducted by state-appointed but privately owned inspection stations (8 states), those with two inspections per year by state-appointed stations (8 states), and those with inspections by state-owned and state-operated inspection stations (2 states).

Tufte's starting point for measuring auto fatalities was *Accident Facts,* a book that lists the number of auto fatalities reported annually by each state in terms of the number of deaths per 100,000 residents. Tufte used these data to produce two different measures of automobile fatality rates in each state. First, he decided to average the fatality rates in each state over a three-year period (he used 1966-1968) to correct for a particularly unusual rate in any one year (perhaps due to a large accident or unusually bad weather). Second, Tufte converted the auto fatality rate per 100,000 residents into a rate per 100 million miles traveled because he reasoned that people drive farther distances in some states than others, making auto accidents more likely in those states. Thus in Tufte's research, two real-world phenomena—state policy regarding automobile inspections and the number of auto fatalities—were empirically observed and measured.

Jacobson's research concerned the impact of campaign spending on the number of votes cast for congressional candidates.[3] His measure of the amount of money spent by congressional candidates was the amount listed by candidates in their reports to the Federal Election Commission. (For 1972 and 1974 Jacobson used summaries of the campaign spending reports compiled by Common Cause; 1976 and 1978 data came from FEC publications.) This approach forced Jacobson to limit his inquiry to elections after 1971. Only since April 7, 1972, have candidates for federal elective office been required to report their campaign expenditures to the federal government.

Jacobson's measures of congressional election returns also came from readily available, published sources: Richard M. Scammon's *America Votes 11: A Handbook of Contemporary American Election Statistics* (published by Congressional Quarterly) and *Congressional Quarterly's Guide to the 1976 Elections: A Supplement to CQ's Guide to U.S. Elections.* In these books are compiled the official returns reported by the state boards of elections. In this case, then, the researcher was able to measure two significant political phenomena by relying on measurements made and published by others.

Sears, Hensler, and Speer were interested in explaining the origins of people's attitudes toward busing.[4] In particular they were interested in whether people's views resulted more from busing's impact on their material well-being or from enduring attitudes—such as racial intolerance and political conservatism—formed early in their lives. Consequently, in their 1972 public opinion survey the researchers had to measure the respondents' material stake in school busing, enduring racial attitudes, and attitudes toward school busing.

Self-interest in the busing issue was measured by the responses to the following three questions:

> In some places, school boards are taking some children out of their closest neighborhood schools and sending them by bus to other schools farther away. Has anything like this happened around here? Have you

heard any talk that this might happen around here in the future?

Do you have any children aged 5-18 who go to school here and who were attending public, rather than private or parochial, school?

Is the grade school/high school nearest you all white, mostly white, about half-and-half, mostly black, or all black?

Racial intolerance was measured with eight questions on the following racial issues: racially restricted housing, segregation in general, a belief in whites' intellectual superiority, fair employment practices, public accommodation, and racial protest. Political conservatism was measured by asking respondents to place themselves on a scale varying from 1 for "extremely liberal" to 7 for "extremely conservative."

The following question measured attitudes toward busing:

There is much discussion about the best way to deal with racial problems. Some people think achieving racial integration of schools is so important that it justifies busing children to schools out of their own neighborhood. Others think letting children go to their neighborhood schools is so important that they oppose busing. Where would you put yourself on this scale, or haven't you thought much about this?

Respondents were then given a seven-point scale on which to place themselves, with a 1 labeled "bus to achieve integration" and a 7 labeled "keep children in neighborhood schools."

The three cases we have discussed are good examples of researchers' attempts to measure important political phenomena (behaviors or attributes) in the real world. Whether the phenomenon in question was state automobile inspection policy, attitudes toward busing, or campaign expenditures by congressional candidates, the researchers devised a measurement strategy that could detect and measure its presence and amount. These observations were then used as the basis for an empirical test of the researchers' hypotheses.

To be useful in providing scientific explanations for political behavior, measurements of political phenomena must correspond closely to the original meaning of a researcher's concepts. They must also provide the researcher with enough information to make valuable comparisons and contrasts. Hence the quality of measurements is judged in terms of both their *accuracy* and their *precision*.

The Accuracy of Measurements

Since we are going to use our measurements to test the validity of explanations for political phenomena, those measurements must be as accurate as possible. Inaccurate measurements may lead to erroneous conclusions since they will interfere with our ability to observe the actual relationship between two or more variables.

Suppose, for example, that you have hypothesized that "courses taught by political scientists are more worthwhile than courses taught by psychologists." During registration time you see a course description for a course in the political science department that looks worthwhile, so you sign up for it. Your friend, on the other hand, signs up for a course in the psychology department. Two weeks after classes start you meet your friend in the campus dining hall and swap evaluations of your courses. Your political science course has turned out to be a dreadful experience, but your friend seems to be enjoying the psychology course.

Does your experience that semester (actually an empirical observation of two cases seemingly relevant to the hypothesis) mean that your hypothesis is wrong? Not necessarily. Suppose the course you had signed up for was not being taught by a political scientist but rather by a historian on loan to the political science department. This would mean that you had inaccurately measured the nature of the course you were taking by assuming that all courses taught in the political science department were taught by political scientists. Thus you were being led to what might, in fact, have been an erroneous conclusion about the quality of courses taught by political scientists. Because of the inaccuracy of your measurement, the comparison you made with your friend turns out to be irrelevant for the hypothesis with which you began.

There are two major threats to the accuracy of measurements. Measures may be inaccurate because they are *unreliable* and because they are *invalid*.

Reliability

Reliability "concerns the extent to which an experiment, test, or any measuring procedure yields the same results on repeated trials. ... The more consistent the results given by repeated measurements, the higher the reliability of the measuring procedure; conversely, the less consistent the results, the lower the reliability." [5]

Suppose, for example, you are given the responsibility of counting a stack of 1,000 paper ballots for some public office. The first time you count them, you obtain a particular result. But as you were counting the ballots you might have been interrupted, two or more ballots might have stuck together, some might have been blown onto the floor, or you might have written the totals down incorrectly. As a precaution, then, you count them five more times and get four other people to count them as well. The consistency of the results of all 10 counts would be an indication of the reliability of the measure.

Or suppose you design a series of questions to measure how cynical people are and ask a group of people those questions. If a few days later you then ask the same questions of the same group of people, the correspondence between the two measures would indicate the reliability of that particular measure of cynicism.

Similarly, suppose you wanted to test the hypothesis that the *New York Times* is more critical of the federal government than the *Wall Street Journal*. This would require you to measure the level of criticism found in articles in the two papers. The reliability of such measures might be assessed by having two people read all the articles, independently measure the level of criticism in them, and then compare their two distinct measures of the news articles. Reliability would be demonstrated if both people reached similar conclusions regarding the content of the articles in question.

The reliability of political science measures can be calculated a number of ways. The *test-retest method* involves applying the same "test" to the same observations after a period of time and then comparing the results of the different measurements. For example, if a series of questions measuring liberalism is asked of a group of respondents two weeks in a row, a comparison of their scores at both times could be used as an indication of the reliability of the measure of liberalism.

This method of measuring reliability is both difficult and problematic since the opportunity to measure the phenomenon at two different points in time is required and the administration of the first measure may affect the second results. For instance, the difference between Scholastic Aptitude Test (SAT) scores the first and second times that individuals take the test ought not be assumed to be a measure of the reliability of the test since test takers might alter systematically their behavior the second time as a result of taking the test the first time.

The *alternative-form method* of measuring reliability also involves measuring the same attribute more than once, but uses two different measures of the same concept rather than the same measure. For example, a researcher could devise two different sets of questions to measure the concept of liberalism, ask the two sets of questions of the same respondents at two different times, and compare the respondents' scores. Using two different forms of the measure prevents the second scores from being influenced by the first measure, but it still requires being able to measure the phenomenon twice.

Finally, the *split-halves method* of measuring reliability involves two measures of the same concept, with both measures applied at the same time. The results of the two measures are then compared. For example, one may devise a measure of liberalism consisting of the responses to 10 questions on a public opinion survey. Half of these questions could be selected to represent one measure of liberalism and the other half selected to represent a second measure of liberalism. If individual scores on the two measures of liberalism are similar, then the 10-item measure may be said to be reliable by the split-halves approach.

The test-retest, alternative-form, and split-halves methods provide a basis for calculating the similarity of results of two or more applications of the same or equivalent measure. The less consistent the results are, the less reliable the measure is. Frankly, the reliability of the measures used by political scientists is frequently suspect and seldom demonstrated. Respondents' answers to survey questions often vary considerably when given at two different times.[6] Usually political scientists simply assume that their measures are reliable rather than assess that reliability empirically.

Validity

Essentially, a valid measure is a measure that does, in fact, measure what it is supposed to measure. Unlike reliability, which depends on whether repeated applications of the same or equivalent measure yield the same result, validity involves the correspondence between the measure and the concept it is thought to measure.

Let us consider first some examples of invalid measures. Suppose a researcher hypothesizes that the larger the police force in a city, the less crime that city will have. This requires the measurement of crime rates in different cities. Now also assume that some police departments systematically over-represent the number of crimes in their cities to persuade the town fathers that crime is a serious problem and that the local police need more resources. If the researcher relied on official, reported measures of crime, the measures would be invalid because they did not correspond closely to the actual amount of crime in some cities.

Or suppose you hypothesize that the more productive a scholar a faculty member is, the better teacher he or she is. This requires measuring different faculty members' teaching abilities. This might be accomplished by asking students to give grades to their instructors based on how good a teacher they think they are. But do students know a good teacher when they see one? Is it possible that students will give good grades to instructors who are personable, humorous, approachable, or easy graders, rather than to instructors who teach them something? If so, such a measurement strategy might well produce an invalid measure of good teaching.

Finally, consider the hypothesis that easy voter registration systems cause more people to vote than difficult voter registration systems do.[7] This requires the accurate measurement of voter turnout. One way of measuring voter turnout is to ask people if they voted in the last election. However, given the social desirability of voting in the United States, will all the people who did not vote in the previous election admit it to an interviewer? More people might say that they voted than actually did, resulting in an invalid measure of voter turnout. In fact, this is what usually happens. Voter surveys commonly overestimate turnout by several percentage points.[8]

A measure's validity is more difficult to demonstrate empirically than its reliability because validity involves the relationship between the measurement of a concept and the actual presence or amount of the concept itself. Information regarding the correspondence is seldom abundant. Nonetheless, there are a number of ways of evaluating the validity of any particular measure.

Face validity may be asserted (not empirically demonstrated) when the measurement instrument appears to measure the concept it is supposed to measure. To assess the face validity of a measure, we need to know the definition of the concept being measured and whether the information being collected is "germane to that concept." [9] For example, suppose a researcher wants to measure the concept "identification with a political party" and devises a question that asks whether the respondent usually thinks of himself or herself as a Democrat, Republican, Independent, or something else. If this measure is given to a group of citizens during a presidential election campaign (as it often is), some people might respond to the question in terms of the particular presidential candidate they are supporting. If this happens, then the measure is measuring two concepts (party identification and candidate support) and is a less valid measure of party identification. Similarly, some have argued that the results of many standard IQ tests measure intelligence and exposure to middle-class white culture, thus making the test results a less valid measure of intelligence.

In general, measures lack face validity when there are good reasons to question the correspondence of the measure to the concept in question. In other words, assessing face validity is essentially a matter of judgment. If there is no consensus about the definition of the concept to be measured, the face validity of one's measure is bound to be problematic.

A second kind of validity test, *content validity*, is similar to face validity. This test (actually a logical argument rather than a test) involves determining the full domain or meaning of a particular concept and then making sure that measures of all portions of this domain are included in the measurement technique. For example, suppose you wanted to design a measure of the extent to which a nation's political system is democratic. As noted earlier, democracy means many things to many people. One way of measuring a concept with multiple meanings is to try and determine the various meanings attached to the concept (such as guarantees for free expression, provision for citizen decisionmaking, agreement between public opinion and public policy, economic equality) and then try to make sure that every one of these meanings is included in the measuring scheme. If this can be accomplished, then the entire domain of the concept has been measured and the measure possesses content validity. Unfortunately, many political science concepts are so abstract and ill-defined that there is little agreement about their domain. This makes content validity less useful to political scientists than it is to other researchers.

A third way to evaluate the validity of a measure is by empirically demonstrating *construct validity*. When a measure of a concept is related to a measure of another concept with which the original concept is thought to be related, construct validity is demonstrated. In other words, a researcher may specify, on theoretical grounds, that two concepts ought to be related (say, political efficacy with political participation, or education with income). The researcher then develops a measure of each of the concepts and determines the relationship between them. If the measures are related, then one measure has construct validity for the other measure. If the measures are unrelated, there is an absence of construct validity. Either the theoretical relationship is in error, one or more of the measures is not an accurate representation of the concept, or the procedure used to test the relationship is inappropriate. The absence of the hypothesized relationship does not tell us for certain that the measure is invalid, but the presence of a relationship gives us some assurance of the measure's validity.

A good example of an attempt to demonstrate construct validity may be found in the Educational Testing Service's booklet describing the Graduate Record Exam, a standardized test required for admission to most graduate schools. Since GRE test scores are supposed to measure a person's aptitude for graduate study, presumably construct validity could be demonstrated if the scores did, in fact, accurately predict the person's performance in graduate school. Over the years ETS has tested the relationships between GRE scores and first-year graduate school grade-point average. The results, shown in Table 4-1, indicate that GRE scores are typically quite poor predictors of this measure of graduate school performance. In short, ETS has found it difficult to demonstrate construct validity for its GRE.[10]

A fourth way in which validity can be demonstrated is through *inter-item association*. This is the type of validity test most often used by political scientists. It relies on the similarity of outcomes of more than one measure of a concept to demonstrate the validity of the entire measurement scheme.

Let us return to the researcher who wants to develop a valid measure of liberalism. First the researcher might measure people's attitudes toward 1) school busing, 2) welfare, 3) protection of the rights of the accused, 4) military spending, 5) government employment programs, 6) social security benefit levels, 7) urban renewal programs, and 8) a progressive income tax. Then the researcher could determine how the

Table 4-1 Construct Validity of Graduate Record Examination
Test Scores

Relationship between GRE test scores, undergraduate grade-point average, and first-year graduate grade-point average		*(n)*
GRE verbal	+.24	(388)
GRE quantitative	+.24	(388)
GRE subject tests	+.32	(144)
Undergraduate GPA	+.28	(366)
GRE verbal + GRE quantitative + undergraduate GPA	+.37	(365)

Source: *GRE Information Bulletin,* 1985-86, 29. Copyright © 1984 by Educational Testing Service. All rights reserved. Reprinted by permission.

Note: The numbers in this table are product-moment correlations—numbers that can vary between −1.0 and +1.0 and that indicate the extent to which one variable is associated with another. The closer the correlation is to ±1.0, the stronger the relationship between the two variables; the closer the correlation is to 0.0, the weaker the relationship. Since all of the correlations in this table are between .2 and .4, the relationship between GRE scores and first-year graduate grade-point average is not very strong. In other words, knowing a student's GRE scores would not be very helpful in predicting accurately a student's first-year grade-point average.

responses to each question relate to the responses to each of the other questions. The validity of the measurement scheme would be demonstrated if there were strong relationships between people's responses across the eight questions.

The results of such inter-item association tests are often displayed in something called a *correlation matrix.* (See Table 4-2.) Such a display shows how strongly related each of the items in the measurement scheme is to all of the other items. In the hypothetical data shown in Table 4-2, we can see that people's responses to six of the eight measures were strongly related to each other while responses to the questions on protection of the rights of the accused and school busing were not part of the general pattern. Thus the researcher would probably conclude that the first six items all measure a dimension of liberalism and that, taken together, they are a valid measurement of the liberalism concept.

Content and face validity are difficult to assess when there is a lack of agreement on the meaning of a concept, and construct validity, which requires a well-developed theoretical perspective, usually yields a less than definitive result. The inter-item association test requires multiple measures of the same concept. Although those validity "tests" provide important evidence, none of them is apt to result in a definite decision concerning the validity of particular measures.

An example of research performed at the Survey Research Center at the University of Michigan illustrates the numerous threats to the

Table 4-2 Inter-Item Association Validity Test of a Measure of Liberalism

	Welfare	Military Spending	Government Spending	Social Security	Urban Renewal	Income Tax	Busing	Rights of Accused
Welfare	x							
Military Spending	.56	x						
Government Spending	.71	.60	x					
Social Security	.80	.51	.83	x				
Urban Renewal	.63	.38	.59	.69	x			
Income Tax	.48	.67	.75	.39	.51	x		
Busing	.28	.08	.19	.03	.30	−.07	x	
Rights of Accused	−.01	.14	−.12	.10	.23	.18	.45	x

Source: Hypothetical data.

Note: The figures in this table are product-moment correlations, explained in the note to Table 4-1. A high correlation indicates a strong relationship between how people answered the two different questions designed to measure liberalism. The figures in the last two rows are considerably closer to 0.0 than are the other entries, indicating that people's answers to the busing and rights of the accused questions did not follow the same pattern as their answers to the other questions. Therefore, it looks like busing and rights of accused are not part of the measure of liberalism accomplished with the other questions.

reliability and validity of political science measures. In 1980 the center conducted interviews with a national sample of eligible voters and measured their income levels with the following question:

Please look at this page and tell me the letter of the income group that includes the income of *all members of your family living here in 1979 before taxes.* This figure should include salaries, wages, pensions, dividends, interest, and all other income."

Respondents were then given the following choices:

A. None or less than $2,000
B. $2,000 - $2,999
C. $3,000 - $3,999
D. $4,000 - $4,999
E. $5,000 - $5,999
F. $6,000 - $6,999
G. $7,000 - $7,999
H. $8,000 - $8,999
J. $9,000 - $9,999
K. $10,000 - $10,999
M. $11,000 - $11,999
N. $12,000 - $12,999
P. $13,000 - $13,999
Q. $14,000 - $14,999
R. $15,000 - $16,999
S. $17,000 - $19,999
T. $20,000 - $22,999
U. $23,000 - $24,999
V. $25,000 - $29,999
W. $30,000 - $34,999
X. $35,000 - $49,999
Y. $50,000 and over

Both the reliability and validity of this method of measuring income are questionable. Threats to the reliability of the measure include the following:

1) Respondents may truly not know how much money they make and therefore incorrectly guess their income.

2) Respondents may also not know how much money other family members make and guess incorrectly.

3) Respondents may know how much they make but carelessly select the wrong categories.

4) Interviewers may circle the wrong categories when listening to the selections of the respondents.

5) Keypunchers may punch the wrong number when entering the answer into the computer.

6) Dishonest interviewers may incorrectly guess the income of a respondent who does not complete the interview.

7) Respondents may not know which family members to include in the income total; some respondents may include only a few family members while others may include even distant relations.

8) Respondents whose income is on the border between two categories may not know which one to pick. Some pick the higher category; some the lower one.

Each of these problems may introduce some error into the measurement of income, resulting in inaccurate measures that are too high for some respondents and too low for others. Therefore, if this measure were applied to the same people at two different points in time we could expect the results to vary.

In addition to these threats to reliability, there are numerous threats to the validity of this measure:

1) Respondents may have illegal income they do not want to reveal and, therefore, systematically underestimate their income.

2) Respondents may try to impress the interviewer, or themselves, by systematically overestimating their income.

3) Respondents may systematically underestimate their before-tax income if they believe too much money is being withheld from their paychecks.

This long list of problems with both the reliability and validity of this fairly straightforward measure of a relatively concrete concept is worrisome. Imagine how much more difficult it is to develop reliable and valid measures when the concept is abstract (for example, intelligence, self-esteem, or liberalism), and the measurement scheme is more complicated.

The reliability and validity of the measures used by political scientists are seldom demonstrated to everyone's satisfaction. Most measures of political phenomena are neither completely invalid or valid nor thoroughly unreliable or reliable, but rather are partially accurate. Therefore, researchers generally present the rationale and evidence that are available in support of their measures and attempt to persuade their audience that their measures are at least as accurate as alternative measures would be. Nonetheless, it must be admitted that demonstrating the accuracy of their measures is not often a high priority of political scientists. A skeptical stance on the part of the reader toward the reliability and validity of political science measures is often warranted.

Reliability and validity are not the same thing. A measure may be reliable without being valid. One may devise a series of questions to measure liberalism, for example, which yields the same result of the same people every time but which misidentifies individuals. A valid measure, on the other hand, will also be reliable since if it accurately measures the concept in question then it should do so consistently across measurements. It is more important, then, to demonstrate validity than reliability, but reliability is usually more easily and precisely tested.

The Precision of Measurements

Measurements should be not only accurate but also precise; that is, measurements should contain as much information as possible about the attribute or behavior being measured. The more precise our measures, the more complete and informative can be our test of the relationships between two or more variables.

Suppose, for example, that we were measuring the height of political candidates to see if taller candidates usually win elections. Height could be measured in many different ways. We could have two categories of the variable height, tall and short, and assign different candidates to the two categories based on whether they were of above-average or below-average height. We could compare the heights of candidates running for the same office and measure which candidate was the tallest, which the next tallest, and so on. Or we could take a tape-measure and measure each candidate's height in inches and record that measure. Clearly, the last method of measurement preserves the most information about each candidate's height and is, therefore, the most precise measure of the attribute.

When we consider the precision of our measurements, we refer to the *level of measurement.* The level of measurement involves the type of information that we think our measurements contain and the type of comparisons that can be made across a number of observations on the same variable. The level of measurement also refers to the claim we are willing to make when we assign numbers to our measurements.

There are four different levels of measurement: *nominal, ordinal, interval,* and *ratio.* Very few concepts used in political science research inherently require a particular level of measurement, so the level used in any specific research project is a function of the imagination and resources of the researcher and the decisions made when the method of measuring each of the variables is developed.

A *nominal* level of measurement is involved whenever the values assigned to a variable represent only different categories or classifications for that variable. In such a case, no category is more or less than another category, simply different. For example, suppose we measure the religion of individuals by asking them to indicate whether they are Protestant, Catholic, Jewish, or something else. Since the four categories or values for the variable "religion" are simply different, this would be a nominal level of measurement.

Nominal level measures ought to consist of categories that are exhaustive and mutually exclusive; that is, the categories should include all of the possibilities for the measure, and they should be differentiated in such a way that a case will fit into one and only one category. For example, the categories of the measure of religion are exhaustive (because of the "something else" category) as well as mutually exclusive (since presumably an individual cannot be of more than one religion). If one attempted to measure "types of political systems," on the other hand, with the categories democratic, socialist, authoritarian, undeveloped, traditional, capitalist, and monarchical, the categories would be neither exhaustive nor mutually exclusive. (In which category do the Soviet Union, Great Britain, and India belong?) The difficulty of deciding the category into which many countries should be put would hinder the very measurement process the variable was intended to further.

An *ordinal* level of measurement assumes that more or less of a variable can be measured and that a comparison can be made on which observations have more or less of a particular attribute. For example, we could create an ordinal measure of formal education completed with the following categories: "8th grade or less," "some high school," "high school graduate," "some college," "college degree or more." Notice that we are not concerned here with the exact difference between the categories of education, but only with whether one category is more or less than another. Or suppose we ask individuals three questions designed to measure social trust, and we believe that an individual who answers all three questions a certain way has more social trust than a person who answers two of the questions a certain way, and this person has more social trust than a person who answers one of the questions a certain way, and so on. We could assign a score of 3 to the first group, a 2 to the second group, a 1 to the first group, and a 0 to those who did not answer any of the questions in a socially trusting manner. In this case, the higher the number, the more social trust an individual had. With an ordinal measure it does not matter whether we assign to the four categories the numbers 0, 1, 2, 3; 5, 6, 7, 8; 10, 100, 1000, 10005; or 100, 101, 107, 111. The intervals between the numbers have no meaning; all that matters is that the higher numbers represent more of the attribute than the lower numbers do.

An *interval* level of measurement is a measuring scheme in which the intervals between the categories or values assigned to the observations have meaning. For interval measures, the value of a particular observation is important not just in terms of whether it is larger or smaller than another value (as in ordinal measures), but also in terms of how much larger or smaller it is. For example, suppose we record the year in which certain events occurred. If we have three observations—1950, 1960, and 1970—we know that the event in 1950 occurred 10 years before the one in 1960 and 20 years before the one in 1970. We also know that the difference between the 1950 and 1970 observations is twice the difference between the 1950 and 1960 or 1960 and 1970 observations. One unit change (the interval) all along this measurement is identical in meaning: the passage of one year's time. This is not necessarily the case for the measure of social trust discussed earlier since we are not certain in that example whether the difference between a score of 1 and a score of 2 is identical with the difference between a score of 2 and a score of 3.

Another characteristic of an interval level of measurement that distinguishes it from the next level of measurement (ratio) is that the zero point is arbitrarily assigned and does not represent the absence of the attribute being measured. For example, many time and temperature scales have arbitrary zero points. Thus, 0 A.D. does not indicate the beginning of time—if this were true there would be no B.C. dates. Nor does 0°C indicate the absence of heat but rather the temperature at which water freezes. For this reason, with interval level measurements we cannot calculate ratios; that is, we cannot say that 60°F is twice as warm as 30°F because it does not represent twice as much warmth.

The final and highest level of measurement is a *ratio* level measure. This type of measurement involves the full mathematical properties of numbers. That is, the values of categories order the categories, tell something about the intervals between the categories, and state precisely the relative amounts of the variable that the categories represent. If, for example, a researcher is willing to claim that an observation with 10 units of a variable possesses exactly twice as much of that attribute as an observation with 5 units of that variable, then a ratio level measurement exists.

The key to making this assumption is that a value of zero on the variable actually represents the absence of that variable. Because ratio measures have a true zero point, it makes sense to say that one measurement is x times another. It makes sense to say a 60-year-old person is twice the age of a 30-year-old person $(60/30 = 2)$, while it does not make sense to say that 60°C is twice as warm as 30°C.[11]

Identifying the level of measurement of variables is important since it affects the kinds of hypotheses that can be tested and the data analysis techniques that can be used. However, the decision is not always a straightforward one, and there is often uncertainty and disagreement among researchers concerning these decisions. Very few phenomena inherently require one particular level of measurement. Often a phenomenon can be measured with any level of measurement, depending upon the particular technique designed by the researcher and the claims that the researcher is willing to make about the resulting measure.

Since distinguishing different levels of measurement is sometimes difficult let us consider an example. Suppose we are interested in measuring how much political freedom exists in different countries. We can design a measure of political freedom by deciding its important dimensions and determining the presence of each in different countries.

For example, does the country have privately owned newspapers; the legal right to form political parties; contested elections for significant public offices; voting rights extended to most of the adult population; and limitations on government's ability to incarcerate citizens? In addition to this checklist, suppose we form a summary index of political freedom by summing the number of conditions thought to exist in each country. The index could vary from 0 to 5 with any integer in between a possible value.

This measure could be a nominal level measure since it groups countries into discrete categories. Could it also be an ordinal measure? That depends on whether the researcher thinks that each of the five activities is equally important for the measurement of political freedom. If so, then the higher the index value, the more political freedom in a country. But if the researcher thinks that some of the attributes are more important than others, then the measure would not be an ordinal one. Does a country with contested elections and privately owned newspapers (an index value of 2) have more political freedom than one with limits on government's ability to incarcerate citizens (an index value of 1)? It is difficult to say.

If it is hard to imagine this measure being ordinal, it is even more difficult to imagine it being interval or ratio. To do so would require claims about 1) the precise amount of freedom represented by an index interval of one everywhere along the index, and 2) whether it is possible to say that a country has two or three (or whatever) times more freedom than another country. Such claims are highly suspect in this case.

For this measure, then, a nominal level measure is certainly acceptable and an ordinal level measure possible. It is unlikely that the measure could be considered interval or ratio.

Political science researchers have measured many concepts at the ratio level. People's ages, unemployment rates, percent vote for a particular candidate, and crime rates are all examples of measures that contain a zero point and represent the full mathematical properties of the numbers used. However, more political science research has probably relied upon nominal and ordinal level measures than interval or ratio level measures. This has restricted the types of hypotheses and analysis techniques that political scientists have been willing and able to use.

Researchers usually try to devise as high a level of measurement for their concepts as possible (nominal being the lowest level of measurement and ratio the highest). The higher the level of measurement, the more informative a hypothesis using the variables will be and the more advanced the data analysis techniques that can be used. Consequently, one might start with a nominal level measure and think of a way to turn it into an ordinal or interval level measure. Since very few concepts may be measured only at the nominal level it is usually possible to turn a nominal level measure into something higher. We might initially think, for example, that living is a nominal level measure: one is either alive or dead—two categories only. Yet it is clear that our legal system is currently having to make more precise determinations than that. Is a fetus living at the point of conception in the same way a newborn is? Is a person alive when on life-support systems even though brain activity is minimal? May living, then, be measured with an ordinal level measure in which some people are more or less alive? The answers are not clear.

Political scientists often begin with a nominal level measure of a concept and then "enrich" that measurement to a higher level. In his study of automobile traffic fatalities, Tufte began with a nominal level measurement of state auto inspection policy (either a state required inspections or it did not). He then found it useful to distinguish between types of state inspection systems by measuring those states that had more rigorous inspections than others. This resulted in an ordinal level measure of inspection policy. Similarly, a researcher investigating the effect of campaign spending on election outcomes could devise an ordinal level measure that simply distinguished between those candidates who spent more or less than their opponent. However, more information would be preserved if a ratio level variable measuring how much more (or less) a candidate spent than the opposition were devised. Researchers measuring attitudes or personality traits also often construct a scale or index that permits at least ordinal level comparisons between observations.

Multi-Item Measures

Many of the measures considered so far in this chapter have consisted of a single item. Jacobson's measures of candidate expenditures and vote totals and Tufte's measures of traffic fatality rates and state auto inspection policy are all derived from single measures of each phenomenon in question. Often, however, researchers devise measures that are combinations of more than one indicator. These multi-item measures are useful because they enhance the accuracy of a measure, simplify a researcher's data by reducing it to a more manageable size, and increase the level of measurement of a phenomenon. In the remainder of this section we will describe two commonly used types of multi-item measures: indexes and scales.

Indexes

An index is a method of accumulating scores on individual items to form a composite measure of a phenomenon. The typical index is constructed by assigning a range of possible scores for a number of items, determining the score for each item for each observation, and then combining the scores for each observation across all of the items. The resulting summary score represents the measurement of a phenomenon with an index.

The researcher interested in measuring how much freedom there is in different countries might devise a list of items germane to such a measure, determine where individual countries score on each of the items, and then add these scores together to get a summary measure. In Table 4-3 such a hypothetical index is used to measure the amount of freedom in countries A through E.

The index in Table 4-3 is a simple, additive one; that is, each of the items counts equally toward the calculation of the index score, and the total score is the summation of the individual item scores. However, indices may be constructed with more complicated aggregation procedures and by counting some items as more important than others. In the preceding example a researcher might consider some indicators of freedom more important than others and wish to have them contribute more to the calculation of the final index score. This could be done either by weighting (multiplying) some item scores by a number indicating their importance or by assigning a higher score than 1 for those attributes considered more important.

Table 4-3   Index for Measuring Freedom in Nations

	Country A	Country B	Country C	Country D	Country E
Does the country possess:					
Privately owned newspapers	1	0	0	0	1
Legal right to form political parties	1	1	0	0	0
Contested elections for significant public offices	1	1	0	0	0
Voting rights extended to most of the adult population	1	1	0	1	0
Limitations on government's ability to incarcerate citizens	1	0	0	0	1
Index Score	5	3	0	1	2

Source: Hypothetical data.

Note: The score is 1 if the answer is yes; 0 if no.

Indexes are often used with public opinion surveys to measure political attitudes. A researcher might measure attitudes toward abortion, for example, by asking respondents to react to the following three statements:

> Abortions should be permitted in the first three months of pregnancy.

> Abortions should be permitted if the woman's life is in danger.

> Abortions should be permitted whenever a woman wants one.

The respondents would then choose one of five possible responses: strongly agree, agree, undecided, disagree, and strongly disagree. An index of attitudes toward abortion could be computed by adding the numerical values of a respondent's answers to these three questions. (The researcher would have to decide what to do when a respondent did not answer one or more of the questions.) The lowest possible score would be a 3, indicating the most extreme pro-abortion attitude, and the highest possible score would be a 15, indicating the most extreme anti-abortion attitude. Scores in between would indicate varying degrees of approval of abortion, although it is not clear what level of measurement such scores would represent.

Indexes are commonly used as measures of all sorts of political phenomena. The FBI Crime Index and Consumer Price Index, for example, as well as many measures of political attitudes, are constructed from indexes. Indexes generally provide a researcher with a more accurate and manageable measure than would a single item.

Scales

Although indexes are often an improvement over single item measures, there is also an element of arbitrariness in their construction. Both the selection of particular items making up the index and the way in which the scores on individual items are aggregated are based on the judgment of the researcher. Scales are also multi-item measures, but the selection and combination of items in them is more systematically accomplished than is usually the case for indexes. Three different kinds of scales are frequently used in attitude research: Likert scales, Thurstone scales, and Guttman scales.

A *Likert scale* score is calculated from the scores obtained on individual items. Each item generally asks a respondent to indicate a degree of agreement or disagreement with the item, as with the abortion questions discussed earlier. A Likert scale differs from an index, however, in that once the scores on each of the items are obtained, then some of the items are selected for inclusion in the calculation of the final score. Those items that allow a researcher to discriminate most readily those scoring high on an attribute from those scoring low will be retained, and a new scale score will be calculated based only on those items.

Thurstone scales attempt to ensure that the items used in the calculation of the scale score represent equally spaced intervals across the range of an attitude. Dozens of questionnaire items are composed. A group of representative "judges" rank orders the questions in terms of how favorable or unfavorable the items are to the attitude being measured, selecting those items that will best cover the entire range of the attitude at equally spaced intervals. This reduced set of items is then administered to the respondents. The responses to this set of items may then be aggregated, usually by summation, to produce Thurstone scale scores.

Guttman scales employ a series of items to produce a scale score for respondents. Unlike the Likert and Thurstone scales, however, a Guttman scale is designed to present respondents with a range of attitude choices that are increasingly difficult to agree with; that is, the items composing the scale range from those easy to agree with to those difficult to agree with. Respondents who agree with one of the "more difficult" attitude items will also generally agree with the "less difficult" ones.

Let us return to the researcher interested in measuring attitudes toward abortion. He or she might devise a series of items ranging from "easy to agree with" to "difficult to agree with." Such an approach might be represented by the following items.

> Do you agree or disagree that abortions should be permitted:
> 1. When the life of the woman is in danger.
> 2. In the case of incest or rape.
> 3. When the fetus appears to be unhealthy.
> 4. When the woman cannot afford to have a baby.
> 5. Whenever the woman wants one.

This array of items seems likely to result in responses consistent with Guttman scaling. A respondent agreeing with any one of the items is likely to also agree with those items numbered lower than that one. This would result in the "stepwise" pattern of responses characteristic of a Guttman scale, and in the scale scores presented in Table 4-4.

A Guttman scale is much more difficult to achieve than either a Thurstone or Likert scale. For a Guttman scale to work, the items must have been ordered and be perceived by the respondents as representing increasingly more difficult responses to the same attitude. If the respondents' pattern of responses fit the Guttman model, however, the resulting scale scores are likely to be an accurate measure of an attitude.

Table 4-4 Guttman Scale of Attitudes toward Abortion

Respon-dent	Life of Woman	Incest or Rape	Unhealthy Fetus	Afford	Anytime	Scale Score
1	Agree	Agree	Agree	Agree	Agree	5
2	Agree	Agree	Agree	Agree	Disagree	4
3	Agree	Agree	Agree	Disagree	Disagree	3
4	Agree	Agree	Disagree	Disagree	Disagree	2
5	Agree	Disagree	Disagree	Disagree	Disagree	1
6	Disagree	Disagree	Disagree	Disagree	Disagree	0

Source: Hypothetical data.

Through indexes and scales, researchers attempt to enhance both the accuracy and precision of their measures. Although these multi-item measures have received their most prevalent use in attitude research, they are often useful in other endeavors as well. Both indexes and scales require researchers to make decisions regarding the selection of individual items and the way in which the scores on those items will be combined to produce more useful measures of political phenomena.

Conclusion

To a large extent, a research project is only as good as the measurements that are developed and used in it. Inaccurate measurements will interfere with the testing of scientific explanations for political phenomena and may lead to erroneous conclusions. Imprecise measurements will limit the extent of the comparisons that can be made between observations and the precision of the knowledge that results from empirical research.

Despite the importance of good measurement, political science researchers often find that their measurement schemes are of uncertain accuracy and precision. Abstract concepts are difficult to measure in a valid way, and the practical constraints of time and money often jeopardize the reliability and precision of measurements. The quality of a researcher's measurements makes an important contribution to the results of his or her empirical research and should not be lightly or routinely sacrificed.

Sometimes the accuracy of measurements may be enhanced through the use of multi-item measures. With indexes and scales, researchers select multiple indicators of a phenomenon, assign scores to each of these indicators, and combine those scores into a summary measure. While these methods have been used most frequently in attitude research, they can also be used in other situations to improve the accuracy and precision of single-item measures.

Notes

1. Edward R. Tufte, *Data Analysis for Politics and Policy* (Englewood Cliffs, N.J.: Prentice-Hall, 1974); Gary C. Jacobson, *Money in Congressional Elections* (New Haven, Conn.: Yale University Press, 1980); Ted Robert Gurr, *Why Men Rebel* (Princeton, N.J.: Princeton University Press, 1970); and David O. Sears, Carl P. Hensler, and Leslie K. Speer, "Whites' Opposition to 'Busing': Self-Interest or Symbolic Politics?" *American Political Science Review* 73 (June 1979): 369-84.
2. Tufte, *Data Analysis*, 8-18.
3. Jacobson, *Money in Congressional Elections*, 38-45.
4. Sears, Hensler, and Speer, "Whites' Opposition to 'Busing,' " 373-74.
5. Edward G. Carmines and Richard A. Zeller, *Reliability and Validity Assessment*, Series on Quantitative Applications in the Social Sciences, No. 07-001, Sage University Papers (Beverly Hills, Calif.: Sage, 1979).
6. Philip E. Converse, "The Nature of Belief Systems in Mass Publics," in David E. Apter, ed., *Ideology and Discontent* (New York: Free Press, 1964); D. M. Vaillancourt, "Stability of Children's Survey Responses," *Public Opinion Quarterly* 37 (Fall 1973): 373-87; J. Miller McPherson, Susan Welch, and Cal Clark, "The Stability and Reliability of Political Efficacy: Using Path Analysis to Test Alternative Models," *American Political Science Review* 71 (June 1977): 509-21; and Philip E. Converse and Gregory B. Markus, "The New CPS Election Study Panel," *American Political Science Review* 73 (March 1979): 32-49.
7. Raymond E. Wolfinger and Steven I. Rosenstone, *Who Votes?* (New Haven, Conn: Yale University Press, 1980).
8. Ibid., Appendix A.
9. Kenneth D. Bailey, *Methods of Social Research* (New York: Free Press, 1978), 58.
10. This is a good example of a situation where the absence of a relationship does not necessarily mean the measure lacks construct validity. Because persons with low GRE scores are generally not admitted to graduate school, we lack performance measures for them. Consequently, the people for whom we can test the relationship between test scores and performance may be of similar ability and may not exhibit meaningful variation in their graduate school performance. Hence the test scores may be valid indicators of ability, but only for a less selective sample of test takers. The lack of a relationship in Table 4-1 undercuts claims of test score validity, but it does not necessarily disprove such claims.

11. The distinction between an interval and a ratio level measure is not always clear, and some political science texts do not distinguish between them. Interval level measures in political science are rather rare, while ratio level measures (money spent, age, number of children, years living in the same location, for example) are more prevalent.

Terms Introduced

Alternative-form. Calculating reliability by repeating different but equivalent measures at two or more points in time.

Construct validity. Demonstrating validity for a measure by showing it is related to the measure of another concept.

Content validity. Demonstrating validity by ensuring that the full domain of a concept is measured.

Correlation matrix. A table showing the relationships among a number of discrete measures.

Face validity. Asserting validity by arguing that a measure corresponds closely to the concept it is designed to measure.

Guttman scale. A multi-item measure in which respondents are presented with increasingly difficult measures of approval for an attitude.

Index. A multi-item measure in which individual scores on a set of items are combined to form a summary measure.

Interval. A measure for which a one unit difference in scores is the same throughout the range of the measure.

Level of measurement. An indication of what is meant by assigning scores or numerals to empirical observations.

Likert scale. A multi-item measure in which the items are selected based on their ability to discriminate between those scoring high and those scoring low on the measure.

Measurement. The process by which phenomena are observed systematically and represented by scores or numerals.

Nominal. A measure for which different scores represent different, but not ordered, categories.

Operational definition. The rules by which a concept is measured and scores assigned.

Ordinal. A measure for which the scores represent ordered categories that are not necessarily equally distant from each other.

Ratio. A measure for which the scores possess the full mathematical properties of the numbers assigned.

Reliability. The extent to which a measure yields the same results on repeated trials.

Split-halves. Calculating reliability by comparing the results of two equivalent measures made at the same time.

Test-retest. Calculating reliability by repeating the same measure at two or more points in time.

Thurstone scale. A multi-item measure in which the goal is to select items that represent the entire range of an attitude at equal intervals.

Validity. The correspondence between a measure and the concept it is supposed to measure.

Exercises

1. Read J. Miller McPherson, Susan Welch, and Cal Clark, "The Stability and Reliability of Political Efficacy: Using Path Analysis to Test Alternative Models," *American Political Science Review* 71 (June 1977): 509-21. With what measurement issue are the authors concerned? What do they conclude about the measure of political efficacy that they analyze?

2. Read Jerald G. Bachman and Patrick M. O'Malley, "When Four Months Equal a Year: Inconsistencies in Student Reports of Drug Use," *Public Opinion Quarterly* 45 (Winter 1981): 536-48. Are the authors concerned with the reliability or validity of their measures? What do they conclude about the adequacy of their measure of drug use? On what is this conclusion based?

3. What would be the level of measurement of the following measures?

a. The unemployment rates of the 50 American states.

b. The region of the country in which people were born.

c. How frequently people attended religious services in the last two months.

d. The number of employees in different government agencies.

e. The number of times incumbent senators voted the way the president wanted them to on 20 key pieces of legislation.

f. The occupation of candidates for public office (for example, lawyer, teacher, farmer, banker).

g. The percent of different corporations' pre-tax profit accounted for by overseas sales.

h. Whether people read the daily newspaper every day, almost every day, frequently, occasionally, seldom, or never.

Suggested Readings

Babbie, Earl R. *Survey Research Methods.* Belmont, Calif.: Wadsworth, 1973.

Carmines, Edward G., and Richard A. Zeller. *Reliability and Validity Assessment.* Series on Quantitative Applications in the Social Sciences. No. 07-001, Sage University Papers. Beverly Hills, Calif.: Sage, 1979.

Kerlinger, Fred N. *Behavioral Research*. New York: Holt, Rinehart & Winston, 1979.

Robinson, John P., Jerrold G. Rusk, and Kendra B. Head. *Measures of Political Attitudes*. Ann Arbor, Mich.: Institute for Social Research, 1969.

Rubin, Herbert J. *Applied Social Research*. Columbus: Northern Illinois University, 1983.

Smith, Barbara, et al. *Political Research Methods*. Boston: Houghton Mifflin, 1976.

5. *Research Design*

A research design is a plan that shows how a researcher intends to fulfill the goals of a proposed study. It indicates the necessary observations that will be made to provide answers to the questions posed by the researcher, how the observations will be made, and the analytical and statistical procedures to be used once the data are collected. If the goal of the research is to test hypotheses, a research design will explain how this is to be accomplished.

A research design has been defined as a plan that "guides the investigator in the process of collecting, analyzing, and interpreting observations. It is a logical model of proof that allows the researcher to draw inferences concerning causal relations among the variables under investigation. The research design also defines the domain of generalizability, that is, whether the obtained interpretations can be generalized to a larger population or to different situations."[1]

Developing the research design is just as important as developing research questions and hypotheses. A poor research design may produce insignificant and erroneous conclusions, no matter how original and brilliant the hypothesis. In this chapter we will discuss various research designs and their advantages and disadvantages and show how a poor research design can result only in tentative and uninformative research.

Many factors affect the choice of a particular research design. One is the purpose of the investigation. Whether the research is intended to be exploratory, descriptive, or explanatory will most likely influence the choice of a research design. Another is the practical limitations on how researchers may test their hypotheses. Some research designs may be unethical, others impossible to implement for lack of data or sufficient time and money. Researchers frequently must balance what is humanly possible to accomplish against what would be ideally done to test a particular hypothesis. Consequently, many of the research designs that researchers actually use are unfortunate but necessary compromises. The conclusions that reasonably may be drawn from most political science research are more tentative and incomplete than they might be.

All research designs to test hypotheses are attempts by researchers to 1) establish a relationship between two or more variables, 2) demonstrate that the results are generally true in the real world, 3) reveal whether one phenomenon precedes another in time, and 4) eliminate as many alternative explanations for a phenomenon as possible. This chapter will explain how various research designs allow or do not allow researchers to accomplish these four objectives. Two different types of designs will be discussed: experimental and nonexperimental.

Experimentation

Experimental research designs differ from nonexperimental designs in that they allow the researcher to have more control over the independent variable, the units of analysis, and the environment in which behavior occurs. Consequently, experimental designs allow researchers to establish causal explanations for political behavior more easily than nonexperimental designs do. However, very few types of significant political behaviors are studied by political scientists with experimentation. Nonetheless, it is important to understand how an experimental research design allows researchers to evaluate causal explanations.

An ideal experiment has five basic characteristics.[2] First, there are experimental groups that receive an experimental or test stimulus and control groups that do not. Second, the researcher determines the composition of the experimental and control groups by choosing the subjects and assigning them to one of the groups. In other words, the researcher can control who experiences the independent variable and who does not. Third, the researcher has control over the introduction of the experimental treatment—the independent variable; that is, the researcher can determine when, and under what circumstances, the experimental group is exposed to the experimental stimulus. Fourth, the researcher is able to measure the dependent variable both before and after the experimental stimulus is given. And finally, the researcher is able to control the environment of the subjects in order to control or exclude extraneous factors that might affect the dependent variable.

In an ideal experiment a researcher can make causal statements and rule out alternative explanations; that is, he or she can argue that manipulation of the experimental stimulus caused the experimental and control groups to differ with respect to the dependent variable. Before we examine some of the types of experimental research designs used by researchers and the advantages and limitations of each, let us consider how we might experimentally test an actual hypothesis.

Suppose you want to test the hypothesis that "watching violence on television causes people to engage in aggressive social behavior." The independent variable, or experimental stimulus, is the amount of violence watched on television, and the dependent variable is the frequency with which people exhibit aggressive social behavior. To test this hypothesis you might ask some people to experience the experimental stimulus (watch a lot of television violence); others you would not permit to experience this same stimulus. In this experiment you would be able to exercise enough control over the participants' lives that you could determine who watched a lot of television violence and who did not. You also could control when, how often, for how long, and under what conditions those in the experimental group would watch violence on television. The next step would be to observe the amount of aggressive social behavior by all participants in the experiment, both before and after the experimental group watched the violent programming. It would be important to ensure that nothing other than the difference in television viewing affected one group and not the other during the course of the experiment.

If all of these conditions could be met, an experiment could be conducted that would shed considerable light on the hypothesis. You would be particularly interested in the amount, and change in the amount, of aggressive behavior for the experimental group compared with the control group and would have some basis for concluding that any difference could be attributed to the experimental stimulus. In other words, if significant differences in the aggressive behavior of the two groups occurred, then you could legitimately conclude that watching television violence was a causal explanation for at least a portion of a group's aggression.

This is a very persuasive kind of evidence for a researcher to have, hence the attraction of experimentation. But problems arise with the conduct of experiments. These problems are often discussed in terms of internal and external validity.[3]

Internal Validity

Internal validity deals with whether the manipulation or variation in the independent variable makes a difference in the dependent variable. The internal validity of experimental research may be adversely affected by history, maturation, testing, statistical regression, and several other factors.

History. As we have seen, one of the characteristics of experimental research is that the researcher has enough control over the environment to make sure that exposure to the experimental stimulus is the only difference between the experimental and control groups. Sometimes, however, events other than the experimental stimulus occur between the pre-treatment and post-treatment measurements of the dependent variable and these affect the dependent variable. For example, suppose that after an automobile safety inspection program is introduced in a state, a crackdown on drunk driving also begins. A decline in the traffic fatality rate could be due to the inspection program, the drunk driving campaign, or a combination of both.

Maturation. The passage of time may also affect subjects and create differences between experimental and control groups. For example, subjects may grow older, or become tired or hungry during the course of an experiment. These changes may affect their reaction to the test stimulus and introduce an unanticipated effect on post-treatment scores.

Testing. The standard experimental research design includes a measurement of the dependent variable both before and after the experimental stimulus. However, the act of measuring the dependent variable prior to the experimental stimulus may itself affect the post-treatment scores of subjects. For example, suppose individuals who do poorly on the Scholastic Aptitude Test enroll in a course to improve their performance (the experimental stimulus), retake the SATs, and obtain higher scores. The improvement could be due to the course, to the experience that taking the SATs initially provided, or to a combination of the initial test and the course. Similarly, suppose a researcher wanted to see if watching a presidential debate makes viewers better informed than those not watching it. If the researcher measures the political awareness of the experimental and control groups prior to the debate, he or she runs the risks of sensitizing the subjects to certain topics or issues and contributing to a more attentive audience than would otherwise be the case. Consequently, we would not know for sure whether any increase in awareness was due to the debate, the pre-test, or a combination of both. Fortunately, some research designs have been developed to separate these various effects.

Statistical Regression. Sometimes a person is selected for participation in an experimental program because of some extreme characteristic such as very high or low reading test scores. These scores may be temporary deviations—due to illness, fatigue, or emotional upset—from what the person would normally measure. After subsequent retesting, the scores would be expected to return to normal and become less extreme regardless of the impact of the person's participation in any special program. If this happens, improvements in scores may be attributed erroneously to the program.

Experimental Mortality. In assigning subjects to experimental and control groups, a researcher hopes that the two groups will be equivalent. If subjects drop out of the experiment, experimental and control groups that may have been the same at the start may no longer be equivalent. Thus differential loss of participants from comparison groups may raise doubts about whether the changes and variation in the dependent variable are due to manipulation of the independent variable.

Instrument Decay. Sometimes the instrument used to measure the dependent variable changes during the experiment so that the pre-test and post-test measures are not made in the same way. For example, a researcher may become tired and not take post-test measurements as carefully as pre-test ones. Or different persons with different biases may conduct the pre-test and post-test. Thus changes in the dependent variable may be due to measurement changes, not to the experimental stimulus.

Selection. If experimental and control group subjects are not equivalent, then differences between the groups at the end of an experiment cannot be attributed conclusively to the independent variable. Bias in the selection of subjects may occur if a researcher does not control assignment of subjects to experimental and control groups or if the researcher personally assigns subjects in a biased manner. A common selection problem occurs when subjects volunteer to participate in a program. Volunteers may differ significantly from nonvolunteers.

Some of the difficulties that may prevent completion of a successful experiment may be anticipated and guarded against by using particular experimental designs. In other cases, however, a researcher cannot rule out all possible threats to internal validity. Nevertheless, because of the characteristics mentioned earlier, experimental research designs are better able to resist threats to internal validity than are other types of research designs.

External Validity

External validity refers to the representativeness of research findings and whether it is possible to generalize from them to other situations. One possible problem is that the same effects may not be found using a different population. For example, findings from an experiment investigating the effects of live television coverage on legislators' behavior in state legislatures with fewer than 100 members may not be generalizable to larger state legislative bodies or to Congress. In general, if a sample population is not representative of a larger population, the ability to generalize about the larger population will be limited.

Another question is whether slightly different experimental treatments will result in similar findings with small differences or in findings that are fundamentally different. For example, a small increase in city spending for neighborhood improvements may not result in a more positive attitude of residents toward their neighborhood or the city. A slightly larger increase, however, may have an effect, perhaps because it resulted in more noticeable improvements.

Threats to the external validity of an experiment also may be caused if the artificiality of the experimental setting makes it hard to generalize about findings in more natural settings. For example, subjects may react to a stimulus differently when they know they are being studied than when they are in a natural setting. Finally, subjects' behavior may be affected by testing. For example, if subjects react to the pre-test (not just to the experimental treatment), the findings may not be applicable to other subjects who are not exposed to a pre-test.

Despite these problems with experimental research designs, experiments are still attractive to researchers because they provide control over the subjects and their exposure to various levels of the independent variable.[4] The purpose of an experiment is to isolate and measure the effects of the independent variable or variables and to exclude other factors that might also influence the dependent variable. Control over the assignment of subjects to the experimental and control groups is used by researchers to exclude as many of these other factors as possible.

Control over Assignment of Subjects

Researchers attempt to exclude extraneous factors by assigning subjects to control and experimental groups in three different ways. One way is to assign subjects to the groups at random under the assumption that extraneous factors will affect all groups equally. *Assignment at random* is the practical choice when the researcher is not able to specify possible extraneous factors in advance or when there are so many that it is not possible to assign subjects to experimental and control groups equally.

Even if a researcher assigns subjects at random, extraneous factors may not be randomly distributed and therefore will affect the outcome of the experiment. This is especially true if the number of subjects is small. Prudent researchers do not assume that all significant factors are randomly distributed just because subjects have been assigned at random. In addition to random assignment, researchers often check to see if the control and experimental groups are, in fact, equal with regard to those factors that are suspected of influencing the dependent variable.

Precision matching is another way to assign subjects to groups in order to control extraneous factors. Precision matching is used if the researcher knows ahead of time that certain factors are related to differences in the dependent variable. In precision matching, the researcher matches pairs of subjects who are as similar as possible and assigns one to the experimental group and the other to the control group. Thus the researcher does not take the chance that random assignment will equalize the groups with respect to these factors. One problem with this method is that the greater the number of factors to be controlled, the more difficult it becomes to match subjects on all relevant characteristics and the larger the pool of prospective subjects required. A second problem is that not all extraneous factors may be identified ahead of time. To guard against bias in the assignment of pairs, members of the matched pairs should be randomly assigned to the control and experimental groups.

A third method of assigning subjects to groups is by *frequency distribution control*. Instead of matching pairs of subjects, the researcher makes sure that the experimental and control groups are identical in the distribution and average value of an extraneous variable. For example, if one wanted to control income as an extraneous factor, one would make sure that the average income of the control and experimental groups was similar. Frequency distribution control requires a smaller subject pool than precision matching, but it has the disadvantage that it can be done only for one variable at a time. Thus it is possible to equalize groups with respect to income and end up with all doctors in one group and all lawyers in another. If occupation were also a suspected extraneous factor, the experiment would be in jeopardy.

One of the biggest obstacles to experimentation in social science research is the inability of researchers to control assignment of subjects to experimental and control groups. This is especially true when public policies are involved. Even though the point of conducting an experiment is to test whether a treatment or program has a beneficial effect, it is often politically difficult to assign subjects to a control group; people assume that the experimental treatment must be beneficial otherwise the treatment or program would not have been proposed as a response to a public policy problem. In setting up experimental and control groups, social scientists generally lack sufficient authority or incentives to offer subjects.

Now that we have discussed experimental research in general and some problems associated with it, let us consider some specific experimental research designs. Each one represents a different attempt by the researcher to retain experimental control while also dealing with the various threats to internal and external validity. Students may not have the immediate opportunity to employ these research designs, but knowledge of them will help in evaluating research and in determining whether the research design employed by the researcher supports the conclusions that are reached.

Experimental Designs

Simple Post-test Design

The simplest experimental design involves two groups and two variables, one independent and one dependent. Subjects are assigned to one or the other of the two groups. One group, the experimental group, is exposed to a "treatment" or stimulus that represents the independent variable. The other group, the control group, is not. Then the dependent variable is measured for each group. This design may be diagrammed as follows:

(Random Assignment)	Treatment	Post-treatment Measurement of Dependent Variable
Experimental group	Yes	Yes
Control group	No	Yes

A researcher using this design can make causal inferences because he or she can make sure that the treatment occurred prior to measurement of the dependent variable. Furthermore, the researcher can argue that any difference between the two groups on the measure of the dependent variable is attributed to the difference in the treatment—in other words, to the introduction of the independent variable—between the groups. This design requires random assignment of subjects to the experimental and control groups, and therefore assumes that extraneous factors were controlled (that is, were the same for both groups). It also assumes that prior to the application of the experimental stimulus, both groups were equivalent with respect to the dependent variable.

A simple example will illustrate this design. Suppose we wanted to test the hypothesis that watching a national nominating convention on television makes people more informed politically. Using this research design, we would take our subjects, randomly assign them to a group that will watch a convention or a group that will not, and measure how well-informed the members of the two groups are after the convention is over. Any difference in the level of awareness between the two groups after the convention would be attributed to the impact of watching convention coverage.

The simple post-test experimental design assumes that the random assignment of subjects to the experimental and control groups creates two groups that are identical in all significant ways prior to the introduction of the experimental stimulus. Although this is a safe assumption, it is not always accurate. Post-treatment differences between the two groups may be the result of pre-treatment differences. Since it is impossible with this design to tell how much of the post-treatment difference is simply a reflection of pre-treatment differences, a second research design is often used.

'Classic' Pre-test and Post-test Design

Unlike the simplest experimental design, the classic experimental design provides for a pre-test of the dependent variable before the experimental stimulus is introduced. This design may be diagrammed this way:

(Random Assignment)	Pre-Treatment Measurement of Dependent Variable	Treatment	Post-Treatment Measurement of Dependent Variable
Experimental group	Yes	Yes	Yes
Control group	Yes	No	Yes

In this design it is possible to determine whether the groups actually are equivalent with respect to the dependent variable prior to the experimental treatment. The extra measurement provided by the pre-test strengthens the validity of the experiment by removing the doubt in the simple post-test design that the groups might not have been equivalent despite random assignment of subjects to groups. Furthermore, any pre-test difference between control and experimental groups can be taken into account when calculating the effect of the experimental stimulus.

For example, let's assume that a researcher wants to test the effect of a candidate's televised campaign commercials on the ability of voters to identify important issues in the campaign. In a post-test only experimental design, subjects would be randomly assigned to experimental and control groups, and one group of subjects would be shown the commercials while the other group would not. After the experimental group has seen the commercials, a test measuring the ability to identify campaign issues would be given to subjects in both groups. Suppose the average score on this test for the experimental group was 9.5 and 7.5 for the control group. The effect of having seen the campaign commercials would seem to be the difference in the two scores (2).

Now suppose a pre-test of issue awareness had also been given to both groups. The experimental group might have had a pre-test score of 8 and the control group a score of 7.5. In this case the presence of a pre-test would reveal to the researcher that the random assignment to the two groups did not create perfectly equivalent groups. Furthermore, the researcher would then realize that the gain in awareness for the experimental group was 1.5 (9-7.5), while the gain in awareness for the control group was 0 (7.5-7.5). Hence the researcher could conclude that the effect of seeing the ads translated into a 1.5 point change on the score of the experimental group, not 2 points as measured in the simple first design.

Pre-test, post-test designs with a control group have another advantage as well. Sometimes a considerable amount of time lapses between the pre-test and post-test. This increases the possibility that extraneous factors may intrude and cause the dependent variable to change. Historical events or maturation processes may take place, for example. If it can be assumed that extraneous factors affect control and experimental groups equally, then the effect of extraneous factors is measured by the change in the dependent variable for the control group. Therefore, change in the dependent variable due only to the experimental stimulus can be calculated as follows:

$$\text{Experimental effect} = \left(\begin{array}{c} \text{Post-test} \\ \text{score for} \\ \text{experimental} \\ \text{group} \end{array} - \begin{array}{c} \text{Pre-test} \\ \text{score for} \\ \text{experimental} \\ \text{group} \end{array} \right) - \left(\begin{array}{c} \text{Post-test} \\ \text{score for} \\ \text{control} \\ \text{group} \end{array} - \begin{array}{c} \text{Pre-test} \\ \text{score for} \\ \text{control} \\ \text{group} \end{array} \right) \quad (5.1)$$

Now assume for a moment that the post-test score for the control group was 8 instead of 7.5 (reflecting the possibility that the control group would increase its issue awareness over time even though it did not watch any political commercials on television). The effect of seeing the campaign commercials would be only a one-point difference in awareness: $(9.5 - 8.0) - (8.0 - 7.5) = 1$.

Although this classic experimental design allows researchers to assess the pre-treatment equivalence of the experimental and control groups, it, too, is vulnerable to a particular problem—namely, *testing* or *instrument reactivity*. In other words, the pre-test itself may sensitize or otherwise affect respondents and cause a change in the dependent variable for both control and experimental groups. For example, if you are in the control group, taking the pre-test may make you more attentive to information touched on in the test in the days and weeks that follow. To minimize the possibility of the pre-test having an enduring effect, researchers often allow a considerable amount of time to lapse between pre-test and post-test measurements. If the effect of the pre-test is equal for both control and experimental groups, any instrument reactivity caused by the pre-test would be factored out along with any other extraneous factors by Equation 5.1. The pre-test may sensitize both the control and experimental groups, but the effect may be greater for the experimental group. The pre-test may cause the experimental group to react differently to the treatment than it would have if there had been no pre-test. If the pre-test affects the experimental and control groups differently, the pre-test, post-test design does not permit precise measurement and adjustment for the effect of the pre-test.

In addition to instrument reactivity, there is another problem with the classic pre-test, post-test design: measurement error. So far we have assumed that all the measurements taken are precise and reliable measures of the independent and dependent variables. However, measurement error may affect the reliability of the difference measure between the pre-test and post-test. If the reliability of the instrument used in the pre-test and post-test is imperfect, the reliability of the measurement of the difference between two imperfect measures will be even less and may be unacceptable for use in drawing any conclusions.[5]

Despite these difficulties, the pre-test, post-test design is useful, particularly where there are several treatment groups with random assignment but no control group. This is often the case in program evaluation studies where researchers are investigating whether the program has produced changes in program participants.[6] If the program is believed to be beneficial, it may be difficult to establish a control group that receives no treatment. The pre-test, post-test design allows the researcher to compare change in two groups receiving different treatments. Any difference in change is attributed to differences in treatments. Without a control group, however, change between a pre-test and post-test does not absolutely establish the factors that caused the change. The researcher can never be sure what might have happened to subjects if no treatment had been given at all.

Multigroup Design

So far we have discussed mainly research involving one experimental and one control group. In multigroup designs the dependent variable is measured for each group, but instead of one experimental group and one control group, more experimental or control groups are added. This is useful if the independent variable can assume several values and if the researcher wants to see the possible effects of manipulating the independent variable in several different ways. Multigroup designs may involve a post-test only or both a pre-test and post-test.

Suppose you were concerned with the problem of how to increase the proportion of respondents who fill out and return mail questionnaires. The proportion of respondents who return questionnaires in a mail survey is usually quite low. Investigators have attempted to increase these response rates by including an incentive or token of appreciation in the survey. Since these add to the cost of the survey, researchers like to know whether the incentives do increase response rates and which ones are most effective and cost efficient.

To test the effect of various incentives, you could use a multigroup post-test design. If you wanted to test the effects of five treatments, you could randomly assign subjects to six groups. One group would receive no reward (the control group); each of the other groups would receive a different reward—for example, 25¢, 50¢, $1.00, a key ring, or a pen. Response rates (the post-treatment measure of the dependent variable) for the groups could then be compared. Table 5-1 presents the results.

The response rates indicate that rewards increase response rates and that monetary incentives have more effect than do token gifts. Furthermore, it seems that the dollar incentive is not cost effective since it did not yield a sufficiently greater response rate than the 50¢ reward to warrant the additional expense. Other experiments of this type could be conducted to compare the effects of prepaid versus promised monetary rewards or the inclusion or exclusion of a prestamped return envelope.

Table 5-1   Mail Survey Incentive Experiment

(Random Assignment)	Treatment	Response Rate
Experimental Group 1	25¢	45.0%
Experimental Group 2	50¢	51.0
Experimental Group 3	$1.00	52.0
Experimental Group 4	pen	38.0
Experimental Group 5	key ring	37.0
Control Group	no reward	30.2

Source: Hypothetical data.

Multigroup Time Series Design

The pre-test must come before the experimental treatment and the post-test must come afterwards, but exactly how long before and how long afterwards? Researchers seldom know for sure. Therefore, a research design including several pre-treatment and post-treatment measures is often used when a researcher is uncertain exactly how quickly the effect of the independent variable should be observed or when the most reliable pre-test measurement of the dependent variable should be taken.

For example, a three-group, four-measurement design might consist of the following:

(Random assignment)	Pre-test First	Pre-test Second	Treatment	Post-test First	Post-test Second
Experimental Group 1	Yes	Yes	Yes	Yes	Yes
Experimental Group 2	Yes	Yes	Yes but different	Yes	Yes
Control Group	Yes	Yes	No	Yes	Yes

One good reason to use this design is to establish pre-treatment trends in the dependent variable. Multiple measurements can be used to check for stability in the dependent variable for all groups prior to treatment. In addition, multiple measurements after treatment allow researchers to see if treatment effects are immediate or delayed and whether the effects are lasting. The issue of lasting effects is often an important one in the evaluation of programs in education, health, and criminal justice. One drawback to this design, however, is that the possibility of instrument reactivity becomes greater when there are multiple measurements of the dependent variable.

An example of a multigroup time series design would be an attempt to test the relationship between watching a presidential debate and support for the candidates. Suppose you conducted a classical experiment, randomly assigning some people to a group that watches a debate and others to a group that does not watch the debate. On the pre- and post-tests you might receive the following scores:

	Predebate Support for Candidate X	Treatment	Postdebate Support for Candidate X
Experimental Group 1	60	Yes	50
Control Group	55	No	50

These scores seem to indicate that the control group was slightly less supportive of Candidate X before the debate (that is, the random assignment did not work perfectly) and that the debate led to a decline in support for Candidate X of 5 percent $(60 - 50) - (55 - 50)$.

Suppose, however, that you had the following additional measures.

	Pre-test				Post-test		
	First	Second	Third	Treatment	First	Second	Third
Experimental Group	80	70	60	Yes	50	40	30
Control Group	65	60	55	No	50	45	40

It appears that support for Candidate X eroded throughout the whole period for both the experimental and control groups and that the rate of decline was consistently more rapid for the experimental group (that is, the two groups were not equivalent prior to the debate). Viewed from this perspective, it seems that the debate had no effect on the experimental group since the rate of decline both before and after the debate was the same.

Factorial Designs

In experiments where researchers are interested in determining the effects of several independent variables on a dependent variable, alone and in combination, factorial designs are used. The simplest factorial design is the 2 x 2 design. In this design there are two independent variables, each of which takes on two values. Factorial designs may involve more than two dimensions and an independent variable may have any number of values or levels.

An example of a 2 x 2 design is an experiment to test the effectiveness of token gifts and follow-up reminders alone and in combination on the response rate in a mail survey. Four hundred respondents are randomly assigned in equal numbers to the four treatment groups shown in Table 5-2.

To examine the effect of each independent variable singly, ignore the individual cell response rates and observe the response rates at the bottom and along the side of the table. There is a 12.5 percentage point

Table 5-2   Response Rates in Mail Survey Experiment

	No Gift	Token Gift	
No Follow Up	30.0% (30/100)	45.0% (45/100)	37.5% (75/200)
Follow Up	50.0% (50/100)	60.0% (60/100)	55.0% (110/200)
	40% (80/200)	52.5% (105/200)	

improvement (52.5 percent − 40 percent) in response rates when a token gift is included with the mail survey. Also a follow-up letter improves response rates. Therefore, each independent variable has a positive effect on response rates. By looking at the individual cell response rates, you can see that the two treatments combine to increase response rates well above any other combination (60 percent).

Solomon Four-Group Design

We have mentioned the possible problem of instrument reactivity caused by using a pre-test. A more complex pattern of reactivity, however, may occur: the pre-test and test stimulus may interact to cause. additional change in the dependent variable, beyond the effects attributable to the pre-test and the test stimulus individually.

Consider this example. An experiment is designed to test the effect of a film on water use and supplies on attitudes about water conservation. Subjects are assigned at random to two groups. Both groups are given a pre-test asking them about their attitudes about water conservation. Then the test group, but not the control group, is shown the film. Sometime later both groups are retested on their attitudes toward water conservation. It is possible that the control group will show a change in attitudes if the pre-test made the subjects more aware of water conservation issues. Suppose the experimental group showed a much larger change. The difference between the control and test groups could be due to the film, but it also could be due to the pre-test and the film. The combination might create a much greater effect than simply the sum of the effect of the pre-test alone and the effect of the film alone. The experimental group may have watched the film differently and responded to it differently than it would have otherwise because it had been given the pre-test. (Perhaps it is easier to understand the concept of measurement interaction by recalling how you may have felt after consuming a little too much pizza or beer. Now how would you have felt if you had had too much pizza and beer at the same sitting?)

The Solomon four-group design is an experimental design that allows a researcher to measure the interaction between a pre-test and test stimulus. The effect of the treatment, the effect of the pre-test on the post-test, and the effect of other extraneous factors can also be measured.[7] Thus, unlike the two-group pre-test, post-test design, extraneous factors are isolated from pre-test factors.

In this design one group is given the pre-test, test stimulus and a post-test. A second group is given the test stimulus, and post-test, but no pre-test. A third group is given a pre-test and post-test, but no experimental stimulus. A fourth group is given only the post-test. The design can be represented as follows:

Random Assignment	*Pre-Test*	*Treatment*	*Post-Test*
Experimental Group 1	Yes	Yes	Yes
Experimental Group 2	No	Yes	Yes
Control Group 1	Yes	No	Yes
Control Group 2	No	No	Yes

The total change in the first experimental group can be summarized as:

$$\text{Change} = \text{Pre-test effect} + \text{treatment effect} + \text{interaction effect} + \text{other factors} \qquad (5.2)$$

Table 5-3 presents the result of this four-group experiment. Total change in Experimental Group 1 equals 10 ($20 - 10$). The pre-test effect is determined by comparing the post-test scores of the two control groups, one of which had a pre-test. Subtracting the post-test of Control Group 2 from that of Control Group 1, we get ($12 - 11$) for a pre-test only effect. The treatment effect can be determined by comparing Experimental Group 2, which received no pre-test and saw only the film, and Control Group 2, which received no pre-test and did not see the film. The treatment effect equals 4 ($15 - 11$). To calculate the effect of other factors only, we need to compare the post-test score for Control Group 2 with the pre-test scores of the groups given a pre-test. Since subjects were assigned at random to all four groups, we can assume that the pre-test score of Control Group 2 is the average of the pre-test scores of the two

Table 5-3 Water Conservation Test

(*Random Assignment*)	*Pre-test*	*Treatment*	*Post-test*
Experiment Group 1	10	Yes	20
Experiment Group 2		Yes	15
Control Group 1	10	No	12
Control Group 2	(assumed to be 10)	No	11

pre-tested groups or 10. Thus the effect of other factors affecting the dependent variable is 1 (11 − 10).

Substituting these numbers into Equation 5.2 and rearranging the terms to solve for interaction, we find that 4 points out of the 10 point change were due to the interaction between the pre-test and the test stimulus.

$$10 = 1 + 4 + \text{interaction effect} + 1$$
$$\text{Interaction effect} = 10 - 1 - 4 - 1 = 4$$

In addition to the six types of experimental designs mentioned here—the simple post-test design; the classic pre-test, post-test design; the multigroup design; the multigroup time series design; the factorial design; and the Solomon four-group design—there are numerous others described in the Suggested Readings listed at the end of this chapter.

Field Experiments

Field experiments are experimental designs applied in a natural setting; thus they are not really a separate kind of design. In field experiments, researchers try to control the selection of subjects, their assignment to treatment groups, and the manipulation of the independent variable. Field experiments differ from laboratory experiments because the environment in which the subjects behave cannot be completely controlled. Thus there is a greater chance for extraneous factors—such as historical events—to intrude and affect experimental results. It may be possible to choose natural settings that are isolated in some respects, thereby approximating a controlled environment, but the researcher can only hope that the environment remains unchanged during the course of a field experiment.

Field experiments should not necessarily be considered inferior to laboratory experiments. The artificial environment of a laboratory or controlled setting may seriously affect the external validity of an experiment. Something that can be shown only in a laboratory may have limited applicability in the real world. A program or treatment that is successful in a controlled setting may not be successful in a natural setting.

An interesting example of a field experiment in political science is the New Jersey experiment in income maintenance funded by the Office of Economic Opportunity and conducted from 1967 to 1971.[8] This effort was the forerunner of other large-scale social experiments designed to test the effects of new social programs. The experiment is a good illustration of the difficulty of mounting a large social experiment.

At the time of the experiment, dissatisfaction with the existing welfare system was high because of its cost and because it was thought to discourage the poor from lifting themselves out of poverty. Families headed by able-bodied men generally were excluded from welfare programs and the income of welfare recipients was taxed at such a rate that many thought there was little incentive for recipients to work.

In 1965 a negative income tax was proposed that would provide a minimum, nontaxable allowance to all families and that would attempt to maintain work incentives by allowing the poor to keep a significant fraction of their earnings. For example, a family of four might be guaranteed an income of $5,000 and would be allowed to keep 50 percent of all its earnings up to a break-even point where it could choose to remain in the program or opt out. If the break-even income was $10,000, a family earning $10,000 could receive $5,000 guaranteed minimum plus half of $10,000 ($5,000) for a total of $10,000 or it could keep all the $10,000 earned and choose not to receive any income from the government. The idea was opposed by those who thought a guaranteed minimum income would induce people to reduce their work effort. Others were concerned about how families would use the cash allowances. Numerous questions also were raised about the administration of the program. Because of these uncertainties, an experiment was designed to test the consequences of a guaranteed minimun income system.

The experimental design included two experimental factors. One was the income guarantee level, expressed as a percent of the poverty line. The level is the amount a family received if other income was zero. The other factor was the rate at which each dollar of earned income was taxed. The design showing the experimental conditions is presented in Table 5-4.

Table 5-4 Experimental Design of New Jersey Income-Maintenance Experiment

Guarantee (percent of poverty line)	Tax Rate		
	30%	*50%*	*70%*
125		X	
100		X	X
75	X	X	X
50	X	X	

Note: X represents experimental conditions actually tested.

This 4 x 3 factorial design allowed researchers to examine the effect of the variation in one factor while the other was held constant. For example, it allowed researchers to examine the effect of varying the tax rate from 30 to 50 to 70 percent while the guarantee remained set at 75 percent of the poverty line.

Certain combinations of experimental treatments were not chosen because they were not realistic policy options or because they increased the cost of the study. In assigning families to cells, there was a tradeoff between the number of families that could be included in the study and the number of families assigned to each cell since some cells were more costly than others. The cells with the most likely national policy options (the 100-50 and 75-50 plans) were assigned more families to make sure that enough families completed the experiment. Finally, for some of the less generous combinations, the researchers experienced difficulty in finding eligible families willing to participate in the experiment. Families placed in these cells were likely to receive at most a small payment because they were near the break-even point. This situation created resentment within the community because it was hoped that participants would benefit from participating in the experiment beyond the nominal payment families were given each time they completed an income report. If the researchers had had complete control over their subjects, assignment problems would have been less. But in research involving human subjects, such control is understandably lacking.

Only families headed by able-bodied males were eligible for the experiment because of the great interest in the possible impact the program would have on the work effort of poor families. Information about the work behavior of females with dependent children was not considered a good indicator of the work response of able-bodied males to public assistance. Very little was known about the work response of males because, as a group, able-bodied men and their families were not entitled to general public assistance.

In the rest of this section we will explore some of the issues and problems faced during this field experiment.

Generalizability.   To limit possible extraneous factors, families were chosen from a fairly homogeneous setting—New Jersey. Because a nationally dispersed sample was not chosen, however, the ability to generalize findings to a national program was limited. Generalizability was also affected by the three-year duration of the experiment. Families knew that the program was not permanent, and this may have affected their behavior.

Instrumentation Difficulties.   The experiment encountered income measurement problems. The income reports asked for gross income, but families had trouble distinguishing between net and gross income. Families in the experimental groups learned more quickly how to fill out the reports correctly than control group families because they were asked to report income every month. Control families (that is, other low-income families) were asked only every three months. As a result, the accuracy of income data changed over time and differentially for experimental and control group families. This one month-three month difference arose because researchers were afraid that too much contact with control families would change their behavior (instrument reactivity) and make them less than true controls. Such are the tradeoffs that researchers must make to avoid the numerous threats to the validity of experiments.

Uncontrolled Environment. In field experiments, unlike laboratory experiments, researchers are not in complete control of subjects' environments. This problem was dramatically illustrated during the New Jersey income-maintenance experiment. In the middle of the experiment, New Jersey adopted AFDC-UP, a public assistance program. Eligible families were those with dependent children and an unemployed parent, male or female. One reason New Jersey originally had been chosen was because it did not have this program. AFDC-UP provided an attractive alternative to some of the experimental cell conditions, and thus many families dropped out of the experiment.

Another problem arose because there were not enough eligible families in the New Jersey communities that were chosen to provide sufficient ethnic diversity. As a consequence, an urban area in northeastern Pennsylvania was included. However, the families in that area faced different conditions than the New Jersey families and varied on some important characteristics such as home ownership. One purpose of the study was to examine whether ethnic groups responded differently to the income-maintenance program. Because whites were represented mostly from one site, it became difficult to separate ethnic differences from site-induced differences.

Ethical Issues. Even though participation in the program was voluntary, the researchers were concerned about the effect of termination of the experiment on families that had been receiving payments. At the start of the experiment, families were given a card with the termination date of payments printed on it. Researchers debated tapering off payments and reminding families of the approaching end. It was decided to remind the families once toward the end, and research field offices remained open as referral agencies in case families needed help. But none requested help. Answers to a questionnaire three months after the last payment indicated that there were no serious adverse effects on the families caused by the experiment.

Major Findings. There was only a 5 to 6 percent reduction in average hours worked by the male heads of families who received negative income tax payments. This reduction occurred only among white men. For black men, average hours increased, although not significantly. For Spanish-speaking men, hours decreased but also not significantly. Researchers were unable to explain this unexpected finding, and therefore it may be unreliable. The behavior of black working wives was not affected, while Spanish-speaking and white working wives reduced their work effort considerably. Experimental families made larger investments in housing and durable goods than control families. There was also an indication that experimental families experienced increased educational attainment.

The experiment failed to provide accurate cost estimates for alternative negative income tax plans or conclusive evidence on the work disincentive of various tax rates. Because of these shortcomings, it did not provide conclusive evidence in favor of or against a negative income tax plan.

This is a good example of the difficulty of studying a political phenomenon both experimentally and in a natural setting. Political scientists seldom have the resources or the control over subjects and other phenomena to conduct experiments on political behavior of the type attempted in New Jersey. Consequently, researchers interested in explaining political phenomena usually have to rely on other kinds of approaches.

Nonexperimental Designs

We described experimental research designs in some detail because they capture the logic of testing the effect of an independent variable and are the standard against which research is often evaluated. In actual practice, however, political scientists seldom use any of these experimental designs. The reason is really quite simple: political scientists seldom have sufficient control over people's behavior and the introduction of experimental stimuli to conduct experimental research.

Suppose, for example, that a researcher wanted to test the hypothesis that poverty causes people to commit robberies. Following the logic of experimental research, the researcher would have to randomly assign people to two groups, measure the number of robberies committed by members of the two groups prior to the experimental treatment, force the experimental group to become poor, and then remeasure the number of robberies committed at some later date. Clearly, people are understandably reluctant to allow researchers to have this much control over their lives. (Witness the difficulties that arose when such an "experiment" was conducted with two people in the movie *Trading Places.*)

As a result of the many obstacles to conducting experimental research, political scientists have developed a number of nonexperimental research designs that are more practical. In these designs only a single group is used or the researcher has no control over the application of the test stimulus or independent variable. A few of these designs are described below.

Pre-test, Post-test Design

The pre-test, post-test design involves only one group that is given a pre-test, a test stimulus, and a post-test. There is no control group, and it is assumed that any change in the dependent variable is due to the test stimulus. Obviously, there is no way of knowing for sure that a change in the dependent variable was due to the experimental factor and not to other factors. Also there is no way to check for pre-test effects and pre-test test stimulus interaction.

Suppose, for example, that we measured the level of political interest for a group of people, had them all watch a televised presidential debate, remeasured levels of political interest, and then observed that the amount of interest increased. Would we be justified in concluding that watching the debate caused an increase in political interest? Clearly, the answer is no because we do not know what would have happened in the absence of watching the debate. The increase in political interest could have been the result of any number of other factors, including the pre-test and participation in the project, as well as a secular trend (for example, political interest in general was on the rise).

Interrupted Time Series Design

An improvement over the single group pre-test, post-test design is the interrupted time series design. In this design numerous measures of the dependent variable are taken both before and after the treatment, but still for only one group. The premeasurements allow a researcher to establish trends in the dependent variable. These trends may be linear (either increasing or decreasing) or cyclical, as illustrated in Figure 5-1. After the trends are established, the researcher introduces (or observes) the experimental stimulus. A change in direction of the dependent variable away from the established trend may indicate that the test stimulus has had an effect. (In Figure 5-1 such an effect is presumably present in examples B and C, but not A.) This assumes that nothing else changed that might have affected the dependent variable and that the trend would have continued undisturbed if not for the test stimulus. Tufte might have used this research design in his study of the impact of auto inspection programs by examining the trends in automobile fatalities in states before and after the introduction of inspection programs.

Time series studies may be affected by numerous threats to internal validity. For example, instrument change may affect the measurement of the dependent variable over time. This is especially possible if the researcher relies on existing data collected by others. For example, time series studies are often used to investigate the impact of governmental programs. City crime rates may be compared for several years before and after a change in police patrol practices. Achievement scores of school

Figure 5-1   Examples of Pre-treatment Trends in the Dependent
Variable

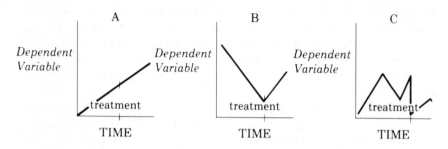

children may be observed before and after a change in the school's reading program. City budgets may be examined before and after reorganization of city departments. In these instances, conclusions may be jeopardized by changes in the method of recording crimes, different achievement tests, or different accounting methods. The longer the time period under study, the more likely instrument change will occur.

Another problem with time series studies is that subjects may react to multiple measurements by becoming bored, tired, or by trying to be consistent. In some cases, however, multiple testing may help a respondent to relax and give more natural answers or to learn what information is desired by the researcher so that more accurate and valid answers may be given.

Finally, since time series studies also lack a control group, we cannot be certain that all post-treatment changes are due only to the experimental stimulus. Other factors present or occurring at approximately the same time can also influence the dependent variable. For example, it is difficult to tell how much public opinion was affected by the civil rights movement, the Vietnam War, and the federal government's War on Poverty since all three "experimental stimuli" occurred during the 1960s and there is no control group that was not appreciably "exposed" to them all.

One of the problems with the two nonexperimental research designs discussed so far is the lack of a control group with which to compare the behavior of the experimental group. In experimental research the researcher can create a control group by preventing exposure to the independent variable. This cannot be done in nonexperimental research, but sometimes researchers can use a control group that exists naturally (that is, without the researcher's interference). The next two research designs are ones in which a control group of sorts is present.

Cross-sectional Design

In a cross-sectional research design, measurements of the independent and dependent variables are taken at the same point in time. The measurements of the independent variable are used to construct quasi-experimental and quasi-control groups that have naturally occurred, and the measurements of the dependent variable are used to assess the differences between the quasi-experimental and quasi-control groups.

For example, to test the hypothesis that "those with more education earn more income" a researcher could divide people into groups with varying amounts of education. In this way the quasi-control group (those with no formal education) and the quasi-experimental group (the others) may be observed. (Notice, however, that the researcher did not control who was in each group by forcing people to have differing amounts of education. The groups were simply naturally occurring and observed.) The income levels for each of these groups could then be measured and contrasted to assess the impact of education on income.

The cross-sectional design is frequently used in political science research. In fact, most of the examples in Chapter 1 of scientific political studies relied on this type of research design. In the study of attitudes toward busing, for example, the researchers used survey data to measure the dependent variable (support for busing) and the independent variables (racial intolerance, political conservatism, and self-interest in the busing issue) at the same point in time.[9] They divided people into groups based on the measures of the independent variable and then observed the amount of the dependent variable in each of the groups. Recall that they found that measures of racial intolerance and political conservatism correlated with support for busing while measures of self-interest in busing did not.

This study and others of this type have several limitations. Because all measures were taken at one point in time, the researchers do not know for sure that racial intolerance or political conservatism preceded attitudes toward busing. Therefore, they cannot say for sure that racial intolerance caused attitudes toward busing, even though there is a strong relationship between the two. The respondents' attitudes toward busing, after all, might have been formed before their racial intolerance. A second problem is that since the subjects were not randomly assigned to treatment groups, the differences between treatment groups might have been due to factors other than the independent variables under consideration.

Researchers attempt to remove the effects of other factors by controlling for them statistically (a process we will describe in Chapter 13); that is, they attempt to make the comparison groups equivalent by holding relevant extraneous factors constant and then observing the relationship between independent and dependent variables. But holding these factors constant is problematic and ultimately impossible, since it is very difficult to be sure that all relevant variables have been controlled for.

Edward Tufte's study of automobile traffic fatalities, introduced in Chapter 1, is also essentially a cross-sectional research design.[10] Recall that the purpose of this study was to find out whether compulsory automobile safety inspection programs help reduce traffic fatalities. Hence the hypothesis tested was "states with inspection programs have fewer automobile deaths than states without inspection programs." Tufte measured the relevant variables at the same time, even though he used the average of auto fatality rates in three years as the dependent variable. Note also that he did not control the assignment of states to different experimental conditions (that is, inspection program or no inspection program). Rather he observed the naturally occurring groups of states with different inspection programs. This research design affects the conclusions that Tufte was able to draw from his study.

The average number of traffic fatalities per 100,000 people for inspected states was 26.1. For uninspected states it was 31.9. Would we be safe to conclude, therefore, that inspection programs caused the lower death rate? Possibly, but there are some problems with this conclusion. First, since the study lacks a pre-test of the dependent variable, it may be that there has always been a difference in the auto death rates of these two groups of states and that the existence or absence of state inspections is irrelevant. Even before adopting inspection programs, some states may have had very low death rates for reasons that have nothing to do with car inspections. Second, because Tufte did not control the assignment of the states to the two groups, he was not able to equalize average death rates for the two groups of states prior to the addition of inspection programs. Consequently, he could not be sure that the groups of states with and without inspection programs were equivalent or that all relevant, extraneous factors were distributed at random. Tufte, you recall, did statistically control for some relevant differences among states—such as population density and number of miles driven. Yet states with inspection programs may still have differed systematically from states without programs in some other way that was related to traffic fatalities. Hence we cannot be certain that any portion of the difference in fatality rates between the two groups of states can be attributed to the effect of an automobile inspection program.

On the other hand, the difference in average death rates between the two groups of states might also understate the benefits of inspection programs. This could be the case if a number of the inspection programs were weak or poorly implemented. This is a possibility since the treatment given the inspection states was not controlled by Tufte and could not be observed as carefully as he might have liked.

Clearly, the lack of a pre-test and of control over the assignment of cases to the experimental and control groups creates difficulties for researchers who use the cross-sectional design. Another research design that attempts to address at least the absence of a pre-test is the panel study.

Panel Study Design

A panel study is a cross-sectional design that introduces a time element. A panel study involves taking measurements of the variables of interest to the researcher on the same units of analysis at several points in time. Panel studies may thus be used to observe changes over time and to provide a pre-test of some phenomenon prior to exposure to the experimental stimulus. A panel study is similar to a cross-sectional study in that measurements of the independent and dependent variables are made at the same time, and the researcher has no control over which subjects are exposed to the experimental stimulus.

Let us return to the classic pre-test, post-test experiment described earlier in this chapter. In that example we were interested in finding out if exposure to a candidate's televised campaign commercials increased the ability of voters to identify the important issues in a campaign. If we used the pre-test, post-test experimental design to test this hypothesis, we would measure pre-exposure issue awareness, randomly assign people to an experimental or control group, expose only the experimental group to the commercials, and then measure post-exposure issue awareness again.

When using a panel research design, a researcher would proceed in a similar, but not identical, fashion. First, pre-exposure issue awareness would be measured for a group of subjects (presumably before any commercials have actually been broadcast). The researcher would wait for time to pass, the campaign to begin, and the commercials to be broadcast. Then the researcher would interview the same respondents again and measure both the amount of exposure to commercials and the post-exposure issue awareness for everyone. Finally, the researcher would use the measure of commercial exposure to construct quasi-experimental and quasi-control groups and compare the change in the amount of issue awareness for the two groups.

The major difference between such a study and the classical experiment is that in the panel study the researcher waits for exposure to the experimental stimulus to occur and then uses the amount of exposure to create naturally occurring experimental and control groups. Hence the researcher observes rather than controls exposure to the experimental stimulus.

Since the panel study has a pre-test and a quasi-control group, it allows the researcher to reach more confident conclusions than are possible with any of the other nonexperimental designs. However, the lack of control over who is exposed to the independent variable and under what conditions creates the problem of nonequivalent experimental and control groups. In our example those who are exposed to more commercials may be more likely to develop issue awareness than those who are not for reasons that have nothing to do with commercial exposure itself.

Panel studies are particularly useful in studies of change in individuals over time. One difficulty with panel studies, however, is *panel mortality*. Individuals may die, move away, or decide to drop out of the study. If these persons differ from those who remain in the study, study findings may be biased and unrepresentative.

Case Study Design

Finally, there is one other nonexperimental research design that is really quite different from any of the others considered thus far. This is the case study design. When little is known about some political phenomenon, researchers may observe initially only one or a few cases of that phenomenon. Careful observation of one or a handful of cases may suggest possible general explanations for the behavior or attributes that are observed. These explanations—in the form of hypotheses—can then be tested more systematically by observing more cases. Carefully observing the origins of political dissent within one group at one location may suggest general explanations for dissent, and observing a handful of incumbent representatives when they return to their districts may suggest hypotheses relating incumbent attributes, district settings, and incumbent-constituency relations.[11]

The case study design is nonexperimental because the researcher has little control over the events under investigation. For example, the researcher is not able to assign subjects or cases to experimental and control groups, manipulate the independent variable, or control contextual and extraneous factors. Like experimental and nonexperimental research designs, the case study design has several variations.

A single case study, although often considered only exploratory or descriptive, may be used for explanatory purposes as well. In some situations a single case may represent a critical test of a theory.[12] For example, in a study of organization innovation, a school with a history of innovation was used to test theories that claimed "barriers to innovation" accounted for innovation failure. The researchers showed that even in the school that did not suffer from these barriers, an innovation failed. The result of this case study was to reorient innovation theory away from a focus on barriers.[13]

Another example that demonstrates the explanatory possibilities of a case study is Jeffrey Pressman's and Aaron Wildavsky's study of the implementation of an economic development program in Oakland.[14] In contrast to other programs whose failure had been documented, the Oakland program lacked certain factors associated with failure: great conflict, excessive publicity, political importance and sensitivity, and insufficient funds. Yet the Oakland program also failed. Pressman and Wildavsky attributed the failure to the fact that numerous approvals and clearances had to be obtained from a variety of participants. These "perfectly ordinary circumstances" led to the unraveling of previous agreements and ultimately the program.[15]

By choosing a case in which implementation looked as if it would be easy, Pressman and Wildavsky were able to shed considerable light on the process of implementation. This type of case study design has been called the *deviant case study,* a case that differs from what prevailing theory would lead the researcher to expect. The researcher looks for factors that may explain why the case differs. Research like this may lead to the revision or clarification of existing theories.

Another good example of a deviant case study is discussed in *Union Democracy* by Seymour Martin Lipset, Martin Trow, and James Coleman.[16] It has long been observed that voluntary organizations conform to Michels' "iron law of oligarchy." [17] Lipset, however, observed that the International Typographical Union (ITU) did not conform to the normal oligarchical pattern in which one group "controls the administration, usually retains power indefinitely, rarely faces organized opposition, and when faced with such opposition often resorts to undemocratic procedures to eliminate it." [18] The ITU had an institutionalized two-party system that regularly presented candidates for chief union posts elected in biennial elections. In *Union Democracy,* the authors attempted to understand this anomaly and in doing so helped explain the workings of democratic processes in general.

Comparative or multiple case studies are more likely to have explanatory power than a single case study because they provide the opportunity for replication; that is, they enable a researcher to test a single theory more than once. For some cases, similar results will be predicted; for others, different results.[19]

The case study approach has been criticized because of the potential for bias in the use of evidence.[20] Typically researchers sift through enormous quantities of detailed information about their cases. In studying contemporary events, a researcher may be the only one to record certain behavior or phenomena. Certainly the potential for bias is not limited to case studies. One way to counteract the charge of bias is careful documentation using a variety of types and sources of evidence. In fact, case studies are often an extremely demanding type of research since they involve the use of multiple methods of collecting evidence.

Conclusion

In this chapter we have discussed why the choice of a research design is an important step in the research process. A research design is a plan that enables the researcher to achieve his or her research objectives. A good research design produces definitive, informative research findings.

Two basic types of research designs—experimental and nonexperimental designs—were presented along with numerous variations of these designs. We discussed their advantages and disadvantages. Experimental designs—which allow the researcher to have control over the independent variable, the units of analysis, and their environment—are preferred over nonexperimental designs because they enable the researcher to establish more easily causal explanations of the phenomena being studied. Therefore, experimental designs are generally stronger in internal validity than nonexperimental ones. Yet it may not always be possible or appropriate to use an experimental design. Thus nonexperimental observation may be used to test hypotheses in a meaningful fashion. For example, careful observation over long periods of time in natural, uncontrolled settings has supported causal statements about geological and astronomical phenomena.

It is rarely possible to study political phenomena using an experimental research design. Nevertheless, the principles and objectives of research designs, whether experimental or nonexperimental, are the same. It is important to understand the strengths of experimental designs in order to choose an appropriate research design from the remaining options.

A single research design may not be able to avoid all threats to internal and external validity. Researchers often use several designs together so that the weaknesses of one can be overcome by the strengths of another. Also, research findings based on research with a weak research design are likely to be more readily accepted if they corroborate findings from previous research that used different research designs.

In the next chapter we will discuss how to conduct background research on a topic you might be interested in studying. One purpose of this process is to discover and evaluate the research designs that other researchers have used to study the topic. Background research may suggest appropriate research designs for you to employ. You may be able to use a research design that results in an improvement over past research. Later chapters will discuss various methods that you can use to collect the data you need to implement your design.

Notes

1. Four components of an ideal experiment are identified by Kenneth D. Bailey in *Methods of Social Research* (New York: Free Press, 1978), 191.
2. See Donald T. Campbell and Julian C. Stanley, *Experimental and Quasi-Experimental Designs for Research* (Chicago: Rand McNally, 1966), 5-6; and Paul E. Spector, *Research Designs* (Beverly Hills, Calif.: Sage, 1981), 24-27.
3. Spector, *Research Designs,* 22.
4. This discussion is based on Bailey, *Methods,* 204-206; and Jarol B. Mannheim and Richard C. Rich, *Empirical Political Science* (Englewood Cliffs, N.J.: Prentice-Hall, 1981), 76-77.
5. Spector, *Research Designs,* 46-47.
6. Ibid., 45-46.
7. Ibid., 60-61; and Campbell and Stanley, *Experimental and Quasi-Experimental Designs,* 24-25.
8. This discussion of the New Jersey experiment is based on Joseph A. Pechman and P. Michael Timapre, eds., *Work Incentives and Income Guarantees: The New Jersey Negative Income Tax Experiment* (Washington, D.C.: The Brookings Institution, 1975), esp. chaps. 2 and 3.
9. David O. Sears, Carl P. Hensler, and Leslie K. Speer, "Whites' Opposition to 'Busing': Self-Interest or Symbolic Politics?" *American Political Science Review* 73 (June 1979): 369-84.
10. Edward R. Tufte, *Data Analysis for Politics and Policy* (Englewood Cliffs, N.J.: Prentice-Hall, 1974), 5-17.
11. See Richard F. Fenno, Jr., *Home Style: House Members in Their Districts* (Boston: Little, Brown, 1978).
12. Robert K. Yin, *Case Study Research: Design and Methods* (Beverly Hills, Calif.: Sage, 1984), 42.
13. Neal Gross, Joseph B. Giacquinta, and Marilyn Bernstein, *Implementing Organizational Innovations* (New York: Basic Books, 1971).
14. Jeffrey L. Pressman and Aaron B. Wildavsky, *Implementation* (Berkeley, Calif.: University of California Press, 1973).
15. Ibid., xii.
16. Seymour Martin Lipset, Martin Trow, and James Coleman, *Union Democracy* (Garden City, N.Y.: Anchor, 1962).
17. Robert Michels, *Political Parties* (New York: Dover, 1959).
18. Lipset, Trow, and Coleman, *Union Democracy,* 1.
19. Yin, *Case Study Research,* 49.
20. Ibid., 21.

Terms Introduced

Assignment at random. Random assignment of subjects to experimental and control groups.

Case study design. Comprehensive and in-depth study of a single case or several cases. Nonexperimental design in which investigator has little control over events.

Classic experimental design. Experiment with random assignment of subjects to experimental and control groups with pre-test and post-test for both groups.

Control group. A group of subjects that does not receive the treatment or test stimulus.

Cross-sectional design. Research design in which measurements of independent and dependent variables are taken at same time; naturally occurring differences in independent variable are used to create quasi-experimental and quasi-control groups; extraneous factors are controlled for by statistical means.

Deviant case study. Study of a case that deviates from other cases and from what prevailing theory would lead the researcher to expect.

Experimental effect. Effect of independent variable on the dependent variable.

Experimental group. A group of subjects receiving treatment or test stimulus.

Experimental mortality. A differential loss of subjects from experimental and control groups that affects equivalency of groups.

Experimentation. Research using an experimental research design in which the researcher has control over the independent variable, the units of analysis, and their environment; used to test causal relationships.

External validity. The ability to generalize from one set of research findings to other situations.

Extraneous factors. Other factors besides independent variable that may cause change in dependent variable.

Factorial design. Experimental design used to measure effect of two or more independent variables singly and in combination.

Field experiments. Experimental designs applied in a natural setting.

Frequency distribution control. When frequency distribution of a characteristic is the same in the experimental group as in the control group.

History. Change in dependent variable due to changes in environment over time; threat to internal validity.

Instrument decay. Change in measurement device used to measure dependent variable producing change in measurements.

Instrument reactivity. Reaction of subjects to pre-test.

Interaction effect. Reaction of subjects to combination of pre-test and test stimulus.

Internal validity. The ability to show that manipulation or variation of the independent variable causes the dependent variable to change.

Maturation. Change in subjects over time that affects dependent variable.

Nonexperimental design. Research design characterized by presence of a single group or lack of researcher control over assignment of subjects to control and experimental groups.

Panel Study. Cross-sectional study in which measurements of variables are taken on the same units of analysis at multiple points in time.

Precision matching. Matching of pairs of subjects with one of pair assigned to experimental group and the other to control group.

Pre-test. Measurement of dependent variable prior to administration of treatment or manipulation of independent variable.

Post-test. Measurement of dependent variable after manipulation of independent variable.

Research design. A plan specifying how the researcher intends to fulfill the goals of the study; a logical plan for testing hypotheses.

Selection. Bias in selection of experimental and control groups.

Statistical regression. Change in dependent variable due to temporary nature of extreme values.

Test stimulus. The independent variable.

Testing. Effect of pre-test on dependent variable.

Time series design. Multiple measurements of dependent variable before or after experimental treatment.

Exercises

1. Redesign Tufte's research plan investigating the impact of state automobile inspection programs. Address the possibility that states that adopted inspection programs had lower traffic death rates prior to the introduction of inspections than states that did not adopt the programs.

2. How would you design a research project to test the effect on turnout of having elections on a Sunday? Discuss the advantages and disadvantages of your design. Specify why you ruled out other possible designs.

3. In the case that follows, what research design is used by the researchers to test the relationship between receiving congressional mail and name recognition of the member of Congress? What problems are inherent in such a research design? The excerpt is from Albert Cover and Bruce S. Brumberg, "Baby Books and Ballots: The Impact of Congressional Mail on Constituent Opinions," *American Political Science Review* 76 (June 1982): 349.

Research Design: The Baby Book Data

Members of Congress like to keep in touch with constituents. Sending out roughly eight pieces of franked mail for every letter received, Congress blankets the nation with a wide variety of reports, speeches, questionnaires, books, and other missives. The volume of franked mail sent from congressional offices has grown rapidly over the last few decades, reaching a total of 523 million pieces in 1980.

One steady contributor to the stream of outgoing franked mail is the 72-page government pamphlet, *Infant Care.* Currently in its sixth edition, this pamphlet is among the most popular government documents available. More than 59 million copies have been printed since the pamphlet was first published in 1914. Of the three million families in the United States who had newborn children last year, roughly one-third received a free copy of the pamphlet in a plain brown wrapper with a congressional frank, i.e., with the signature of the member whose signature replaces normal postage. . . . In one office willing to discuss its procedures for handling these baby books, lists of newborns are collected each month from district hospitals. Parents are tracked down and sent a copy of the pamphlet along with a brief letter of congratulation signed by the member. The pamphlet is also stamped on its inside cover, "Best Wishes, Congressman X," offering one final opportunity for member X to let recipients know that he has been thinking of them. Finally, about a year later the parents receive a second government publication in a franked wrapper, Your Child From One to Six. Like the first pamphlet, this one has the member's name and best wishes stamped inside.

Focusing on the electoral impact of these childcare pamphlets has one major advantage over focusing on franked mail in general; the narrower focus means that we will be dealing with a reasonably standardized form of communication with constituents. . . . To overcome the recall and design problems, however, requires an extraordinary degree of cooperation from a congressional office in giving researchers access to potentially sensitive information on communications with constituents. Fortunately, in return for a promise of anonymity, one House member who was curious about what impact his mail had on constituents provided this cooperation.

Congressman X's office usually sends out a monthly batch of *Infant Care* booklets. In May and June of 1980, however, the office simply collected the list of newborns from district hospitals. A total of 216 names were collected. At the end of this period the parents of these newborns were randomly divided into two groups. One group was immediately sent its copy of

Infant Care. For the other groups the mailing was withheld. After the first group had received its copy, telephone interviews were conducted with *both* groups.... [I]n general they dealt with Congressman X's saliency and reputation. Thus, in this part of the study we can compare potential electoral support for Congressman X in two groups, one that had just received a copy of *Infant Care* and another that had not.

Suggested Readings

Campbell, Donald T., and Julian C. Stanley. *Experimental and Quasi-Experimental Designs for Research.* Chicago: Rand McNally, 1966.

Spector, Paul E. *Research Designs.* Beverly Hills, Calif.: Sage, 1981.

Yin, Robert K. *Case Study Research: Design and Methods.* Beverly Hills, Calif.: Sage, 1984.

6. Conducting a Literature Review

So far we have discussed the initial stages of any research project: hypothesis formation, conceptualization, measurement, and the development of a suitable research design. At some point early in the research process it is also important for a researcher to spend some time reading others' reports of similar research. We refer to this enterprise as conducting background research or a literature review.

A literature review should be undertaken near the outset of a research effort if for no other reason than to make sure that your research is not exactly duplicating someone else's. This chapter will discuss this and other reasons for background research and explain how to conduct a review.

Reasons for a Literature Review

All sound research involves reviewing what has been written about a research topic. Among the reasons for such a review are 1) to develop general explanations for observed variations in a behavior or phenomenon; 2) to identify potential relationships between concepts and to identify researchable hypotheses; 3) to learn how others have defined and measured key concepts; 4) to identify data sources that other researchers have used; 5) to develop alternative research designs; and 6) to discover how a research project is related to the work of others. Let us examine some of these reasons more closely.

Often a novice researcher will start out by expressing only a general interest in a topic, such as childhood socialization or the siting of hazardous waste facilities. At this stage the researcher will not have formulated a research question (for example, "How soon in childhood does socialization begin?" or "What are the characteristics of communities most likely to oppose hazardous waste facilities, and what tactics are most commonly used to successfully oppose hazardous waste disposal in one's community?") A review of the previous research will help sharpen a research topic by familiarizing the researcher with the major research questions that have been asked by others. After reading the published work in an area, a researcher may decide that previous work has not answered a question satisfactorily. Thus a research project may be designed to answer an "old" question in a new way. Published research reports often are sources of important questions and untested hypotheses that need to be researched. Thus an investigation may follow up on one of these research ideas.

Other times, researchers may begin a research project with a hypothesis or with a desire to explain a relationship that has already been observed. Here a literature review may reveal reports of similar observations by researchers and may also help a researcher develop general explanations for the relationship by identifying theories that explain the phenomenon of interest. The value of one's research will be higher if a general explanation of the observed or hypothesized relationship can be provided rather than simply a report of the empirical verification of a relationship.

In addition to seeking theories that support the plausibility and increase the significance of a hypothesis, a reseacher should be alert for competing or alternative hypotheses. One may start out with a hypothesis specifying a simple relationship between two variables. Since it is rare for one political phenomenon to be related to or caused by just one other phenomenon, it is important to look for other possible causes of the dependent variable and to look for other variables that may affect in some way the relationship specified in the researcher's own hypothesis. Data collection should include measurement of these other relevant variables so that in subsequent data analysis the researcher may rule out competing explanations or at least indicate more clearly the nature of the relationship between the variables in the original hypothesis.

For example, suppose a researcher hypothesized that people become active in politics because they have some serious dissatisfaction with government policy. A review of the literature on political participation might show that participation is related to years of formal education, attitudes of citizen duty, and beliefs in one's own ability to affect political affairs. Thus it would be wise for the researcher to include measures of these variables in the research design so that the policy dissatisfaction explanation may be compared with the other explanations for political participation.

A researcher also may compare his or her concept definitions with the way other researchers have defined the same or similar concepts. Using the same definitions of a concept as other researchers will lead to greater comparability of research findings on the same topic. Furthermore, the validity of a researcher's measures may be improved if the literature reveals that other researchers' definitions of a concept are ambiguous or combine two or more concepts that need to be treated separately. For example, in his study of political participation of French peasants, Sidney Tarrow found that it was important to separate the concept "support for political parties" from the concept "interest in politics." [1] The concept "interest in politics" was interpreted by French peasants to include the idea of approval of existing parties. Because French peasants did not approve of the parties, they denied they were interested in politics despite their high levels of voter turnout. Hence in this case it was advisable to measure political interest and party support separately.

A researcher may also discover the opposite problem: he or she may be using overly narrow definitions that fail to capture important dimensions of a concept. For example, if you were conducting a survey to measure support for democratic values, you would be missing numerous definitions of this concept if you simply defined it as a belief in regular elections. A review of other studies on democratic values would alert you to other definitions.

Research reports provide a researcher with valuable information about viable research designs, measurement strategies, and data collection methods. A note of caution is necessary, however. Dead ends and "bone head" mistakes are rarely reported. Published research reports usually imply that the research process proceeds in an orderly, non-problematical, "textbook" fashion. Thus some of the more obvious alternatives in research design, measurement, and data collection may have been tried by other researchers and rejected for good reasons. Sometimes, however, an author will discuss possible improvements and explain why they were not incorporated into his or her own research. Although reading previous research will not necessarily tell you everything other researchers have tried and rejected, it still might suggest to you ways of improving your research design and measurements and help you turn your study into a more interesting and successful research project.

As an example of the benefits of a literature review, let us look at a review conducted by a political scientist who was interested in the impact of television news on the political opinions and behavior of the American public. In particular he wondered if watching the news affected people's beliefs about the utility of political participation.

A review of the literature on political participation revealed four main pieces of information that were germane to the inquiry. First, it was discovered that previous researchers had developed a concept that was relevant to the hypothesis. It was called *political efficacy* or *sense of civic competence*. This concept had been defined in a number of similar ways, including:

> the feeling that political and social change is possible, and that the individual citizen can play a part in bringing about this change;[2]

the timeless theme of democratic theory that members of a democratic regime ought to regard those who occupy positions of political authority as responsive agents and that the members themselves ought to be disposed to participate in the honors and offices of the system;[3]

an individual's belief in the value of political action and the probability of success in this action;[4]

belief in the efficacy of one's own political action, consisting of 1) a belief that public officials can be and are influenced by ordinary citizens, 2) some knowledge about how to proceed in making this influence felt, and 3) sufficient self-confidence to try to put this knowledge to work at appropriate times and places.[5]

This looked to the author like a concept that might be influenced by watching television news shows.

Second, it was discovered that political efficacy had recently been divided into two different types of belief: *internal political efficacy,* or "the level of perceived personal power in the political system"[6] and *external political efficacy* or "the feeling that an individual and the public can have an impact on the political process because government institutions will respond to their needs."[7] This division meant that a researcher might want to specify which aspect of political efficacy is involved in any given hypothesis.

Third, the literature review revealed ways in which both internal and external political efficacy had been measured by other researchers. A set of six to eight questions on public opinion surveys had originally been used to measure efficacy in general; later a smaller set of questions was found to measure internal and external political efficacy separately.

Fourth, the literature review turned up numerous studies that had tested different explanations for variations in people's political efficacy. (See Table 6-1.) These explanations focused on individuals' personality, social status, social cohesion, and political experiences, and consequently they represented rival hypotheses for efficacy that did not depend upon television news viewing. The researcher was then able to include some of these alternative explanations in his research design so that the television news hypothesis could be evaluated more completely.

At the conclusion of this literature review, then, the researcher had become familiar with the conceptualization and measurement of a phenomenon relevant to his original hypothesis, had discovered sources of data that included at least some of the measures of interest, and had been alerted to competing hypotheses that would have to be taken into consideration in testing the link between political efficacy and television news exposure. One can readily see that literature reviews further the conceptual, empirical, and theoretial aims of most research projects.

Table 6-1 Explanations for Political Efficacy Concepts
Used as Independent Variables

Personality

Political cynicism	Self-competence/personal efficacy
Opinion intensity	Political interest
Interpersonal trust	Cosmopolitanism

Social Status

Education	Religion
Region	Sex
Size and place of residence	Race
Age	Relative deprivation
Income	IQ
Occupation	

Social Cohesion

Marital status	Organization membership/ leadership
Number of children	
Years of residence	Political, social participation
Church attendance	Size of community

Political Environment/Experiences/Interaction

Newspaper exposure	Ideology
Incumbent support	Political milieu (exposure to corrupt urban politics
Partisan domination	
Partisan competition	Political subculture
Political success	Exposure to political agitation
Events/period/history	Attitudes of friends
Accumulation of democratic experience	Attitudes of parents
Party Identification	Attitudes of teachers

Source: Richard Joslyn, "The Portrayal of Government and Nation on Television Network News: Content and Implications" (Paper delivered at the annual meeting of the Midwest Political Science Association, Cincinnati, Ohio, 1981).

Conducting a Literature Review

How you conduct a literature review depends on the main purpose of the review and the stage of development of the research topic. If you are starting with only a general interest in a subject and not a specific hypothesis you want to test, then it might be a good idea to locate a textbook covering the subject, read the appropriate sections, and then check out the sources cited in the footnotes. A perusal of the subject card catalog in your library will also help you identify books that broadly address your topic. From there you can begin to develop and refine a more specific research question. Another approach to get you started would be to skim the contents of a few professional journals likely to have articles in your area of interest.

A thorough literature search includes anything published on your topic in professional journals, magazines, books, newspapers, government publications and documents, and conference proceedings. To guide you in this endeavor, we have listed in the remainder of this chapter a number of professional journals in political science, with comments on their content. Also listed are indexes and bibliographies that will help you locate materials related to your topic.[8] Your library's reference librarian will undoubtedly be able to provide you with additional information and guidance on the particular library sources available.

Advances in computer technology have significantly improved a researcher's ability to search for and find published material. Computerized literature searches produce more up-to-date citations than printed indexes since the computer data base can be updated more easily and more frequently. Computer-assisted searches can also be quite specific; it is usually possible to use several key words to narrowly identify a subject. This reduces the necessity in most literature searches of eliminating citations that are not really related to the research topic. Finally, a computerized literature search may produce a printed list of citations. This reduces the amount of tedious labor required to do a thorough literature search by hand.

It is wise to check with a reference librarian in your library on the availability of computerized searches. Some universities provide this service to students at no charge; others charge a fee. Depending on the time you have and your particular topic and research goals, a computerized search may be well worth the cost.

Professional Journals in Political Science and Related Fields

Any good literature review will include research reports published in professional political science journals. It is a sign of the information explosion and of academic pressures to publish that there are now an increasing number of journals with political science-related articles. The following list is not complete, but it includes the major, general political science journals, a representative selection of journals that specialize in some aspect of political science, multidisciplinary journals, and some major journals in related disciplines.

Journals of National and Regional Political Science Associations

American Political Science Review. 1906-
 The official journal of the American Political Science Association.
American Journal of Political Science. 1957-
 Primarily American government and politics articles.

Journal of Politics. 1939-
    Primarily American government and politics articles.
Polity. 1968-
    Articles on American politics, comparative politics, international relations, and political philosophy.
Social Science Quarterly. 1920-
    Articles on a wide range of topics in the social sciences.
Western Political Quarterly. 1948-
    Broad coverage of political science and public administration.

Specialized or Multidisciplinary Journals

Annals (American Academy of Political and Social Sciences). 1899-
    Each issue focuses on a single topic.
American Politics Quarterly. 1973-
    Articles on American political behavior.
Comparative Political Studies. 1969-
    Interdisciplinary articles on cross-national comparative studies.
Comparative Politics. 1968-
    Broad coverage of comparative politics topics.
Foreign Affairs. 1922-
    Foreign policy focus, especially on current issues in American foreign policy.
Foreign Policy. 1970-
    Wide-ranging coverage of foreign affairs.
International Affairs. 1922-
    Emphasis on political and social aspects of international affairs.
International Organization. 1947-
    Focus on practical and theoretical problems of international organizations.
International Studies Quarterly. 1957-
    Multidisciplinary articles related to transnational phenomena.
Journal of Conflict Resolution. 1957-
    Articles on international and intranational conflicts.
Policy Studies Journal. 1972-
    Theoretical and practical articles addressing important public policy problems.
Policy Studies Review. 1981-
    Articles related to current public policy issues.
Political Science Quarterly. 1886-
    Articles on American politics, comparative politics, and international relations.
Presidential Studies Quarterly. 1971-
    Focus on the American presidency.

Public Administration Review. 1940-
   Focus on municipal and state management issues.
Public Opinion Quarterly. 1937-
   All aspects of public opinion and polling.
Public Policy. 1953-
   Articles on public policy formulation.
Publius: The Journal of Federalism. 1971-
   Intergovernmental relations in federal systems; multidisciplinary articles.
Urban Affairs Quarterly. 1965-
   Interdisciplinary articles on urban affairs.
World Politics. 1948-
   Current international affairs articles.

Major Journals in Related Disciplines

American Economic Review. 1911-
   Major economics journal.
American Journal of Sociology. 1895-
   Wide-ranging coverage of topics in sociology and related fields.
American Psychologist. 1946-
   Official journal of the American Psychological Association; current issues in psychology.
American Sociological Review. 1936-
   Official journal of American Sociological Association; general articles in field of sociology.

Indexes, Bibliographies, and Abstracts

A literature search will also utilize the information contained in indexes, bibliographies, and collections of abstracts. There are numerous indexes to periodical literature, books, and government publications. Some are quite comprehensive, others are more selective. It is a good idea to check the description of a particular index—usually contained in the front of the index—before using it.

Unfortunately, there is a time lag between publication of a periodical or book and its entry in an index. However, you may discover that articles of interest are concentrated among a few journals. To identify articles related to you topic that have not yet been indexed, skim the table of contents of the latest issues of these journals.

The first time you conduct a comprehensive literature search, you may be overwhelmed by the number of citations you discover. Managing them systematically may present a major problem. It may help to put each relevant citation on a separate 3 x 5 index card. If the citation proves to be useful, then complete bibliographic information can be entered later on the card in the form you will be using for your bibliography. These cards can be sorted according to various needs. This method preserves the fruits of a literature search in a form that will be useful to you, and it saves the step of writing the citation information onto a list and then transferring it to a card.

After you have located a number of sources pertinent to your research project, you will want to become familiar with this literature in the most efficient way possible. Each researcher develops a strategy best suited to the situation at hand, but we offer here three suggestions. First, locate the most important and relevant research reports immediately and concentrate on them rather than trying to read all of the numerous research reports you have discovered, some of which are of only peripheral concern. Abstracts are helpful here. Abstracts are short summaries of the contents of books and articles. These will aid in identifying those sources most relevant to your topic and improve the efficiency of your literature review. Collections of abstracts are included in our list of indexes and bibliographies.

Second, start with the most recent publications. They will contain references to past literature. Even when the content of past work is not discussed, repeated reference to a work will indicate that it is considered by many to be important. Thus you should probably review the work early on in your review.

A final strategy is to take a number of works that you know are directly related to your topic. Using the citation index of the *Social Sciences Citation Index,* locate the author and work. Below this entry will be a list of all subsequent publications that have referenced the work. These publications are likely to be closely related to your topic as well. The number of times a work is cited by others is a rough indication of its significance (or controversiality). This may guide your decisions about which works to read first.

The following is a list of indexes, bibliographies, and collections of abstracts and other sources of use to political science researchers conducting a literature search. Although each source is briefly described, you will ultimately be the judge of whether the work is a useful source for your own literature review.

ABC Pol Sci: A Bibliography of Contents. 1969-

Timely index with tables of contents of about 300 international journals in the original language of the fields of political science, sociology, economics, policy studies, and law. Author, title, and subject indexes. Updated quarterly.

America: History and Life. 1964-

Abstracts and citations of articles on U.S. and Canadian history from prehistory to present. Volume O includes abstracts from *Historical Abstracts,* 1954-65. Updated quarterly.

Combined Retrospective Index to Scholarly Journals in Political Science. 1886-1974
An index of articles from 531 journals in history, political science, and sociology. Arranged by subject. Also includes author index.

Current Contents/Social and Behavioral Science. 1974-
Weekly index with tables of contents of journals arranged by broad discipline headings. Good for searching for recent articles. Includes author and title word index.

Current Law Index. 1980-
Monthly index of some 700 periodicals.

Dissertation Abstracts International: Humanities and Social Sciences. 1938-
Monthly compilation of abstracts of doctoral dissertations from cooperating U.S., Canadian, and European institutions. Formerly called *Dissertation Abstracts and Microfilm Abstracts.* Change in title reflects increased coverage.

Index to Legal Periodicals. 1908-
Monthly index with annual cumulation.

Index to Periodical Articles Related to Law. 1958-
Quarterly index of journals not covered by *Current Law Index* or *Index to Legal Periodicals.* Therefore does not cover law journals or directly law-related publications.

Index to U.S. Government Periodicals. 1970-
Quarterly index of approximately 200 out of more than 2,000 government periodicals.

International Bibliography of the Social Sciences-Political Science. 1953-
Covers international journals in political science, updated yearly.

Magazine Index. January 1970-
Microfilm index, updated, monthly, of 400 magazine titles.

Monthly Catalog of United States Government Publications. 1895-
Most complete index to U.S. government publications.

Public Affairs Information Service Bulletin. 1915-
Biweekly index of policy-oriented literature. Includes periodicals, books, and government documents.

Public Affairs Information Service Bulletin: Foreign Language Index. 1972-
Foreign language counterpart of *PAIS Bulletin,* updated quarterly.

Readers' Guide to Periodical Literature. 1900-
Semimonthly index of 180 popular newsstand periodicals.

Sage Urban Studies Abstracts. 1973-
Quarterly collection of articles international in scope. No cumulated indexes.

Social Sciences Citation Index. 1973-
An index, updated three times a year, of 2,000 journals. Subject, source and citation indexes.

Social Sciences Index. 1974-
Quarterly index of 260 frequently used journals in the social sciences.

Sociological Abstracts. 1953-
Extensive coverage of publications in and related to sociology. Supplements include papers presented at sociological meetings, updated five times a year.

Women Studies Abstracts. 1972-
Updated quarterly.

Universal Reference System: Political Science Series. 1969-
Annual supplements commence in 1969. A 10-volume set arranged by broad topic headings indexes material prior to 1969. Includes abstracts.

USPD, United States Political Science Documents. 1975-
Indexes and abstracts articles from political science journals; updated yearly.

Urban Affairs Abstracts. 1971-
Updated weekly with semiannual and annual cumulations.

Newspaper Indexes

Newspaper articles may be a source of background information as well as of explanations and hypotheses about politics. These major newspapers have indexes:
Christian Science Monitor
New York Times
Times (London)
Wall Street Journal
Washington Post
There is also a microfilm index, the *National Newspaper Index*, that indexes since January 1979 the *Christian Science Monitor*, the *New York Times* and the *Wall Street Journal*. The *Washington Post* was added in September 1982 and the *Los Angeles Times* in October 1982. Your library may also have an on-line computer newspaper index.

Book Reviews

You may find it helpful to know how others have evaluated key books related to your research topic. Reviewers often critique the books, compare them with other works in the field, and offer interpretations and explanations that differ from those of the author.

Book Review Digest. 1905-

Book Review Index. 1965-

Combined Retrospective Index to Book Reviews in Scholarly Journals. 1886-1974.

Current Book Review Citations. 1976-

Monthly index to book reviews published in more than 1,200 periodicals.

Perspective. 1972-

Monthly review of new books.

Political Science Reviewer. 1971-

Conference Proceedings

Frequently research is presented at professional conferences before it is published in a professional journal. Thus if you want to be extremely up-to-date or if a research topic is quite new, it may be worthwhile to investigate papers given at professional conferences.

The *Index to Social Sciences & Humanities Proceedings* (1979-) indexes published proceedings. However, the proceedings of the annual meetings of the American Political Science Association (APSA) and regional political science associations have not been published. Summer issues of the APSA's *PS* contain the preliminary program for the forthcoming annual meeting. The program lists authors and paper titles. The *International Studies Newsletter* publishes preliminary programs for International Studies Association meetings. Copies of programs for other political science and related conferences (frequently announced in *PS*) may be obtained from the sponsoring organization. Abstracts for some fields, for example *Sociological Abstracts,* include papers presented at conferences. Once promising papers presented at professional conferences have been located, copies of the papers may then usually be obtained by writing to the authors directly.

Conclusion

No matter what the original purpose of your literature search, it should be thorough. In your research report you should discuss those sources that provide explanations for the phenomena you are studying and that support the plausibility of your hypotheses. You should also discuss how your research relates to other research and use the existing literature to document the significance of your research. An example of a literature review is contained in the research report in Chapter 14.

Notes

1. Sidney Tarrow, "The Urban-Rural Cleavage in Political Involvement: The Case of France," *American Political Science Review* 65 (June 1971): 341-57.
2. Angus Campbell, Gerald Gurin, and Warren E. Miller, *The Voter Decides* (Evanston, Ill.: Row, Peterson, 1959), 187.
3. David Easton and Jack Dennis, "The Child's Acquisition of Regime Norms: Political Efficacy," *American Political Science Review* 61 (March 1967): 26.
4. Robert Weissberg, *Political Learning, Political Choice and Democratic Citizenship* (Englewood Cliffs, N.J.: Prentice-Hall, 1974), 470.
5. Donald R. Matthews and James W. Prothro, *Negroes and the New Southern Politics* (New York: Harcourt, Brace & World, 1966), 526.
6. Jerome D. Becker and Ivan L. Preston, "Media Usage and Political Activity," *Journalism Quarterly* 46 (Spring 1969), 130.
7. Arthur H. Miller, Edie N. Goldenberg, and Lutz Erbring, "Type-Set Politics: Impacts of Newspapers on Public Confidence," *American Political Science Review* 73 (March 1979): 67.
8. A source of much of the commentary in this chapter on journals, indexes, bibliographies, and abstracts was Bill Katz and Linda Sternberg Katz, *Magazines for Libraries,* 4th ed. (New York: R. R. Bowker, 1982). Appreciation also goes to Margaret G. Bronner, reference librarian at the University of Delaware, for her assistance in compiling this information.

Exercises

1. Using the citation index of the 1983 *Social Sciences Citation Index* determine the number of times Stephen J. Wayne's book, *The Road to the White House,* has been cited. Then use the source index to obtain complete information on the first source that cites the book.

2. How many issues of *Legislative Studies Quarterly* are cited in *ABC Pol Sci* 1983? Give the year, volume, and issue number for each issue. Give the name and author of the first article in the first issue cited.

3. Using volume 9 of the *Social Sciences Index* determine the number of sources listed for one of the following topics: acid rain, television and children, social surveys, international organizations.

4. Using the same topic you chose in Exercise 3, list the other suggested topic headings (if any) in volume 9 of the *Social Sciences Index.*

7. Sampling

This chapter examines a decision that all researchers have to make sooner or later: the selection of observations to evaluate a proposed hypothesis. Whatever the hypothesis under consideration, a researcher must decide what observations are appropriate for testing it. Furthermore, researchers must decide whether they will measure the concepts in question for all or for only some of the pertinent observations. If data are collected on only some of the observations, then care must be taken to ensure that the observations selected are appropriate for the inquiry. We will illustrate the nature of this choice by returning to our examples of political science research.

Recall that Edward Tufte was interested in the relationship between automobile inspection policies and traffic fatalities in the United States. The American state was the unit of analysis, and inspection policy and traffic fatalities (as well as other variables) had to be measured. Tufte also had to decide whether to perform this measurement (that is, collect the data) for all 50 states or for only some of the states. He chose to collect data for all 50 states.

Gary Jacobson was interested in the relationship between campaign spending and vote totals for congressional candidates. He, too, had to decide whether to measure these phenomena for all congressional candidates or for only some. He chose to collect data for all candidates for the U.S. Congress (but only in certain years).

Finally, David Sears, Carl Hensler, and Leslie Speer were interested in explaining the variation in attitudes toward school busing in America. They decided that to test their hypotheses it was necessary to collect data on only some rather than all Americans.

In the first two cases, then, the researchers decided to collect data on all of the observations covered by the hypothesis. This is called the *population* of cases. In the latter case, however, the researchers decided to collect data on only some of the pertinent observations. In this case, a *sample* of observations was taken. In the remainder of this chapter we will discuss the differences between a population and a sample and the numerous ways in which a sample may be chosen.

Population or Sample?

A researcher's choice between collecting data for a population or for a sample is usually made on practical grounds. If time, money, and other costs were not considerations, it would almost always be better to collect data for a population. However, since research is costly, researchers must weigh the advantages and disadvantages of collecting data on a sample. The advantages of taking a sample are usually savings in time and money. The disadvantages are that the researcher's information usually is less accurate than it would be had data on the entire population of observations been collected.

In political research, investigators often collect data on a sample if the population is large or difficult to observe. For example, interviewing every adult in the United States to collect data for testing a hypothesis about adult political behavior would require a great many interviewers. Finding and paying enough qualified interviewers would pose quite a problem. Substituting inexperienced, less expensive interviewers would increase the chances of making mistakes in asking questions and recording answers.[1] Also such a survey would take a very long time to complete. In the meantime, unanticipated events could cause the responses of persons interviewed late in the process to differ from the responses of those interviewed earlier. Thus the cost of such an endeavor would be prohibitive and the validity of the data collected would be questionable.

Consider another example of the decision whether to collect data on a population or a sample. One researcher wanted to test some hypotheses regarding the content of televised political campaign commercials. This would require collecting data on the content of commercials, the unit of analysis in this case. Clearly, from the standpoint of accuracy, it would be preferable to have data on the population of televised commercials (in other words, to have available for measurement every campaign commercial ever aired on television). However, data collection on the population is simply impossible. No such collection exists anywhere, nor does anyone know how many commercials have been televised across the country in the last 30 years. Consequently, the researcher relied on a sample of commercials to test his hypotheses—a decision that was practical, necessary, and less costly, but also apt to yield a less accurate result.[2]

Thus for reasons of necessity and convenience, political science researchers often collect data on a sample of observations. In fact, public opinion and voting behavior researchers *always* rely on samples. This means, however, that they must know how to select good samples and must appreciate the implications of relying on samples for testing hypotheses.

The Basics of Sampling

A sample is simply a subset of a larger population. If the sample is selected properly, the information collected about the sample may be used to make statements about the whole population. Since sampling is always used in public opinion surveys, it is often thought of in connection with that type of data. However, issues of sampling arise whenever a researcher takes measurements on a subset of those observations covered by the hypothesis being tested. Several different types of samples will be described in this chapter. Before we discuss various sampling procedures, it will be helpful to review some terms commonly used in discussions of sampling.[3]

An *element* is the entity about which a researcher collects information or the unit of analysis in a research project. Elements in political science research are often individuals, but they also can be states, cities, agencies, countries, campaign advertisements, political speeches, social or professional organizations, crimes, or legislatures.

The term *population* refers to elements in the aggregate. A population is the collection of elements of interest to a researcher. For example, a population may consist of all campaign speeches given by major candidates for president in the last four presidential elections. Notice that the description of the population should be fairly specific. You may refer to presidential campaign speeches as the focus of your research, but at some point you should make clear which presidential campaign speeches are included in the population.

For reasons that we will discuss shortly, a population may be stratified—that is, subdivided or broken up into groups of similar elements or *strata* before a sample is drawn. For example, you may divide the population of presidential campaign speeches in the last four presidential elections into four strata, each stratum containing speeches from one of the four presidential elections in the study. In a study of students' attitudes, particularly at a university, the student body may be stratified in terms of their class, major, and grade-point average. The strata that are chosen usually are characteristics or attributes thought to be related to the dependent variables under study.

The population from which a sample is actually drawn is called a *sampling frame*. Technically speaking, all elements that are part of the population defined to be of interest to the research question should be part of the sampling frame. If they are not, any data collected may not be representative of the population studied. Often, however, sampling frames are incomplete as the following example illustrates. Suppose community opinion about snow removal is evaluated by interviewing every fifth adult entering a local supermarket. The sampling frame would consist of all adults entering the supermarket while the researcher was standing outside. This sampling frame could hardly be construed as including all adult members of the community unless all adult members of the community made a trip to the supermarket when the researcher was there. (In a few communities this might be a valid assumption.) Furthermore, use of such a sampling frame would probably introduce bias in survey results. Perhaps many of the people who stayed at home rather than going to the supermarket considered the trip too hazardous because of poor snow removal. Therefore, the closer the sampling frame is to the target population, the better.

Sometimes lists of elements exist that constitute the sampling frame. For example, a university may have a list of all students, or the Conference of Mayors may have a list of current mayors of cities with 500,000 residents or more. The existence of a list may be enticing to a researcher since it removes the need to create one from scratch. But lists may represent an inappropriate sampling frame if they are out of date, incorrect, or do not really correspond to the population of interest. A common example would be if a researcher used a telephone directory as the sampling frame for interviewing sample households within the service area. Households with unlisted numbers would be missed, other numbers would no longer be working, and recently assigned numbers would not be included. Consequently, the telephone book would constitute an inaccurate sampling frame for the population in that area. Researchers should carefully check their sampling frames for potential omissions or erroneously included elements. Consumers of research should also carefully examine sampling frames to see that they match the populations researchers claim to be studying.

A famous example of a poll that relied on an incomplete sampling frame is the *Literary Digest* poll of 1936. It predicted that the winner of the presidential election would be Alf Landon, not Franklin D. Roosevelt. This poll imprudently relied on a sample drawn from telephone directories and automobile registration lists. At that time telephone and automobile ownership was not as widespread as it is today. Thus the sampling frame overrepresented the wealthy.[4] The problem was compounded by the fact that in the midst of the Depression an unprecedented number of poor people voted, and they voted overwhelmingly for Roosevelt.

In many instances a list of the population may not exist or it may not be feasible to create a list of all elements. It may be possible, however, to create a list of *groups*. Then the researcher could sample from among the groups and enumerate the elements only in the selected groups. In this case the initial sampling frame would consist of a list of groups, not elements.

For example, suppose you wanted to collect data on the attitudes and behavior of civic and social service volunteers in a large metropolitan area. Rather than initially developing a list of all such volunteers—a laborious and time-consuming task—you could develop a list of all organizations known to have volunteers. Next a subset of these organizations could be selected and then a list of volunteers secured for only this subset, hence avoiding listing the volunteers in the nonselected organizations.

The *sampling unit* is the entity listed in a sampling frame. In simple cases the sampling unit is the same as an element. In more complicated sampling designs it may be a collection of elements.

Types of Samples

Researchers make a basic distinction among types of samples according to the amount of control over *sample bias* they provide. We mentioned earlier that political scientists often select a sample, collect information about the sample, and then use that information to talk about the population from which the sample was drawn. In other words, they make inferences about the whole population from what they know about a smaller group. If a sampling frame is incomplete or inappropriate, the sample will be unrepresentative of the population of interest to the researcher. But sample bias may also be caused by a biased selection of elements, even if the sampling frame is a complete and accurate list of elements.

Suppose that in the survey of opinion on snow removal every adult in the community did enter the supermarket while the researcher was there. And suppose that instead of selecting every fifth adult who entered, the researcher avoided individuals who appeared in a hurry or in a poor humor (perhaps because of snowy roads). The researcher's sample could easily be biased, then, and not representative of public opinion in that community.

Because of the concern over sample bias it is important to distinguish between two basic types of samples: probability and nonprobability samples. A *probability sample* is simply a sample for which each element in the total population has a known probability of being selected. This allows a researcher to calculate how accurately the sample reflects the population from which it is drawn. A *nonprobability sample* is a sample for which each element in the population has an unknown probability of being selected, thus preventing the calculation of how accurate the sample is. Ordinarily, probability samples are preferred to nonprobability samples although sometimes the latter are the only ones possible.

In this section different types of probability samples will be considered; simple random samples, systematic samples, stratified samples (both proportionate and disproportionate), cluster samples, and telephone samples. We then will discuss nonprobability samples and the situations in which they are used.

Simple Random Samples

In a random sample, each element and combination of elements must have an equal chance of being selected. A list of all the elements in the population must be available, and a method of selecting those elements must be used that ensures that each element has an equal chance of being selected.[5] Two common ways of selecting a simple random sample will be reviewed so that you can see how elements are given an equal chance of selection.

One way of selecting elements at random from a list is by assigning a number to each element and using a *random numbers table* to select numbers. A portion of a random numbers table is shown in Table 7-1.

If we have a population of 1507 elements and wish to draw a sample of 150, we can select any four adjacent columns on the random numbers table and look down those columns of numbers. Each time a number between 0001 and 1507 appears, that element is selected. If a number appears more than once, that number is ignored after the first time, and we simply go on to another number on the random numbers table. (This is called sampling without replacement.) If we start with the first four columns in Table 7-1 and go down the columns, elements 0799, 1016, and 0084 would be included. As long as we do not deliberately look for a certain number, we may start anywhere and use any system to move through the table. Random numbers may be generated by computer programs as well. It is not acceptable to generate four-digit numbers in one's head, however, since these are likely to be biased in some way.

The second way of selecting a random sample is with the *lot* method. In this method all the elements in the population are tossed in a hat (or some analogous procedure), and elements are randomly drawn out until the desired sample size has been reached. This procedure requires that the elements "in the hat" are continuously and thoroughly mixed so that

Table 7-1   Portion of a Random Numbers Table

37	52	35	15	80
07	99	95	64	06
21	28	31	42	72
10	16	69	93	08
00	84	65	56	29

Source: Hypothetical data.

each element has an equal chance of being selected. This procedure can be quite cumbersome when the population size is large. It does, however, eliminate the necessity of assigning a number to each element in the sampling frame.

Whichever method of selection is used, simple random sampling requires a list of the total population. For example, a random sample of members of Congress could be drawn from a list of all 100 senators and 435 representatives. A random sample of countries could be chosen from a list of all of the countries in the world. A random sample of American cities with more than 50,000 people could be selected from a list of all such cities in the United States. In other words, whenever an accurate and complete list of the target population is available and is of manageable size, a simple random sample can usually be drawn quite easily from that list.

Systematic Samples

Systematic sampling, an alternative to simple random sampling, also requires a list of the target population. Assigning numbers to all elements in a list and then using a random numbers table to select elements may be a cumbersome procedure. But in systematic sampling, elements are chosen off the list systematically·rather than randomly. That is, every jth element on the list is selected where j is the number that will result in the desired number of elements being selected; j is called the *sampling interval*.

For example, suppose we wanted to draw a sample of 100 names from a list of all 5,000 students attending a particular college. If we were going to use systematic sampling, we would first calculate the *sampling interval* by dividing the number of elements in the list by the sample size. In this case dividing the list of 5,000 names by the desired sample size of 100, we would get a sampling interval of 50. Then we would systematically go through the list and select every fiftieth student (hence selecting 100 names). To determine where on the list to start, a number between 1 and 50 is selected at random using a random numbers table. (This is called a *random start*.) Thus if the number 31 is randomly selected, students 31, 81, and 131 would be included in the sample.

Systematic sampling is very useful when dealing with a long list of population elements. It is often used in product testing. Suppose you have been given the job of ensuring that a firm's tuna fish cans are properly sealed before they are delivered to grocery stores. And assume that your resources permit you to test only a sample of tuna fish cans rather than the entire population of tuna fish cans. It would be much easier to systematically select every jth tuna fish can as it rolls off the assembly line than to collect all the cans in one place and randomly select some of them for testing.

Despite its advantages, systematic sampling may result in a biased sample in two situations.[6] One occurs if elements on the list have been ranked according to a characteristic. In that situation the position of the random start will affect the average value of the characteristic for the sample. For example, if students were ranked from the lowest to the highest grade-point average, a systematic sample with students 1, 51, and 101 would have a lower grade-point average than a sample with students 50, 100, and 150. Each sample would yield a grade point average that presents a biased picture of the student population.

The second situation that may lead to bias occurs if the list contains a pattern that corresponds to the sampling interval. Suppose you were conducting a study of the attitudes of children from large families and you were working with a list where the children in each family were listed by age. If the families included in the list all had six children and your sampling interval was 6 (or any multiple of 6), then systematic sampling would result in a sample of children who were all in the same position among their siblings. If attitudes varied with birth order, then your findings would be biased.

A survey of soldiers conducted during World War II is a good example of a case in which a pattern in the list used as the sampling frame interfered with the selection of a systematic sample.[7] The list of soldiers was arranged by squad, with each squad roster arranged by rank. The sampling interval and squad size were both 10. Consequently, the sample consisted of all persons who held the same rank, in this case squad sergeant. Clearly, sergeants might not be representative of all soldiers serving in World War II.

Stratified Samples

Stratified sampling takes advantage of the principle that the more homogeneous the population, the easier it is to select from it a representative sample. Also if a population is relatively homogeneous, the size of the sample needed to produce a given degree of accuracy will be smaller than for a heterogeneous population. In stratified sampling, sampling units are divided into strata with each unit appearing in only one stratum. Then a simple random sample or systematic sample is taken from each stratum.

Proportionate Sampling. Let's assume we have a total population of 500 colored balls: 50 each of red, yellow, orange, and green balls and 100 each of blue, black, and white balls. We wish to draw a sample of 100 balls. To ensure a sample with each color represented in proportion to its presence in the population, we would first stratify the balls according to color. To determine the number of balls to sample from each stratum, we calculate the *sampling fraction,* which is the size of the desired sample divided by the size of the population. In this example the sampling fraction is 100/500 or one-fifth of the balls. Therefore we must sample one-fifth of all the balls in each stratum.

Since there are 50 red balls, we want one-fifth or 10 red balls. We could select these 10 red balls at random or select every fifth ball with a random start between 1 and 5. If we followed this procedure for each color, we would end up with a sample of 10 each of red, yellow, orange, and green balls and 20 each of the blue, black, and white balls. Note that if we select a simple random sample of 100 balls, there is a finite chance (albeit slight) that all 100 balls will be blue or black or white. Stratified sampling guarantees that this cannot happen, and that is why stratified sampling results in a more representative sample.

Sytematic sampling of an entire stratified list, rather than sampling from each stratum, will yield a sample in which each stratum is represented roughly proportional to its representation in the population. Some deviation from proportional representation will occur, depending on the sampling interval, the random start, and the number of sampling units in a stratum.

In selecting characteristics on which to stratify a list, you should choose characteristics that are expected to be related to or affect the dependent variables in your study. If you are attempting to measure the average income of households in a city, for example, you might stratify the list of households by education, sex, or race of household head. Because income may vary by education, sex, or race, you would want to make sure that the sample is representative with respect to these factors. Otherwise the sample estimate of average household income might be biased.

If you were selecting a sample of members of Congress to interview, you might want to divide the list of members into strata consisting of the two major parties, or the length of congressional service, or both. This would ensure that your sample accurately reflected the distribution of party and seniority in Congress. Or if you were selecting a sample of television news stories to analyze, you might want to divide the population of news stories into three strata based on the network of origin to ensure that your sample contained an equal number of stories from NBC, CBS, and ABC.

Some lists may be inherently stratified. Telephone directories are stratified to a degree by ethnic groups since certain last names are associated with particular ethnic groups. Lists of social security numbers arranged consecutively are stratified by geographical area since numbers are assigned based on the applicant's place of residence.

Disproportionate Sampling. In the examples of stratified sampling we have considered so far, we assured ourselves of a more representative sample in which each stratum was represented in proportion to its size in the population. There may be occasions, however, when we wish to take a disproportionate sample.[8]

For example, suppose we are conducting a survey of 200 students at a college, and there are 500 liberal arts majors, 100 engineering majors, and 200 business majors, for a total of 800 students at the college. If we sampled from each major (the strata) in proportion to its size, we would have 125 liberal arts majors, 25 engineering majors, and 50 business majors. If we wished to analyze the student population as a whole, this would be an acceptable sample. But if we wished to investigate some questions by looking at students in each major separately, we would find that 25 engineering students was too small a sample for statistical analysis.

To get around this problem we could sample disproportionately—for example, 100 liberal arts majors, 50 engineering students, and 50 business majors. Then we would have enough engineering students for separate analyses. The problem now becomes evaluating the student population as a whole since our sample is biased due to an undersampling of liberal arts majors and an oversampling of engineering majors. Suppose engineering students have high grade-point averages. Our sample estimate of the student body's grade-point average would be biased upward because we have oversampled engineering students. Therefore, when we wish to analyze the total sample, not just a major, we need some method of adjusting our sample so that each major is represented in proportion to its real representation in the total student population.[9]

Table 7-2 shows the proportion of the population of each major and the mean grade-point average (GPA) for each group in the sample. To calculate an unbiased estimate of the overall mean GPA for the college, we would multiply the mean GPA for each major by the proportion or weighting factor.[10] Thus the mean GPA would be

$$.625 (2.5) + .125 (3.3) + .25 (2.7) = 2.65$$

Table 7-2   Stratified Sample of Student Majors

	Liberal Arts	Engineering	Business	Total
Number of students	500	100	200	800
Proportion or weight	.625	.125	.25	1.00
Size of sample	100	50	50	200
Sample mean grade-point average	2.5	3.3	2.7	

Source: Hypothetical data.

Disproportionate stratified samples allow a researcher to represent more accurately the elements in each stratum and ensure that the overall sample is an accurate representation of important strata within the target population. This is done by weighting the data from each stratum when the sample is used to estimate characteristics of the target population. Of course, to accomplish disproportionate stratified sampling, the proportion of each stratum in the target population must be known.

Cluster Samples

Thus far we have considered examples in which a list of elements in the sampling frame existed. There are, however, situations where a sample is needed but no list of elements exists and to create one would be prohibitively expensive. Since only some of the elements are to be included in the sample, it is unnecessary to be able to list all elements. Cluster sampling is used to address the problem of having no list of the elements in the target population. In cluster sampling, groups or clusters of elements are identified and listed. Next a sample is drawn from this list of sampling units. Then for the sampled units only, elements are identified and sampled. For example, let's take an opinion poll of 1,000 persons in a city. Since there is no complete list of city residents, we might begin by obtaining a map of the city and identifying and listing all blocks. This list of blocks becomes the sampling frame from which a number of blocks are sampled at random or systematically. Next we would go to the selected blocks and list all the dwelling units in those blocks. Then a sample of dwelling units would be drawn from each block. Finally, the households in the sampled dwellings would be contacted, and someone in each household would be interviewed for the opinion poll. Suppose there are 500 blocks, and from these 500 blocks 25 are chosen at random. On these 25 blocks, 4,000 dwelling units or households are identified. One-quarter of these households will be contacted because a sample of 1,000 individuals is desired. These 1,000 households could be selected with a random sample or a systematic sample.

Note that even though we did not know the number of households ahead of time, each household is given an equal chance of being selected. This probability is equal to the probability of one's block being selected times the probability of one's household being selected or $25/500$ x $1000/4000 = 1/80$. Thus cluster sampling conforms to the requirements of a probability sample.

Our example involved taking only two samples or levels (the city block and the household). Some cluster samples involve many levels or stages and thus many samples. For example, in a national opinion poll the researcher might list and sample states, list and sample counties within states, list and sample municipalities within counties, list and sample census tracts within municipalities, list and sample blocks within census tracts, and finally list and sample households—a total of six stages.

Cluster sampling allows researchers to get around the problem of acquiring a list of elements in the target population. Cluster sampling also reduces fieldwork costs because it produces respondents who are close together. For example, in a national opinion poll respondents will not come from every state. This reduces travel and administrative costs.

A drawback to cluster sampling is that there is more imprecision. Sampling error occurs at each stage of the cluster sample. For example, a sample of states will not be totally representative of all states, a sample of counties will not be totally representative of all counties, and so on. The sampling error at each level must be added together to arrive at the total sampling error for a cluster sample.

In cluster sampling, the researcher must decide how many elements to select from each cluster. In the previous example, the researcher could have selected two individuals from each of the 500 blocks (hence requiring no selection of blocks), or 1,000 individuals from one of the blocks (hence making the selection of the particular block terribly important), or some other combination in between (40 individuals from 25 blocks, 25 individuals from 40 blocks, and so on). But how does the researcher decide how many units to sample at each stage?

We know that samples are more accurate when drawn from homogeneous populations. Generally, elements within a group are more similar than are elements from two different groups. Thus households on the same block are more likely to resemble each other than households on different blocks. Sample size can be smaller for homogeneous populations than for heterogeneous populations and still be as accurate. (If a population is totally homogeneous, a sample of one element will be accurate). Therefore, sampling error could be reduced by selecting many blocks but interviewing only a few households from each block. Following this reasoning to the extreme, we could select all 500 blocks and sample two households from each block. This, however, would be very expensive since every household in the city would have to be identified and listed, which defeats the purpose of a cluster sample. The desire to maximize the accuracy of a sample must be balanced by the need to reduce the time and cost of creating a sampling frame—a major advantage of cluster sampling. Stratification of clusters can reduce sampling error. States can be grouped by region, census tracts by average income, and so forth.

Systematic, stratified (both proportionate and disproportionate), and cluster samples are acceptable and often more practical alternatives to the simple random sample. In each case the probability of a particular element being selected is known, and consequently the accuracy of the sample can be determined. The type of sample chosen depends upon the resources a researcher has available and the availability of an accurate and comprehensive list of a well-defined target population.

Telephone Samples

Telephone surveys are becoming a common sample survey practice. As we have mentioned, telephone directories are generally incomplete sampling frames. However, there is quite a bit of debate about how inaccurate they are and whether it is always advisable to develop a different sampling frame.[11] A procedure called *random digit dialing* (RDD) can be used to contact a sample of all telephone owners, whether they have listed numbers or not.[12] However, keep in mind that not all households have telephones. Therefore a sampling frame consisting of randomly generated telephone numbers is still an incomplete listing of households. It is estimated that 90 to 98 percent of all households have telephones.[13] Therefore if the survey population is *all* households in the United States, a telephone sample will not be entirely satisfactory.

Nonprobability Samples

Probability samples are usually preferable to nonprobability samples because they represent fairly accurately a large population, and it is possible to calculate how accurate an estimate the sample is of that population. However, in some situations probability sampling may be too expensive to justify (in exploratory research, for example), or the target population may be too ill-defined to permit probability sampling (this was the case with the television commercials example discussed earlier). Researchers may feel that they can learn more by studying carefully selected and perhaps unusual cases than by studying representative ones. A brief description follows of some of the types of nonprobability samples.

With *purposive* or *judgmental samples* a researcher exercises considerable discretion over what observations to include in the data collection. Here the goal is more typically to study a diverse and usually limited number of observations than to study a sample representative of a larger target population. Richard Fenno's *Home Style*, which describes the behavior of 18 incumbent representatives, is an example of research based on a purposive sample.[14] Likewise, a study of journalists that concentrated on the most prominent journalists in Washington or New York would be a purposive rather than a representative sample of all journalists.

In *convenience* or *haphazard samples,* elements are included because they are convenient or easy for a researcher to select. A public opinion sample in which interviewers haphazardly select whomever they wish is this type of sample. A sample of campaign commercials that consists of those advertisements that a researcher is able to acquire is also this type. A study of the personalities of politicians dependent upon those who have sought psychoanalysis is also a convenience sample, as is any public opinion survey consisting of those who volunteer their opinions. Convenience samples are most appropriate when the research is exploratory or when a target population is impossible to define or locate. But like other nonprobability samples, convenience samples do not provide accurate estimates of the attributes of target populations.

In *quota sampling,* elements are sampled in proportion to their representation in the population, and thus it is similar to proportionate stratified sampling. The difference between quota and stratified sampling is that the elements in the quota sample are not chosen in a probabilistic manner. Instead they are chosen in a purposive or haphazard or convenient fashion until the appropriate number of each type of element (quota) has been found. Because of the lack of probability sampling of elements, quota samples are apt to be biased estimates of the target population. Even more important, it is impossible to calculate the accuracy of a quota sample.

A researcher who decided to conduct a public opinion survey of 550 women and 450 men and who instructed his interviewers to select whomever they pleased until these quotas were reached would be drawing a quota sample. A famous example of an error-ridden quota sample is the one in 1948 by Gallup and other pollsters that predicted that Thomas Dewey would defeat Harry Truman for president.[15]

In *snowball sampling,* respondents are used to identify other persons who might qualify for inclusion in the sample.[16] These people are then interviewed and asked to supply appropriate names for further interviewing. This process is continued until enough persons are interviewed to satisfy the researcher's needs. Snowball sampling is particularly useful to study a relatively select or rare population such as draft evaders, campaign contributors, political protesters, or even home gardeners who use sewage sludge on their gardens—a group estimated to constitute only 3 percent to 4 percent of households.[17]

We have discussed the various types of samples that political science researchers use in their data collection. Samples allow researchers to save time, money, and other costs. However, this benefit is a mixed blessing, for by avoiding these costs researchers must rely on information that is less accurate than if they had collected data on the entire target population. Now we will consider the type of information that samples provide.

Sample Information

At best, samples provide us with estimates of attributes of, or relationships within, the target population. For example, a finding that 30 percent of a random sample of members of Congress did not accept campaign contributions from political action committees does not mean that exactly 30 percent of all members refused such contributions; it means that approximately 30 percent refused them. In other words, researchers sacrifice some precision of information whenever they decide to rely on samples for their empirical observations. How much precision is lost depends on how the sample has been drawn. The accuracy of the estimates gleaned from sample data can be calculated for probability samples but not for nonprobability samples. The accuracy of these sample estimates for probability samples is expressed in terms of what are known as the *margin of error* and the *confidence level*.

When a researcher measures some attribute in a sample, the result of that measurement is called the *sample statistic*. However, the researcher is usually not interested in the measurement of that attribute for the sample only but in the incidence of the attribute in the target population (called the *population parameter*). The sample statistic provides the basis for estimating the incidence of the attribute of interest in the target population. Around the sample statistic is placed a mathematically calculated range (the margin of error) within which the population parameter is likely to fall.

For example, suppose a researcher is interested in the proportion of Americans of voting age who believe the United States should send troops to El Salvador. A cluster sample is drawn, and it is discovered that 40 percent of the respondents in the sample think that the troops should be sent. This 40 percent (the sample statistic) is only an estimate of the attitudes of the target population (the population parameter). Around this 40 percent a mathematically calculated margin of error will be calculated, and that range will constitute the estimate of the population parameter. If the margin of error were ± 3 percent, then the sample result would provide an estimate that somewhere between 37 percent and 43 percent of the target population believes that U.S. troops should be committed to El Salvador. The sample information cannot tell us exactly where, within the range defined by the margin of error, the population parameter exists.

Associated with the margin of error is the *confidence level*. This number, also mathematically calculated for probability samples, indicates the degree of certainty that the population parameter falls within the margin of error. A certainty level of 95 percent is the convention used by social science researchers; this indicates 95 percent certainty that the population parameter falls within the margin of error of the sample statistic. It also means that there is a 5 percent chance that the population parameter falls outside the margin of error. Most researchers find 95-to-5 odds acceptable.

Sampling Error

The margin of error and the confidence level together constitute *sampling error*. They are mathematically related so that the calculation of one determines the calculation of the other. Thus sampling error is expressed in this way: "With 95 percent certainty the target population is within ±3 (or whatever) of the sample."

Ideally, sample estimates of the target population are as accurate and precise as possible. The margin of error should be small and the confidence level high. However, the only way to eliminate sampling error entirely is to collect data from the whole target population (in other words, not rely on a sample at all). Sampling error is the price researchers pay for reducing the costs involved in measuring some attribute of the target population.

You may have seen reports of sample-based information that imply that the sample results are precise estimates of the target population. During election campaigns, for example, newspaper headlines may declare: "Reagan leads Mondale, 55% to 45%." Such reports are misleading and erroneous. No probability sample can produce precise estimates of the national voting-age population. While the results for the cluster sample may have been 55 percent to 45 percent, the estimate of presidential preferences in the target population is always subject to some sampling error.

Error is possible whenever a researcher relies on a sample. For example, any measurements of attributes in samples of members of Congress, convention delegates, census tracts, or nation-states are estimates of the target population of members, convention delegates, census tracts, or nation-states, and therefore are subject to sampling error. Sampling error is not applicable only to public opinion surveys.

The most important factor in the sampling error of probability samples is the size of the sample. The larger the sample, the smaller the sampling error. However, there is an exponential rather than a linear relationship between sample size and sampling error. For example, to cut sampling error in half, the sample size must be quadrupled. This means that researchers must balance the costs of increasing sample size with the size of the sampling error they are willing to tolerate. Table 7-3 shows the relationship between sample size and the margin of error for Gallup Poll-type samples.

Sampling error is also dependent on the type of sample drawn. For a given sample size, a simple random sample provides a more accurate estimate of the target (that is, a smaller margin of error) than a cluster sample does. Sampling error is also smaller for an attribute that is shared by almost all elements in the sample than for an attribute that is distributed across half the sample elements.

Table 7-3 The Relationship between Sample Size and Sampling Error

Sample Size	Confidence Interval
4,000	±2%
1,500	±3
1,000	±4
600	±5
400	±6
200	±8
100	±11

Source: Charles W. Roll, Jr., and Albert H. Cantril, *Polls* (New York: Basic Books, 1972), 72.

Note: This table is based on a 95% confidence level and is derived from experience with Gallup Poll samples.

Finally, sampling error is reduced if the sample is a significant proportion of the target population (called the *sampling fraction*). However, this does not pertain unless the sample represents more than one-fourth of the target population, so the effect of the sampling fraction on sampling error is usually minuscule.

Of all the factors that reduce sampling error, sample size is usually the easiest for researchers to control. But in research based on public opinion surveys, increasing sample size may be too costly. Public opinion researchers usually draw samples of 1,500 to 2,000 people (regardless of the size of the target population). This yields a margin of error (about ±3 percent) and a confidence level (95 percent) at a cost that is within reach for at least some survey organizations. Reducing the sampling error appreciably in this kind of research would mean incurring costs that are prohibitive for most researchers.

Conclusion

In this chapter we have discussed what it means to select a sample out of a target population, the various types of samples that political scientists use, and the kind of information that a sample yields. The following guidelines may help researchers who are deciding whether to rely on a sample and students evaluating research based on a sample:

1) If cost is not a major consideration and the validity of one's measures will not suffer, it is generally better to collect data for one's target population than for a sample thereof.

2) If cost or validity considerations dictate that a sample be drawn, a probability sample is usually preferable to a nonprobability

sample. It is only for probability samples that the accuracy of sample estimates can be determined. If the desire to accurately represent a target population is not a major concern or is impossible to achieve, then a non-probability sample may be used.

3) Remember that probability samples yield estimates of the target population. All samples are subject to sampling error; no sample, no matter how well drawn, can provide an exact measurement of an attribute of, or relationship within, the target population.

4) Finally, keep in mind that the accuracy of sample estimates is expressed in terms of the margin of error and the confidence level. Sampling error is dependent mainly on sample size, but it is also somewhat dependent on the distribution of the attribute being measured, the type of probability sample, and the sampling fraction.

In the next chapter we will discuss in more detail one type of data collection procedure involving sampling—the public opinion survey. In Chapter 11 we will illustrate how to mathematically calculate sampling error.

Notes

1. Earl R. Babbie, *Survey Research Methods* (Belmont, Calif.: Wadsworth, 1973), 74.
2. Richard A. Joslyn, *Mass Media and Elections* (Reading, Mass.: Addison-Wesley, 1984).
3. This discussion of terms used in sampling is drawn primarily from Babbie, *Survey Research Methods*, 79-81.
4. Ibid., 74-75.
5. Strictly speaking, to ensure an equal chance of selection, *replacement* is required; that is, putting each selected element back on the list before the next element is selected. In *simple* random sampling, however, elements are selected without replacement. This means that on each successive draw, the probability of an element being selected increases because there are fewer and fewer elements remaining. But for each draw the probability of being selected is equal among the remaining elements. If the sample size is less than one-fifth the size of the population, the slight deviation from strict random sampling caused by sampling without replacement is acceptable. See Hubert M. Blalock, Jr., *Social Statistics* (New York: McGraw-Hill, 1972), 513-14.
6. Ibid., 515.
7. Babbie, *Survey Research Methods*, 93.
8. Two reasons for disproportionate sampling in addition to including enough cases for statistical analysis of subgroups are a high cost of sampling some strata and differences in the heterogeneity of some strata and thus differences in sampling error. A researcher might want to minimize sampling where it

was costly and increase sampling from heterogeneous strata while decreasing it from homogeneous strata. See Blalock, *Social Statistics*, 518-19.

9. Ibid., 521-22.
10. We could have obtained the same results by multiplying the GPA of each student by the weighting factor associated with the student's major and then calculating the mean GPA for the whole sample.
11. C. L. Rich, "Is Random Digit Dialing Really Necessary?" *Journal of Marketing Research* 14 (August 1977): 300-305.
12. For various methods of RDD, see E. L. Landon, Jr. and S. K. Banks, "Relative Efficiency and Bias of Plus-One Telephone Sampling," *Journal of Marketing Research* 14 (August 1977): 294-99; K. M. Cummings, "Random Digit Dialing: A Sampling Technique for Telephone Surveys," *Public Opinion Quarterly* 43 (Summer 1979): 233-44; R. M. Groves and R. L. Kahn, *Surveys by Telephone* (New York: Academic Press, 1979); and J. Waksberg, "Sampling Methods for Random Digit Dialing," *Journal of the American Statistical Association* 73 (March 1978): 40-46.
13. James H. Frey, *Survey Research by Telephone* (Beverly Hills, Calif.: Sage, 1983), 22.
14. Richard F. Fenno, Jr., *Home Style: House Members in Their Districts* (Boston: Little, Brown, 1973).
15. Babbie, *Survey Research Methods*, 75.
16. Snowball sampling is generally considered to be a nonprobability sampling technique, although strategies have been developed to achieve a probability sample with this method. See Kenneth D. Bailey, *Methods of Social Research* (New York: Free Press, 1978), 83.
17. J. W. Bergsten and S. A. Pierson, "Telephone Screening for Rare Characteristics Using Multiplicity Counting Rules," *1982 Proceedings of the American Statistical Association Section on Survey Research Methods*, 145-50.

Terms Introduced

Cluster sample. A probability sample used when no list of elements exists. Sampling frame initially consists of clusters of elements.

Confidence level. The probability that the population parameter actually falls within the margin of error of a sample statistic.

Convenience sample. A nonprobability sample in which the selection of elements is determined by the researcher's convenience.

Disproportionate sample. A stratified sample in which elements sharing a characteristic are underrepresented or overrepresented in a sample.

Element. Entity about which information is collected or the unit of analysis.

Margin of error. The range around a sample statistic within which the population parameter is likely to fall.

Nonprobability sample. A sample for which each element in the total population has an unknown probability of being selected.

Population. All of the cases or observations covered by a hypothesis; all the units of analysis to which a hypothesis applies.

Population parameter. The incidence of a characteristic or attribute in a population (not a sample).

Probability sample. A sample for which each element in the total population has a known probability of being selected.

Purposive or judgmental sample. A nonprobability sample in which a researcher uses discretion in selecting elements for observation.

Quota sample. A nonprobability sample in which elements are sampled in proportion to their representation in the population.

Random digit dialing. A procedure used to improve the representative-ness of telephone samples by giving listed and unlisted numbers a chance of selection.

Random numbers table. A list of random numbers.

Random start. Selection of a number at random to determine where to start selecting elements in a systematic sample.

Sample. A subset of all the observations or cases covered by a hypothesis; a portion of a population.

Sample bias. The bias that occurs whenever some elements of a population are systematically excluded from a sample. It is usually due to an incomplete sampling frame or a nonprobability method of selecting elements.

Sample statistic. The estimate of a characteristic or attribute in a sample.

Sampling error. The confidence level and the margin of error taken together.

Sampling fraction. The proportion of the population included in a sample.

Sampling frame. The population from which a sample is drawn. Ideally it is the same as the total population of interest to a study.

Sampling interval. The number of elements in a sampling frame divided by the desired sample size.

Sampling unit. The entity listed in a sampling frame. It may be the same as an element, or it may be a group or cluster of elements.

Simple random sample. A probability sample in which each element has an equal chance of being selected.

Snowball sample. A sample in which respondents are asked to identify additional members of a population.

Stratified sample. A probability sample in which elements sharing one or more characteristics are grouped, and elements are selected from each group in proportion to the group's representation in the total population.

Stratum. A subgroup of a population that shares one or more characteristics.

Systematic sample. A probability sample in which elements are selected from a list at predetermined intervals.

Weighting factor. A mathematical factor used to make a disproportionate sample representative.

Exercises

1. If there are 10,000 elements in a sampling frame and a simple random sample of 1,000 elements is taken, what is the chance of an element being included in the sample? What is this chance called?

2. If a systematic sample of 250 elements is taken from a sampling frame of 1,500 elements, what is the sampling interval? How would one decide where to start?

3. Suppose you are drawing a sample of candidates running for your state legislature. You would like your sample to be representative of incumbents and challengers and of both parties. You determine that there are 350 incumbent Republicans, 350 Democratic challengers, 150 incumbent Democrats, and 150 Republican challengers. Your sample size is 100. How many of each group of candidates must you sample?

4. A researcher has collected data on voter turnout rates for city council elections in a sample of cities. To analyze his data by region, he found it necessary to oversample in some regions. Now he would like to calculate the overall mean turnout for his sample as a whole. Based on the information below, complete the table and calculate the overall mean turnout rate for the sample.

City Council Election Voter Turnout

	South	Northeast	Midwest	West	Total
Number of cities	100	400	300	200	1,000
Proportion					1.00
Size of sample	50	50	50	50	200
Mean percent turnout	18.5	22.0	25.0	21.0	

5. Suppose a cluster sample has been taken for a study of the contents of editorials in newspapers with a daily circulation of at least 10,000. First a sample of 10 states was taken. Then within the selected states, all the newspapers meeting the qualifications were listed for a total of 500 newspapers. Then a sample of 100 newspapers was selected. What is the probability of a newspaper being included in the study?

6. A research project has been established to investigate the potential for increased support by voluntary service organizations for social service activities. Increased private support for these activities is being

sought because governmental programs have been cut drastically due to a severe state budget shortfall. A survey of members is planned to investigate members' perceptions of the need for certain programs and their willingness to devote their organization's resources to these programs. It is estimated that there are 1,000 local organizations across the state and about 500,000 members. A sample size of 1,000 has been decided. How would you go about selecting a probability sample? Explain your decision.

Suggested Readings

Babbie, Earl R. *Survey Research Methods.* Belmont, Calif.: Wadsworth, 1973.

Backstrom, Charles H., and Gerald Hursh-Cesar. *Survey Research,* 2d ed. New York: John Wiley & Sons, 1981.

Blalock, Hubert M., Jr. *Social Statistics,* 2d ed. New York: McGraw-Hill, 1972.

Groves, Robert M., and Robert L. Kahn. *Surveys by Telephone.* New York: Academic Press, 1979.

Kalton, Graham. *Introduction to Survey Sampling.* Beverly Hills. Calif.: Sage, 1983.

8. Making Empirical Observations: Survey Research and Elite Interviewing

In the preceding chapters we have discussed the nature of scientific explanation and the initial stages of a social science research project: formulating testable hypotheses, selecting a suitable research design, and conducting background research. The difficulties associated with measuring political phenomena and with sampling techniques also have been described. In this and the next two chapters we address the task of making the empirical observations with which to implement our research design and test our hypotheses. This is what is generally called the *data collection* stage of a research project.

We have said that empirical observations are necessary to test the hypotheses that we have devised, but so far we have not explained how those observations are made and what the implications are of making the observations in particular ways. Political scientists tend to use three broad types of observations or data, depending on the phenomena they are interested in studying.

Types of Data and Collection Techniques

Interview data, the subject of this chapter, are data derived from written or verbal questioning of some group of respondents. This type of data collection may involve interviewing a representative cross-section of the national adult population or a select group of political actors, such as committee chairmen in Congress. It may involve face-to-face interviews or interviews conducted over the phone or through the mail. It may involve highly structured interviews in which a questionnaire is closely followed or a less structured, open-ended discussion. Regardless of the particular type of interview setting, however, the essentials of the data collection method are the same: the data come from responses to verbal or written cues of the researcher and the respondent knows these responses are being recorded.

In addition to interview data, political scientists rely heavily on data that exist in various archival records. In this type of data collection, known as *document analysis* (the subject of Chapter 9), researchers rely on the record-keeping activities of government agencies, private institutes, interest groups, media organizations, and even private citizens. What sets this type of data collection apart from data based on interviews is that the researcher is usually not the original collector of the data and the original reason for the collection of the data is not to further a scientific research project. The record keepers are usually unaware of how the data they collect will ultimately be used, and the phenomena they record are not generally the personal beliefs and attitudes collected through interviews.

Finally, data may be collected through *direct observation,* which will be discussed in more detail in Chapter 10. In this type of data collection the researcher collects data on political behavior either by observing the behavior itself or some physical trace of the behavior. Unlike interviewing, this method of data collection does not rely on people's verbal responses to verbal stimuli presented by the researcher. Furthermore, those whose behavior is being directly observed may be unaware that they are being observed or the reason for the observation.

A political scientist's choice of a data collection method depends upon a number of factors. One important consideration is the *validity* of the measurements that a particular method will permit. For example, a researcher who wants to measure the crime rate of different cities may feel that the crime rates reported by local police departments to the FBI are not sufficiently accurate to base a research project upon them. The researcher may be concerned that some departments over-report and some under-report various criminal acts, hence rendering that method of collecting data and measuring the crime rate unacceptable. Therefore, the researcher may decide that a more accurate indication of the crime rate can be secured by interviewing a sample of citizens in different cities and asking them how much crime they have experienced themselves.

A political scientist is also influenced by the *reactivity* of a data collection method—the effect of the data collection itself on the phenomena being observed. When people know their behavior is being observed and know or can guess the purpose of the observation, they may alter their behavior. As a result, the observed behavior may be an unnatural reaction to the process of being observed. People may be reluctant, for example, to admit to an interviewer that they are anti-Semitic or have failed to vote in an election. For this reason many researchers prefer unobtrusive or nonreactive measures of political behavior because they believe that the resulting data are more natural or real.

The *population* covered by a data collection method is also an important consideration for a researcher. The population determines whose behavior is observed. One type of data may be available for only a few, while another type may permit more numerous, interesting, and worthwhile comparisons. A researcher studying the behavior of political consultants, for example, may decide that relying on the published memoirs of a handful of consultants will not adequately cover the population of consultants (not to mention the validity problems) and that it would be better to seek out a broad cross-section of consultants and interview them. Or a researcher interested in political corruption might decide that interviewing a broad cross-section of politicians charged with various corrupt practices is not feasible and that data (of a different kind) could be obtained for a more diverse set of corrupt acts from accounts published in the mass media.

Finally, *cost* and *availability* are crucial elements in the choice of a data collection technique. Some types of data collection are simply more expensive than others, and some types of observations are more readily made than others. Large-scale interviewing, for example, is very expensive and time-consuming, and the types of questions that can be asked and behaviors observed are limited. Data from archival records are usually much less expensive since the record-keeping entity has borne most of the cost of collecting and publishing the data. The disadvantage, however, is that the data are not under the researcher's control but must be made available by the record-keeping agency, which can take a long time. Finally, direct observation can be time-consuming (if the researcher does it) or expensive (if the researcher pays others to do it). And again there are physical, legal, and ethical limits to what can be observed.

After weighing the importance of each of the above factors, the researchers select a particular method or methods of data collection. Often practical considerations (such as cost and availability) necessitate the use of data that are suspect on other grounds (such as validity and reactivity). If possible, it is preferable to use different data collection methods and cross-check the results.

In this and the following two chapters, the relative advantages and disadvantages of each of the major data collection methods will be examined with respect to the factors of validity, reactivity, population coverage, and cost and availability. We begin here with a discussion of the information political scientists garner from written polls and oral interviews.

Survey Research

Survey research or opinion polling is one of the most familiar research methods. Scarcely a day goes by in which we are not told the results of one poll or another. There are presidential performance and popularity polls. Businesses use polling to determine satisfaction with products and services. Nonprofit organizations conduct polls to find out about their public image and how to increase contributions. Candidates for public office use polls to help map campaign strategies; polls tell them what appeals to make to constituents, what issues to stress, and which to avoid. Interest groups conduct public opinion polls to determine public support for their issue positions. Public officials use surveys to evaluate the effectiveness of the programs they administer or to learn more about problems in the population that need to be addressed by new programs. Social scientists also use surveys to explore and test theories about human beliefs and activities.

As the use of surveys as a research method has grown, so has the amount of research on the method itself increased. This research is concerned with the validity and reliability of survey results and the costs of survey research. We now know more about many aspects of survey research than when the method was first used, much to the benefit of researchers and consumers of survey research.

To construct a good questionnaire, a researcher must write well-worded questions, choose the appropriate type of question (either closed or open-ended), and place questions in the appropriate order. A clearly defined research purpose and well-developed hypotheses will help eliminate unnecessary questions, thereby reducing respondent effort and survey costs. A well-constructed questionnaire is easy for both the interviewer and the respondent to follow, resulting in correctly administered and completed interviews.

We shall begin our review of the survey research method by discussing how to construct a survey instrument or questionnaire. We will then discuss surveys by mail, telephone, and personal interview, rating their relative advantages and disadvantages and mentioning issues of particular importance to the application of each. Finally we will conclude with a discussion of the special difficulties involved in interviewing elite respondents.

Question Wording

The goal of survey research is to measure accurately people's attitudes, beliefs, and behavior by asking them questions. Success greatly depends on the quality of the questions. Good questions prompt accurate answers; poor questions provide inappropriate stimuli and result in unreliable or inaccurate responses. When writing questions, researchers should avoid double-barreled, ambiguous, vague, or leading questions and should use appropriate vocabulary. Failure to do so may result in uncompleted questionnaires by frustrated or offended respondents and meaningless data for the researcher.

Double-barreled questions are really two questions in one, such as "Do you agree with the statement that the Soviet Union is ahead of the United States in the arms race and that the United States should increase defense spending?" How does a person answer who believes that the Soviets are superior in military capacity, but does not wish an increase in defense spending? And how does the researcher interpret an answer to such a question? The researcher does not know if the respondent meant his or her answer to apply to both components or if one component was given precedence over the other.

Despite a conscious effort by researchers to define and clarify concepts, words with multiple meanings or interpretations may creep into questions. An example of an ambiguous question is "What is your income?" Is the question asking for family income or just the personal income of the respondent? Is the question asking for earned income (salary or wages), or should interest and stock dividends be included? Similarly, the question "Do you prefer Brand A or Brand B?" is ambiguous. Is the respondent telling us which brand is purchased or which brand would be purchased if there were no price difference between the brands?

After the 1976 debate between presidential contenders Jimmy Carter and Gerald Ford, respondents to one poll were asked to rate the performance of the two debaters as good, bad, or indifferent. This vague question confused respondents, who then asked whether the ratings were to be made 1) by comparing the debate with other, unspecified, political debates that they had witnessed; 2) by comparing the debate with the one between John F. Kennedy and Richard Nixon; 3) by comparing Carter and Ford with each other; or 4) by measuring the candidates against the respondent's predebate expectations. Respondents also were unsure whether performance meant style, substance, or something else.[1]

As we have seen, poorly worded questions may be double-barreled, ambiguous, or vague. They also may lead the respondent to choose a particular response because the question indicates that the researcher expects it. The leading question "Don't you think there is a serious energy shortage?" implies that to think otherwise would be unusual. Choice of words may also lead respondents. Research has shown that people are more willing to help "the needy" than those "on welfare." Asking people if they favor socialized medicine rather than national health insurance is bound to decrease affirmative responses. Moreover, linking personalities or institutions to issues can affect responses. For example, whether or not a person liked the governor would affect responses to the question, "Would you say that Governor Burnett's energy program for promoting solar heating of private homes has been very effective, fairly effective, not too effective, or not effective at all?"[2] There are numerous additional ways of leading the respondent, such as by characterizing one response as the preference of others, and thereby creating an atmosphere that is anything but neutral.[3]

Polls conducted by political organizations and politicians often include leading questions. For example, a 1980 poll for the Republican National Committee asked: "Recently the Soviet armed forces openly invaded the independent country of Afghanistan. Do you think the U.S. should supply military equipment to the rebel freedom fighters?" [4] Before accepting any interpretation of survey responses, check the full text of a question to make sure that it is neither leading nor biased.

Use of inappropriate wording is another mistake often made by researchers. Technical words, slang, and unusual vocabulary should be avoided since their meaning may be misinterpreted by respondents. Questions including words with several meanings will result in ambiguous answers. For example, the answer to the question "How much bread do you have?" depends on whether the respondent thinks of bread as coming in loaves or dollar bills.

In cross-cultural research the use of appropriate wording is especially important. For researchers to compare answers across cultures, questions should be equivalent in meaning. For example, the question "Are you interested in politics?" may be interpreted as "Do you vote in elections?" or "Do you belong to a political party?" The interpretation would depend on the country or culture of the respondent.

Questions also should be personal and relevant to the respondent. For example in a questionnaire on abortion, the question "Have you ever had an abortion?" could be changed to "Have you [your wife, girl friend] ever had an abortion?" This will permit the researcher to include the responses of men as well as women.

Questions should also be worded and selected for the research purpose and survey population at hand. This does not mean, however, that every researcher must formulate questions anew, as Seymour Sudman and Norman Bradburn point out.[5] They advise researchers to review questions asked by others. Copies of questionnaires are included in book-length research reports or may be obtained by writing to the authors of journal articles. The following general sources include survey questions:

New York Times Index (for CBS)/*New York Times* polls);

The Gallup Poll: Public Opinion, 1935-1971 (Gallup, 1972) and *The Gallup Poll: Public Opinion, 1972-1977* (Gallup, 1978);

General Social Surveys, 1972-80: Cumulative Codebook (National Opinion Research Center, 1980);

Index to International Public Opinion, 1978-1979 (Hastings & Hastings, 1980);

Measures of Political Attitudes (Robinson, Ruse, & Head, 1968);

Public Opinion (opinion roundup section);

Public Opinion Quarterly (polls section);

Survey Data for Trend Analysis: An Index to Repeated Questions in U.S. National Surveys (Roper Public Opinion Research Center, 1974).[6]

Using existing questions has numerous benefits for the researcher. Replication and the ability to compare research results with previous research is an important aspect of accumulating scientific knowledge. Repeated use of questions in similar contexts with similar results indicates reliability of measurement. Repeated use also may allow estimates of trends.[7] Before using a question, a researcher should check to see if permission is needed; usually it is not.

Attention to these basic guidelines for question wording increases the probability that respondents will interpret a question consistently and as intended, yielding reliable and valid responses.

Question Type

The form or type of question as well as its specific wording is important. There are two basic types of questions: open-ended and closed-ended. Closed-ended questions provide the respondent with responses from which to choose. "Do you agree or disagree with the statement that the government ought to do more to help farmers?" and "Do you think that penalties for drunk driving are too severe, too lenient, or just about right?" are two examples of closed-ended questions.

A variation of the closed-ended question is a question with multiple choices for the respondent to either accept or reject. A question with multiple choices is really a series of closed-ended questions. Consider the following example: "Numerous strategies have been proposed concerning the war in Vietnam. Please indicate whether you find the following alternatives acceptable or unacceptable: unilateral withdrawal, staged withdrawal, limited withdrawal, continue fighting, renew bombing of North Vietnam, attack North Vietnam, drop A-bomb on North Vietnam."

In an open-ended question, the respondent is not provided with any answers from which to choose. The respondent or interviewer writes down the answer. Examples of open-ended questions are "What do you think is the biggest problem facing the country today?" and "Is there anything you particularly like about Candidate A?"

Closed-ended Questions: Advantages and Disadvantages. The main advantage of a closed-ended question is that it is easy to answer and takes little time. Also the answers can be precoded (that is, assigned a number) and the code then easily transferred from the questionnaire to a computer. Another advantage is that answers are easy to compare since all responses fall into a fixed number of predetermined categories. These advantages aid in the quick statistical analysis of data. In open-ended questions, on the other hand, the researcher must read each answer, decide which answers are equivalent, decide how many categories or different types of answers to code, and assign codes before the data can be computerized.

Another advantage of closed-ended questions over open-ended ones is that respondents are usually willing to respond on personal or sensitive topics (for example, income, age, frequency of sexual activity, or political views) by choosing a category rather than stating the actual answer. This is especially true if the answer categories include ranges rather than ask the respondent to provide the exact number. Finally, closed-ended questions may help clarify the question for the respondent, thus avoiding misinterpretations of the question and unusable answers for the researcher.

Critics of closed-ended questions charge that they force a respondent to choose an answer category that may not accurately represent his or her position. Therefore, the response has less meaning and is less useful to the researcher. Also closed-ended questions often are phrased so that a respondent must choose between alternatives or state which one is preferred. This may result in an oversimplified and distorted picture of public opinion. A closed-ended question with multiple choices does not force a respondent to choose between alternatives. The information produced by the question indicates which alternatives are acceptable to a majority of respondents. This knowledge may be much more useful to policymakers in fashioning a policy that is acceptable to most people.

Just as the wording of a question may influence responses, so may the wording of response choices. Changes in the wording of question responses can result in different response distributions. An example of this problem is a question concerning troop withdrawal from Vietnam.[8] A June 1969 Gallup Poll question asked:

> President Nixon has ordered the withdrawal of 25,000 United States troops from Vietnam in the next three months. How do you feel about this—do you think troops should be withdrawn at a faster rate or a slower rate?

The answer "same as now" was not presented but was accepted if given. The response distribution was: faster, 42 percent; same as now, 29 percent; slower, 16 percent; no opinion, 13 percent. Compare the responses with those to a September-October 1969 Harris Poll. Respondents were asked:

> In general, do you feel the pace at which the president is withdrawing troops is too fast, too slow, or about right?

Responses to this question were: too slow, 28 percent; about right, 49 percent; too fast, 6 percent; no opinion, 18 percent.

Thus, depending on the question, support for presidential plans varied from 29 percent to 49 percent. This clearly shows the effect of question wording. The difference in response is a result of whether respondents were directly given the choice of agreeing with presidential policy or had to mention such a response spontaneously.

Response distributions may also be affected by whether a question asks the respondent to agree or disagree with a single substantive statement or offers the respondent two substantive choices. An example of a one-sided question is:

> Do you agree or disagree with the idea that the government should see to it that every person has a job and a good standard of living?

The two-sided question is:

> Do you think that the government should see to it that every person has a job and a good standard of living, or should it let each person get ahead on his own?

With a single-sided question there is a tendency for a larger percentage of respondents to agree with the statement given. Forty-four percent of the respondents to the single-sided question agreed that the government should guarantee employment, while only 30.3 percent of the respondents given the two-sided question chose this position.[9] It has also been found that presenting two substantive choices reduces the proportion of respondents giving no opinion.[10]

Closed-ended questions may provide inappropriate choices, thus leading many respondents not to answer or to choose the "other" category. Unless space is provided to explain "other" (which then makes the question resemble an open-ended one), it is anybody's guess what "other" means. Another problem is that errors may enter into the data if the wrong response code is marked. With no written answer, inadvertent errors cannot be checked. A problem also arises with questions having a great many possible answers. It is time consuming to have an interviewer read a long list of fixed responses that the respondent may forget. A solution to this problem is use of a *response card*. Responses are typed on a card that is handed to the respondent to read and choose from.

Open-ended Questions: Advantages and Disadvantages. Unstructured, free-response questions allow respondents to state what they know and think. They are not forced to choose between fixed responses that do not apply. Open-ended questions allow the respondent to tell the researcher how he or she defines a complex issue or concept. As one survey researcher in favor of open-ended questions points out, "Presumably, although this is often forgotten, the main purpose of an interview, the most important goal of the entire survey profession, is to let the respondent have his say, to let him tell the researcher what he means, not vice versa. If we do not let the respondent have his say, why bother to interview him at all?" [11]

Sometimes researchers are unable to specify in advance all possible responses to a question. In this situation, an open-ended question is appropriate. Open-ended questions are also appropriate if the researcher is trying to test the knowledge of respondents. Respondents are better able to *recognize* names of candidates in a closed-ended question (that is, pick the candidates from a list of names) than they are able to *recall* names in response to an open-ended question about candidates. Using only one question or the other would yield an incomplete picture of citizen awareness of candidates.

Paradoxically, a disadvantage of the open-ended question is that respondents may respond too much or too little. Some may reply at great length about an issue—a time-consuming and costly problem for the researcher. If open-ended questions are included on mailed surveys, some respondents with poor writing skills may not answer. This may bias responses. Thus the use of open-ended questions depends upon the type of survey. Another problem is that interviewers may err in recording a respondent's answer. Recording answers verbatim is tedious. Furthermore, unstructured answers may be difficult to code, interpretations of answers may vary (affecting the reliability of data) and processing answers may become time consuming and costly. For these reasons, open-ended questions are often avoided, although unnecessarily in Patricia Labaw's opinion:

> I believe that coding costs have now been transferred into data-processing costs. To substitute for open questions, researchers lengthen their questionnaires with endless lists of multiple choice and agree/disagree statements, which are then handled by sophisticated data-processing analytical techniques to try to massage some pattern or meaning out of the huge mass of precoded and punched data. I have found that a well-written open-ended question can eliminate the need for several closed questions, and that subsequent data analysis becomes clear and easy compared to the obfuscation provided by data massaging.[12]

Question Order

The order in which questions are presented to respondents may influence the reliability and validity of answers. In ordering questions, the researcher should consider the impact on the respondent of the previous question, the likelihood of the respondent completing the questionnaire, and the need to select out groups of respondents for certain questions. In many ways, answering a survey is a learning situation, and previous questions can be expected to influence subsequent answers. This presents problems as well as opportunities for the researcher.

The first several questions are usually designed to "break the ice." They are general questions that are easy to answer. Complex, specific questions may cause respondents to terminate an interview or not complete a questionnaire because they think it will be too hard. Questions on personal or sensitive topics usually are left to the end. Otherwise some respondents may suspect that the purpose of the survey is to check up on them rather than to find out public attitudes and activities in general. In some cases, however, it may be important to collect demographic information first. In a study of attitudes toward abortion, one researcher used demographic information to infer the responses of those who terminated the interview. She found that older, low-income women were most likely to terminate the interview on the abortion section. Since their group matched those who completed the interviews and who were strongly opposed to abortion, she concluded that termination expressed opposition to abortion.[13]

One problem to avoid is known as a *response set* or *straight-line responding*. A response set may occur when there is a series of questions with the same answer choices. A person finding himself "agreeing" with the first several statements may skim over subsequent statements and also check "agree." This is likely to happen if statements are on related topics. To avoid the response set phenomenon, statements should be worded so that the respondent may agree with the first, disagree with the second, and so on. This way the respondent is forced to read each statement carefully before responding.

Additional *question-order effects* include saliency, redundancy, consistency, and fatigue.[14] Saliency refers to the fact that specific mention of an issue in a survey may cause a respondent to mention the issue in response to a later question. The earlier question makes the issue foremost in the respondent's mind. For example, a researcher should not be surprised if respondents mention crime as a problem in response to a general question on problems affecting their community if the survey had earlier asked them about crime in the community. Redundancy is the reverse of saliency. Some respondents, unwilling to repeat themselves, may not say crime is a problem in response to the general query if earlier they had indicated that crime was a problem. Respondents may also strive to appear consistent. An answer to a question may be constrained by an answer given earlier. Finally, fatigue may cause respondents to give perfunctory answers to questions late in the survey. In lengthy questionnaires, response set problems often arise due to fatigue.[15]

Lee Sigelman has explored the effects of question order in presidential popularity polls.[16] He found that early placement of the presidential popularity item elicited more "no opinion" answers than when it was asked toward the end of the interview. This is explained by the tendency of respondents to respond in a safe or socially desirable way early in an interview before their critical faculties have been fully engaged and before they begin to trust the interviewer. Since presidential popularity is measured in terms of all Gallup Poll respondents, including those with no opinions, the percentage of people approving or disapproving of a president will be deflated by early placement of the question.

Another study tested the assumption that specific questions create a saliency effect that influences answers to more general questions.[17] Persons were found to express significantly more interest in politics and religion when these questions followed specific questions on political and religious matters. However, persons' evaluations of the seriousness of energy and economic problems were not affected by previous questions about these problems. Perhaps interest is more easily influenced by question order than is evaluation because evaluation questions require more discriminating, concrete responses than do interest questions. The study also suggests that if specific questions about behavior are asked first, they give respondents concrete, behavioral references for answering later on a related, more general question.[18] For example, the answer to "How actively do you engage in sports?" may depend on whether the respondent had first been asked about participation in a number of specific sporting activities.

The learning that takes place during an interview may be an important aspect of the research being conducted. The researcher may purposely use this process to find out more about the respondent's attitudes and potential behavior. Labaw refers to this as "leading" the respondent and notes it is used "to duplicate the effects of information, communication and education on the respondent in real life." [19] The extent of a respondent's favorability or opposition on an issue may be clarified as the interviewer introduces new information about the issue.

In some cases this must be done to elicit needed information on public opinion. For example one study set out to evaluate public opinion on ethical issues in biomedical research.[20] Because the public is generally uninformed about the issues, some way had to be devised to enable respondents to make meaningful judgments. The researchers developed a procedure of presenting "research vignettes." Each vignette described or illustrated a dilemma actually encountered in biomedical research. A series of questions asking respondents to make ethical judgments followed each vignette. Such a procedure was felt to provide an appropriate decisionmaking framework for meaningful, spontaneous answers and a standard stimulus for respondents. A majority of persons were able to express meaningful and consistent opinions, even those with less than a high school education.

If there is no specific reason for placing questions in a particular order, researchers may vary questions randomly to control question order bias. Computerized word processing of questionnaires makes this an easier task.[21]

Question order also becomes an important consideration when the researcher wants to sort respondents into subgroups and direct these subgroups to different parts of the questionnaire using branching questions. This is called *routing respondents*. For example, a marketing survey on new car purchases may sort people into several groups: one that has bought a car in the past year, one that is contemplating buying a car in the next year, and one that is not anticipating buying a car in the foreseeable future. For each group a different set of questions about automobile purchasing may be appropriate. Questions that sort people into different groups are called *filters*, a valuable tool to prevent the uninformed from answering questions. For example, respondents in the 1980 National Election Study were given a list of presidential candidates and asked to mark those names they had never heard of or didn't know much about. Respondents were then asked questions about only those names that they hadn't marked.

Branching questions increase chances for interviewer and respondent error.[22] Questions to be answered by all respondents may be missed. However, careful attention to questionnaire layout, clear instructions to interviewer and respondent, and well-ordered questions will minimize the possibility of confusion and lost or inappropriate information.

Questionnaire Design

The term *questionnaire design* refers to the physical layout and packaging of the questionnaire. An important goal of questionnaire design is to make the questionnaire attractive and easy for the interviewer and respondent to follow. This increases the likelihood that the questionnaire will be completed properly. Another important goal may be the easy transfer of data from the questionnaire to the computer for analysis.

Design considerations are most important for mailed questionnaires. First, the researcher must make a favorable impression based almost entirely on the questionnaire materials mailed to the respondent. Second, because there is no interviewer present to explain the questionnaire to the respondent, a mailed questionnaire must be self-explanatory. Poor design will increase respondent error and nonresponse. Whereas telephone and personal interviewers can and should familiarize themselves with questionnaires before administering them to a respondent, it cannot be expected that a recipient of a mailed questionnaire will spend much time trying to figure out a poorly designed form.

Mailed Questionnaires and Personal and Telephone Interviews

Now that we have considered basic aspects of survey instrument construction, let us turn our attention to the three major ways of administering surveys. In a mailed survey, questionnaires are mailed to the respondent to be filled out at his or her convenience without the presence of the researcher or interviewer. In the personal and telephone interviews, an interviewer asks the respondent questions and records answers. Until recently, survey research connoted personal interviews: telephone and mailed surveys were considered inferior. Now, however, some consider telephone and mailed surveys superior to the personal interview in certain situations.

The three types of surveys will be compared with respect to response rate, representativeness or population coverage, response quality, and cost and administrative requirements. These four factors account for much of the debate and research on the relative merits of the survey types. Of course, a researcher must make compromises in choosing a survey instrument. As Don Dillman notes, "The use of any of the three [types] requires accepting less of certain qualities to achieve others, the desirability of which cannot be isolated from a consideration of the survey topic and the population to be studied." [23]

Response Rate.   Response rate refers to the proportion of persons selected for participation in a survey who actually participate. If this proportion is low, either because persons cannot be reached or because they refuse to participate, the ability to make statistical inferences for the population being studied may be limited. Also those who do participate may differ systematically from those who do not, thereby biasing survey results. Increasing the size of the survey sample to compensate for low response rates may increase costs.

At one time, response rates were clearly superior for personal interview surveys of the general population than for other types of surveys. Response rates of 80 percent to 85 percent were often required by federally funded surveys.[24] Higher response rates were not uncommon. During the last decade, however, response rates for personal interview surveys declined. In 1979, it was reported that in "the central cities of large metropolitan areas the final proportion of repondents that are located *and* consent to an interview is declining to a rate sometimes close to 50 percent." [25]

In general, the decrease in response rates for personal interview surveys has been attributed to both an increased difficulty in contacting respondents and an increased reluctance among the population to participate in surveys. There are more households now in which all adults work outside the home, which makes it difficult for interviewers to get re- sponses. In large cities, nonresponse is due to a number of additional factors: respondents are less likely to be home and are more likely to speak foreign languages; interviewers are less likely to enter neighbor- hoods after dark; and security arrangements in multiple-unit apartment buildings make it difficult for interviewers to reach potential respon- dents.[26] Because of poor working conditions, it is hard to find skilled and experienced interviewers to work in large cities. In smaller cities and towns, people have shown an increased tendency to refuse to participate in surveys.[27]

Higher refusal rates may be due to greater distrust of strangers and fear of crime as well as to the increased number of polls. For example, in one study of respondents' attitudes toward surveys, about one-third did not believe that survey participation benefited the respondent or influenced government.[28] An equal number thought that too many surveys were conducted and that they asked too many personal questions. Some survey researchers feared that the National Privacy Act, which requires researchers to inform respondents that their participation is voluntary, would lead to more refusals. However, one study found that privacy concerns and past survey experience were more frequent reasons for refusals than reminders of the voluntary nature of participation.[29]

Some of these findings about why people do not participate in personal interview surveys raise the possibility that survey research of all types may become increasingly difficult. The effect of increased nonresponse has been to reduce the advantage of the personal interview over mailed and telephone surveys. In fact, response rates rivaling those for personal interviews have been achieved by Don Dillman using his "total design method" for mail and telephone surveys.[30] He concludes that the chance someone will agree to be surveyed is best for the personal interview. Telephone interviews are a close second, followed by mailed surveys. Other research comparing response rates of telephone and personal interview surveys have found little difference.[31]

It is often thought that personal interviews can obtain higher response rates because the interviewer can ask neighbors the best time to contact a respondent who is not at home thus making return visits more efficient and effective. But repeated efforts by interviewers to contact respondents in person are expensive. Much less expensive are repeated telephone calls, even long distance ones, if special telephone services like WATS lines are used.

Two norms of telephone usage contribute to success in contacting respondents and completing telephone interviews.[32] First, most people feel compelled to answer the phone when it rings. A telephone call represents the potential for a positive social exchange. With the advent of telephone solicitation and surveys, this norm may be revised, however. A potential obstacle to telephone surveys is something called *common channel interoffice signalling* (CCIS).[33] Developed in response to junk phone calls, this system permits a person to know the origin of an incoming call, and it can be used to screen and redirect unwanted calls. If CCIS becomes more widely available, telephone surveys may become more difficult to conduct.

A second norm of telephone usage is that the initiator should terminate the call. This norm gives the interviewer the opportunity to introduce himself or herself. And in a telephone interview the introductory statement is crucial. Because the respondent lacks any visual cues about the caller, there is uncertainty and distrust. Unless the caller can quickly alleviate the respondent's discomfort, the norm of caller termination may be short lived, and the respondent may hang up. For this reason telephone interviews are more likely to be terminated before completion than personal interviews. It is harder to ask the interviewer to leave than it is to hang up the phone.

One advantage of mailed surveys is that designated respondents who have changed their address may still be reached since the postal service forwards mail for about a year; it is not as easy in phone surveys to track down persons who have moved. In personal and telephone interviews it is also harder to change the minds of those who initially refuse to be interviewed since personal contact is involved and respondents may view repeated requests as harassment. Mailed recontacts are less personal.[34]

Because of the importance attached to high response rates, much research on how to achieve them has been conducted. For example, an introductory letter sent prior to a telephone interview was found to reduce refusal rates.[35] Researchers have also investigated the best times to find people at home. One study found that for telephone interviews, evening hours are best (6:00 p.m. to 6:59 p.m. especially), with little variation by day (weekends excluded).[36] Another study concluded that the best times for finding someone at home were late afternoon and early evening during weekdays; Saturday up until 4 p.m. was the best day overall.[37]

Since mailed surveys usually have the poorest response rates, many researchers have investigated ways to increase responses to them.[38] Incentives (money, pens, and other token gifts) have been found to be effective, and prepaid incentives are better than promised incentives. Follow-up, precontact, type of postage, sponsorship, and title of person signing the letter of accompaniment are also important factors in improving response rates.[39] A telephone call prior to mailing a survey may increase response rates by alerting a respondent to its arrival. Telephone calls also are a quick method of reminding respondents to complete and return questionnaires. Good follow-up procedures allow a researcher to distinguish between respondents who have replied and those who have not without violating the anonymity of respondents' answers.[40]

In sum, response rates are an important consideration in survey research. When evaluating research findings based on survey research, you should check the response rate and what measures, if any, were taken to increase it. Should you ever conduct a survey of your own, there is a wealth of information that will help you to achieve adequate response rates.

Representativeness of Respondents. Bias can enter survey results either through the initial selection of respondents or through incomplete participation of those selected. In each of the survey methods, these problems arise to varying degrees. If all members of a population can be listed, there is an equal opportunity for all members to be included in the sample. This is rarely the case, however. Personal interviews based on area probability sampling that gives each household an equal chance of being selected are likely to be more representative than mailed or telephone surveys based on published lists that are often incomplete. *Random digit dialing* (the use of randomly generated telephone numbers instead of telephone directories) and correcting for households with more than one number has improved the representativeness of telephone samples. Thus people who have unlisted numbers or new numbers may be included in the sample. Otherwise a telephone survey may be biased by the exclusion of these households. Estimates of the number of households in the United States that do not have phones vary from 10 percent to 2 percent, while only about 5 percent of the dwelling units are missed with personal interview sampling procedures.[41]

Sometimes researchers make substitutions if respondents cannot or will not participate. Substituting another member of a household may bias results if the survey specifically asks about the respondent rather than the respondent's household. Substituting another household from the same block for personal surveys is better than substituting another telephone number since city blocks tend to be homogeneous whereas one has no way of estimating the similarity of households reached by telephone. Substitution of respondents in mailed surveys may pose a special problem. The researcher cannot control whether the intended respondent or another member of the household completed the questionnaire. The extent of bias thus introduced by substitution of respondents depends on the nature of the survey.

As mentioned earlier, one of the major reasons for concern over response rates is the possibility that those who do not respond will differ from those who do.[42] There is ample evidence that those who refuse to participate differ from respondents. Blacks have been found more likely to refuse telephone interviews.[43] Refusals are also more common among older, middle-class persons, urban residents, and westerners.[44]

For personal and telephone interviews, techniques to randomly select a member of the household to participate in the survey are often used. They may not result in perfect random selection of respondents, however. One method, the Troldahl-Carter method, bases selection on the number of adult males living at the address. Some females living alone feel threatened by this question, though, and refuse to participate. The next-birthday method, which selects the adult having the next birthday, results in fewer refusals and therefore less bias in selecting households.[45]

The amount of bias introduced by nonresponse due to refusal or unavailability varies depending on the purpose of the study and the explanatory factors stressed by the research. For example, if urbanization was a key explanatory variable and refusals were concentrated in urban areas, the study could misrepresent respondents from urban areas because the urban respondents who agreed to participate could differ systematically from those who refused. The personal interview provides the best direct opportunity to judge the characteristics of refusers and estimate whether their refusal will bias the survey.[46]

Response Quality. The opportunities to obtain quality responses differ according to the type of survey used. Mailed surveys may have an advantage in obtaining truthful answers to threatening or embarrassing questions. Anonymity can be assured and answers given in privacy. A mailed survey also permits the respondent to complete it at his or her leisure and allows for interruptions; this enables the respondent to check records to provide accurate information, something that is harder to arrange for telephone and personal interviews.

Disadvantages to the mailed survey include problems with open-ended questions. Some respondents may lack writing skills or find answering at length a burden. There is no interviewer present to probe for more information or to clear up confusion over complex or baffling questions. Further drawbacks to mailed surveys include length limitations, inability to control the sequence in which the respondent answers questions, inability to motivate the respondent to answer tedious or boring questions, and inability to control contamination of answers by others.

Personal and telephone interviews share many advantages and disadvantages with respect to obtaining quality responses, although there are also some important differences. Several of the advantages of personal and telephone interviews over mailed surveys stem from the presence of an interviewer. As noted earlier, an interviewer may lead to better quality data by explaining questions, by probing for more information to open-ended questions, and by making observations about the respondent and his or her environment (for example, for a personal interview, quality of furnishings and housing as an indicator of income; for a telephone interview, amount of background noise that might affect the respondent's concentration).

In a personal interview, the interviewer may note that another household member is influencing a respondent's answers and take steps to avoid it. Influence by others is generally not a problem with telephone interviews since only the respondent hears the questions. One response quality problem that does occur with telephone interviews is that the respondent may not be giving the interviewer his or her undivided attention. This may be difficult for the interviewer to detect and correct.

Interviewers are expected to motivate the respondents. Generally it has been thought that warm, friendly interviewers who develop a good rapport with respondents motivate them to give quality answers and to complete the survey. Yet some research has begun to question the importance of rapport.[47] Friendly, neutral, "rapport-style" interviews in which interviewers give only positive feedback no matter what the response may not be good enough, especially if the questions involve difficult reporting tasks. Feedback that is both positive ("yes that's the kind of information we want") and negative ("that's only two things") may improve response quality.[48] Interviewers also may need to instruct respondents about how to give complete and accurate information. This more businesslike, task-oriented style has been found to lead to better reporting than the rapport style interview.[49]

Interviewer style appears to make less difference in telephone interviews, perhaps because of the lack of visual cues for the respondent to judge the interviewer's sincerity.[50] Even something as simple as intonation, however, may affect data quality: interviewers whose voices go up rather than down at the end of a question appear to motivate a respondent's interest in reporting.[51]

Despite the advantages of interviewers in improving response quality, the interviewer-respondent interaction may bias a respondent's answers. The interviewer may give a respondent the impression that certain answers are expected or "right." For example, interviewers who anticipate difficulties in persuading respondents to respond or to report sensitive behavior have been found to obtain lower response and reporting rates.[52] The age, sex, or race of the interviewer may affect the respondent's willingness to give honest answers. For example, on racial questions, respondents interviewed by a member of another race have been found to be more deferential to the interviewer (that is, try harder not to cause offense) than when interviewed by a member of their own race.[53] Education has an impact on race-of-interviewer effects: less educated blacks are more deferential than better educated blacks and better educated whites more deferential than less educated whites.[54]

Interviewer bias may have a larger impact on telephone surveys than on mailed surveys.[55] The efficiency of telephone interviewing requires fewer interviewers to complete the same number of interviews as personal interviews. Also telephone interviewers, even for national surveys, do not need to be geographically dispersed, so that the same interviewers can be used for a greater number of interviews. Centralization of telephone interviewing operations, however, allows closer supervision and monitoring of interviewers, making it easier to identify and control interviewer problems. For both personal and telephone interviewers, interview training and practice is an essential part of the research process.

A number of studies have compared response quality for personal and telephone interviews. One expected difference is in answers to open-ended questions. Telephone interviewers lack visual cues for probing. Thus telephone interviews tend to be quickly paced; pausing to see if the respondent adds more to an answer is more awkward on the telephone than in person. Research findings, however, have been mixed. One study found that shorter answers were given to open-ended questions in telephone interviews, especially among respondents who typically give complete and detailed responses; another study found no differences between personal and telephone interviews in the number of responses to open-ended questions.[56] Asking an open-ended question early in a telephone survey helps to relax the respondent, reduce the pace of the interview, and ensure that the respondent is thinking about his or her answers.[57]

Response quality for telephone interviews may be lowered because of the difficulty of asking complex questions or questions with many response categories over the phone. Research has found more acquiescence, evasiveness, and extremeness in telephone survey responses than in personal survey responses. In addition, phone respondents give more contradictory answers to checklist items and are less likely to admit to problems.[58] This finding contradicts the expectation that telephone interviews result in more accurate answers to sensitive questions due to reduced personal contact.

As we mentioned earlier, one advantage attributed to mailed questionnaires is greater privacy for the respondent in answering sensitive questions. Consequently, researchers using personal and telephone interviews have developed a number of techniques to obtain more accurate data on sensitive topics.[59] Many of these techniques depend on proper wording. For example, when asking questions about socially desirable behavior, a casual approach reduces the threat by lessening the perceived importance of the topic. The question "Did you happen to read any books this past month?" will likely result in more accurate answers than "What books did you read last month?" Giving respondents reasons for not doing something perceived as socially desirable also reduces threat and may cut down on overreporting.

A very different approach to the problem of obtaining accurate answers to sensitive questions is the *randomized response technique* (RRT).[60] This technique may reduce the disadvantage of personal and telephone interviews for asking sensitive questions. RRT is designed to allow respondents to answer sensitive questions truthfully without the interviewer knowing the question being answered. For example, the interviewer gives the respondent a card with two questions, one sensitive and one nonsensitive. A device such as a coin or a box with two colors of beads is used to randomly determine which question the respondent will answer. If a coin is used, the respondent will be instructed to answer one question if the tossed coin is a "heads" and the other if a "tails" shows up. The respondent flips the coin and without showing the interviewer the outcome of the toss answers the appropriate question. To calculate the proportion of yes answers to the sensitive question, the expected proportion of yes answers to the nonsensitive question must be known. Thus the nonsensitive question could be "Were you born in July?" Assuming that birthdays are distributed equally among the months, one-twelfth of the respondents would be expected to say yes to the nonsensitive question. Or the proportion of persons exhibiting the nonsensitive behavior could be estimated by asking a sample population a direct question about the nonsensitive behavior.[61] The proportion of respondents answering "yes" to the sensitive question can be calculated using the formula:

$$R_{yes} = P(S_{yes}) + (1 - P)(N_{yes}) \qquad (8.1)$$

Where

R_{yes} = probability of obtaining yes answer to random question
P = probability of respondent choosing sensitive question
$1 - P$ = probability of respondent choosing nonsensitive question
S_{yes} = proportion of respondents exhibiting sensitive behavior
N_{yes} = proportion of respondents exhibiting nonsensitive behavior

Therefore

$$S_{yes} = \frac{R_{yes} - (1 - P)(N_{yes})}{P}$$

Let's assume that out of 1,000 respondents, we get 500 "yes" responses and that we have estimates showing that 80 percent of our sample should answer "yes" to the nonsensitive question. If a balanced coin is used, P equals .5. Making the substitutions, we get

$$S_{yes} = \frac{500/1000 - (1 - .5)(.80)}{.5} = \frac{.5 - .5(.80)}{.5} = .20 \text{ or } 20\% \qquad (8.2)$$

The accuracy of RRT depends on the assumption that a respondent will answer both the sensitive and nonsensitive questions truthfully. The success in obtaining accurate information depends on the respondent's ability to understand the method and follow instructions and his or her belief that the random-choice device is not rigged.[62] The technique seems to work better when the nonsensitive question deals with a socially positive activity, thus further reducing the stigma attached to a "yes" response.[63]

Research has found RRT superior to other methods of asking threatening questions such as having the respondent answer a direct question and return it in a sealed envelope.[64] For example, use of RRT produced higher estimates of abortion than previous measures.[65] RRT can be used for telephone as well as personal interviews. Random-choice devices can be supplied by the respondent—thus eliminating suspicion that the device is fixed—or they can be mailed by the researcher to the respondent.[66]

Cost and Administrative Requirements. When deciding between personal or telephone interviews or mailed surveys, cost and administrative considerations are important. Personal interview surveys are the most expensive due to the cost of hiring experienced, well-qualified interviewers who are willing to tolerate working conditions that are becoming less attractive. National surveys also incur greater administrative costs. Regional supervisory personnel must be hired and survey instruments mailed back and forth between the researcher and interviewers. Mailed surveys are the least expensive, especially if the survey population is dispersed, because the cost of postage does not increase with distance within the United States. Telephone surveys lie somewhere in between mail and personal surveys in cost.[67] One comparison of the sampling and data collection costs of telephone and personal interviews found that telephone interview costs were 45 percent to 64 percent of the personal interview costs, depending on the sampling design.[68]

Compared with personal interview surveys, telephone surveys have numerous administrative advantages.[69] Despite the cost of long-distance calls, centralization of survey administration is advantageous. Training of telephone interviewers is easier, and flexible working hours are attractive. But the real advantages to telephone survey administration begin after interviewing starts. Greater supervision of interviewers and quick feedback to them is possible. Also interviewers can easily inform researchers of any problems they encounter with the survey. Coders can begin coding data immediately. If they discover any errors, they can inform interviewers before a large problem emerges. With proper facilities, interviewers may be able to code respondents' answers directly on computer terminals. In some cases, the whole interview schedule may be computerized, with questions and responses displayed on a screen in front of the interviewer. These are known as *computer assisted telephone interviews* (CATI). The development of computer and telephone technologies give telephone surveys a significant time advantage over personal interviews and mailed surveys. Telephone interviews may be completed and data analyzed almost immediately.[70]

As researchers and research organizations gain experience in telephone surveys, further developments are likely to occur that will reduce the cost of this method. For example, advances continue to be made in improving the efficiency of random digit dialing.[71] The efficiency of telephone surveys was also improved by a study that found that almost

97 percent of households are reached with four rings and over 99 percent with five rings; extra rings waste time and money.[72]

Telephone surveys are particularly good for situations in which statistically rare subgroups must be reached or estimated. For example, a telephone survey was used to estimate the disabled population in an area (the only problem being that the hearing impaired were underestimated).[73] A large sample was required to obtain enough disabled persons for the survey. Where large samples are required, telephone surveys are one-half to one-third the cost of personal interviews.[74] Telephone interviews cut down on the cost of screening the population. In some cases telephone surveys may be used to locate appropriate households, and then the survey itself may be completed by personal interview. Telephone surveys are also best if the research must be conducted in a short period of time. Personal surveys are not as fast, and mail surveys are quite slow.

The type of survey chosen by a researcher will depend on the population to be reached, response quality issues, representativeness of completed interviews, and cost and time factors. No one type of survey is superior in all situations. Sometimes a single factor may dictate the type of survey to be used. In other situations the choice will be less clear cut. In many situations researchers will communicate with respondents by mail, by telephone, and in person to ensure that data collection results in a high response rate and quality responses from a representative group of respondents.

Elite Interviewing

Elite interviewing is a special form of the personal interview. In his classic book *Elite and Specialized Interviewing,* Lewis Dexter defines an elite as anyone "who in terms of the current purposes of the interviewer is given special, nonstandardized treatment." [75]

Elite interviews usually differ substantially from the highly structured, standardized format of survey research discussed earlier.[76] There are a number of reasons for this difference. First, a researcher may lack sufficient understanding of events to be able to design an effective, structured survey instrument. The only way for researchers to learn about certain events is to interview participants or eyewitnesses directly. Second, a researcher is usually especially interested in an elite interviewee's own interpretation of events or issues and does not want to lose the valuable information that an elite "insider" may possess by constraining the interviewee's responses. As one researcher put it, "A less structured format is relatively exploratory and stresses subject rather than researcher definitions of a problem." [77]

Finally, elite interviewees may resent being asked to respond to a standardized set of questions. In her study of Nobel laureates, for example, Harriet Zuckerman found that her subjects soon detected standardized questions. Because these were people used to being treated as individuals with minds of their own, they resented "being incased in the straightjacket of standardized questions." [78] Therefore, those who interview elites often vary the order in which topics are broached and the exact form of questions asked from interview to interview. Eliciting valid information from elites may require variability in approaches.[79]

Elite interviewing is not as simple as lining up a few interviews and chatting for a while. Researchers using elite interviews must consider numerous logistical and methodological questions. Advance preparation is extremely important. The researcher should study all available documentation of events and pertinent biographical material before interviewing elites.

Advance preparation serves numerous purposes. First, it saves the interviewee's time by eliminating questions that can be answered elsewhere. The researcher may ask the interviewee, however, to verify the accuracy of the information obtained from other sources. Second, it gives the researcher a basis for deciding what questions to ask and in what order. Third, advance preparation helps the researcher interpret and understand the significance of what is being said, to recognize a remark that sheds new light on a topic, and to catch inconsistencies between the interviewee's version and other versions of events. Fourth, it impresses the interviewee with the researcher's serious interest in the topic. At no time, however, should the researcher dominate the conversation to show off his or her knowledge. Finally, good preparation buoys the confidence of the novice researcher interviewing important people.

The ground rules that will apply to what is said in an interview should be made clear at the start.[80] When requesting the interview and at the beginning of the actual interview, the researcher should mention whether a confidential interview is desired. If confidentiality is promised, the researcher should be careful not to reveal a person's identity when writing descriptions of interviewees. A touchy problem in confidentiality may arise if questions are based on previous interviews. It may be possible for an interviewee to guess the identity of the person whose comments must have prompted a particular question.

A researcher may desire and promise confidentiality in the hope that the interviewee will be more candid.[81] Interviewees may request confidentiality if they fear they may reveal something damaging to themselves or to others. Some persons may want to approve anything written based on what they have said. Even if they do not, it often is beneficial to the researcher to give interviewees a chance to review what was written about them. This gives them an opportunity to clarify and expand on what was said. Sometimes a researcher and interviewee may disagree over what was said or its interpretation. If the researcher agreed to let an interviewee have final say on the use of an interview, the agreement should be honored. Otherwise the decision is the researcher's. In making this decision, the researcher should consider his or her need and others' need for future access to elites.

Sometimes gaining access to elites is difficult. They may want further information about the purpose of the research or need to be convinced of the professionalism of the researcher. Important people often have "gatekeepers" who limit access to them. It is advisable to obtain references from people who are known to potential interviewees. Sometimes a person who has already been interviewed will assist a researcher in gaining access to other elites.

Who to interview first is a difficult decision for a researcher. Interviewing first the persons of lesser importance in an event or lower rank in an organization allows a researcher to become familiar with special terminology used by an elite group and more knowledgeable about a topic before interviewing key elites. It also may bolster a researcher's experience and confidence. Lower level personnel may be more candid and revealing about events because they are able to observe major participants and have less personal involvement. On the other hand, talking to superiors first may indicate to subordinates that being interviewed is permissible. Moreover, interviewing key elites first may provide a researcher with important information early on and make subsequent interviewing more efficient. Other factors such as age of respondents, availability, and convenience also may affect interview order.

A tape recorder or handwritten notes may be used to record an interview. There are numerous factors to consider in choosing between the two methods. Tape recording allows the researcher to think about what the interviewee is saying, to check notes, and to formulate follow-up questions. If the recording is clear, it removes the possibility of error about what is said. Disadvantages include the fact that everything is recorded. The material must then be transcribed (an expense) and read before useful data are at hand. Much of what is transcribed will not be useful, a problem of elite interviewing in general. A tape recorder may make some interviewees uncomfortable, and they may not be as candid even if promised confidentiality; there can be no denying what is recorded. Sometimes the researcher will be unfamiliar with recording equipment and appear awkward.

Many researchers rely on handwritten notes taken during an interview. It is very important to write up interviews in more complete form soon after the interview while it is still fresh in the researcher's mind. Typically this takes much longer than the interview itself, so enough time should be allotted. Too many interviews should not be scheduled in one day. After two or three, the researcher may not be able to distinctly recollect individual conversations.

How researchers go about conducting interviews will vary by topic, by researcher, and by respondent. Although elite interviews are usually not rigidly structured, researchers still may choose to exercise control and direction in an interview. Many researchers conduct what is called a *semistructured* or *focused interview*. They prepare an interview guide including topics, questions, and the order in which they should be raised. Sometimes alternative forms of questions may be prepared. Generally the more exploratory the purpose of the research, the less topic control exercised by the researcher. Researchers who desire information about specific topics should communicate this need to the person being interviewed and exercise more control over the interview to keep it on track.

Elite interviewing is difficult work. A researcher must listen, observe nonverbal behavior, think, and take notes all at the same time. Maintaining appropriate interpersonal relations is also required. A good rapport between the researcher and interviewee facilitates the flow of information, although it may be difficult to establish. For example, Zuckerman relates that one Nobel laureate she interviewed sat about four feet from her in a chair with rollers. By the end of the interview he had moved an additional ten feet away.

How aggressive should a researcher be in questioning elites? This question is often debated. Although aggressive questioning may yield more information and allow the researcher to ferret out misinformation, it also may alienate or irritate the interviewee. Zuckerman used the tactic of rephrasing interviewee comments in extreme form to elicit further details. In some cases the Nobel laureates expressed irritation that she had not understood what they had already said.[82]

Establishing the meaningfulness and validity of the data collected through elite interviewing is very important. Interview data may be biased by the questions and actions of the interviewer. Interviewees may give evasive or untruthful answers. As noted earlier, advance preparation may help an interviewer recognize remarks that differ from established fact. The validity of an interviewee's statements also may be determined by examining their plausibility, checking for internal consistency, and through corroboration from other interviewees. John Dean and William Whyte argue that a researcher should understand an interviewee's "mental set" and how it might affect his or her perception and interpretation of events.[83] Raymond Gordon stresses the value of being able to empathize with interviewees to understand the meaning of what they are saying.[84] Lewis Dexter warns that interviewing should be used only if "interviewers have enough relevant background to be sure that they can make sense out of interview conversations or unless there is reasonable hope of being able to ... learn what is meaningful and significant to ask." [85]

Conclusion

This chapter has introduced three main types of data—interview data, archival records, and data collected through direct observation—and discussed the two principal types of interviews—survey research and elite interviewing. Whether the interview is conducted over the phone, through the mail, or in person, the researcher attempts to elicit information that is accurate and informative. This goal is advanced by being attentive to how question wording, question type, question order, and questionnaire design affect the responses of those interviewed. The choice of an in-person, telephone, or mailed survey can also affect the quality of the data collected. Interviews of elite populations require attention to a special set of issues and generally result in a less structured type of interview.

Although you may never be in a position to conduct a survey of your own, the information in this chapter should help you evaluate the survey research of others. Polls, surveys, and interview data have become so prevalent in American life that an awareness of the decisions made and problems encountered by survey researchers is necessary for rendering an independent judgment of survey results.

Notes

1. Doris A. Graber, "Problems in Measuring Audience Effects of the 1976 Debate," in George F. Bishop, Robert G. Meadow, and Marilyn Jackson-Beeck, eds., *The Presidential Debates: Media, Electoral and Policy Perspectives* (New York: Praeger, 1978), 116.
2. Charles H. Backstrom and Gerald Hursh-Cesar, *Survey Research*, 2d ed. (New York: John Wiley & Sons, 1981), 142, 146.
3. Ibid., 141.
4. Republican National Committee, *1980 Official Republican Poll on U.S. Defense and Foreign Policy.*
5. Seymour Sudman and Norman M. Bradburn, *Asking Questions: A Practical Guide to Questionnaire Design* (San Francisco: Jossey-Bass, 1982), 15.
6. Ibid., 16-17.
7. Ibid., 16.
8. John P. Dean and William Foote Whyte, "How Do You Know if the Informant Is Telling the Truth?" in Lewis Anthony Dexter, *Elite and Specialized Interviewing* (Evanston, Ill.: Northwestern University Press, 1970), 127.
9. Raymond L. Gordon, *Interviewing: Strategy, Techniques, and Tactics* (Homewood, Ill.: Dorsey Press, 1969), 18.
10. Dexter, *Elite and Specialized Interviewing*, 17.

11. Patricia J. Labaw, *Advanced Questionnaire Design* (Cambridge, Mass.: Abt Books, 1980), 132.

12. Ibid., 132-33.

13. Ibid., 117.

14. Norman M. Bradburn and W. M. Mason, "The Effect of Question Order on Responses," *Journal of Marketing Research* 1 (1964): 57-64.

15. A. Regula Herzog and Jerald G. Bachman, "Effects of Questionnaire Length on Response Quality," *Public Opinion Quarterly* 45 (1981): 549-59.

16. Lee Sigelman, "Question-Order Effects on Presidential Popularity," *Public Opinion Quarterly* 45 (1981): 199-207.

17. Sam G. MacFarland, "Effects of Question Order on Survey Responses," *Public Opinion Quarterly* 45 (1981): 208-15.

18. Ibid., 213, 214.

19. Labaw, *Advanced Questionnaire Design,* 122.

20. Glen D. Mellinger, Carol L. Huffine, and Mitchell B. Balter, "Assessing Comprehension in a Survey of Public Reactions to Complex Issues," *Public Opinion Quarterly* 46 (1982): 97-109.

21. William D. Perrault, Jr., "Controlling Order-Effect Bias," *Public Opinion Quarterly* 39 (1975): 544-51.

22. Donald J. Messmer and Daniel T. Seymour, "The Effects of Branching on Item Nonresponse," *Public Opinion Quarterly* 46 (1982): 270-77.

23. Don A. Dillman, *Mail and Telephone Surveys: The Total Design Method* (New York: John Wiley & Sons, 1978), 40.

24. Earl R. Babbie, *Survey Research Methods* (Belmont, Calif.: Wadsworth, 1973), 171.

25. Robert M. Groves and Robert L. Kahn, *Surveys by Telephone: A National Comparison with Personal Interviews* (New York: Academic Press, 1979), 3.

26. Charlotte G. Steeh, "Trends in Nonresponse Rates, 1952-1979," *Public Opinion Quarterly* 45 (1981): 40-57.

27. Ibid.

28. Laure M. Sharp and Joanne Frankel, "Respondent Burden: A Test of Some Common Assumptions," *Public Opinion Quarterly* 47 (1983): 36-53.

29. Theresa J. DeMaio, "Refusals: Who, Where and Why," *Public Opinion Quarterly* 44 (1980): 223-33.

30. Dillman, *Mail and Telephone Surveys.*

31. See Theresa F. Rogers, "Interviews by Telephone and in Person: Quality of Responses and Field Performance," *Public Opinion Quarterly* 39 (1975): 51-64; and Groves and Kahn, *Surveys by Telephone.* Response rates are affected by different methods of calculating rates for the three types of surveys. For example, nonreachable and ineligible persons may be dropped from the total survey population for telephone and personal interviews before response rates are calculated. Response rates to mailed surveys are depressed because all nonresponses are assumed to be refusals, not ineligibles or nonreachables. Telephone response rates may be depressed if nonworking but ringing numbers are treated as nonreachable but eligible respondents. Telephone companies vary in their willingness to identify working numbers. If non-eligibility is likely to be a problem in a mailed survey, ineligibles should be

asked to return the questionnaire anyway so that they can be identified and distinguished from refusals.

32. James H. Frey, *Survey Research by Telephone* (Beverly Hills, Calif.: Sage, 1983), 15-16.
33. Ibid., 175.
34. Herschel Shosteck and William R. Fairweather, "Physician Response Rates to Mail and Personal Interview Surveys," *Public Opinion Quarterly* 43 (1979): 206-17.
35. Don A. Dillman, Jean Gorton Gallegos, and James H. Frey, "Reducing Refusal Rates for Telephone Interviews," *Public Opinion Quarterly* 40 (1976): 66-78.
36. Gideon Vigderhous, "Scheduling Telephone Interviews: A Study of Seasonal Patterns," *Public Opinion Quarterly* 45 (1981): 250-59.
37. M. F. Weeks et al., "Optimal Times to Contact Sample Households," *Public Opinion Quarterly* 44 (1980): 101-14.
38. See J. Scott Armstrong, "Monetary Incentive in Mail Surveys," *Public Opinion Quarterly* 39 (1975): 111-16; Arnold S. Linsky, "Stimulating Responses to Mailed Questionnaires: A Review," *Public Opinion Quarterly* 39 (1975): 82-101; James R. Chromy and Daniel G. Horvitz, "The Use of Monetary Incentives in National Assessment Households Survey," *Journal of the American Statistical Association* 73 (1978): 473-78; Thomas A. Heberlein and Robert Baumgartner, "Factors Affecting Response Rates to Mailed Questionnaires," *American Sociological Review* 43 (1978): 447-62; R. Kenneth Godwin, "The Consequences of Large Monetary Incentives in Mail Surveys of Elites," *Public Opinion Quarterly* 43 (1979): 378-87; Kent L. Tedin and C. Richard Hofstetter, "The Effect of Cost and Importance Factors on the Return Date for Single and Multiple Mailings," *Public Opinion Quarterly* 46 (1982): 122-28; Anton J. Nederhof, "The Effects of Material Incentives in Mail Surveys: Two Studies," *Public Opinion Quarterly* 47 (1983): 103-11; Charles D. Schewe and Norman G. Cournoyer, "Prepaid vs. Promised Monetary Incentives to Questionnaire Response: Further Evidence," *Public Opinion Quarterly* 40 (1976): 105-107; James R. Henley, Jr., "Response Rate to Mail Questionnaire with a Return Deadline," *Public Opinion Quarterly* 40 (1976): 374-75; Thomas A. Heberlein and Robert Baumgartner, "Is a Questionnaire Necessary in a Second Mailing?" *Public Opinion Quarterly* 45 (1981): 102-108; and Wesley H. Jones, "Generalized Mail Survey Inducement Methods: Population Interactions with Anonymity and Sponsorship," *Public Opinion Quarterly* 43 (1979): 102-11.
39. Linsky, "Stimulating Responses."
40. For detailed instructions on improving the response rate to mailed surveys, see Dillman, *Mail and Telephone Surveys.*
41. Groves and Kahn, *Surveys by Telephone,* 214; Frey, *Survey Research by Telephone,* 22.
42. For research estimating amount of bias introduced by nonresponse due to unavailability or refusal, see F. L. Filion, "Estimating Bias Due to Nonresponse in Mail Surveys," *Public Opinion Quarterly* 39 (1975): 482-92; Michael J. O'Neil, "Estimating the Nonresponse Bias Due to Refusals in Telephone Surveys," *Public Opinion Quarterly* 43 (1979): 218-32; and Arthur

L. Stinchcombe, Calvin Jones, and Paul Sheatsley, "Nonresponse Bias for Attitude Questions," *Public Opinion Quarterly* 45 (1981): 359-75.

43. Carol S. Aneshensel et al., "Measuring Depression in the Community: A Comparison of Telephone and Personal Interviews," *Public Opinion Quarterly* 46 (1982): 110-21.

44. DeMaio, "Refusals," 223-33; and Steeh, "Trends in Nonresponse Rates," 40-57.

45. Charles T. Salmon and John Spicer Nichols, "The Next-Birthday Method of Respondent Selection," *Public Opinion Quarterly* 47 (1983): 270-76.

46. Dillman, *Mail and Telephone Surveys*.

47. See Willis J. Goudy and Harry R. Potter, "Interview Rapport: Demise of a Concept," *Public Opinion Quarterly* 39 (1975): 529-43; and Charles F. Cannell, Peter V. Miller and Lois Oksenberg, "Research on Interviewing Techniques," in Samuel Leinhardt, ed., *Sociological Methodology 1981* (San Francisco: Jossey-Bass, 1981), 389-437.

48. Cannell, Miller, and Oksenberg, "Research on Interviewing Techniques."

49. Theresa F. Rogers, "Interviews by Telephone and in Person: Quality of Responses and Field Performance," *Public Opinion Quarterly* 39 (1975): 51-65.

50. Ibid.; and Peter V. Miller and Charles F. Cannell, "A Study of Experimental Techniques for Telephone Interviewing," *Public Opinion Quarterly* 46 (1982): 250-69.

51. Arpad Barath and Charles F. Cannell, "Effect of Interviewer's Voice Intonation," *Public Opinion Quarterly* 40 (1976): 370-73.

52. Eleanor Singer, Martin R. Frankel, and Marc B. Glassman, "The Effect of Interviewer Characteristics and Expectations on Response," *Public Opinion Quarterly* 47 (1983): 68-83; and Eleanor Singer and Luane Kohnke-Aguirre, "Interviewer Expectation Effects: A Replication and Extension," *Public Opinion Quarterly* 43 (1979): 245-60.

53. Patrick R. Cotter, Jeffrey Cohen, and Philip B. Coulter, "Race-of-Interviewer Effects in Telephone Interviews," *Public Opinion Quarterly* 46 (1982): 278-84; and Bruce A. Campbell, "Race of Interviewer Effects among Southern Adolescents," *Public Opinion Quarterly* 45 (1981): 231-44.

54. Shirley Hatchett and Howard Schuman, "White Respondents and Race-of-Interviewer Effects," *Public Opinion Quarterly* 39 (1975): 523-28; and Michael F. Weeks and R. Paul Moore, "Ethnicity of Interviewer Effects on Ethnic Respondents," *Public Opinion Quarterly* 45 (1981): 245-49.

55. See Singer, Frankel, and Glassman, "The Effect of Interviewer Characteristics and Expectations on Response"; Groves and Kahn, *Surveys by Telephone;* Dillman, *Mail and Telephone Surveys;* and John Freeman and Edgar W. Butler, "Some Sources of Interviewer Variance in Surveys," *Public Opinion Quarterly* 40 (1976): 79-91.

56. See Groves and Kahn, *Surveys by Telephone;* and Lawrence A. Jordan, Alfred C. Marcus, and Leo G. Reeder, "Response Styles in Telephone and Household Interviewing," *Public Opinion Quarterly* 44 (1980): 210-22.

57. Dillman, *Mail and Telephone Surveys*.

58. Jordan, Marcus, and Reeder, "Response Styles in Telephone and Household Interviewing"; and Groves and Kahn, *Surveys by Telephone*. See also Rogers,

"Interviews by Telephone and in Person."

59. For example, see Sudman and Bradburn, *Asking Questions*, 55-86; and Jerald G. Bachman and Patrick M. O'Malley, "When Four Months Equal a Year: Inconsistencies in Student Reports of Drug Use," *Public Opinion Quarterly* 45 (1981): 542.

60. RRT was first proposed by S. L. Warner in "Randomized Response," *Journal of the American Statistical Association* 60 (1965): 63-69.

61. S. M. Zdep and Isabelle N. Rhodes, "Making the Randomized Response Technique Work," *Public Opinion Quarterly* 40 (1976): 531-37.

62. Frederick Wiseman, Mark Moriarty, and Marianne Schafer, "Estimating Public Opinion with the Randomized Response Model," *Public Opinion Quarterly* 39 (1975): 507-13.

63. Zdep and Rhodes, "Making the Randomized Response Technique Work."

64. Ibid.

65. Iris M. Shimizu and Gordon Scott Bonham, "Randomized Response Technique in a National Survey," *Journal of the American Statistical Association* 73 (1978): 35-39.

66. Robert G. Orwin and Robert F. Boruch, "RRT Meets RDD: Statistical Strategies for Assuring Response Privacy in Telephone Surveys," *Public Opinion Quarterly* 46 (1982): 560-71.

67. For a comparison of costs, see Frey, *Survey Research by Telephone*, 30-31.

68. Groves and Kahn, *Surveys by Telephone*.

69. Ibid.; and Frey, *Survey Research by Telephone*.

70. Frey, *Survey Research by Telephone*, 24-25.

71. Joseph Waksberg, "Sampling Methods for Random Digit Dialing," *Journal of the American Statistical Association* 73 (1978): 40-46; and K. Michael Cummings, "Random Digit Dialing: A Sampling Technique for Telephone Surveys," *Public Opinion Quarterly* 43 (1979): 233-44.

72. Raymond J. Smead and James Wilcox, "Ring Policy in Telephone Surveys," *Public Opinion Quarterly* 44 (1980): 115-16.

73. Howard E. Freeman et al., "Telephone Sampling Bias in Surveying Disability," *Public Opinion Quarterly* 46 (1982): 392-407.

74. Ibid.

75. Dexter, *Elite and Specialized Interviewing*, 5.

76. There are exceptions to this general rule, however. See John Kessel, *The Domestic Presidency* (Belmont, Calif.: Duxbury Press, 1975). Kessel administered a highly structured survey instrument to Richard Nixon's Domestic Council staff.

77. Joseph A. Pika, "Interviewing Presidential Aides: A Political Scientist's Perspective," in George C. Edwards III and Stephen J. Wayne, eds., *Studying the Presidency* (Knoxville: University of Tennessee Press, 1982), 282.

78. Harriet Zuckerman, "Interviewing an Ultra-Elite," *Public Opinion Quarterly* 36 (1972): 167.

79. Gordon, *Interviewing*, 49-50.

80. Dom Bonafede, "Interviewing Presidential Aides: A Journalist's Perspective" in *Studying the Presidency*, 269.

81. Richard F. Fenno, Jr., *Home Style: House Members in Their Districts* (Boston: Little, Brown & Co., 1978), 280.

82. Zuckerman, "Interviewing an Ultra-Elite," 174.
83. Dean and Whyte, "How Do You Know if the Informant Is Telling the Truth?" 127.
84. Gordon, *Interviewing*, 18.
85. Dexter, *Elite and Specialized Interviewing*, 17.

Terms Introduced

Ambiguous question. A question containing a concept that is not clearly defined.

Closed-ended question. A question with response alternatives provided.

Direct observation. A data collection method in which researcher directly observes a behavior or physical traces of the behavior.

Document analysis. Data collection based on records kept by institutions or individuals.

Double-barreled question. A question that is really two questions in one.

Elite interviewing. Interviewing respondents in a nonstandardized, individualized manner.

Filter question. A question used to screen respondents so that subsequent questions will be asked only of certain respondents for whom the questions are appropriate.

Focused interview. A semistructured or flexible interview schedule used when interviewing elites.

Interviewer bias. Interviewer influence on respondent's answers; an example of reactivity.

Interview data. Observations derived from written or verbal questioning of respondent by researcher.

Leading question. A question that leads respondent to choose a particular response.

Mailed questionnaire. Survey instrument mailed to respondent for completion and return.

Open-ended question. A question with no response alternatives from which respondent may choose.

Personal interview. Face-to-face questioning of respondent.

Question order effect. The effect on responses of question placement within a questionnaire.

Questionnaire design. The physical layout and packaging of a questionnaire.

Randomized response technique (RRT). A method of obtaining accurate answers to sensitive questions that protects respondent's privacy.

Reactivity. The effect of data collection on the phenomenon being observed.

Response quality. The extent to which responses provide accurate and complete information.

Response rate. The proportion of respondents selected for participation in a survey who actually participate.

Response set. The pattern of responding to a series of questions in a similar fashion without careful reading of each question.

Single-sided question. A question with only one substantive alternative provided for respondent.

Survey instrument. Schedule of questions to be asked of respondent.

Survey research. Research based on interview method of data collection.

Telephone interview. Questioning of respondent via telephone.

Termination. Respondent refusal to finish interview.

Two-sided question. A question with two substantive alternatives provided for respondent.

Unobtrusive measure. A measure of phenomenon that does not involve reaction to measurement.

Suggested Readings

Aberbach, Joel D., James D. Chesney, and Bert A. Rockman. "Exploring Elite Political Attitudes: Some Methodological Lessons." *Political Methodology* 2 (1975): 1-27.

Backstrom, Charles H. and Gerald Hursh-Cesar. *Survey Research.* 2d ed. New York: John Wiley & Sons, 1981.

Converse, Jean M., and Howard Schuman. *Conversations at Random: Survey Research as Interviewers See It.* New York: John Wiley & Sons, 1974.

Dillman, Don A. *Mail and Telephone Surveys.* New York: John Wiley & Sons, 1978.

Frey, James H. *Survey Research by Telephone.* Beverly Hills, Calif.: Sage, 1983.

Labaw, Patricia J. *Advanced Questionnaire Design.* Cambridge, Mass.: Abt Books, 1980.

Payne, Stanley. *The Art of Asking Questions.* Princeton, N.J.: Princeton University Press, 1971.

Sudman, Seymour, and Norman M. Bradburn. *Asking Questions: A Practical Guide to Questionnaire Design.* San Francisco: Jossey-Bass, 1982.

9. Document Analysis: Using the Written Record

Political scientists use three major methods of collecting the data they need to test their hypotheses: *interviewing, document analysis,* and *observation.* Of the three methods, interviewing and document analysis are the most frequently used. In the last chapter we discussed interviewing techniques; here we will describe how empirical observations can be made using written documents, records, and personal materials.

Political scientists turn to the written record when the political phenomena that interest them cannot be observed through personal interviews, questionnaires, or by observation. For example, the last two methods are of limited utility to researchers interested in phenomena that are the result of large-scale collective behavior (such as the national government's budget allocations), or in phenomena that are distant in time (Supreme Court decisions during the Civil War), or in phenomena that are geographically distant (defense spending by different countries).

The political phenomena that have been observed through written records are many and varied—for example, judicial decisions concerning the free exercise of religion, voter turnout rates in gubernatorial elections, the change over time in Soviet military expenditures, and the incidence of political corruption in the People's Republic of China.[1] However, not all portions of the written record are equally useful to political scientists. This chapter will discuss the major components of the written record of interest to political scientists and how they are used to measure significant political phenomena.

Types of Written Records

Some written records are ongoing and cover an extensive period of time; others are more episodic. Some are produced by public organizations at taxpayers' expense; others are produced by business concerns or are created by private citizens. Some are carefully preserved and indexed; other records are written and forgotten. In this section we will discuss two different types of written records: the episodic record and the running record.

The Episodic Record

Records that are not part of an ongoing, systematic record-keeping program but are produced and preserved in a more casual, personal, and accidental manner are called *episodic records*. Good examples are personal diaries, memoirs, manuscripts, correspondence, and autobiographies; biographical sketches and other biographical materials; the temporary records of organizations; and media of temporary existence, such as brochures, posters, and pamphlets. The episodic record is of particular importance to political historians since much of their subject matter can be studied only through this data. Also political scientists often base their analyses on the episodic record.

To use written records, researchers must 1) gain access to the materials, and 2) code and analyze them. In the case of the episodic record, gaining access is particularly difficult.[2] Locating suitable materials can easily be the most time-consuming aspect of the whole data collection exercise, as the following example illustrates.

Historian Sandra Frances Van Burkleo became interested in Kentucky politicians' response to the financial panic of 1819. In particular, she wanted to find out how the panic altered banking practices and land law, the relationship between Kentucky and Virginia, and Kentucky's view of the judiciary. Her research led her to consult historical documents in four Kentucky archives—a quest that points out the difficulties and opportunities presented by the episodic record.

> At my first stop . . . I reviewed legislative journals and statute books while trying to learn something about the contents of several steel warehouses. A glance at the finding aids, prepared years before and patched together by untrained personnel, suggested inaccuracy—especially because so much was stacked in packing crates. Through conversations, I gradually gained familiarity with the repository's criteria for collecting materials, and gathered clues about the crates' contents. . . .
>
> I also discovered several hundred bound volumes of banking records—unrecorded in any manuscript guide—and was given a preliminary inventory, which was only partly accurate: size was recorded properly, while substance was not. "Record books," for example, variously meant ledgers, minute books, and miscellaneous volumes. . . .
>
> The staff granted me permission to photocopy. I spent two weeks reading, selecting pages, making lists and cross references, and expanding the search into hinterland branch records as clues emerged—only to learn that archival policy had changed. Photocopying of selections was disallowed. I could choose between staff microfilming of selections at a steep price, or using the cameras myself for much less cost, provided that I filmed whole volumes rather than selected pages and left the master

behind. I tried to remain calm, donned a technician's coat, and found myself behind sophisticated microfilming equipment under hot floodlights in a dank warehouse. Two weeks later, I had filmed over 10,000 pages, garnered prints, finished other research, and moved on to another repository. . . .

My second stop was a state historical society, where I was greeted by friendly volunteers, a classically southern librarian, and a small horde of genealogists. . . . At night, I studied names in local histories; by day, I searched collections. Soon, a network of kin and business associates appeared. . . .

I gained permission to use the original governor's papers and saw that the inventory had been prepared in the 1940s by a volunteer. Nobody knew anything about her. But whole boxes were missing and the numbers of bundles inside boxes did not tally with the inventory. . . .

Finally, I discovered, through a volunteer, that the "storeroom" held material that nobody had ever used. Why not, I asked? She didn't know. I was granted permission to roam in the mysterious "storeroom"—a place reminiscent of another small room in a Carolina library called "the coffin." There were cobwebs, boxes, and old books buried beneath boxes. I lifted, gently moved, and dug. There was an unlabeled register of monies received by the treasury, linked to landholdings in ways that were not clear, and the volume had not been indexed because it lacked a title page. I found five amazing minute books, kept by the Senate clerk during five sessions after 1821—but in a curious shorthand, complete with splendid caricatures of Senate speakers in the margins. . . . I quickly photocopied them. These volumes were a reasonable substitute for long-lost legislative proceedings, providing I could penetrate the shorthand system. They listed individual votes on bills; they summarized speeches. In my hotel room, I read about early American shorthand and eventually deciphered the clerk's alphabetic coding.

At a third repository, located at a state university, another two days were given over to conversation with staff and to generalized poking and digging in finding aids. Again, I wanted to learn something about criteria for collecting, the degree of bibliographic control, the quality of calendars and descriptive inventories. And I hoped to locate someone familiar with the contents of three huge family paper collections which had never been inventoried formally. I found a junior staff member who had processed two of the collections, and had been curious enough to absorb and jot some of the contents. She was thoughtful and meticulous. I trusted her notes and memory, and eliminated considerable searching. . . .

I had been gone well over two months, and it was clear that I would not be able to visit both repositories remaining on my list. Already I was reduced to two meals a day. I aborted a plan to drive to a small western college in order to survey three family paper collections, fragments of which had been explored in the state historical society and had proved irrelevant, and decided to concentrate remaining resources upon a private historical society in Louisville. . . .

My weeks at this final archive were the most instructive of all. The society was underbudgeted and understaffed—an increasingly typical archival condition, but the staff was dedicated. And they chose to befriend me. Over lunch, I heard horror stories (very like those told elsewhere) about visiting scholars—the "loot and pillage" variety who storm a repository with pockets filled with dimes for photocopying, and who leave without acknowledging a debt; dependent scholars who expect curatorial workers to conduct research *for* them; lethargic historians who, when confronted with hundreds of relevant entries in a card catalog, simply leave; or gratuitous visitors who view archivists as failed historians or bright clerks. The staff habitually responded in kind, usually by refusing to volunteer information.[3]

As Van Burkleo's saga suggests, locating episodic records can be a time-consuming and frustrating task yet a rewarding one as well.

Researchers generally use episodic records to illustrate phenomena rather than as the basis for numerical measures. Consequently, quotations and other excerpts from research materials are often used as evidence for a thesis or hypothesis.

Over the years, social scientists have conducted some exceptionally interesting and imaginative studies of political phenomena based on the episodic record. We will describe three particular studies that used the episodic record to illuminate an important political phenomenon.

Deviance in the Massachusetts Bay Colony. Twenty years ago sociologist Kai Erikson studied deviance in the Puritans' Massachusetts Bay Colony during the seventeenth century.[4] He was interested in the process by which communities decide what constitutes deviant behavior. In particular, he wished to test the idea that communities alter their definitions of deviance over time and use deviant behavior to reaffirm and establish the boundaries of acceptable behavior. Contrary to the conventional view that deviant behavior is uniformly harmful, Erikson believed that the identification of and reaction to deviant behavior can serve a useful social purpose for a community.

Obviously, no one is still alive who could be interviewed about the Puritan form of justice in the colony. Consequently, Erikson had to search existing historical documents for evidence relating to his thesis. He found two main collections germane to his inquiry: *The Records of the Governor and Company of the Massachusetts Bay in New England* and *The Records and Files of the Quarterly Courts of Essex County, Massachusetts, 1636-1682.*[5] With these documents Erikson was able to weave together a fascinating tale of crime and punishment, Puritan style, during the mid-1600s.

Erikson's primary concern was with the identification of acts judged deviant in the Massachusetts Bay Colony. From the records of the Essex County courts he was able to collect information on all 1,954 convictions reached between 1651 and 1680. This data allowed Erikson to investigate the frequency of criminal behavior and to calculate a crude crime rate for the Bay Colony during this period.

Erikson's analysis of these historical records was not altogether straightforward. For example, he discovered that the Puritans were extremely casual about how they spelled people's names. One man named Francis Usselton made many appearances before the Essex County Court, and his name was spelled at least 14 different ways in the court's records. This did not present insurmountable difficulties in his case because his name was so distinctive. However, Erikson had a more difficult time deciding whether Edwin and Edward Batter were the same man and whether "the George Hampton who stole a chicken in 1649" was "the same man as the George Hampden who was found drunk in 1651." [6]

A second problem with the Puritans' record keeping was that they often passed the same name from generation to generation. Hence it was sometimes unclear whether two crimes 20 years apart were committed by the same person or by a father and a son. Between 1656 and 1681, for example, John Brown was convicted of seven offenses. However, since John Brown's father and grandfather were also named John Brown, it was unclear who committed which crimes.[7]

Despite these difficulties, Erikson's research is a testimonial to the ability of historical records to address important contemporary issues. Without the foresight of those who preserved and printed these records, an important aspect of life in Puritan New England would have been measurably more difficult to piece together.

Economics and the U.S. Constitution. In 1913 historian Charles Beard wrote a book about the U.S. Constitution in which he made imaginative use of the episodic record.[8] Beard's thesis was that economic interests prompted the movement to frame the Constitution. He reasoned that if he could show that the framers and pro-Constitution groups were familiar with the economic benefits that would ensue upon ratification of the Constitution, then he would be able to argue that economic considerations were central to the Constitution debate. If, in addition, he could show that the framers themselves benefited economically from the system of government established by the Constitution, the case would be that much stronger. This thesis, which has stimulated a good deal of controversy in the intervening years, was tested by Beard with a variety of data from the episodic record.

The first body of evidence presented by Beard measured the property holdings of those present at the 1787 Constitutional Convention. These measures, which Beard admits are distressingly incomplete, are derived largely from six different types of sources: biographical materials, such as James Herring's multivolume *National Portrait Gal-*

lery, and the *National Encyclopedia of Biography;* census materials, in particular the 1790 census of heads of families, which showed the number of slaves owned by some of the framers; U.S. Treasury records, including ledger books containing lists of securities; records of individual state loan offices; records concerning the histories of certain businesses, such as the *History of the Bank of North America,* and the *History of the Insurance Company of North America;* and collections of personal papers stored in the Library of Congress.

From these written records Beard was able to discover the occupations, land holdings, securities, mercantile interests, and slaves owned by many of the framers. This allowed him to establish a plausible case that the framers were not economically disinterested when they met in Philadelphia to "revise" the Articles of Confederation.

Beard coupled his inventory of the framers' personal wealth with a second body of evidence concerning their political views. His objective was to demonstrate that the framers realized and discussed the economic implications of the Constitution and the new system of government. By using the existing minutes of the debate at the convention, the personal correspondence and writings of some of the framers, and *The Federalist Papers* by James Madison, Alexander Hamilton, and John Jay, which were written to persuade people to vote for the Constitution, Beard was able to demonstrate that the framers were concerned about, and cognizant of, the economic implications of the Constitution they wrote.

A third body of evidence allowed Beard to analyze the distribution of the vote for and against the Constitution. Where the data permitted, Beard measured the geographical distribution of the popular vote in favor of ratification and compared this with information about the economic interests of different geographical areas in each of the states. He also attempted to measure the personal wealth of those present at the state ratification conventions and then related those measures to the vote on the Constitution. This data was gleaned from the financial records of the individual states and the U.S. Treasury Department and from historical accounts of the ratification process in the states.

Through this painstaking and time-consuming reading of the historical record, Beard constructed a persuasive (although not necessarily proven) case for his conclusion that "the movement for the Constitution of the United States was originated and carried through principally by four groups of personalty interests which had been adversely affected under the Articles of Confederation: money, public securities, manufactures, and trade and shipping." [9]

Presidential Personality. A third good example of the use of the episodic record may be found in James David Barber's *The Presidential Character.* Because of the importance of the presidency in the American political system and the extent to which that institution is shaped by its sole occupant, Barber was interested in understanding the personalities of the individuals who have occupied the office during the twentieth century. Ideally, he would have had a chance to observe directly and personally the behavior of the 14 presidents who held office between 1908 and 1984; instead, he was forced to rely on the available written materials about them.

For Barber, discerning a president's personality means understanding his style, character, and world view. Style is *"the President's habitual way of performing his three political roles: rhetoric, personal relations, and homework."* A president's world view is measured by his *"primary, politically relevant beliefs, particularly his conceptions of social causality, human nature, and the central moral conflicts of the time."* And character *"is the way the President orients himself toward life."* [10] Barber believes that a president's style, character, and world view "fit together in a dynamic package understandable in psychological terms" and that this personality "is an important shaper of his Presidental behavior on nontrivial matters." But how is one to measure the style, character, and world view of presidents who are either dead or who will not permit a political psychologist access to their thoughts and deeds? This is an especially troublesome question when one believes, as Barber does, that "the best way to predict a President's character, world view, and style is to see how they were put together in the first place . . . in his early life, culminating in his first independent political success." [11]

Barber's solution to this problem was to use available materials on the twentieth-century presidents, including biographies, memoirs, diaries, speeches, and, in the case of Richard Nixon, tape recordings of presidential conversations. Barber did not use all the available biographical materials. For example, he "steered clear of obvious puff jobs put out in campaigns and of the quickie exposés composed to destroy reputations." [12] He quotes frequently from the biographical materials as he builds his case that a particular president was one of four basic personality types. Had these materials been unavailable or of questionable accuracy (a possibility that Barber glossses over in a single paragraph), measuring presidental personalities would have been a good deal more difficult if not impossible.

Barber's analysis of the presidential personality is exclusively qualitative; there is not a single table or graph in his entire 500-page book. He uses the biographical material to categorize each president as one of four personality types and to show that the presidents with similar personalities exhibited similar behavioral patterns when in office. In brief, Barber uses two dimensions—activity-passivity (how much energy does the man invest in his presidency?) and positive-negative affect (how does he feel

Table 9-1   Presidential Personality Types

Activity-Passivity

Postive-Negative Affect	Active	Passive
Positive	Franklin D. Roosevelt Harry S Truman John F. Kennedy Gerald Ford Jimmy Carter	William Howard Taft Warren Harding Ronald Reagan
Negative	Woodrow Wilson Herbert Hoover Lyndon Johnson Richard Nixon	Calvin Coolidge Dwight Eisenhower

about what he does?)—to define the four types of presidential personality. (See Table 9-1.)

Barber's research is a provocative and imaginative example of the use of the episodic record—in this case, biographical material—as evidence for a series of generalizations about presidential personality. Although Barber does not empirically test his hypotheses in the ways that we have been discussing in this book, he does accumulate a body of evidence in support of his assertions and present his evidence in such a way that the reader can evaluate how persuasive it is.

The Running Record

Unlike the episodic record, the running record tends to be produced by organizations rather than private citizens, is carefully stored and easily accessed, and is available for long periods of time. The portion of the running record that is concerned with political phenomena is extensive and growing. The data collection and reporting efforts of the U.S. government alone are impressive, and if one adds to that the written records collected and preserved by state and local governments, interest groups, publishing houses, research institutes, and commercial concerns, the quantity of politically relevant written records increases quickly. Reports of the U.S. government, for example, now cover everything from electoral votes to electrical rates, taxes to taxi cabs, and, in summary form, fill one thousand pages in the *Statistical Abstract of the United States,* published annually by the U.S. Bureau of the Census.

In this section we will summarize the main types of running records of interest to political scientists.

Election Returns. Election returns have been collected, tabulated, and published for almost 200 years. They are available for most federal offices and some statewide offices at the state and county levels. Commonly used sources of such data are the *America Votes* series (published biennially since 1956 by the Elections Research Center and Congressional Quarterly) and the Inter-University Consortium for Political and Social Research (ICPSR) at the University of Michigan.

Congressional Voting. Votes of members of the U.S. Congress since 1789 are available from the ICPSR. Congressional roll call votes since 1945 and a plethora of other records concerning individual members of Congress (presidential support scores and party support scores, for example) are published annually in the *Congressional Quarterly Almanac. Politics in America,* published biennially by Congressional Quarterly since 1972, contains more detailed information on individual members, including data on each member's district or state, political career, and voting record, as rated by a variety of interest groups.

Judicial Decisions. Summaries of all state and federal judicial decisions are reported in the *Decennial Digest* (published by West Publishing Co.) and the text of all Supreme Court decisions may be found in *United States Reports,* published by the U.S. Government Printing Office. In addition, the ICPSR has information on the votes cast in the 4,573 cases decided by the U.S. Supreme Court between 1946 and 1969. The ICPSR also has more limited collections of data on topics such as civil and criminal federal court cases (1962-63), plea bargaining in felony cases in Alaska (1974-76), state criminal court cases (1962), and U.S. Supreme Court certiorari decisions (1947-56).

Governmental Policy. For information on public policy, researchers have a wide variety of sources. The laws passed each year by the federal government are summarized in the *Congressional Quarterly Almanac* and cited in full in the *United States Statutes at Large.* Data on federal expenditures are included in the *Congressional Quarterly Almanac* as well as the *Statistical Abstract of the United States.* Measures of public policy at the state and local levels may be found in *The Book of the States* (published biennially by the Council of State Governments), the *County and City Data Book* (published by the U.S. Bureau of the Census), the *Statistical Abstract of the United States,* and the U.S. Census Bureau's *Annual Survey of Governments.*

The ICPSR also has useful data describing government policy at the national, state, and local levels. *Annual Time Series Statistics for the U.S.* describes federal expenditures by various departments, agencies, and commissions from 1929 to 1968. Four separate studies contain information on state policymaking and governmental expenditures; one covers 1950 to 1964, one provides data at decennial points from 1890 to 1960, one covers 1956 to 1965, and one has select data from both the nineteenth and twentieth centuries. At the local level, ICPSR has data for 676 incorporated urban places with populations of 25,000 or more during the 1960s and other data since 1960 for 130 incorporated cities with populations greater than 100,000.

The *Statistical Abstract of the United States* is a treasure trove of data on American society. It contains summaries of all of the major data collection efforts of the national government. Between its covers you will find information on health care expenditures, drug use, crime and victimization rates, numbers of arrests and prisoners, air quality, weather, environmental control expenditures, leisure time activities, state and local government finances, federal government personnel and expenditures, veterans' benefits, unemployment, occupational injury rates, the consumer price index, banking and publishing activities, number of foreign-owned U.S. firms, energy production and consumption, transportation revenues, motor vehicle accidents, crop production, housing construction, public housing, department store sales, foreign assistance, and exports and imports. Such a publication is truly an archival researcher's delight! Another useful guide to government records is Andrew Hacker's *U/S: A Statistical Portrait*.[13]

Crime Statistics. One particular area of American life that has attracted a huge record-keeping enterprise is the criminal justice system. Some crime data may be found in the *Statistical Abstract*. The ICPSR also has data describing many aspects of crime and the criminal justice system. These include:

> The FBI's *Uniform Crime Reports* (data from 1966 to 1976 on the eight index crimes—murder, forcible rape, robbery, aggravated assault, burglary, larceny-theft, motor vehicle theft, and manslaughter);
> National Crime Surveys (victimization data, 1972-80;
> National Jail Census (data on local jails, 1970, 1972, 1978);
> Census of Correctional Facilities (1974 and 1979);
> Survey of Jail Inmates (1972 and 1978);
> Criminal Case Processing in Metropolitan Courts (1976);
> Pretrial Release Practices in the U.S. (1976-78);
> Expenditure and Employment Data for the Criminal Justice System (1971-1979).

Campaign Spending. For decades, political scientists have been interested in the role of money in election campaigns. However, it is only within the past 15 ·years that reliable and comprehensive data on campaign spending have been available to researchers. As a result of the

Federal Election Campaign Act of 1971, a federal agency—the Federal Election Commission—was established and given the responsibility of collecting data on the fund-raising and campaign spending practices of candidates for federal elective office. Political scientists now have a rich new source of archival data on a consequential area of political life.

Speeches. There is also an ongoing written record of the public statements of politicians. Presidential campaign speeches, for example, are contained in a variety of publications, including those published by individual candidates (such as *Nixon Speaks Out,* published by the Nixon-Agnew Campaign Committee) and those published for every president (such as *Public Papers of the Presidents of the United States,* published annually by the U.S. Government Office of the Federal Register). Presidential debate transcripts for 1960, 1976, 1980, and 1984 are also available.[14]

Speeches given on the floor of the U.S. Congress are recorded in the *Congressional Record,* although since members are allowed to excise, revise, and add to what they actually said this record is not completely accurate. *National Party Platforms,* published by the University of Illinois Press, contains a collection of the documents put together every four years since 1840 by the American political parties.

Mass Media Materials. The output of news organizations is a running record of daily events and public affairs. The types of stories written, the political issues and personalities covered, the photographs taken, and the opinions expressed may all be considered as a written record of our political and social life. This record has been difficult to use simply because it is so massive, disorganized, and hard to retrieve, yet now with the development of newspaper and television indices a sizable portion of the news is both enduring and readily accessible. The *New York Times* has been indexed since 1851, the *Wall Street Journal* since 1957, the *Christian Science Monitor* since 1960, and the *Washington Post* since 1971. Television network news coverage has been indexed since 1968.

Local libraries often have extensive collections of local newspapers. The Philadelphia Free Library, for example, has preserved the *Philadelphia Inquirer* since 1860, the *Evening-Bulletin* for 1847-1982, the *Public Ledger* for 1836-1934, and the *North American* for 1839-1925 (the last three papers went out of business in 1982, 1934, and 1925, respectively).

If a researcher is interested in a phenomenon that can be measured using newspaper content, the running news record is well-preserved and extensive. But the running record for broadcast news is less satisfactory. Television network news coverage has been preserved and indexed only since 1968. And, as far as we know, there is no archive or collection of radio news or local television news that could be used by researchers.

Foreign Affairs.   Researchers interested in comparative politics and international relations have collected a variety of data on an array of subjects, including the socioeconomic and political attributes of nations; instances of political dissent, conflicts, or violence within different nations; events of conflict and cooperation between nations; trade and arms transfers between nations; and defense expenditures and use of military force by nations. These data represent a rich and readily accessible archival source of observations that would be time-consuming and difficult to collect oneself.

Biographical Data.   Finally, biographical data is part of the running record. Using biographical publications such as *Who's Who in America* and the *Social Register,* researchers have been able to trace the origins and relationships among people in various positions of power and influence and to contrast different types of elite groups.[15] The ICPSR has biographical data on higher echelon federal executive appointees (1932-65), arms control bureaucrats, higher civil servants in American federal agencies (1963), state and federal supreme court judges (1955), U.S. Supreme Court justices (1789-1958), members of the Congress of the Confederate States of America (1862-65), and members of the U.S. Congress (1789-1980). Biographical data also exist on selected foreign elites. The ICPSR has data on political elites in Eastern Europe (1971), Kenya (1966-67), Tanzania (1964-68), the Soviet Union (1966), France and Germany (1964), Brazil (1960), and Uganda (1964-68).

The Running Record and Episodic Record Compared

There are three primary advantages to using the running record over the episodic record. The first is cost, in terms of both time and money. Since the costs of collecting, tabulating, storing, and reporting the data in the running record are generally borne by the record keepers themselves, political scientists are usually able to use this data very inexpensively. In contrast to the time-consuming and expensive research of the episodic record described earlier by the historian interested in early nineteenth-century Kentucky, researchers can often use the data stored in the running record by photocopying a few pages of a reference book, purchasing a government report, or acquiring a computer tape. In fact, the recent expansion of the data collection and record-keeping activities of the national government has been a financial boon to social scientists of all types.

A second, related advantage is the accessibility of the running record. Instead of searching packing crates, deteriorated ledgers, and musty storerooms, as users of the episodic record often do, users of the running record more often handle reference books, government publications, computer printouts, and computer tapes. Many political science research projects have been completed with only the data stored in the reference books and government documents of a decent research library.

A third advantage of the running record is that by definition it covers a more extensive period of time than the episodic record does. This permits the type of longitudinal analysis and before-and-after research designs discussed in Chapter 5. Although the episodic record helps explain the origins of and reasons for a particular event, episode, or period, the running record allows the measurement of political phenomena over time.

The running record is not without its defects, however. One is that a researcher is at the mercy of the data collection practices and procedures of the record-keeping organizations themselves. Researchers are rarely in a position to influence record-keeping practices; they must rely instead on what organizations such as the U.S. Census Bureau, Federal Election Commission, and the Roper Center for Public Opinion Research decide to do. There is often a tradeoff between ease of access and researcher influence over the measurements that are made.

Another related disadvantage of the running record is that some organizations are not willing to share their raw data with researchers. The processed data that they do release may reflect calculations, categorizations, and aggregations that are inaccurate or uninformative.

Finally, it is sometimes difficult for researchers to find out exactly what the record-keeping practices of some organizations are. Unless the organization publishes a description of its procedures, a researcher may not know what decisions have guided the record-keeping process. This can be a special problem when these practices change, altering in an unknown way the measurements reported.

Although the running record has its disadvantages, often political scientists must rely on it if they wish to do any empirical research on a particular topic. For years, for example, the only reasonable way of conducting research on crime in the United States was to use the *Uniform Crime Reports* (UCR) of the Federal Bureau of Investigation. We conclude this section on types of written records with a description of some of the limitations in the *Uniform Crime Reports,* one of the longest and most often used portions of the running record.

The Uniform Crime Report

First issued in 1930, the *Uniform Crime Report* is the only enduring, national compilation of statistics on crime in the United States and consequently the basis for numerous research reports on crime and police behavior. In recent years, however, the accuracy and precision of the measures reported in the UCR have been called into question and the report has been criticized by many of its users.

The FBI's measure of criminal activity is based on the reports it receives from thousands of law enforcement agencies across the country. State and local police departments voluntarily submit these reports; the FBI has never been given the power to enforce participation. Each police agency must bear the cost and responsibility of providing the information, although the FBI does provide instructions and assistance to participating police departments. The FBI's intent, then, is to produce a report representing the *population* of police departments; no sampling is done.

Police departments are asked to report two types of information: the number of criminal acts of seven different kinds that come to their attention ("Part I" crimes) and the number of arrests that they make for many other types of crimes ("Part II" crimes). Part I crimes include criminal homicide, forcible rape, robbery, aggravated assault, burglary, larceny, and auto theft. Part II crimes include other assaults; forgery and counterfeiting; embezzlement and fraud; buying, receiving, or possessing stolen property; carrying or possessing weapons; prostitution and commercialized vice; sex offenses; offenses against the family and children; violations of narcotics drug laws; violations of liquor laws; drunkenness; disorderly conduct; vagrancy; gambling; driving while intoxicated; violation of road and driving laws; parking violations; other violations of traffic and motor vehicle laws; all other offenses; and suspicion.[16] Trends in crime over time are reported, as well as rates of crimes per 100,000 people.

In this section we will discuss the flaws in the UCR that have led to questionable measures of criminal activity in the United States. The most obvious problem is that not all crimes are reported to the police and therefore are never included in the UCR.[17] There are numerous reasons why victims do not report a crime: they may be unable to do so (for example, they may have been murdered), they may fear reprisal by the accused, they may think that nothing will be done by the police, they may wish to hide their own participation in criminal activity, they may consider their losses too minor to justify the inconvenience, they may be reluctant to publicize their victimization, and they may be able to secure compensation from other sources (for example, from an insurance company).[18] Many crimes are reported elsewhere: to military officials, prosecutors, and regulatory agencies with judicial power, such as the Securities and Exchange Commission. Violations of federal laws, misrepresentation in advertising, restraints of trade, and manipulation of prices and markets are not the kinds of crimes reported to state and local police forces.[19]

Moreover, the police themselves may neglect, either by accident or intention, to report crimes to headquarters or to the FBI. Manpower is often scarce, records poorly kept, and employees incompetent and inefficient. In addition, the police may purposely try to protect the reputation of their coworkers, superiors, precincts, and municipality by failing to report criminal acts. If they know that the UCR statistics are going to be used to compare the safety of their city with that of another, they may be tempted to underreport crime.[20] Who wants to be a policeman in the city dubbed "the murder capital of the world"?

Another problem with the UCR is that Part II crimes are included only if an arrest is made. This is because it is known that many Part II crimes are never reported to the police, thus making UCR reports of these crimes even less reliable than they are for Part I crimes.[21]

Just as some crimes go unreported, some crimes are reported that never took place. After all, the courts, not the victim, decide that someone is guilty of committing a crime. Yet the UCR assumes that any criminal act reported to the police did, in fact, happen, regardless of the eventual disposition of the case. Crimes may be overreported, then, as well as underreported.[22]

The FBI asks that crimes be reported in one of 27 categories—7 Part I crimes, 20 Part II crimes. The behavior that constitutes each of these crimes, however, varies widely across the many police departments represented in the UCR. Assault and larceny are often used as substitutes for robbery, for example, and there is tremendous variation in what constitutes drunkenness, disorderly conduct, prostitution, vagrancy, assault and battery, and aggravated assault.[23] What may be considered criminal behavior by a minority youth in a center city precinct might simply engender a stern warning and a free ride home when committed by a white youth in a privileged suburban community.[24] Yet there is no way that the FBI can force state and local police departments to maintain uniformity in either law or practice. As long as individual state and local legislatures are the ones defining crimes and state and local police are the ones enforcing these laws, there will be no uniformity in how criminal acts are reported.[25]

By the late 1960s, most police departments had joined the UCR system, amounting to coverage of areas containing 96 percent of the U.S. population.[26] In earlier years, however, participation was much less, resulting in the absence of crime statistics for large areas of the country. Thus UCR measures of over-time trends, if not based on identical reporting areas, are suspect.

One criminal incident may involve the breaking of several laws. Yet the FBI has decided that the UCR should reflect only the most serious offense in a multiple-offense episode. For example, if someone breaks into a home, steals $300 worth of jewels, kills an occupant, injures a bystander, and steals a car with which to make an escape, only the murder will be recorded. Obviously this systematically underestimates the number of criminal acts committed or laws broken.[27]

Beginning in 1958, the UCR included an "index" of criminal activity calculated by summing the Part I crimes reported. The rationale for calculating such an index was that Part I crimes are the most serious and the most likely to be reported to the police.[28]

The crime index has been the subject of two major criticisms. First, by excluding Part II crimes, the index does not reflect many crimes that are serious and cause major physical harm (such as arson, kidnapping, and assault and battery) or substantial financial loss and property damage (such as embezzlement, malicious mischief, and disorderly conduct).[29] Second, by summing the number of Part I crimes, the index effectively treats each crime, regardless of its type, equally. A murder counts the same as an auto theft in calculating the crime index. Since the FBI believes that the seven Part I crimes may be rank-ordered in terms of severity, the equally weighted index would seem to be inconsistent with the FBI's own approach to crime reporting.[30]

In short, one must be careful about the inferences drawn from the crime index. The index does not represent all crime, or all crimes reported to the police, or even all serious crimes reported to the police. Nor do changes in the crime index necessarily mean that crime has become any more or less serious. Since the index is composed of many very different kinds of crime but not all crimes, exactly what it does measure is unclear.

As we have seen, the validity and reliability of the *Uniform Crime Reports* are jeopardized by numerous shortcomings in the FBI's record-keeping system. Nevertheless, this running record is a valuable source of information about political phenomena that are impossible to observe in any other way.

Content Analysis

Acquiring or gaining access to the written records necessary to sustain an empirical research project is really only the beginning of document analysis. Once the appropriate written records have been located and gathered, they must be organized and used to inform an empirical analysis. This often requires *data reduction;* that is, distillation of a voluminous amount of raw material to a more manageable and informative set of observations.

Sometimes researchers extract excerpts, quotations, or examples from the written record to support an observation or relationship. Users of the episodic record, such as Charles Beard and James David Barber, often use the written record in this way. Other times researchers use numerical measures calculated by record keepers and presented in the written record without altering these measures in any appreciable fashion. Users of the *Uniform Crime Reports,* for example, often simply use the crime rates reported there as their independent and dependent variables, as do users of the Federal Election Commission's campaign spending reports. With both of these written records, a minimum of conversion is done by the researcher.

Researchers, however, may wish to extract numerical measures from an extensive written record in non-numerical form. For example, a researcher might want to study the news coverage of a presidential campaign to measure how favorable the tone of the coverage was for different candidates. This might require reducing hundreds of newspaper articles and news programs to a handful of numerical measures of the tone of news stories.

To derive numerical measures from a non-numerical written record, researchers commonly use a technique called *content analysis*. This procedure enables them to "take a verbal, nonquantitative document and transform it into quantitative data." A researcher "first constructs a set of mutually exclusive and exhaustive categories that can be used to analyze documents, and then records the frequency with which each of these categories is observed in the documents studied." [31]

Content Analysis Procedures

The first step in content analysis is deciding what *sample of materials* to include in the analysis. If a researcher is interested in the political values of those desiring public office, a sample of political party platforms and campaign speeches might be suitable. If the level of sexism in a society is of interest, then a sample of television entertainment programs and films might be drawn. Or if a researcher is interested in what liberals are thinking about, liberal opinion magazines might be sampled. Actually, two tasks are involved at this stage: selecting materials germane to the researcher's subject (in other words, choosing the appropriate *sampling frame*) and sampling the actual material to be analyzed from that sampling frame. Once the appropriate sampling frame has been selected, then all of the possible types of samples described in Chapter 7—random, systematic, stratified, cluster, and nonprobability— could be used.

The second task in any content analysis is to *define the categories* of content that are going to be measured. A study of the prevalence of crime in the news, for example, might measure the amount of news content that either deals with crime or does not. Content that deals with crime might be further subdivided into the kinds of crimes covered. A study of news coverage of a presidential campaign might measure whether news content concerning a particular presidential candidate is favorable, neutral, or unfavorable. Or a study might measure the personality traits of various prime-time television characters—such as strength, warmth, integrity, humility, and wisdom—and the sex, age, race, and occupation of those characters. This process is in many respects the most important part of any content analysis because the researcher must measure the content in such a way that it relates to the research topic, and he or she must define this content so that the measures of it are both valid and reliable.

The third task is to choose the *recording unit*. For example, from a given document, news source, or other material, the researcher may want to code 1) each word, 2) each theme, 3) each character or actor, 4) each sentence, 5) each paragraph, or 6) each item in its entirety. When measuring concern with crime in the daily newspaper, the recording unit might be the article. When measuring the favorableness of news coverage of presidential campaigns in news weeklies, the recording unit might be the paragraph. And when measuring the amount of attention focused on different governmental institutions on television network news, the recording unit might be the story.

In choosing the recording unit, the researcher usually considers the ease of identifying the unit (words, sentences, and paragraphs are easier to identify than stories and themes) and the correspondence between the unit and the content categories (stories may be more appropriate than words in determining whether crime is a topic of concern, while individual words or sentences rather than larger units may be more appropriate for measuring the traits of political candidates). Generally, if the recording unit is too small, each case will be unlikely to possess any of the content categories. Furthermore, small recording units may obscure the context in which a particular content appears. For example, counting the number of mentions of "Geraldine Ferraro" would lump together "Geraldine Ferraro continues to be haunted by questions about her financial affairs" with "Geraldine Ferraro addressed another wildly enthusiastic rally today." On the other hand, if the recording unit is too large, it will be difficult to measure the single category of a content variable that it possesses (in other words, the case will possess multiple values of a given content variable). The selection of the appropriate recording unit is often a matter of trial and error, adjustment, and compromise in the pursuit of measures that capture the content of the material being coded.

Finally, a researcher has to devise a *system of enumeration* for the content being coded. The presence or absence of a given content category can be measured or the "frequency with which the category appears," or the "amount of space allotted to the category," or the "strength of intensity with which the category is represented." [32] For example, suppose we were coding the presence of Hispanics in televised entertainment programming, with the *program* the recording unit. For each program we could count 1) whether there was at least one Hispanic present or not, 2) how many Hispanics there were, 3) how much time Hispanics were on the screen, and 4) how favorable or how important the portrayal of Hispanics was for the overall story.

The validity of a content analysis can usually be enhanced with a precise explanation of the procedures followed and content categories used. Usually the best way to demonstrate the reliability of content analysis measures is to show *intercoder reliability*. Intercoder reliability simply means that more than one analysts, using the same procedures and definitions, agree on the content categories applied to the material analyzed. The more agreement that can be shown, the more confident the researcher can be that the meaning of the content is not heavily dependent on the particular person doing the analysis. If different coders disagree frequently, then the content categories have not been defined with enough clarity and precision.

If you have never done a formal content analysis, the following example may be helpful. Suppose you were interested in studying 1984 presidential campaign coverage by *Time* and *Newsweek* (the sampling frame). You could decide to analyze every article about the campaign from September 1 to election day, with the article the recording unit. The content categories could be 1) the subject of the paragraph (that is, the "who"); 2) the topic of the paragraph (that is, the "what"); and 3) the tone of the paragraph (was it unfavorable or favorable?). To encode the content you could devise a coding sheet like the one presented in Table 9-2. It shows the content variables, the categories for each variable, the recording unit, and the system of enumeration. This is the type of sheet that would be used to quantify the data.

Table 9-2   Coding Sheet for Hypothetical Content Analysis of Presidential Campaign Coverage

---

Magazine   1. Time_____   2. Newsweek_____

Date _____

Page no. _____

No. of paragraphs _____

No. of paragraphs devoted
to each candidate: 1. Mondale _____   3. Reagan _____

                                         2. Ferraro _____   4. Bush _____

Primary focus
of article:

                1. Candidate prospects _____   3. Policy issues _____

                2. Campaign events _____   4. Personalities _____

Overall tone
of article:

                For Reagan/Bush: Negative 1 2 3 4 5 6 7 Positive

                For Mondale/Ferraro: Negative 1 2 3 4 5 6 7 Positive

---

Although political scientists have used content analysis sparingly, it is a useful technique in some areas of inquiry. We will conclude this section with an example of a content analysis performed by two political scientists.

News Coverage of Presidential Campaigns

A frequent subject of content analysis is press coverage of election campaigns. Given the importance of how candidates are presented and how the electoral process is treated in the news, political scientists have been interested for some time in accurately and systematically describing and explaining campaign news coverage. Most of these studies have investigated whether candidates receive favorable or unfavorable coverage, whether news coverage relays useful information to the American electorate, whether the press accurately presents the complex and lengthy presidential nomination process, and whether journalists are, in general, objective, accurate, fair, and informative.

One good example of a content analysis of this type is a study by Michael J. Robinson and Margaret A. Sheehan of presidential campaign coverage in 1980.[33] We will discuss the procedures they followed and some of the strengths and weaknesses of their analysis.

At the beginning Robinson and Sheehan had to select the news coverage for their study. Given the overwhelming quantity of print and broadcast coverage that a presidential election campaign stimulates, there was no way that they could carefully analyze it all. In 1980 there were more than 1,000 daily newspapers and 6,000 broadcast stations in the United States. Consequently, they had to select, or sample, a portion of the news coverage to analyze. Six different decisions were involved in choosing the sample.

First, the researchers decided what type of medium to analyze. Primarily because of their estimates of the audience reached by different media, they chose national network television and newspaper wire service copy.[34] In the process, they decided not to select several regional daily newspapers and the news weeklies, as had been done in a study of the 1976 campaign, and not to draw a representative sample of daily newspapers, as had been done in a study of the 1974 congressional elections.[35]

Second, because Robinson's and Sheehan's resources were limited, they had to decide which of the media outlets to select. In other words, which television network and which wire service would be chosen? Based again on audience size, as well as professional prestige, they selected CBS and Associated Press (AP). But AP refused to cooperate—an example of one of those disturbing yet all too frequent developments that cause the best laid research plans to go awry. Consequently, the researchers switched reluctantly to United Press International (UPI), even though it had far fewer clients and generally placed fewer stories in daily newspapers. CBS and UPI, then, became their case studies for 1980.[36]

What products of these two media outlets should be included in the study? This was the third decision facing Robinson and Sheehan. CBS produces several versions of the nightly news as well as morning news shows, mid-day news shows, news interviews, and news specials. And UPI offers several news services, among them an "A" wire, which is the national wire; a city wire, and a radio wire. The "A" wire itself has two versions: the night cycle, which runs from noon to midnight, and the day cycle, which runs from midnight to noon. The researchers decided to use the day "A" wire, for reasons of scope of coverage as well as accessibility, and the CBS nightly news (the 7 p.m. Eastern time edition) primarily for financial reasons and convenience.[37]

Fourth, they had to decide which of the material from these news shows and wire copy to include. They decided to include only campaign or campaign-related stories. Thus they used any story that "mentioned the presidential campaign, no matter how tangentially; mentioned any presidential candidate in his campaign role; mentioned any presidential candidate or his immediate family in a noncampaign, official role (almost always a story about the president); or discussed to a substantial degree any campaign lower than the presidential level." [38] Just over 5,500 stories on UPI and CBS—22 percent of UPI and CBS total news coverage—met these selection criteria.[39]

Fifth, Robinson and Sheehan had to decide what time period to include in their study. Although a presidential campaign has a fairly clear ending point, election day, the beginning date of the campaign is uncertain. The researchers decided to include coverage every weekday in 1980 (that is, from January 1 to December 30). They give no justification for excluding the weekend news.[40]

Finally, Robinson and Sheehan made an important decision to exclude some of the content of both CBS's and UPI's news coverage. They decided not to include any photographs, film, videotape, amd live pictures and to rely exclusively on verbal (CBS) or written (UPI) expression. They defended this decision on the grounds that it is more difficult to interpret the meaning of visuals and that the visual message usually supports the verbal message. Moreover, comparing the visual component of CBS with that of UPI would be difficult.[41]

Having selected the news content to be analyzed, Robinson and Sheehan then decided what unit of analysis to use when coding news content. They always use the *story,* although at times they analyze the content sentence by sentence and word by word. Most content analyses of this type have also used the story as the unit of analysis, but it is unfortunate that Robinson and Sheehan did not explain this choice in any detail or discuss how difficult it was to tell where one story ended and another began.[42]

We now will consider the most important decision in any content analysis: the selection of the content categories to be encoded and the definitions of the values for these content categories. Robinson and Sheehan coded some 25 different aspects of each 1980 campaign story. Some of these were straightforward, such as the story's date, length, and reporter.[43] Other categories, which pertained to the central subject matter of the study, were not as readily defined or measured.

The researchers were primarily concerned with five questions: Were CBS and UPI 1) objective, 2) equitable in providing access, 3) fair, 4) serious, and 5) comprehensive? We will discuss each of these questions in turn.

Robinson and Sheehan measured the objectivity of the press's coverage in four ways: by the number of explicit and unsupported conclusions made by journalists about the personal qualities of the candidates; by the number of times the journalists expressed personal opinions concerning the issues of the campaign; by counting the number of sentences that were either descriptive, analytical, or judgmental; and by counting the number of verbs used by journalists that were either descriptive, analytical, or insinuative. Clearly, each of these content categories involved judgments by researchers concerning what constituted an explicit and unsupported conclusion, what constituted a personal opinion, what constituted a descriptive versus an analytical sentence. The researchers provide examples of different types of coded content, and they also give some curt definitions of what each of the categories meant to them: for example, *descriptive sentences* "present the who, what, where, when of the day's news, without any meaningful qualification or elaboration," *analytical sentences* "tell us *why* something occurs or predicts as to whether it might," and *judgmental sentences* "tell us how something ought to be or ought not to be." [44]

To determine whether the press granted appropriate access to each of the presidential candidates, Robinson and Sheehan quantitatively measured how much coverage (in terms of seconds for CBS and column inches for UPI) each of the candidates received. They do not say whether this coding procedure presented any difficulties, although they do evaluate whether the amount of access granted each candidate was justified.

Determining whether press coverage was fair was much more difficult than measuring access since an evaluation of fairness requires that the tone of campaign coverage be measured. Establishing tone in a reliable and valid way is not easy. Robinson and Sheehan define tone and fairness in these terms:

Tone pertains not simply to the explicit message offered by the journalist but the implicit message as well. Tone involves the overall (and admittedly subjective) assessment we made about each story: whether the story was, for the major candidates, "good press," "bad press," or something in between. "Fairness," as we define it, involves the sum total of a candidate's press tone; how far from neutrality the candidate's press score lies.[45]

They evaluated content in terms of whether it represented good press (a story that had three times as much positive information as negative information about a candidate) or bad press (a story that had three times as much negative as positive information). But they never discuss how they determined what constituted positive and negative information. Furthermore, in their effort to restrict their analysis to the behavior of journalists, Robinson and Sheehan excluded information about political events (such as the failure of the Iranian hostage rescue mission), polls, comments made by partisans, remarks of "criminals and anti-Americans" (such as Fidel Castro and the Ayatollah Khomeini), and statements made by the candidates themselves.[46] In short, their measurement of fairness depended upon the wisdom of a number of decisions regarding the encoding of campaign stories. Some of these decisions are highly questionable, such as using an arbitrary 3-to-1 ratio to determine good press/bad press and excluding political events, polls, and the words of the candidates themselves from the analysis.

The seriousness of press coverage was measured by coding each story and, at times, each sentence, according to whether they represented policy issues, candidate issues, "horse-race coverage," or something else. *Policy issues* were ones that "involve major questions as to how the government should (or should not) proceed in some area of social life," *candidate issues* "concern the personal behavior of the candidate during the course of his or her campaign," and *horse-race coverage* focuses on "any consideration as to winning or losing."[47] Because of difficulty in encoding entire stories into only one of these categories, the researchers shifted to the more exacting sentence-by-sentence analysis. Some sentences did not fit into one and only one of these categories, but "the majority of sentences were fairly easy to classify as one form of news or another."[48] The seriousness of UPI and CBS campaign coverage in 1980 was then measured by comparing their amount of policy issues coverage with the policy issues coverage in other media in previous presidential election years.

Finally, to evaluate how comprehensive press coverage was in 1980, Robinson and Sheehan coded campaign stories in terms of the level of office covered: presidential, vice-presidential, senatorial, congressional, and gubernatorial. More than 90 percent of both CBS and UPI campaign coverage was of the presidential and vice-presidential races.[49]

Over the Wire and on TV represents one of the most thorough content analyses ever performed by political scientists. Certainly, in terms of the time period covered and the sheer quantity of material analyzed, it is an ambitious study. The value of the study is weakened, however, by the inadequate explanation of content analysis procedures. The definitions of the categories used are brief and the illustrative material sketchy. Furthermore, Robinson and Sheehan dispense with the issue of measurement quality in only one paragraph, where they report that intercoder reliability figures among four members of the coding team averaged about 95 percent agreement.[50] However, they fail to report any details about how this reliability was measured or about the agreement scores for different content categories. Despite these shortcomings, this study exemplifies how content analysis can reveal useful information about a significant political phenomenon. It also illustrates how practical limitations—such as AP's refusal to participate and financial constraints—all too often delimit what researchers can actually accomplish.

Advantages and Disadvantages of the Written Record

Using documents and records, or what we call the *written record*, has several advantages for researchers. First, it allows them *access* to subjects that may be difficult or impossible to research through direct, personal contact, either because they pertain to the past or to phenomena that are geographically distant. For example, the record keeping of the Puritans in the Massachusetts Bay Colony during the seventeenth century allowed Eriksen to study their approach to crime control, and late eighteenth-century records permitted Beard to advance and test a novel interpretation of the framing of the U.S. Constitution. Neither of these studies would have been possible had there been no records available from these periods.

A second advantage of data gleaned from archival sources is that the raw data are usually *nonreactive*. In other words, those writing and preserving the records are generally unaware of any future research goal or hypothesis or, for that matter, that the fruits of their labors will be used for research purposes at all. The record keepers of the Massachusetts Bay Colony were surely unaware that their records would ever be used to study how a society defines and reacts to deviant behavior. Similarly, state loan officers during the late 1700s had no idea that two hundred years later a historian would use their records to discover why some people were in favor of revising the Articles of Confederation. This nonreactivity has the virtue of encouraging more accurate and less self-serving measures of political phenomena.

Record keeping is not completely nonreactive, however. Record keepers are less likely to create and carefully preserve records that would be embarrassing to them, their friends, or their bosses; that would reveal illegal or immoral actions; that would disclose stupidity, greed, or other demeaning attributes. Richard Nixon, for example, undoubtedly wishes that he had destroyed the infamous Watergate tapes that revealed the extent of his administration's knowledge of the 1972 break-in at Democratic National Committee headquarters. Today many record-keeping agencies employ paper shredders to ensure that a portion of the written record does *not* endure. Researchers should be aware of the possibility that the written record has been selectively preserved to serve the record keepers' own interests. As noted earlier, police may underreport crimes because they know that the crime statistics they report to the FBI will be used to rate the relative safety of their cities.

A third advantage of using the written record is that sometimes the record has existed long enough to permit analyses of political phenomena *over time*. The before-and-after research designs discussed in Chapter 5 may then be used. For example, suppose you are interested in the impact of the 55-mile-per-hour speed limit (gradually adopted by the states) on the rate of traffic accidents. Assuming that the written record contains data on the incidence of traffic accidents over time in each state, you could compare the accident rate before and after the introduction of a 55 mph limit in those states that lowered their speed limit. These changes in the accident rate could then be compared with the changes occurring in states in which no change in the speed limit took place. The rate changes could then be "corrected" for other factors that might affect the rate of traffic accidents. (We will discuss how this is done in Chapter 13.) In this way an *interrupted time series research design* could be used, a research design that has some important advantages over cross-sectional designs. Because of the importance of time, and of changes in phenomena over time, for the acquisition of causal knowledge, a data source that supports longitudinal analyses is a valuable one. The written record more readily permits longitudinal analyses than either interview data or direct observation generally do.

A fourth advantage to researchers of using the written record is that it often enables them to *increase sample size* above what would be possible through either interviews or direct observation. For example, it would be terribly expensive and time-consuming to observe the level of spending by all candidates for the House of Representatives in any given year. Interviewing candidates would require either a lot of travel, long-distance phone calls, or the design of a mail questionnaire to secure the necessary information. Direct observation would also require gaining access to many campaigns and traveling across the country. How much easier and less expensive to contact the Federal Election Commission in Washington and request the print-out of campaign spending for all House candidates! Without this written record, resources might permit only the inclusion of a handful of campaigns in a study; with the written record, all 435 campaigns can easily be included.

This raises the fifth main advantage of using the written record: *cost.* Since the cost of creating, organizing, and preserving the written record is borne by the record keepers, researchers are able to conduct research projects on a much smaller budget than would be the case if they had to bear the cost themselves. In fact, one of the major beneficiaries of the record-keeping activities of the federal government and of news organizations is the research community.[51] It would cost a prohibitive amount for a researcher to measure the amount of crime in all cities larger than 25,000 or to collect the voting returns in all 435 congressional districts. Both pieces of information are available at little or no cost, however, because of the record-keeping activities of the FBI and the Elections Research Center, respectively.

Similarly, using the written record often saves a researcher considerable *time.* It is usually much quicker to consult printed government documents, reference materials, computerized data, and research institute reports than it is to accumulate data from scratch. Requesting and reading printed materials or computer tapes takes far less time than collecting data on one's own.

The written record is a veritable treasure for researchers. Collecting data in this manner, however, is not without some disadvantages.

One problem mentioned earlier is *selective survival.* For a variety of reasons, record keepers may not preserve all pertinent materials but rather selectively save those that are the least apt to be embarrassing, controversial, or problematic. It would be surprising, for example, if political candidates, campaign consultants, and public officials saved correspondence and memoranda that cast disfavor on themselves. Obviously, whenever a person is selectively preserving portions of the written record, the accuracy of what remains is suspect. This is less of a problem the less the connection between the record keeper's self-interest and the subject being examined by the researcher.

A second, related disadvantage of the written record is its *incompleteness,* not necessarily because of the selectivity of the record keeper, but for other reasons. There are large gaps in many archives due to fires, losses of other types, personnel shortages that hinder record-keeping activities, and the failure of the record maker or record keeper to regard a record as worthy of preservation. We all throw out personal records every day; political entities do the same. It is very difficult to know what kinds of records a future researcher will need, and it is often impossible for the record keeper to bear the costs of maintaining and storing voluminous amounts of material.

Another reason why records may be incomplete is simply because no person or organization is responsible for preserving them. For example, before 1930 national crime statistics were not collected by the FBI, and before the creation of the Federal Election Commission in 1971 records on campaign expenditures by candidates for the U.S. Congress were spotty and inaccurate.

A third disadvantage of the written record is that its content may be *biased.* Not only may the record be incomplete or selectively preserved, but it also may be inaccurate or falsified, either inadvertently or on purpose. For example, memoranda or copies of letters that were never sent may be filed, events may be conveniently forgotten or misrepresented, the authorship of documents may be disguised, and the dates of written records may be altered. Scholars (and investigators) attempting to reconstruct the actions in the Watergate episode have been hampered by alterations of the record by those worried about the legality of their role in it. Often historical interpretations rest upon who said or did what, and when. To the extent that falsifications of the written record lead to erroneous conclusions, the problem of record-keeping accuracy can bias the results of a research project. The main safeguard against bias is the one used by responsible journalists: confirming important pieces of information from more than one, dissimilar source.

A fourth disadvantage is that some written records are *unavailable* to researchers. Documents may be classified by the federal government; they may be sealed (that is, not made public) until a legal action has ceased or the political actors involved have passed away; or they may be or stored in such a way that they are difficult to use. Other written records—such as the memoranda of multinational corporations, campaign consultants, and Supreme Court justices—are seldom made public because there is no legal obligation to do so and the authors benefit from keeping them private.

Finally, the written record may *lack a standard format* because it is kept by different people. For example, the Chicago budget office may have different budget categories for public expenditures than the San Francisco budget office does. Or the Chicago budget office may have had different budget categories before 1960 than it had after 1960. Or the French may include different items in their published military defense expenditures than the Chileans do. Consequently, a researcher often must expend considerable effort to ensure that the formats in which records are kept by different record-keeping entities can be made comparable.

Political scientists have generally found that the advantages of using the written record outweigh the disadvantages. The written record often supplements the data they collect through interviews and direct observation, and in many cases it is the only source of data on historical and contemporary political phenomena.

Conclusion

The written record includes personal records, archival collections, organizational statistics, and the products of the news media. Researchers interested in historical research, or in a particular event or time in the life of a polity, generally use the episodic record. Gaining access to the appropriate material is often the most resource-consuming aspect of this method of data collection, and the hypothesis testing that results is usually more qualitative and less rigorous (some would say more flexible) than with the running record.

The running record of organizations has become a rich source of political data as a result of the record-keeping activities of governments at all levels and of interest groups and research institutes concerned with public affairs. The running record is generally more quantitative than the episodic record and may be used to conduct longitudinal research. Measurements using the running record can often be obtained inexpensively, although the researcher frequently relinquishes considerable control over the data collection enterprise in exchange for this economy.

One of the ways in which a voluminous, non-numerical written record may be turned into numerical measures and then used to test hypotheses is through a procedure called content analysis. Content analysis is most frequently used by political scientists interested in studying media content, but it has been used to advantage in studies of political speeches, statutes, and judicial decisions.

Through the written record researchers may observe political phenomena that are geographically, physically, and temporally distant from them. Without such records, our ability to record and measure historical phenomena, crosscultural phenomena, and political behavior that does not occur in public would be seriously hampered.

Notes

1. Frank Way and Barbara J. Burt, "Religious Marginality and the Free Exercise Clause," *American Political Science Review* 77 (September 1983): 652-65; Samuel C. Patterson and Gregory A. Caldeira, "Getting Out the Vote: Participation in Gubernatorial Elections," *American Political Science Review* 77 (September 1983): 675-89; William Zimmerman and Glenn Palmer, "Words and Deeds in Soviet Foreign Policy: The Case of Soviet Military Expenditures," *American Political Science Review* 77 (June 1983): 358-67; and Alan P. L. Liu, "The Politics of Corruption in the People's Republic of China," *American Political Science Review* 77 (September 1983): 602-23.

2. Charles Beard reports that he was able to use some records in the U.S. Treasury Department in Washington "only after a vacuum cleaner had been brought in to excavate the ruins." See Beard, *An Economic Interpretation of the Constitution of the United States* (London: MacMillan, 1913), 22.

3. Sandra Van Burkleo, "My Own 'Desperate Deeds and Desperate Motives': How the Project Evolved," in W. Phillips Shively, ed., *The Research Process in Political Science*. Copyright © 1984. Reprinted with permission of the publisher, F. E. Peacock Publishers, Inc., Itasca, Ill.

4. Kai T. Erikson, *The Wayward Puritans* (New York: John Wiley & Sons, 1966).

5. The records of the governor were edited by Nathaniel B. Shurtleff and printed by order of the Massachusetts legislature in 1853-54; the records of the courts were edited by George Francis Dow and published by the Essex Institute in Salem, Massachusetts.

6. Erikson, *The Wayward Puritans*, 209-10.

7. Ibid.

8. Beard, *An Economic Interpretation*.

9. Ibid., 324.

10. James David Barber, *The Presidential Character*, 3d ed. (Englewood Cliffs, N.J.: Prentice-Hall, 1985), 5.

11. Ibid., 4.

12. Ibid., 1st ed. (1972), ix.

13. Andrew Hacker, *U/S: A Statistical Portrait* (New York: Viking, 1983).

14. George F. Bishop, Robert G. Meadow, and Marilyn Jackson-Beeck, eds., *The Presidential Debates* (New York: Praeger, 1980); Sidney Kraus, ed., *The Great Debates* (Gloucester, Mass.: Peter Smith, 1978); *Congressional Quarterly Weekly Report*, September 27, 1980, 2863-69; *Congressional Quarterly Almanac*, 1980, 127B-137B; and *Congressional Quarterly Almanac*, 1984, 107B-127B.

15. See C. Wright Mills, *The Power Elite* (New York: Oxford University Press, 1956); G. William Domhoff, *Who Rules America?* (Englewood Cliffs, N.J.: Prentice-Hall, 1967); and Andrew Hacker, "The Elected and the Annointed: Two American Elites," *American Political Science Review* Vol. 55 (September 1961): 539-49.

16. Marvin E. Wolfgang, "Uniform Crime Reports: A Critical Appraisal," *University of Pennsylvania Law Review* 111 (April 1963): 717-18.

17. Ibid.; Sophia M. Robison, "A Critical View of the Uniform Crime Reports," *Michigan Law Review* 64 (April 1966); Marvin E. Wolfgang, "Urban Crime," in James Q. Wilson, ed., *The Metropolitan Enigma* (Garden City, N.Y.: Doubleday, 1970): 280; and U.S. President's Commission on Law Enforcement and Administration of Justice, *The Challenge of Crime in a Free Society* (New York: Dutton, 1968): 97.

18. Peter P. Lejins, "Uniform Crime Reports," *Michigan Law Review* 64 (April 1966): 1018.

19. Robison, "A Critical View," 1041-42.

20. Wolfgang, "Uniform Crime Reports," 715, Wolfgang, "Urban Crime," 280-81; President's Commission, *The Challenge*, 107-12; and Robison, "A Critical View," 1033-37.

21. Wolfgang, "Uniform Crime Reports," 709-10.
22. Lejins, "Uniform Crime Reports," 1019-20.
23. Wolfgang, "Uniform Crime Reports," 714, 716; and Robison, "A Critical View," 1040-41.
24. Robison, "A Critical View," 1042.
25. Wolfgang, "Urban Crime," 279.
26. Wolfgang, "Uniform Crime Reports," 710.
27. Ibid., 721-24; and Wolfgang, "Urban Crime," 281.
28. Wolfgang, "Uniform Crime Reports," 709-10.
29. Ibid., 719-20; and Robison, "A Critical View," 1043-45.
30. Ibid., 721.
31. Kenneth D. Bailey, *Methods of Social Research,* 2d ed. (New York: Free Press, 1982), 312-13.
32. Ibid., 319.
33. Michael J. Robinson and Margaret A. Sheehan, *Over the Wire and on TV* (New York: Russell Sage, 1983).
34. Ibid., 13-17.
35. On the 1976 campaign, see Thomas Patterson, *The Mass Media Election: How Americans Choose Their President* (New York: Praeger, 1980). On the 1974 congressional elections, see Arthur Miller, Edie Goldenberg, and Lutz Erbring, "Type-Set Politics: Impact of Newspapers on Public Confidence," *American Political Science Review* 73 (March 1979): 67-84.
36. Robinson and Sheehan, *Over the Wire and on TV,* 17-19.
37. Ibid., 20, 23-24.
38. Ibid., 20.
39. Ibid., 21.
40. Ibid., 20.
41. Ibid., 26-27.
42. Ibid., 21.
43. Ibid.
44. Ibid., 49-50.
45. Ibid., 92.
46. Ibid., 94-95.
47. Ibid., 144, 145, 155.
48. Ibid., 145.
49. Ibid., 173.
50. Ibid., 22.
51. The proposed national budget for fiscal year 1986 includes the following amounts (in millions of dollars) for the major data collection agencies of the national government: Bureau of the Census, $88.0 (53 percent increase over 1981); National Center for Health Statistics, $48.0 (37 percent increase over 1981); Bureau of Justice Statistics, $16.7 (14 percent increase over 1981); Bureau of Labor Statistics, $148.3 (44 percent increase over 1981); and National Archives and Records Administration, $99.4 (17 percent increase over 1981). See Consortium of Social Science Associations, *Washington Update,* vol. II, No. 3, February 15, 1985.

Terms Introduced

Content analysis. A procedure by which verbal, nonquantitative records are transformed into quantitative data.

Episodic record. The portion of the written record that is not part of a regular, ongoing record-keeping enterprise.

Running record. The portion of the written record that is enduring and covers an extensive period of time.

Written record. Documents, reports, statistics, manuscripts, and other written, oral, or visual materials available and useful for empirical research.

Exercises

1. Find a recent volume of *The Statistical Abstract of the United States* and glance through its contents. Devise a testable hypothesis that could be evaluated with data contained therein.

2. Suppose the United Nations asked each member nation to supply data about its rates of illiteracy, infant mortality, and malnutrition. What problems would there be with using such records as the basis for a measure of health in different nations?

3. Read Appendix D of Raymond Wolfinger and Steven Rosenstone's *Who Votes?* (New Haven, Conn.: Yale University Press, 1980). What difficulties did Wolfinger and Rosenstone encounter in using the written record to devise measures of election law in each of the states? Do you think that their measures are both reliable and valid? Please explain your answer.

Suggested Readings

Hacker, Andrew, ed. *U/S: A Statistical Portrait of the American People.* New York: Viking, 1983.

Kalvelage, Carl, and Morley Segal. *Research Guide in Political Science.* 2d ed. Glenview, Ill.: Scott, Foresman, 1976.

Van Burkleo, Sandra. "My Own 'Desperate Deeds and Desperate Motives': How the Project Evolved." In *The Research Process in Political Science,* edited by W. Phillips Shively. Ithaca, Ill.: F. E. Peacock, 1984.

Webb, Eugene J., et al. *Nonreactive Measures in the Social Sciences.* 2d ed. Boston: Houghton-Mifflin, 1981.

10. Observation

In the preceding two chapters we have discussed the two sources of data used most frequently by political scientists: interviews or questionnaires and the written record. In this chapter we consider a third method of collecting data about political phenomena: observation. Although observation is more generally a research tool of anthropologists, psychologists, and sociologists, political scientists have used it to good advantage as well. For example, observation has been used by political scientists to study political campaigning, community politics, leadership and executive decisionmaking, program implementation, judicial proceedings, the U.S. Congress, and state legislatures. In fact, any student who has had an internship, kept a daily log or diary, or written a paper based on his or her experiences has used this method of data collection.

Every day of our lives, we "collect data" using observational techniques. We observe some attribute or characteristic of people and infer some behavioral trait from that observation. For example, we watch the car in front of us sway between the traffic lanes and conclude that the driver has been drinking; we observe the dress, physical features, and facial expressions of a student in one of our classes and decide that the person is someone we would like to meet; or we decide not to try and sell a set of encyclopedias at a house that is dilapidated and surrounded by junk. The observational techniques used by political scientists are really only extensions of this method of data collection. They resemble everyday observations in daily life, but are usually more self-conscious and systematic.

Observations may be classified in at least four different ways: *direct* or *indirect, participant* or *nonparticipant, overt* or *covert,* and *structured* or *unstructured.* The most basic distinction is whether an observation is direct—the actual behavior, verbal or nonverbal, is observed firsthand—or indirect—the results or physical traces of behavior are observed.[1] For example, an indirect method of observing college students' favorite studying spots in classrooms and office buildings would be to arrive on campus early in the morning before the custodial staff and measure the amount of food wrappers, soda cans, and other debris at various locations. A direct method of observing the same thing would be to go around the buildings and notice where students are.

In participant observation, the investigator is a regular participant in the activities or group being observed. For example, someone who studies political campaigns by becoming actively involved in them is a participant observer. A nonparticipant observer does not participate in group activities or become a member of the group or community. For example, an investigator studying children at play might sit quietly in the background and make no attempt to become a part of the play activity.

A third way to characterize observation is whether it is overt or covert. In overt observation, those being observed are aware of the investigator's presence and intentions. In covert observation, the investigator's presence is hidden or undisclosed and his or her intentions are disguised. For example, two social scientists studying student conversations once hid under beds in students' rooms.[2] Covert observation may be the only way to observe some phenomena, but as you might imagine, the method often raises important ethical questions.

In structured observation, the investigator looks for and systematically records the incidence of specific behaviors. In unstructured observation, all behavior is considered relevant, at least at first, and recorded. Only later, upon reflection, will the investigator distinguish between important and trivial behavior.

In this chapter we shall discuss observation as a method of data collection and some of the ethical issues associated with it. As we will see observation, like other research methods, has both advantages and disadvantages.

Direct Observation

The vast majority of observation studies conducted by political scientists have been the result of direct observation, either in a laboratory or in a natural setting.

Laboratory Settings

Observation in a laboratory setting gives a researcher the advantage of control over the environment of the observed. Thus the researcher may be able to employ more rigorous experimental designs than are possible in a natural, uncontrolled setting. Also observation may be easier and more convenient to record and preserve since one-way windows, videotape machines, and other observational aids are more readily available in a laboratory.

A disadvantage of laboratory observation is that subjects usually know they are being observed and therefore may alter their behavior, raising questions about the validity of the data collected. The use of aids that allow the observer to be physically removed from the setting and laboratories that are designed to be as inviting and as natural as possible may lead subjects to behave more naturally and less self-consciously. In some cases, researchers have deceived subjects about the true purpose of the observation so that they will behave more naturally. This, of course, may be viewed as unethical.

A good example of an attempt to create a natural-looking laboratory setting may be found in Stanley Milgram and R. Lance Shotland's book *Television and Antisocial Behavior*.[3] These researchers were interested in the impact of television programming on adult behavior, specifically in the ability of television drama to stimulate antisocial acts such as theft. They devised four versions of a program called "Medical Center," each with a different plot, and showed the versions in a theater to four different audiences. Some of the versions showed a character stealing money, and the versions differed in whether the person was punished for his theft or not. The participants in the study were then asked to go to a particular office at a particular time to pick up a free transistor radio, their payment for participating in the research study. When they arrived in the office (the laboratory), they encountered a sign that said the radios were all gone. The researchers were then interested in how people would react and specifically in whether they would imitate any of the behaviors in the versions of "Medical Center" that they had seen (such as the theft of money from see-through plastic collection dishes). Their behavior was observed covertly via a one-way mirror. Once the subjects left the office, they were directed to another location where they were, in fact, given the promised radio.

Laboratory observation may be structured or unstructured. Only specific behaviors may be of interest and recorded, or all behavior may be recorded because it is considered potentially relevant. Recording aids in laboratory settings are helpful in this regard.

Researchers interested in child development often use laboratory observation to study parent-child interaction and other aspects of child behavior. The standard procedure in studies of the impact of violent movies or television programs on children is to divide the children into two groups, expose each group to a different type of video presentation, and then observe the play of the two separated groups, looking for instances of aggressive, violent, or antisocial behavior.[4]

Laboratory observation also has frequently been used to study group dynamics and the development of and response to power and authority. In Milgram's well-known study of obedience to authority, individuals were enlisted to help in an experiment. The purpose of the experiment, they were told, was to test the learning response of the subjects. The task of the individuals was to administer electric shocks to the subjects as instructed by the researcher. Actually the researcher's helpers were the real subjects and, unknown to the helpers, the electric shocks were fake. Many of the helpers complied with the researcher's requests to administer electric shocks despite the screams of the subjects: to have done otherwise, they thought, would have ruined the experiment. The real purpose of the study was to test obedience to authority even if it meant inflicting harm on others.[5] As you might imagine, this study has raised numerous ethical concerns, which we will discuss later in this chapter.

Field Studies

Political scientists have used direct observation as a data collection technique in natural settings or *field studies* more than in the laboratory. The advantage of observing people in a natural setting rather than in the artificiality of a laboratory setting is that people can generally be expected to behave as they would ordinarily. Furthermore, field studies permit the investigator to observe people for longer periods of time than would be possible in a laboratory. In fact, one of the striking features of field studies is the considerable amount of time an investigator may spend in the field. It is not uncommon for investigators to live in the community they are observing for a year or more. William F. Whyte's fascinating study of life in an Italian slum, *Street Corner Society,* was based on three years of observation (1937-40) and Marc Ross's study of political participation in Nairobi, Kenya, took more than a year of field observation.[6] To study the behavior of U.S. representatives in their districts, Richard Fenno traveled intermittently for almost seven years, making 36 separate visits and spending 110 working days in 18 congressional districts.[7]

Sometimes researchers have no choice but to observe political phenomena as they occur in their natural setting. Written records of events may not exist, or the records may not cover the behavior of interest to the researcher. Relying on personal accounts of participants may be unsatisfactory because of participants' distorted views of events, incomplete memories, or failure to observe what is of interest to the researcher.

Like laboratory observation, observation in field studies may be structured or unstructured. Hugh Lytton conducted a structured field study to compare parent-child interaction in families with twins and families with a single child. His assistants in this study learned an elaborate system of codes for various kinds of behaviors (for example, Code F57C3: Father romps with child, but in a gentle manner).[8] The codes were then quietly dictated into a tape machine. Another tape recorder taped the verbal interaction of family members. Dictation instead of note-taking allowed the observers to see more, while the taped interaction provided a check on coded observation. Observer reliability was promoted through extensive training and by the use of a second observer on occasion. The two-tape-recorder method proved to be less intrusive than a video-tape camera, which the observers discovered could not easily be kept focused on all relevant subjects anyway.

Lytton felt it was important to observe in the home since a laboratory setting would have reduced the validity of the observations. Data validity was further protected by conducting several lengthy observation sessions; it was felt that the families would be unlikely to maintain a front for the entire time period.

The term *field study* usually refers to open-ended and wide-ranging rather than structured observation in a natural setting. The studies by Whyte and Fenno were of this nature. Open-ended, flexible observation is appropriate if the research purpose of the field study is one of description and exploration. For example, Fenno's research purpose was to study "representatives' perceptions of their constituencies while they are actually in their constituencies. . . ." [9] As Fenno explains, his visits with representatives in their districts

> were totally open-ended and exploratory. I tried to observe and inquire into anything and everything these members did. I worried about whatever they worried about. Rather than assume that I already knew what was interesting, I remained prepared to find interesting questions emerging in the course of the experience. The same with data. The research method was largely one of soaking and poking or just hanging around. [10]

In these kinds of field studies, researchers do not start out with particular hypotheses that they want to test. They often do not know enough about what they plan to observe to establish lists and specific categories of behaviors to look for and record systematically. The purpose of the research is to discover what these might be.

Some political scientists have used observation as a preliminary research method. [11] For example, James Robinson's work in Congress provided firsthand information for his studies of the House Rules Committee and of the role of Congress in foreign policymaking. [12] Ralph Huitt's service on Lyndon B. Johnson's Senate majority leader staff gave Huitt inside access to information for his study of Democratic party leadership in the Senate. [13] And David Minar served as a school board member and used his experience to develop questionnaires in his comparative study of several school districts in the Chicago area. [14]

Most field studies involve participant observation. An investigator cannot, like "a fly on the wall," observe a group of people for long periods of time. Usually he or she must assume a role or identity within the group that is being studied and participate in the activities of the group.

Acceptance by the group is necessary if the investigator is going to benefit from the naturalness of the research setting. An investigator who remains a stranger or complete outsider is unlikely to be privy to natural behavior, particularly behavior that is sensitive and could cause embarrassment or other harm if revealed to an outsider. If the observer can gain the trust of the observed, greater opportunities for observation arise. As noted earlier, many political scientists who have studied Congress have worked as staff members on committees and in congressional offices.

Field work using participant observation is also commonly referred to as *ethnography.* Cultural anthropologists and sociologists frequently use this method. Some well-known examples in addition to Whyte's study are Margaret Mead's *Coming of Age in Samoa,* Elliot Liebow's *Tally's Corner,* Herbert Gans's *The Levittowners,* and Arthur J. Vidich's and Joseph Bensman's *Small Town in Mass Society.*[15]

Investigators using participant observation often depend on members of the group they are observing to serve as *informants,* persons who are willing to be interviewed about their activities and behavior and those of the group to which they belong. An informant also helps the researcher interpret behavior. A close relationship between the researcher and informant may help the researcher gain access to other group members, not only because an informant may familiarize the researcher with community members and norms, but also because the informant, through close association with the researcher, will be able to pass on information about the researcher to the community.[16] Some participant observation studies will have one key informant; others will have several. For example, Whyte relied on the leader of a street corner gang whom he called "Doc" as his key informant, while Fenno's 18 representatives all could be considered informants.

Although a valuable asset to researchers, informants may present problems. A researcher should not overly rely on one or a few informants since they may give a biased view of a community. And if the informant is associated with one faction in a multifaction community or is a marginal member of the community (and thus more willing to associate with the researcher) the researcher's affiliation with the informant may inhibit rather than enhance access to the community.[17]

Participant observers may be covert or overt about their activities. In covert observation, the participant investigator does not reveal his or her research purpose on the assumption that the presence of a researcher would not be accepted or that it would alter the behavior of the observed. In overt observation, members of the group are aware that they are being studied and are informed of the general purpose of the study. The line between covert and overt observation is not entirely clear, however. Those being observed may be told only in a general way the purpose of the research—not because the investigator wishes to deceive the group, but due to the open-ended nature of the research. In fact, the investigator may not decide on the actual direction of the research until much later.

As Fenno puts it, "Only after prolonged, unstructured soaking is the problem formulated. Indeed, the reformulation of a problem or a question may be the end product of the research." [18] In other cases a researcher will be deliberately vague about the intended direction of the study for fear of rejection.

Some social scientists oppose covert observation as unethical. The pursuit of knowledge does not justify deceit, they claim, even though researchers might not gain entry to a group or be able to observe natural, unaffected behavior if their research purposes were revealed. [19] Subjects of the research may be harmed if they reveal damaging information about themselves—information they would have concealed if they had been aware that they were being studied. A second argument against covert participant observation is that subsequent revelation of deceit will lead to a backlash against social research and limit opportunities for other researchers. [20]

Finally, a third argument against covert observation is that it is an unreliable and unsound research method. Deceit may alter the nature of the interaction between observed and observer. [21] For example, covert participant observation of a flying saucer cult whose members predicted the end of the world probably damaged the validity of the data collected. In the study the researchers posed as cult members and believers. Since the cult was small in size, deceit very likely altered the behavior of the cult by reinforcing the beliefs of cult members. With enhanced expectations, harm to cult members was also increased when the prophesied end did not materialize. Thus ethical issues were raised as well. [22]

Participant observation offers the advantages of a natural setting, the opportunity to observe people for lengthy periods of time so that interaction and changes in behavior may be studied, and a degree of accuracy impossible with recall data. However, there are some noteworthy limitations to the method as well.

The main problem with direct, participant observation as a method of empirical research for political scientists is that many significant instances of political behavior are not accessible for observation. The privacy of the voter in the voting booth is legally protected, U.S. Supreme Court conferences are not open to anyone but the justices themselves, political consultants and bureaucrats do not usually wish to have political scientists privy to their discussions and decisions, and most White House conversations and deliberations are carefully guarded. Occasionally physical traces of these private behaviors become public—such as the Watergate tapes of Richard Nixon's conversations with his aides—and disclosures about some aspects of government decisionmaking, such as congressional committee hearings and Supreme Court oral arguments; but typically access is the major barrier to directly observing consequential political behavior.

Another disadvantage of participant observation is lack of control over the environment. A researcher may be unable to isolate individual factors and observe their effect on behavior. Efforts to manipulate interactions among informants or subjects may be awkward and conflict with the expectations of subjects that the participant observer should remain a passive member of the social group. For example, to gain favor with a key member of a street gang, Whyte took the side of the member in a gang discussion. This antagonized the other side, and his plan backfired. Perceiving that Whyte was on his side, the member decided that he need not make an effort to establish closer relations with him. Thus Whyte failed to achieve his aim of greater rapport with this gang member.

Participant observation is also limited by the small number of cases that are usually involved. For example, Fenno observed only 18 members or would-be members of Congress—too few for any sort of statistical analysis. He chose "analytical depth" over "analytical range"; in-depth observation of 18 cases was the limit that Fenno thought he could manage intellectually, professionally, financially, and physically.[23] Whyte observed one street-corner gang in-depth, although he did observe others less closely. Because of the small numbers of cases, the representativeness of the results of participant observation has been questioned.

Unstructured participant observation also has been criticized as invalid and biased. A researcher may selectively perceive behaviors, noting some, ignoring others. The interpretation of behaviors may reflect the personality and culture of the observer rather than the meaning attributed to them by the observed themselves. Moreover, the presence of the observer may alter the behavior of the observed no matter how skillfully the observer attempts to become accepted as a nonthreatening part of the community.

Field workers attempt to minimize these possible threats to data validity by immersing themselves in the culture they are observing and by taking copious notes on everything going on around them no matter how seemingly trivial. Events without apparent meaning at the time of observation may become important and revealing upon later reflection. Of course, copious note-taking leads to what is known as a *high dross rate:* much of what is recorded is not relevant to the research problem or question as it is finally formulated. It may be painful for the investigator to discard so much of the material that was carefully recorded, but this is a standard practice with this method.

Another way to attain more valid data is to allow the observed to read and comment on what the investigator has written and point out events and behavior that may have been misinterpreted. This check on observations may be of limited or no value if the observed cannot read or if the written material is aimed at persons well-versed in the researcher's discipline and therefore is over the observed's head.

Researchers' observations may be compromised, however, if the researchers begin to overidentify with their subjects or informants. "Going native," as this phenomenon is known, may lead them to paint a more complimentary picture of the observed than is warranted. Researchers combat this problem by returning to their own culture to analyze their data and by asking colleagues or others to comment on their findings.

By now you should have some understanding of various types of field studies and their advantages and disadvantages. We now will focus on four common aspects of all fieldwork experiences: gaining access, learning the ropes, maintaining relations, and leaving the field.[24] This section should be especially helpful to novice researchers and to students doing observational studies as part of an internship.

How to Conduct Fieldwork

If you have served as an intern for a government agency, a private organization, or an elected representative, you may recall your initial uneasiness as you learned your way around and became acquainted with your coworkers. If you were supposed to write a report based on your internship experiences, you may have felt additional pressure to understand what was going on and to be accepted. Those you were observing as part of your internship may have attempted to influence information you obtained, the content of your report, or the audience to whom it would be given. Perhaps this description of the rigors of fieldwork rings true with your own experience in the field:

> Fieldwork must certainly rank with the more disagreeable activities that humanity has fashioned for itself. It is usually inconvenient, to say the least, sometimes physically uncomfortable, frequently embarrassing and, to a degree, always tense. Sociologists and anthropologists, among others in the social sciences, have voluntarily immersed themselves for the sake of research in situations all but a tiny minority of humanity goes to great lengths to avoid. . . .
>
> For most researchers the day-to-day demands of fieldwork are regularly fraught with feelings of uncertainty and anxiety. The process of becoming immersed over an extended period of time in a way of life that is often both novel and strange exposes the researcher to situations and experiences that are usually accompanied by an intense concern with whether the research is conducted and managed properly.[25]

As this quote indicates, doing fieldwork can be a physically and mentally demanding task. The first challenge usually involves *gaining access* to those you wish to study. There is no single way of gaining entry; access depends on the characteristics of the fieldworker and of his or her subjects. Usually a fieldworker must receive permission to observe activities or assume a role within the group that allows the opportunity for observation. Fenno used the direct approach of writing letters to members of Congress. In the letter he described his research topic in general terms, gave personal references, and requested permission to accompany the representative on district visits. After he had conducted several district visits, his letters included references to representatives whom he had already accompanied.[26]

But such a direct approach will not always work. Those you wish to study may not comprehend or sympathize with your research needs, or they may suspect you as an outsider (even Fenno experienced these problems). Here access may be facilitated by a member of the subject group who acts as a reference or initial go-between. Whyte gained access to the street-corner gang by talking to social workers in the local settlement house. One of the social workers introduced him to Doc who became his key informant and entrée into the community. Doc also provided tips on appropriate behavior for Whyte. Commenting on his success, Whyte explains, "At the time I found it hard to believe that I could move in as easily as Doc had said with his sponsorship. But that indeed was the way it turned out." [27]

Whyte's previous efforts at gaining entry had not been successful. In one attempt he followed a Harvard colleague's suggestion that access could be obtained by picking up a young woman at a local bar.

> There I encountered a situation for which my adviser had not prepared me. There were women present all right, but none of them was alone. Some were there in couples, and there were two or three pairs of women together. I pondered this situation briefly. I had little confidence in my skill at picking up one female, and it seemed inadvisable to tackle two at the same time. Still, I was determined not to admit defeat without a struggle. I looked around me again and now noticed a threesome: one man and two women. It occurred to me that here was a maldistribution of females which I might be able to rectify. I approached the group and opened with something like this: "Pardon me. Would you mind if I joined you?" There was a moment of silence while the man stared at me. He then offered to throw me downstairs. I assured him that this would not be necessary and demonstrated as much by walking right out of there without any assistance.[28]

In other cases a researcher may assume a role within a community before making the research role known (if ever). For example, Laud Humphreys studied homosexual behavior in public restrooms by assuming the role of a "lookout" (someone who watches for the approach of police, youths, or others who may harass homosexuals). David A. Karp hung around Times Square to study behavior in public places. And William Chambliss claimed to be a truck driver and frequented an amusement parlor in Seattle's skid-row area to begin his study of crime in that city.[29]

Gaining entry is only the first step in achieving access. In *learning the ropes,* a researcher must learn appropriate behavior and gain acceptance from those being studied. Rapport must be established between the observer and the observed. Without a mutual feeling of trust and understanding, a researcher may move into a community, not be threatened or asked to leave, yet be unable to carry out his or her research. For example, Myron and Penina Glazer moved to Chile to study the professional and political attitudes of Chilean University students, but they found that students were extremely suspicious of North Americans and were reluctant to agree to be interviewed.[30] Fenno found that he had to establish rapport with representatives' gatekeepers (wives, friends, district staff) as well as with the representatives. Acceptance was facilitated by his active participation in district activities, such as telephone polling and handing out campaign material, and his willingness to be patient and not compete with gatekeepers for access to a member of Congress.

Gaining acceptance may require changes in a researcher's behavior and attitudes. For example, in her study of army life, Arlene K. Daniels found that she had to conform with military officers' ideas of appropriate female behavior and change her critical attitude toward career officers before she could conduct her research.[31] It is not always necessary for the researcher to behave exactly as the researched, however. The researcher may be accepted without assuming the language and behavior of those being studied. Whatever the circumstances and conditions of the field-work, this is a stressful stage for the researcher since the success of the research effort hinges on the ability to establish rapport.

Maintaining relations is the process of building upon the rapport the researcher has established with the observed. A researcher must take care not to speak or act in a way that will damage this rapport. If confidentiality has been promised to informants, the researcher must be careful not to reveal knowledge to other members of the informants' group that will violate that confidence.

Appropriate behavior for the researcher may change as the informants' views of the researcher evolve. In their study of the Unification Church and the anticult organization called the National Ad Hoc Committee Engaged in Freeing Minds, David Bromley and Anson Shupe found that rapport diminished as they became more knowledgeable about the organizations. Both groups "developed a sense of uneasiness that we had seen so much and yet remained unconvinced, and the failure to embrace their respective points of view tended to threaten their faiths (and our positions, dependent as they were on our informants' cooperation and good will) in the self-evident rightness of their causes." [32]

Another problem in maintaining relations may stem from achieving too much rapport. In his study of members of Congress, Fenno preferred to create and maintain business friendships rather than personal friendships with his informants. In one case where Fenno was treated as a personal friend, he found that he could not ask probing questions important for his research. The representative was in a close reelection contest and would have considered such behavior by a personal friend unacceptable and callous.[33]

In some situations a researcher has to choose between engaging in unacceptable or illegal behavior and losing rapport. For example, Harold Pepinsky chose not to expose a policeman who to save face used a trumped-up charge against a youth. Pepinsky didn't disclose the crime because he wanted to maintain relations with the police on whom he depended for his dissertation research.[34] Whyte became so involved in one election in Cornerville that he cast four votes for his candidate and came close to being arrested.[35]

In *leaving the field* a researcher may confront a new set of problems.[36] Some researchers report that it is difficult to adjust, that they miss their research settings.[37] In overt participation observation, terminating relationships and coping with personal obligations that may have developed during a study may be difficult. A researcher may feel he or she is abandoning the observed. Yet usually the observed understand that the researcher has come into a setting to study it, not to stay. Some investigators continue friendships with informants and find that they enjoy these friendships more after completion of their research since they are freed from the role of observer.[38]

Of course, those who are covertly observed do not have expectations concerning the researcher's activities and departure. The researcher may find natural reasons for leaving the field and choose not to continue contact for fear of revealing his or her true identity. Leaving the field in covert observation may be problematic if the researcher is not in control of his or her departure. A researcher's cover role may be terminated before the completion of the research. If the cover role is terminated by the group being observed, gaining reentry may be extremely difficult.

A major problem associated with leaving the field is the writing and publication of the research findings. Researchers must confront the possibility that their observations will offend the observed. Caution must be exercised to honor promises of anonymity and confidentiality given to informants. If the research report takes a long time to complete and informants have been promised a copy, the researcher may avoid contact with the informants until the report is in hand, further exacerbating the awkwardness of leaving the field.

One professor who observed the filming of a series of political commercials encountered great hostility upon the publication of his report.³⁹ This professor was asked by a friend and former student to go to the Southwest and help him film a series of commercials for a congressional candidate, a series the former student was hoping would further his own career as a film-maker. Based on his participant observation, the professor wrote a report, published in an academic journal, that criticized the whole filming enterprise and elicited a highly negative reaction from his former student. It is most unlikely that the professor will ever be invited, by his former student at least, to observe the same type of activity again.

All researchers engaged in observational studies face some problems in gaining entry, learning the ropes, maintaining rapport, and leaving the field. But these problems must be weathered if the full advantages of gaining knowledge and understanding through participant observation are to be realized.

Another demanding yet essential part of a field study is *taking field notes*. Note-taking can be divided into three phases: mental notes, jotted notes, and field notes.⁴⁰ *Mental note-taking* involves orienting one's consciousness to the task of remembering things one has observed, such as "who and how many were there, the physical character of the place, who said what to whom, who moved about in what way, and a general characterization of an order of events." ⁴¹ Since mental notes may fade rapidly, researchers use *jotted notes* to preserve them. Jotted notes consist of short phrases and key words that will activate a researcher's memory later when the full field notes are written down.

Since note-taking may disrupt observation, researchers often use restrooms, cars, and other private settings to make jotted notes. Note-taking may be especially awkward while gaining rapport. Once rapport has been achieved field researchers may be able to jot down field notes or to use a recording device during observation. Field researchers may arrange interviews with informants to probe for desired information. For example, after Chambliss had spent a considerable amount of time in the bar and in the entertainment district in Seattle, he revealed his true identity and purpose to a bar manager and arranged interviews with a number of individuals engaged in criminal activity. Chambliss recorded these interviews and later revealed them to his informants, giving them the choice to keep the tapes. Only one informant who had revealed a murder refused to allow Chambliss to keep the recorded conversation.⁴²

Taped interviews do not constitute full *field notes,* which should include a running description of conversations and events. John Lofland advises that researchers should be factual and concrete, avoid making inferences, and employ participants' descriptive and interpretative terms. Full field notes should include material previously forgotten and subsequently recalled. Lofland suggests that researchers distinguish between verbal material that is exact recall, paraphrased or close recall, and reasonable recall.[43]

Field notes should also include a researcher's analytic ideas and inferences, personal impressions and feelings, and notes for further information.[44] Because events and emotional states in a researcher's life may affect observation, they should be recorded. Notes for further information provide guidance for future observation, either to fill in gaps in observations, call attention to things that may happen, or test out emerging analytic themes.

Full field notes should be legible and should be reviewed periodically, since the passage of time may present past observations in a new light to the researcher or reveal a pattern worthy of attention in a series of disjointed events. Creating and reviewing field notes is an important part of the observational method. Consequently, a fieldworker should expect to spend as much time on field notes as is spent observing in the field.

Indirect Observation

Indirect observation, the observation of physical traces of behavior, is essentially detective work.[45] Based on physical traces, inferences about people and their behavior can be drawn. An unobtrusive research method, indirect observation is nonreactive: subjects do not change their behavior because they do not know they are being studied. Among indirect observation methods, Webb et al. distinguish between *erosion measures,* created by selective wear on some material, and *accretion measures,* created by the deposition and accumulation of materials.

Erosion Measures

An example of an erosion measure is the selective wearing of floor tiles in a museum.[46] Tiles around popular exhibits will tend to be more worn than those around less popular exhibits. Similarly, the rate at which carpeting and stairs are worn will indicate relative use. We know of at least one university where campus planners observed paths worn in grassy areas and then rerouted paved walkways to correspond to the most heavily trafficked routes. Other examples of natural erosion measures include wear on library books, wear and tear on selected articles within volumes, depletion of items in stores, and wear on upholstery.

In some cases the researcher may intervene in an erosion measure without impairing its nonreactivity. This may be done to reduce the problem of materials that erode too slowly to be measured in the desired time frame or to make sure that the materials are equivalent before the wearing activity occurs. For example, in a study measuring the activity level of children by how quickly their shoes wear out, children could be given identical shoes.[47]

Accretion Measures

Archeologists and geologists commonly use accretion measures in their research by measuring, mapping, and analyzing accretion of materials. Other professions find them useful as well. Webb et al. report a study in which mechanics in an automotive service department recorded radio dial settings to estimate radio station popularity.[48] This information was then used to select radio stations to carry the dealer's advertising. Popularity of television programs could be measured by drops in water levels during commercials since for very popular shows viewers tend to use the toilets only during commercials. Similarly, declines in telephone usage could indicate television program popularity. The presence of fingerprints and nose prints on glass display cases may indicate interest as well as reveal information about the size and age of those attracted to the display. The effectiveness of various antilitter policies and conservation programs could also be measured using physical trace evidence, and the amount and content of graffiti may represent an interesting measurement of the beliefs, attitudes, and mood of a population.

One of the most well-known examples of the use of accretion measures is W. L. Rathje's ongoing study of people's garbage.[49] He has been studying people's behavior from what they discard in their trash cans. One project involved investigating whether poor people waste more food than those better off: they do not.

Indirect observation typically raises fewer ethical issues than direct observation since the measures of individual behavior are taken after the individuals have left the scene, thus assuming anonymity. But Rathje's studies of garbage raised ethical concerns because some discarded items (such as letters and bills) identified the source of the garbage. Although the court ruled in Rathje's favor by declaring that when people discard their garbage, they have no further legal interest in it, one might consider sorting through one's garbage an invasion of privacy. In a study in which data on households were collected, consent forms were obtained, and codes were used to link household information to garbage data and then the codes were destroyed. Rathje's assistants in another garbage study were instructed not to examine closely any material.

It is also possible that garbage may contain evidence of criminal wrongdoing. Twice during Rathje's research, body parts were discovered, although not in the actual bags collected as part of the study. Rathje has taken the position that evidence of victimless crimes should be ignored; evidence of serious crimes should be reported.[50] Of course, the publicity surrounding Rathje's garbage study may deter disposal of such evidence. This raises the problem of reactivity: to what extent might people change their garbage-disposing habits if they know there is a small chance that what they throw away will be examined?

This example also illustrates the possibility that indirect observation of physical traces of behavior may border on direct observation of subjects if the observation of physical traces quickly follows their creation. In some situations, extra measures may have to be taken to preserve the anonymity of subjects.

Another good example of the use of accretion measures is Kurt and Gladys Lang's study of the MacArthur Day parade in Chicago in 1951.[51] Gen. Douglas MacArthur and President Harry S Truman were locked in an important political struggle at the time, and the Langs wanted to find out how much interest there was in the parade. They used data on mass-transit passenger fares, hotel reservations, retail store and street vendor sales, parking lot usage, and the volume of tickertape on the streets to measure the size of the crowd attracted by MacArthur's appearance.

Validity Problems with Indirect Observation

Although physical-trace measures generally are not subject to reactivity as are participant observation and survey research, threats to the validity of these measures do exist. Also erosion and accretion measures may be biased. For example, certain traces are more likely to survive because the materials are more durable. Thus physical traces may provide a selective, rather than complete, picture of the past. Differential wear patterns may not be due to variation in use, but to differences in material. Researchers studying garbage must be careful not to infer that garbage reflects all that is used or consumed. Someone who owns a garbage disposal, for example, will generally discard less garbage than someone who doesn't.

Researchers should exercise caution in linking changes in physical traces to particular causes. Other factors may account for variation in the measures. Webb et al. suggest that several physical-trace measures be used simultaneously or that alternative data collection methods be used to supplement physical-trace measures.[52] For example, physical-trace measures of use of recreational facilities, such as which trash cans in a park fill up the fastest, could be supplemented with questionnaires to park visitors on facility usage.

Caution should also be used in making inferences about the behavior that caused the physical traces. For example, wear around a particular museum exhibits could be indicative of many people viewing the exhibit or of a few people spending considerable time at the exhibit shuffling their feet.[53] Direct observation could determine the answer; but in cases where the physical-trace measures occurred in the past, this solution is not possible.

Examples of the use of indirect observation in political science research are not numerous. Nevertheless, this method has been used profitably, and you may be able to think of cases where it would be appropriate, such as in a study of the number of campaign posters put up in communities, how long they remained posted, and how long before they were defaced. A comparative measure of the number of visitors and office activity of elected representatives might be obtained by noting carpet wear in office entryways. This would not be as precise as counting visitors, but it would avoid posting observers or questioning office staff.

Indirect observation, when used ingeniously, can be a low-cost research method free from many of the ethical issues that surround direct observation. Let us now turn to a consideration of some of these ethical issues that develop in the course of fieldwork and in simple, nonexperimental laboratory observations.

Ethical Issues in Observation

Ethical dilemmas arise primarily when there is a potential for harm to the observed. They also may arise if researchers observe behavior or conditions that they feel they should report but in reporting would jeopardize their research. For example, what if a researcher during the course of observation views a crime? Should it be reported, or is the researcher obligated not to report it if he or she has requested and received permission to observe activities that are not normally accessible to an outsider? Or, for example, what if researchers observe deplorable living conditions or severe political repression? Should they abandon their research to devote their efforts to the improvement of the conditions? Or is it acceptable to continue the research by rationalizing that it will ultimately benefit the observed? [54]

The potential for serious harm to subjects in most observational studies is quite low. Observation generally does not entail investigation of highly sensitive, personal, or illegal behavior because people are reluctant to be observed in those circumstances. In addition, fieldwork and simple laboratory observation do not involve experimental manipulations of subjects and exposure to risky experimental treatments. Nonetheless, harm or risks to the observed may result. They include 1) negative repercussions from associating with the researcher due to the researcher's sponsors, nationality, or outsider status; 2) invasion of privacy; 3) stress during the research interaction; and 4) disclosure of behavior or information to the researcher resulting in harm to the observed during or after the study. Each of these possibilities will be considered in turn.

In some fieldwork situations, contact with outsiders may be viewed as undesirable behavior by an informant's peers. Cooperation with a researcher may violate community norms. For example, a researcher who studies a group known to shun contact with outsiders exposes informants to the risk that they will be censured by their group.

Social scientists from the United States have encountered difficulty in conducting research in countries with hostile relations with the United States.[55] Informants and researchers may be accused of being spies, and informants may be exposed to harm for appearing to sympathize with "the enemy." Harm may result even if hostile relations develop after the research has been conducted. Government, military, or CIA sponsorship of research may particularly endanger the observed.

A second source of harm to the observed results from the invasion of privacy that observation may entail. Even though a researcher may have permission to observe, the role of observer may not always be remembered by the observed. In fact, as a researcher gains rapport, there is a greater chance that informants may reveal to the researcher as a friend something that could prove to be damaging. A researcher does not always warn, "Remember, you're being observed!" Furthermore, if a researcher is being treated as a friend, such a warning may damage rapport. Researchers must consider how they will use the information gathered from subjects. They must judge whether use in a publication will constitute a betrayal of confidence.[56]

Some harm to informants may occur if a researcher encourages them to talk about topics that cause them anxiety or embarrassment. Although informants can exercise control over what they say, they may reveal something in the flow of a conversation that they later regret.[57]

In some situations, informants may welcome the opportunity to talk to a sympathetic listener even if the subject is a painful one. For example, in her study of American widows, Helena Lopata found that widows were not reluctant to discuss widowhood. Protective relatives and friends, however, tried to keep Lopata from interviewing some widows because they feared the subject would upset them.[58]

The potential for harm to those being observed is the greatest in covert observation studies, which, by definition, involves an invasion of privacy. Mary Henle and Marian B. Hubbler's eavesdropping in dormitory rooms mentioned at the beginning of the chapter is clearly an unacceptable invasion of privacy, but is eavesdropping and observation in public places unethical? Consider the ethics of Humphreys' study of homosexual encounters in park restrooms.[59] Humphreys disguised himself and assumed the role of a lookout. Then, with the cooperation of authorities who were not aware of the nature of his research, Humphreys traced automobile license plate numbers to identify and locate participants. Was this a legitimate use of this information? A year later Humphreys had a number of these men included in a community health study so he could interview them without their ever being aware of his knowledge of their homosexual activities.

Humphreys' study has been criticized for the risk of discovery he created for these homosexuals. Public or family discovery of their homosexual encounters could have resulted in serious harm to these men. Luckily, Humphreys exercised a great deal of caution and was never required by law enforcement officials to disclose his subjects' identities, but the risk was real.[60] Humphreys conducted his research out of sympathy for homosexuals, and he presented a sympathetic portrait of these men as posing no threat to others. Yet would they have agreed to take the personal risk of participation in the study in return for the possibility that they would be better understood and persecuted less? Even if Humphreys had acted as a lookout and not followed through on his observations, was this unjustifiable snooping? Some critics think so.[61] Finally, should Humphreys be criticized for not reporting observed illegal behavior to the authorities?

In Milgram's violence/obedience experiment, subjects were deceived about the purpose of their participation. The harm to the subjects stemmed from their awareness that they had been obedient to an authority even to the extent of "harming" another person. Milgram has contended that his subjects were not harmed.[62] When interviewed after the experiment, his subjects claimed they were happy to have participated. Milgram's experiment also might be condoned by some on the grounds that knowledge about obedience to authority is socially beneficial. Others, however, conclude that balancing harms against benefits is off target; his subjects were wronged, they contend, by being exposed "to unwanted and unasked-for self-knowledge," whether or not they were harmed.[63] This position is similar to the one that arises when an informant reveals embarrassing information or experiences psychological stress during or after a conversation with an investigator. Questions that are potentially embarrassing or stressful are potentially harmful. Even if no harm is felt and no deceit is involved, do researchers have the right to expose subjects to the possibility of harm? [64]

Much of the harm to subjects in fieldwork occurs as a result of publication. They may be upset at the way they are portrayed, subjected to unwanted publicity, or depicted in a way that embarrasses the larger group to which they belong. Moreover, disclosures about individuals or groups may be used by others in an exploitative manner.[65] Carelessness in publication may result in the violation of promises of confidentiality and anonymity. And value-laden terminology may offend those being described.[66]

Although subjects may be upset at discovering how they are perceived by others, published research has helped individuals see and change their objectionable qualities.[67] For example, Whyte depicted one Cornerville individual as self-centered, ambitious, and insensitive to others. While this portrayal hurt the feelings of the person who recognized himself, he accepted Whyte's description and appeared to alter his behavior in response.[68]

Carole Johnson has prepared the following guidelines for the "ethical proofreading" of manuscripts prior to publication. To diminish the potential for harm to the observed, researchers should keep in mind these nine points:

1) Assume that both the identities of the location studied and the identities of individuals will be discovered. What would the consequences of this discovery be to the community? To the individuals? What would the consequences be both within the community and outside the community? Do you believe that the importance of what you have revealed in your publication is great enough to warrant these consequences? Could you, yourself, live with these consequences should they occur?

2) Look at the words used in your manuscript. Are they judgmental or descriptive? How accurate are the descriptions of the phenomena observed? A judgment, for example, would be to say that a community is backward. A description might be to say that 10% of the adult population can neither read nor write. The latter is preferable both scientifically and ethically. . . .

3) Where appropriate in describing private or unflattering characteristics, consider generalizing first and then giving specifics. . . . This tends to make research participants feel less singled out. It also adds to the educational value of the writing.

4) Published data may affect the community studied and similar communities in a general way even though the identities of the community and individuals may remain unknown. In the case of West's book on Plainville, for example, people were described as backward. Some people were said to live like animals. Some men were said to be as dirty as animals. West also related that many people from Plainville left the community to seek employment in the cities. What if such descriptive information about rural communities affected individuals' opportunities for employment due to the creation of negative stereotypes about people from rural areas? Therefore, ask yourself how your information might be used in a positive way? In a negative way? And again ask if the revelations are worth the possible consequences.

5) Will your research site be usable again or have you destroyed this site for other researchers? Have you destroyed other similar sites? Is such destruction worth the information obtained and disseminated?

6) What was your perspective toward subjects? What were your biases? How did your perspective and biases, both positive and negative, affect the way you viewed your subjects and wrote about them?. . .

7) In what ways can research participants be educated about the role of fieldworkers and the nature of objective reporting of fieldwork? It may be advisable to caution your subjects at various stages of the research that it is not easy to read about oneself as one is described by another.

8) When conducting research within a larger project, know the expectations of other project members concerning what each member will be permitted to publish both in the short and long run, i.e., are there any limitations? If not, what limits ought ethically to be imposed? Who will have the final say about publication? Who will own the data? Who will have access to the data and on what terms? What will happen to the data after publication? Most important, see that agreements are set forth in writing in a legally enforceable contract.

9) Have several people do "ethical proofreading" of your manuscript. One or two of those people might be your subjects. They should read it for accuracy and should provide any general feedback they are inclined to offer. One or two of your colleagues should also read the manuscript. Preferably those colleagues should not be ones who are particularly supportive or sympathetic to your research but colleagues who can be constructively critical.[69]

Ethical proofreading of manuscripts will protect informants from some of the worst examples of researcher carelessness or insensitivity, but it does not protect the observed from the harm that might arise during observation. Protecting the observed against harm and assessing the potential for harm to the observed prior to starting observation may be difficult. The risk to subjects posed by observation cannot be precisely estimated, nor may concrete measures to avoid all harm be easily specified and enforced. It is up to the researcher to behave in an ethical manner. An appropriate ethical framework for judging fieldwork should be "constructed on respect for the autonomy of individuals and groups based on the fundamental principle that persons always be treated as ends in themselves, never merely as means" to a researcher's own personal or professional goals.[70]

Conclusion

Observation is an important research method for political scientists. Observational studies may be direct or indirect. Indirect observation is less common but has the advantage of being a nonreactive research method. Direct observation of people by social scientists has produced numerous studies that have enhanced knowledge and understanding of human beings and their behavior. Fieldwork—direct observation by a participant observer in a natural setting—is the best known variety of direct observation, although direct observation may take place in a laboratory setting. Observation tends to produce data that are qualitative rather than quantitative. Because the researcher is the measuring device, this method is subject to particular questions about researcher bias and data validity. Since there is an evolving relationship between the observer and the observed, participant observation is a demanding and often unpredictable research endeavor. Part of the demanding nature of fieldwork stems from the difficult ethical dilemmas it raises.

As a student you may find yourself in the position of an observer, but it is more likely that you will be a consumer and evaluator of observational research. In this position you should base your evaluation on a number of considerations: Does it appear that the researcher influenced the behavior of the observed or was biased in his or her observation? How many informants were used? A few or only one? Does it appear likely that the observed could have withheld significant behavior of interest to the researcher? Are generalizations from the study limited because observation was made in a laboratory setting or because of the small number of cases observed? And were any ethical issues raised by the research? Could they have been avoided, and what would you have done in a similar situation? These questions should help you evaluate the validity and ethics of observational research.

Notes

1. Eugene J. Webb et al., *Nonreactive Measures in the Social Sciences,* 2d ed. (Boston: Houghton Mifflin, 1981).
2. Mary Henle and Marian B. Hubble, "Egocentricity in Adult Conversation," *Journal of Social Psychology* 9 (May 1938): 227-34.
3. Stanley Milgram and R. Lance Shotland, *Television and Antisocial Behavior: Field Experiments* (New York: Academic Press, 1973).
4. H. J. Eysenck and D. K. B. Nias, *Sex, Violence and the Media* (New York: Harper & Row, 1978).
5. Stanley Milgram, "Behavioral Study of Obedience," *Journal of Abnormal and Social Psychology* 67 (October 1963): 371-78.
6. William F. Whyte, *Street Corner Society: The Social Structure of an Italian Slum,* 3d ed. (Chicago: University of Chicago Press, 1981); and Marc H. Ross, *Grassroots in an African City: Political Behavior in Nairobi* (Cambridge, Mass.: MIT Press, 1975).
7. Richard F. Fenno, Jr., *Home Style: House Members in Their Districts* (Boston: Little, Brown, 1978).
8. Hugh Lytton, *Parent-Child Interaction: The Socialization Process Observed in Twin and Singleton Families* (New York: Plenum Press, 1980), 295.
9. Fenno, *Home Style,* xiii.
10. Ibid., xiv.
11. Jennie-Keith Ross and Marc Howard Ross, "Participant Observation in Political Research," *Political Methodology* 1 (Winter 1974): 65-66.
12. James A. Robinson, *The House Rules Committee* (Indianapolis: Bobbs-Merrill, 1963); and James A. Robinson, *Congress and Foreign Policy-making* (Homewood, Ill.: Dorsey Press, 1962). Also extensive firsthand observations

of Congress are reported in many of the articles in Raymond E. Wolfinger, ed., *Readings on Congress* (Englewood Cliffs, N.J.: Prentice-Hall, 1971).

13. Ralph K. Huitt, "Democratic Party Leadership in the Senate," *American Political Science Review* 55 (June 1961): 333-44.

14. David W. Minar, "The Community Basis of Conflict in School System Politics," in Scott Greer et al., eds., *The New Urbanization* (New York: St. Martin's Press, 1968), 246-63.

15. Margaret Mead, "Coming of Age in Samoa," in *From the South Seas* (New York: Morrow, 1939); Elliot Liebow, *Tally's Corner* (Boston: Little, Brown, 1967); Herbert Gans, *The Levittowners: Ways of Life and Politics in a New Suburban Community* (New York: Pantheon, 1967); Arthur J. Vidich and Joseph Bensman, *Small Town in Mass Society: Class, Power and Religion in a Rural Community* (Princeton, N.J.: Princeton University Press, 1958).

16. Ross and Ross, "Participant Observation," 70.

17. Ibid.

18. Fenno, *Home Style*, 250.

19. Joan Cassell, "Harms, Benefits, Wrongs and Rights in Fieldwork," in Joan E. Sieber, ed., *The Ethics of Social Research: Fieldwork, Regulation and Publication* (New York: Springer-Verlag, 1982), 18.

20. Ibid., 19.

21. Ibid., 18.

22. Leon Festinger, Henry Riecken, and Stanley Schacter, *When Prophecy Fails* (Minneapolis: University of Minnesota Press, 1956).

23. Fenno, *Home Style*, 255.

24. These categories are the same as those used by William B. Shaffir, Robert A. Stebbins, and Allan Turowitz, eds., *Fieldwork Experience: Qualitative Approaches to Social Research* (New York: St. Martin's Press, 1980). For a discussion of fieldwork experiences, see also Myron Glazer, *The Research Adventure: Promise and Problems of Fieldwork* (New York: Random House, 1972).

25. Shaffer, Stebbins and Turowitz, *Fieldwork Experience*, 3.

26. Fenno, *Home Style*, 257-58.

27. Whyte, *Street Corner Society*, 293.

28. Ibid., 289.

29. Laud Humphreys, *Tearoom Trade: Impersonal Sex in Public Places* (Chicago: Aldine, 1970); David A. Karp, "Observing Behavior in Public Places," in *Fieldwork Experience*, 82-97; and William J. Chambliss, *On the Take: From Petty Crooks to Presidents* (Bloomington, Ind.: Indiana University Press, 1978).

30. Glazer, *The Research Adventure*, 21.

31. Ibid., 32-36.

32. David G. Bromley and Anson D. Shupe, Jr., "Evolving Foci in Participant Observation: Research as an Emergent Process," in *Fieldwork Experience*, 201.

33. Fenno, *Home Style*, 272-73.

34. The youth pleaded guilty in exchange for a small fine. Harold E. Pepinsky, "A Sociologist on Police Patrol," in *Fieldwork Experience*, 201.

35. See account in Whyte, *Street Corner Society*, 313-17.

36. In general, see Shaffer, Stebbins, and Turowitz, *Fieldwork Experience,* 257-310.
37. Alan Roadburg, "Breaking Relationships with Research Subjects: Some Problems and Suggestions" in *Fieldwork Experience,* 257-310.
38. Peter Letkemann, "Crime as Work: Learning the Field" in *Fieldwork Experience,* 281-90.
39. Thomas W. Benson, "Another Shooting in Cowtown," *Quarterly Journal of Speech* 67 (November 1981): 347-406.
40. John Lofland, *Analyzing Social Settings: A Guide to Qualitative Observation and Analysis* (Belmont, Calif.: Wadsworth Publishing Co., 1971), 102-103.
41. Ibid., 102.
42. Chambliss, *On the Take,* 49.
43. Lofland, *Analyzing Social Settings,* 105.
44. Ibid., 106-107.
45. Webb et al., *Nonreactive Measures,* 4.
46. Ibid., 7.
47. Ibid., 24.
48. Ibid.. 10-11.
49. See discussion of Rathje's work in ibid., 15-17.
50. Ibid., 17.
51. Kurt Lang and Gladys Engel Lang, *Politics and Television* (Chicago: Quadrangle, 1968).
52. See Webb et al., *Nonreactive Measures,* 27-32.
53. Ibid., 8.
54. See Glazer, *The Research Adventure,* 59-72.
55. Ibid., 25-48, 97-124.
56. See Fenno, *Home Style,* 272.
57. Myron Glazer, "The Threat of the Stranger: Vulnerability, Reciprocity, and Fieldwork," in *The Ethics of Social Research,* 50-53.
58. Helena Znaniecki Lopata, "Interviewing American Widows," in *Fieldwork Experience,* 68-81.
59. Humphreys, *Tearoom Trade.*
60. See Glazer's account in *The Research Adventure,* 107-116.
61. Cassell, "Harms, Benefits," 18.
62. Ibid., 21.
63. Ibid.
64. Ibid.
65. Carole Gaar Johnson, "Risks in the Publication of Fieldwork," in *The Ethics of Social Research.*
66. For a discussion and examples of value-laden terminology in published reports of participant observers, see ibid.
67. See Brian Miller and Laud Humphreys, "Keeping in Touch: Maintaining Contact with Stigmatized Subjects," in *Fieldwork Experience,* 212-22.
68. Whyte, *Street Corner Society,* 350-54.
69. Johnson, "Risks," 87-88.
70. Cassell, "Harms and Benefits," 14.

Terms Introduced

Accretion measures. Indirect observation of the accumulation of materials.

Covert observation. The observer's presence or purpose is kept secret from those being observed.

Direct observation. Actual observation of behavior.

Erosion measures. Indirect observation of selective wear of some material.

Ethnography. Participant observation in a natural setting.

Field study. Observation in a natural setting.

Indirect observation. Observation of physical traces of behavior.

Overt observation. Those being observed are informed of the observer's presence and purpose.

Participant observation. Observation in which observer becomes regular participant in the activities of those being observed.

Structured observation. Systematic observation and recording of the incidence of specific behaviors.

Unstructured observation. Observation in which all behavior and activities are recorded.

Suggested Readings

Fenno, Richard F., Jr. *Home Style: House Members in Their Districts.* Boston: Little, Brown, 1973. See the Introduction and Appendix "Notes on Method: Participant Observation."

Glazer, Myron. *The Research Adventure: Promise and Problems of Field Work.* New York: Random House, 1972.

Ross, Jennie-Keith and Marc Howard Ross. "Participant Observation in Political Research." *Political Methodology* (Winter 1974): 63-88.

Shaffir, William B., Robert A. Stebbins, and Allan Turowitz, eds. *Fieldwork Experience: Qualitative Approaches to Social Research.* New York: St. Martin's Press, 1980.

Sieber, J. E., ed. *The Ethics of Social Research: Fieldwork, Regulation, and Publication.* New York: Springer-Verlag, 1982.

Whyte, William Foote. *Street Corner Society.* 3d ed. Chicago: University of Chicago Press, 1981. See Appendix A, "On the Evolution of *Street Corner Society.*"

11. Univariate Data Analysis and Descriptive Statistics

In the preceding chapters we have discussed the initial stages of a social scientific research project. We have examined the nature of scientific knowledge, the formulation of testable hypotheses, the development of a suitable research design, the process of measuring variables, and the many ways in which empirical observations may be made and data collected. The remainder of this book will cover the final steps of a research project: analyzing the data that have been collected and putting together a research report.

The major purpose of making empirical observations is to test hypotheses about political phenomena and behavior. Before researchers test their hypotheses, however, they often take a preliminary look at their data and try to summarize or describe it one variable at a time. This activity is called *univariate data analysis. Descriptive statistics* are used to summarize the measurements of one variable.

You are undoubtedly already familiar with quite a few instances of univariate data analysis and descriptive statistics. For example, a grade point average is a descriptive statistic that describes and summarizes a scholastic record as reflected by course grades. Charting the unemployment rate over time to see if it is rising or falling is also a case of univariate data analysis where the unemployment rate is a descriptive statistic.

Descriptive statistics are simply ways of mathematically summarizing numerous observations in a clear and meaningful fashion. Often the meaning of many measurements is not discernible from individual measurements. Descriptive statistics allow a researcher to "boil down" masses of data into manageable proportions so that some sense can be made of them. For example, if someone asked you to describe your academic performance in college, you could recite each course you took and each grade you received. But after about 10 courses, the listener might have a hard time formulating a clear understanding of your overall performance (unless you received the same grade in every course).

Descriptive statistics are intended to simplify the task of describing a great many observations. They can communicate trends and give an overall impression of a collection of measurements.

Summarizing data with descriptive statistics has a disadvantage, however: information about single measurements is inevitably lost. For example, if you say you have a grade-point average of 3.0 (in a 4.0 grade scale), it is not possible to learn from that single descriptive statistic whether you have excelled in some courses and struggled in others or whether you have been a consistent student receiving all B's. To minimize the loss of information, researchers often use several descriptive statistics to summarize their data in different ways. When used together, these descriptive statistics yield a clearer picture of the individual measurements than could be obtained by a single statistic.

Two different types of descriptive statistics are commonly used to summarize a collection of measurements: one measures *central tendency* (that is, what value is most frequent, common, or central in the distribution of data values); the other measures *dispersion* (that is, how closely or remotely data values are distributed around the most common, middle, or central value). Different descriptive statistics are appropriate for different types of measures. We will discuss those that are appropriate for nominal, ordinal, and interval or ratio level measures.

Nominal Level Measures

A nominal level measure is one that divides observations into arbitrarily ordered categories. Summarizing nominal level data is quite simple and straightforward. They are commonly summarized using a *frequency distribution,* shown in Table 11-1, which indicates the number of observations (or frequencies) for each category of a variable. Frequencies are often represented by the small letter f.

A frequency distribution reveals the central tendency and dispersion of the data. For nominal level data, the measure of central tendency is called the *mode* or *modal category*—the category with the greatest frequency of observations. In Table 11-1 (a), female is the modal category. In Table 11-1 (b), it is the color green. For nominal level data, the greatest amount of dispersion occurs when the observations are distributed equally among the categories. In Table 11-1 (a), the data are quite dispersed since there is an almost equal number of males and females. The dispersion in Table 11-1 (b) is not as high as it could be since there are only relatively few observations in the red category. A total lack of dispersion is indicated if all the observations fall into one category.

In univariate analysis, it is possible to discover characteristics of the data that may present substantial obstacles to further data analysis. For

Table 11-1 A Frequency Distribution: Two Examples

Categories (Values)	Frequency (Number of Observations)
A. Variable: sex	
Male	117
Female	124
Total	241
B. Variable: color perceived as most restful	
Blue	55
Red	17
Green	72
Yellow	60
Total	204

Source: Hypothetical data.

example, suppose you set out to study the relationship between sex and occupation and found the frequency distribution of sex in the sample survey to be male, 300; female, 0. Since there is a total lack of dispersion (that is, no variation in one of the key variables, sex), no comparisons can be made. This problem occurred in the New Jersey negative income tax experiment cited in Chapter 5. There was a lack of cases or observations in some categories for key variables of interest to the study. The moral to remember is "no variation, no comparison." You may discover an interesting uniformity, but you can't explore relationships between variables when one of the variables doesn't vary. Some simple univariate analysis as your data are being collected—such as looking at a frequency distribution—may alert you to impending disaster!

Proportions and *percentages* are frequently used to summarize the distribution of nominal data. Proportions are calculated by dividing the number of observations in each category by the total number of observations. Percentages are calculated by multiplying proportions by 100. Proportions and percentages communicate information that is often more meaningful and easier to remember than a frequency distribution. Table 11-2 presents the frequency distribution, proportion, and percentage of delegate votes at the 1984 Democratic National Convention for the three major presidential candidates, Walter Mondale, Gary Hart, and Jesse Jackson.

Proportions and percentages may also be preferred to frequency distributions because they make it easier to compare two populations of

Table 11-2 Frequency Distribution, Proportion, and Percentage for Delegate Votes, 1984 Democratic National Convention

Categories (Values)	Frequency	Proportion	Percentage
Variable: Roll call vote for 1984 Democratic presidential nomination			
Mondale	2,191.0	.568	56.8
Hart	1,200.5	.311	31.1
Jackson	465.5	.121	12.1
Total	3,857.0	1.000	100.0

Source: *New York Times,* July 20, 1984, A12.

Note: Abstentions, absences, and votes for others are not included. Fractions are rounded off to tenths of a delegate.

different size. For example, Table 11-3 shows two hypothetical student populations of different size, but with the same proportions of selected majors. It would be difficult to discern this fact from the frequency distributions alone. The percentages reveal this information immediately. In many tables, only percentages will be shown for each category. Frequency distributions are omitted, but the total number of observations is always given, making it possible to calculate a frequency distibution.

    Bar graphs and *pie diagrams* are another way to describe nominal level data. A bar graph is a series of bars; each bar represents the number or percentage of observations that are in a category. Figure 11-1 is a bar graph of student majors in college A from Table 11-3. Figure 11-2 is a pie chart of the roll call vote for the 1984 Democratic presidential nomination shown in Table 11-2.

Table 11-3 Frequency Distribution and Percentage for Student Populations

Categories (Values)	College A		College B	
	f	%	f	%
Variable: Student majors				
Political science	35	25.9	105	25.9
Biology	30	22.2	90	22.2
English	45	33.3	135	33.3
Math	25	18.5	75	18.5
Total	135	99.9	405	99.9

Source: Hypothetical data.

Note: Percentages do not add to 100 due to rounding.

Figure 11-1 Bar Graph of Frequencies of Student Majors (College A)

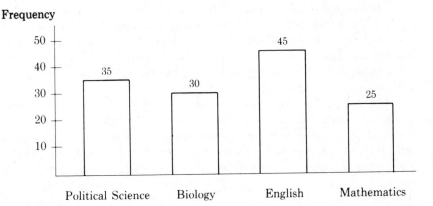

Source: Hypothetical data.

Figure 11-2 Pie Chart of Roll Call Vote on 1984 Democratic Presidential Nomination (N = 3857)

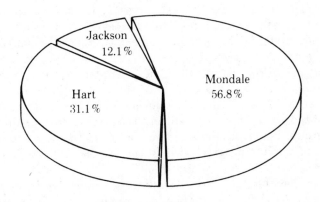

Source: *New York Times*, July 20, 1984, A-12.

Visual displays should be honest representations of data that clarify rather than distort the data's meaning. One common mistake is to use a two-dimensional picture to illustrate one-dimensional data. An excellent discussion of this problem and other aspects of data graphics is Edward Tufte's book, *The Visual Display of Quantitative Information.*[1]

Ordinal Level Measures

The same univariate descriptive statistics used to summarize nominal level data may also be used for ordinal level data. Ordinal level data involve categories of observations that are ordered (from more of some attribute to less of some attribute). Thus, there are some additional permissible descriptive statistics that summarize information about the ordering of measurements.

The *median* as well as the *mode* is used to indicate the central tendency of an ordinal measure. The median is the category or value in a distribution of values above and below which one-half of the frequencies fall. Put in another way, it is the category to which the middle observation belongs.[2] For example, age of respondents may be measured ordinally by grouping ages as shown in Table 11-4. With 729 respondents, the middle observation number is 364.5. Respondents 364 and 365 fall into the "35-44" category, so this is the median age group.

Dispersion for ordinal measures may be indicated by the *range,* the distance between the highest and lowest observations or the range of categories into which observations fall. The range of ages in Table 11-4 is "18-24" to "60 and over." One extreme observation may cause the range to be quite large even when most of the observations are included in only a small range of categories. For this reason, the *interquartile range,* which is not as sensitive to a few observations at the extreme ends of a scale, is the preferred measure of dispersion. The interquartile range reflects the middle 50 percent of the observations: 25 percent are above, 25 percent are below. To calculate the interquartile range, remove the bottom quarter and the top quarter of the observations. For example, one-quarter of 729 is 182.25 and removing 182.25 respondents from the low end of the age scale puts one end of the interquartile range in the "25-34" age group. Removing the same number from the high end puts the other end of the interquartile range in the "45-59" age group. Thus the interquartile range is "25-35" to "45-59."

Notice that the descriptive statistics for ordinal level measures are more informative than those for nominal level measures. For ordinal level measures, the central tendency of a frequency distribution may be judged with both the mode and the median; for nominal level measures, only the

Table 11-4 Ordinal Grouping of Age of Respondents

Ages	18-24	25-34	35-44	45-59	60 and over	Total
Number	91	196	128	154	160	729

Source: Hypothetical data.

mode is appropriate. For ordinal level measures, the dispersion of a frequency distribution may be indicated with the range and the inter-quartile range, while for nominal level measures, dispersion can only be "sensed" by looking across all the categories. That is one reason why higher levels of measurement are preferred to lower levels.

Interval and Ratio Level Measures

Interval and ratio level measures are rarely summarized using frequencies, percentages, bar graphs, or pie charts. Because interval and ratio measures are numerical values, not just categories, there may be such a large number of different observed values that frequencies and percentages do not summarize the data efficiently. Nor are bar graphs practical to use when there are numerous bars. However, when an interval or ratio level variable takes on a relatively small number of different values, a type of bar graph called a *histogram*, shown in Figure 11-3, may be used to illustrate the frequency distribution of the observations. Each bar represents an observed value. The height of the bar indicates the number of times the value has been observed in the data. For example, eight students took no social science course. The vertical bars touch each other because equal differences in scale values are numerically equal for interval and ratio level measures.[3] For example, the difference between one and two courses and between two and three courses is one course in both cases.

Figure 11-3   Histogram of the Number of Social Science Courses Taken per Year for 100 Freshmen

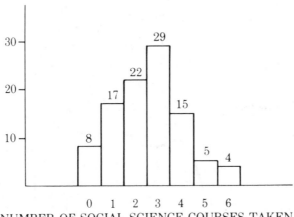

NUMBER OF SOCIAL SCIENCE COURSES TAKEN

Source: Hypothetical Data.

Instead of a histogram, a *frequency curve* also may be used to describe interval and ratio level measures. A frequency curve may be created from a histogram by connecting the midpoints of the bars with straight lines. Frequency curves also may be created by placing a dot on a graph representing the frequency of each value and connecting the dots. Generally a frequency curve is used for distributions of data values that are continuous, or assumed to be, whereas histograms are used if the data are discrete. For example, average daily temperature is a continuous variable; it can take on any number of degree values or fractions thereof. Number of children in a family or number of social science courses taken are discrete values since observations are whole values only, not fractions.

Frequency curves come in an unlimited number of shapes. As Figure 11-4 shows, they may be symmetrical (a, b, f) or asymmetrical (c, d, e). A symmetrical distribution is the same shape on either side of the midpoint in the range of observed values. Asymmetrical distributions may be positively skewed (c) or negatively skewed (d). In a positively skewed distribution, there are fewer observations to the right of the midpoint. In a negatively skewed distribution, there are fewer observations on the left part of the curve.

Figure 11-4   Six Examples of Frequency Curves

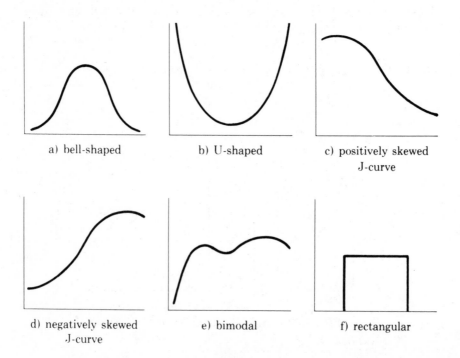

a) bell-shaped   b) U-shaped   c) positively skewed
                                                  J-curve

d) negatively skewed   e) bimodal   f) rectangular
   J-curve

Measures of central tendency for interval and ratio level measures are the mode, median, and the *arithmetic mean*. The arithmetic mean or average is the sum of the values of a variable divided by the number of values. This is represented algebraically as follows:

$$\bar{X} = \frac{X_1 + X_2 + \ldots + X_N}{N} = \frac{\Sigma X}{N} = \frac{\text{sum of scores}}{\text{number of scores}} \qquad (11.1)$$

Where
  $\bar{X}$ = the mean and is referred to as X bar
  X = a raw score in a set of scores
  N = the number of scores, and
  Σ = sigma and directs us to sum the score[4]

The mean may be a misleading indicator of central tendency if there is an extreme value. For example, the incomes in two hypothetical communities shown in Table 11-5 are identical except for the income of one person. The mean income of Community A is $37,500, Community B, $20,500. Knowing just the mean income of the communities would give you the erroneous impression that people in Community A are much better off than people in Community B, when in reality there is only one person in A who is much better off than anyone in B. In this case the median is a better indicator of central tendency than the mean. The median income in both communities is the same: $21,000. If the mean and the median are not close in value, one or a few extreme values are affecting the value of the mean.

Table 11-5 Incomes for Two Communities

	Community A	Community B
1.	$ 10,000	$10,000
2.	10,000	10,000
3.	12,000	12,000
4.	18,000	18,000
5.	20,000	20,000
6.	22,000	22,000
7.	25,000	25,000
8.	28,000	28,000
9.	30,000	30,000
10.	200,000	30,000
	$\bar{X} = 37,500$	$\bar{X} = 20,500$

Source: Hypothetical data.

Indicators of dispersion for interval and ratio level data include *mean deviation, variance,* and *standard deviation* as well as the range and interquartile range discussed earlier. For interval and ratio level data each of the last two indicators is represented by a single number (rather than a range of values as with ordinal data) because of the mathematical properties of the level of measurement. For example, if the highest score on a test was 100 and the lowest was 25, the range of test scores would be $100 - 25$ or 75. If 25 percent of the test scores were above 80, and 25 percent were below 60, then the interquartile range would be $80 - 60$ or 20. If the range of scores on another test was 90, and the interquartile range was 40, this would indicate a greater dispersion of scores on the second test. The range and interquartile range are less useful indicators of variability in scores than the mean deviation, variance, and standard deviation, and consequently they are used less often as indicators of dispersion with interval and ratio level measures.

The mean deviation (MD) is a measure of dispersion that is based on the deviation of each score from the mean. Its calculation is shown in Table 11-6. If we take each score and subtract it from the mean, we calculate the amount each score deviates from the mean (Column 2). The sum of these deviations is always zero—an important mathematical property of the mean. (Check this by adding the numbers in Column 2 for

Table 11-6   Distribution, Deviation, and Mean Deviation of Incomes in Community

X		$X - \bar{X}$	$\lvert X - \bar{X} \rvert$
1.	$10,000	−10,500	10,500
2.	10,000	−10,500	10,500
3.	12,000	−8,500	8,500
4.	18,000	−2,500	2,500
5.	20,000	−500	500
6.	22,000	1,500	1,500
7.	25,000	4,500	4,500
8.	28,000	7,500	7,500
9.	30,000	9,500	9,500
10.	30,000	9,500	9,500

$\bar{X} = 20,500$

$\Sigma(X - \bar{X}) = 0$

$\Sigma \lvert X - \bar{X} \rvert = 65,000$

$MD = \dfrac{65,000}{10} = 6,500$

Source: Hypothetical data.

yourself.) Because we are interested only in the amount of deviation and not the direction or sign of the deviation, we add up the *absolute values* of the deviations (Column 3). Then we take this sum and divide by the number of scores, to find the mean deviation of scores from the mean. The larger the mean deviation, the greater the dispersion of scores around the mean.

The equation for the mean deviation is:

$$MD = \frac{\Sigma \mid X - \bar{X} \mid}{N}$$

Where

$\mid \mid$ = the symbol for an absolute value

Even though the mean deviation does indicate dispersion, the standard deviation and the variance are used more often than the mean deviation. One reason for this is that the standard deviation and variance are used in advanced statistics, which we discuss later in this chapter and in Chapters 12 and 13.[5]

The *variance* (s^2) is the sum of the squared deviations from the mean divided by the number of scores:

$$s^2 = \frac{\Sigma(X - \bar{X})^2}{N}$$

The *standard deviation* (s) is the square root of the variance:

$$s = \sqrt{\frac{\Sigma(X - \bar{X})^2}{N}}$$

The greater the dispersion of data points about the mean, the higher the value of s^2 and s. This means that if all the data points are the same, s^2 and s will be equal to zero.

To calculate the variance and standard deviation, follow these seven steps:

1) Calculate the mean.

2) Calculate the distance between the mean and each value.

3) Square the distances calculated in step 2.

4) Multiply the squared distances by the frequency of observations for each value.

5) Sum the squared distances calculated in step 4.

6) Divide the sum of squares from step 5 by N. This equals the variance.

7) Take the square root of the number calculated in step 6. This equals the standard deviation.

A sample calculation of the variance and standard deviation is presented in Table 11-7.[6]

Table 11-7   Sample Calculation of Variance and Standard Deviation

f	X	X − X̄	(X − X̄)²	f(X − X̄)²
2	1	−2	4	8
1	2	−1	1	1
4	3	0	0	0
1	4	1	1	1
2	5	2	4	8

$\overline{X} = 30/10 = 3$
$f(X - \overline{X})^2 = 18$
$s^2 = 18/10 = 1.8$
$s = \sqrt{1.8} = 1.34$

Source: Hypothetical data.

The standard deviation is an important statistic, especially in conjunction with the normal or bell-shaped distribution, which we will discuss in the next section.

The Normal Distribution

The normal distribution is a symmetrical, bell-shaped frequency curve with two interesting properties. First, the mean, the mode, and the median all coincide at the peak of the curve. Second, a fixed proportion of observations or cases lies between the mean and any distance from the mean measured in terms of the standard deviation. This is shown in Figure 11-5. Thus 34.13 percent of the cases in any normal distribution lie between the mean and one standard deviation to the right of the mean. Since the normal curve is symmetrical, we know that 68.26 percent of the cases lie between the mean and plus or minus one standard deviation from the mean. Also 95.44 percent of the cases lie between the mean and plus or minus two standard deviations. It is not necessary to use only even multiples of the standard deviation. For example, exactly 95 percent of the cases lie between the mean and 1.96 standard deviations on either side of the mean. Ninety-nine percent lie within plus or minus 2.58 standard deviations of the mean.

Relationship of Normal Distribution to Probability Sampling

The normal distribution and its properties are important to probability sampling. If we take a large number of random samples and calculate the mean of each sample, the distribution of these sample means (the *sampling distribution*) will resemble a normal curve. In other

Figure 11-5 Normal Distribution and Percent of Cases between
Selected Points under the Curve

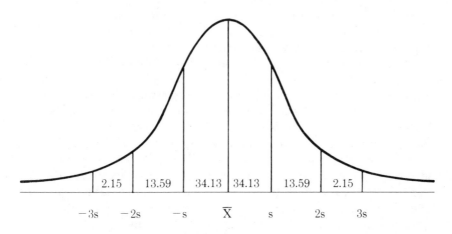

words, most of the sample means will cluster around the mean of all the
sample means. Furthermore, according to the *Central Limit Theorem,*
the mean of all the sample means will be equal to the mean of the
population (designated by the Greek letter mu or μ).[7]

Most of the sample mean values will cluster around the true
population mean, although the mean of some samples may differ
substantially from the true population mean. Thus, we can use the
information that we get from one sample to estimate the mean of the
population. (For a discussion of confidence levels and margins of error,
see Chapter 7.)

In order to estimate the mean of the population from sample
information, we need to calculate the standard deviation of the distribution of the sample means around the population mean. This is called the
standard deviation of the mean or *standard error* (S.E. or σ) and is equal
to $\sigma/\sqrt{N}$ where σ is the standard deviation of the population and N is the
size of each of the samples.

In probability sampling, a proportion of the population is selected at
random and then a population parameter is estimated. For example, we
can estimate the mean amount of student financial aid. In a sample
survey of 100 college students, let's say the mean amount of financial aid
($\overline{X}$) is $750, and the standard deviation (s) is 50. What does this tell us
about the mean amount of financial aid received by all students in the
college? How certain are we that our sample estimate of the mean is
accurate? Luckily mathematics tells us that where our sample size is
large, we may substitute s (the sample standard deviation) for σ in the
formula for standard error. Therefore the standard error is

$$\text{S.E.} = s/\sqrt{N} \text{ or } 50/\sqrt{100} \text{ or } \$5 \qquad (11.5)$$

Because the sample distribution is a normal curve, roughly 68 percent of the sample estimates will lie between the mean and plus or minus one standard error. (Remember that the standard error is a standard deviation, which is why we can substitute standard error for standard deviation in this discussion of the normal distribution.) Therefore, we can say that we are 68 percent confident that the true population mean, or average financial aid award, is \$750 ± \$5, or between \$745 and \$755. We are about 95 percent certain that the true average financial aid award is between \$740 and \$760 (750 ± 2 S.E.).

To emphasize this important aspect of probability sampling, we will explain the process slighty differently. Three different distributions are involved: the distribution of a characteristic in a population, the distribution of the same characteristic in a single sample taken from the population, and the sampling distribution, that is, the distribution of sample means if we take many samples and calculate a mean for each sample.

For each distribution a standard deviation can be calculated. For the population, it is called σ, and normally its numerical value is unknown. For the sample it is s, and it can be calculated. For the sampling distribution we can calculate the standard deviation of the sample means around the mean of all the sample means. This is called the standard error.

Since the sampling distribution is normally distributed, we can calculate the probability of obtaining a single sample mean that lies between the mean of all sample means and any number of standard errors from it. The formula for the standard error is $\sigma \sqrt{N}$. We know the value of N (the size of the sample), but we do not know σ (the standard deviation of the population), nor do we know the mean of all sample means. But we may substitute the mean of the sample, $\bar{X}$, for the mean of all sample means (which equals the mean of the population), and the standard deviation of the sample, s, for the standard deviation of the population σ. Because a probability sample can be linked to the normal distribution in this way, the characteristics of the normal distibution can be used to estimate the accuracy of a probability sample.

The Standard Normal Distribution

Standard normal distributions are normal distributions with a mean of zero and a standard deviation and variance of one. We can convert any normal distribution into a standard normal distribution by converting scores into *z scores*. A z score is the number of standard deviations that a score varies from the mean. The calculation for a z score is represented by

$$Z = \frac{X - \bar{X}}{s} \tag{11.6}$$

Where

    X = a single score
    $\bar{X}$ = mean of all scores
    s = standard deviation of scores

For example, in Table 11-7, where $\bar{X}$ = 3 and s = 1.34, the z score for X = 5 would be (5 − 3)/1.34 = 2/1.34 = 1.49. Thus the observation X=5 is 1.49 standard deviations from the mean.

All z scores have some of the properties of a standard normal distribution; that is, the mean of the z scores is zero, and the standard deviation and variance of z scores are equal to one. Z scores will also be normally distributed if the original scores are normally distributed. Converting raw data scores to z scores will not normalize a non-normal distribution, however.[8]

Z scores make it easier to compare groups of scores or variables. For example, suppose a group of people were given three tests, and the scores for each test are normally distributed. One individual who received scores of 80, 85, and 87 is interested in comparing his performance on each test to the performance of the others.

For each test, a mean grade and standard deviation are calculated. For the first test, $\bar{X}$=80, s=3. For the second test, $\bar{X}$=75, s=5. For the third test, $\bar{X}$=80, s=3.5. The individual's scores can be converted to z scores of 0, 2, and 2. Thus the individual is zero standard deviations from the mean score on the first test, two on the second, and two on the third. This means that while the individual was closer to the mean on the third test than the second (7 points versus 10 points), his relative performance compared with the rest of the group was the same. The individual outperformed 97.72 percent of the group in both tests. The normal distribution tells us that 97.72 percent of all test scores fall below (or to the left of) two standard deviations above the mean (50 + 34.13 + 13.59 = 97.72). Z scores also have an important role in more advanced statistical analysis of data.

Conclusion

In this chapter we have discussed a number of univariate descriptive statistics that are used to summarize data in an efficient and meaningful way. Descriptive statistics should clarify and reveal important characteristics of a collection of measurements. Univariate descriptive statistics indicate the central tendency, the dispersion, and the distribution of data values for a single variable. A single number or a few numbers communicate these important characteristics and thus make the task of describing large amounts of data more manageable. In some situations data may be summarized and depicted using graphic displays such as bar graphs and pie charts. Different methods of displaying data and different univariate statistics are appropriate for use with nominal, ordinal, and interval or ratio level data.

Of the statistics that were discussed, the mean, the standard deviation, and their relationship to the normal distribution are among the most important because they provide a foundation for more complex statistical analyses and for exploring relationships between variables. This chapter has focused on ways to analyze a single variable at a time. In Chapters 12 and 13, we will discuss statistical analyses that allow researchers to test for relationships between two or more variables.

Notes

1. Edward R. Tufte, *The Visual Display of Quantitative Information* (Cheshire, Conn.: Graphics Press, 1983).
2. Kirk W. Elifson, Richard P. Runyon, and Audrey Haber, *Fundamentals of Social Statistics* (Reading, Mass.: Addison-Wesley, 1982), 100.
3. Ibid., 60.
4. Ibid., 95.
5. Ibid., 118.
6. For other computing formulas for the standard deviation that involve fewer rounding errors, see Hubert M. Blalock, Jr., *Social Statistics*, 2d ed. (New York: McGraw-Hill, 1972), 82-83.
7. Ibid., 181.
8. Elifson, Runyon, and Haber, *Fundamentals*, 133.

Terms Introduced

Bar graph. A type of graphic display of frequency or percentage distribution of data.

Central tendency. The most frequent, common, or central value in the distribution of values of a variable.

Descriptive statistic. Mathematical summary of measurements for one variable.

Dispersion. The distribution of data values around the most common, middle, or central value.

Frequency curve. A line graph indicating frequency distribution.

Frequency distribution (f). The number of observations per value or category of a variable.

Histogram. The type of bar graph used to depict interval and ratio level measures.

Interquartile range. The middle 50 percent of observations.

Mean. The sum of the values of a variable divided by the number of values.

Mean deviation. A measure of dispersion of data points for interval and ratio level data.

Median. The category or value above and below which one-half of observations lie.

Mode. The category with the greatest frequency of observations.

Negatively skewed. A distribution of values in which more observations lie to the left of the middle value.

Normal distribution. A frequency curve showing a symmetrical, bell-shaped distribution in which the mean, mode, and median coincide and in which a fixed proportion of observations lies between the mean and any distance from the mean measured in terms of the standard deviation.

Percentage distribution. The percent of observations per category of variable.

Pie graph. A type of graphic display of frequency distribution.

Positively skewed. A distribution of values in which more observations lie to the right of the middle value.

Range. The distance between highest and lowest values or the range of categories into which observations fall.

Standard deviation (s). The measure of dispersion of data points about the mean for interval and ratio level data.

Standard error. The standard deviation of sample means about the mean of sample means.

Standard normal distribution. Normal distribution with mean of zero and standard deviation and variance of one.

Univariate data analysis. Analysis of a single variable.

Variance (s^2). The measure of dispersion of data points about the mean for interval and ratio level data.

Z score. The number of standard deviations that a score deviates from the mean score.

Exercises

1. Draw a line graph and describe the shape of the curve for the following data points: 1, 1, 2, 5, 1, 1, 4, 1, 2, 3, 2, 3, 2, 3, 1, 4.

2. Find the mean, mode, median, range, and interquartile range for the data points in Exercise 1. Locate these on the line graph. Is the mean to the left or the right of the mode?

3. Calculate the mean and standard deviation for the following scores: 011, 222, 3333, 444, 55, 6. Calculate the z score for the score of 4. What does this tell you about the score of 4 with respect to the mean?

4. In a normally distributed population of scores with a mean of 50 and standard deviation of 5, what percent of the scores are between 45 and 55? If a score is 1.2 standard deviations above the mean, what is this score?

5. Calculate the percentages for the following frequency distribution of partisan affiliation. Calculate the appropriate measures of central tendency and dispersion.

Strong Democrat	Moderate Democrat	Weak Democrat	Weak Republican	Moderate Republican	Strong Republican
123	156	64	80	125	60

6. A researcher gathered data on the number of school strikes 50 cities had experienced in the last five yeras. The frequency distribution that resulted is shown below. Calculate the mode, median, mean, and standard deviation for the frequency distribution. (You may express the standard deviation in terms of a fraction and/or square root sign if necessary.) What does the comparison of the median and mean tell you? Is this a normal distribution?

Number of School Strikes	Number of Observations
0	8
1	18
2	5
3	2
4	1
5	2
6	3
7	4
8	7

Suggested Readings

Blalock, Hubert M., Jr. *Social Statistics*. Rev. 2d ed. New York: McGraw-Hill, 1979.

Elifson, Kirk W., Richard P. Runyon, and Audrey Haber. *Fundamentals of Social Statistics*. Reading, Mass.: Addison-Wesley, 1982.

Tufte, Edward R. *The Visual Display of Quantitative Information*. Cheshire, Conn.: Graphics Press, 1983.

12. *Measuring Relationships and Testing Hypotheses: Bivariate Data Analysis*

In this and the next chapter we will discuss how to test the hypotheses that we have developed and refined. To do this five general questions must be addressed: Is there a *relationship* between the independent and dependent variables in the hypothesis? What is the direction or shape of the relationship? How strong is the relationship? Is the relationship statistically significant? And is the relationship a causal one? Each of these questions will be considered in turn.

A relationship exists if the values that observations take on for the independent variable are associated with the values that they take on for the dependent variable. For example, if as people get older they vote more frequently, then the cases (people) take on a value for the dependent variable (voting or not voting) that is associated with a value for the independent variable (age). Therefore, the values for the two variables are related.

Once it is established that there is some pattern in the observed values for the independent and dependent variables, the nature of that pattern becomes important. The direction or shape of a relationship tells the researcher which values of the independent variable are associated with which values of the dependent variable, rather than simply whether the two are connected. For example, if the chances of people voting change as their ages change, there is a relationship between age and turnout. However, the direction of the relationship tells us which values of the independent variable (age) are associated with which values of the dependent variable (turnout). The shape of the relationship tells us whether the relationship is linear, exponential, logarithmic, or something else. To conclude that "the younger you are, the more likely you are to vote" is quite different from concluding that "the older you are, the more likely you are to vote." In both cases there is a relationship between the two variables, but the nature of the relationship is different.

A relationship is strong if most of the observed values for the independent variable are connected with values for the dependent variable. If only a few of the observed values show this association, then we refer to the relationship as a weak one. The notion of strength, therefore, depends upon how many of the observed values of the dependent variable may be understood, accounted for, or explained with values of the independent variable.

There is always a possibility that a relationship observed in a researcher's data is due only to chance. A sample from some target population may be an inaccurate indication of what we would have observed in the entire population. We test the possibility that an observed relationship is the result of chance rather than systematic factors by measuring the relationship's *statistical significance*. This measurement tells us the probability that we could have observed the results we did even if there were no real relationship between the two variables. When working with sample data, we calculate the probability that no relationship exists in the target population given the observed relationship in our sample. If the relationship observed in the sample is too weak for us to be confident that there is a relationship in the population, then we discount the importance of our sample results. When working with nonsample data, we must also generally be concerned with the statistical significance of our results since observed results may also be the product of random chance alone.

Just because a relationship exists between independent and dependent variables does not necessarily mean that the independent variable is a cause of the dependent variable. There are a number of other possible reasons for the existence of such a relationship. For example, there is a relationship between the league of the baseball team that wins the World Series in presidential election years and the political party that wins the U.S. presidency: when National League teams win, a Democratic presidential candidate tends to win. No one seriously thinks that one causes the other, however. The observation of a relationship, then, is really only the beginning of the search for causal knowlege, a search that is generally a lengthy and difficult one.

In this chapter we will show you how to answer the first four questions. Observing the existence, direction, strength, and statistical significance of a relationship is a fairly objective process in which there are well-established analytical techniques and sensible conventions for evaluating evidence. Reaching conclusions about causal relationships, however, is more subjective and problematic and will be discussed in Chapter 13.

The procedure for measuring relationships and testing hypotheses depends upon the level of measurement of the independent and dependent variables. When the independent and dependent variables are both nominal or ordinal level measures, *contingency table analysis* (also called *crosstabulation*) is used. When one of the variables is nominal or ordinal and the other is interval or ratio, the *difference of means test* or *analysis of variance* is the preferred technique. And when both variables are interval or ratio level measures, *regression* or *correlation* analysis is used.

Crosstabulation

A crosstabulation or "crosstab" takes each case and displays the value of that case for both variables in a table. This is done by putting the values for one of the variables along one side of the table and the values for the other variable along the other side of the table. Each case is then placed in the cell in the table that corresponds to the case's values for both variables.

Suppose, for example, a researcher is interested in testing the hypothesis that blondes are more apt to vote Republican than brunettes. Data are collected that measure the hair color and vote choice of a sample of voters. The first 10 cases in this sample look like this:

Case Number	Hair Color	Vote
1	Blonde	Republican
2	Blonde	Democrat
3	Blonde	Republican
4	Brunette	Democrat
5	Brunette	Republican
6	Blonde	Republican
7	Brunette	Democrat
8	Brunette	Democrat
9	Brunette	Democrat
10	?	Republican

We can construct a table showing each case's value for both variables by putting the independent variable across the top and the dependent variable down the side. (This is the conventional format, but the independent variable could instead be located down the side.) In Table 12-1 (a), the cases have been placed in the appropriate box or cell in the crosstab.

Now, what is important in testing the hypothesis is not which cases have particular values for the independent and dependent variables, but how many cases have each combination of values. The number of observations in each cell is shown in Table 12-1 (b).

How does Table 12-1 (b) help us measure a relationship and test the hypothesis? The hypothesis with which we began was that blondes vote differently from brunettes. We have separated the blondes from the brunettes so that we can compare their voting behavior. Our expectation is that blondes will be more likely to vote Republican than brunettes are.

Table 12-1   Relationship between Hair Color and Vote: A Simple
Crosstabulation

Dependent Variable:	Independent Variable: Hair Color		
Vote	Blonde	Brunette	Total
a.			
Republican	1, 3, 6	5	
Democrat	2	4, 7, 8, 9	
b.			
Republican	3	1	4
Democrat	1	4	5
Total	4	5	9

Source: Hypothetical data.

Note: Case no. 10 is not included because hair color is unknown.

Of the four blondes in the table, three or 75 percent voted Republican. Of
the five brunettes in the table, one or 20 percent voted Republican.
Therefore, a greater proportion of blondes voted Republican (75 percent)
than did brunettes (20 percent), indicating that blondes and brunettes
did vote differently. Therefore, the value of the independent variable
matters (whether blonde or brunette) and knowing a case's hair color
would help us account for that case's presidential vote.

Crosstabs almost always contain many more than nine cases and
often contain more than four cells. No matter what the number of cases
and categories, however, the procedure remains the same: 1) separate the
cases into groups based on their values for the independent variable, 2)
compare the values of the dependent variable for those groups, and 3)
decide if the values for the dependent variable are different for the
different groups of cases.

Now let us take a slightly more complicated crosstab and see how we
would use it to assess the existence, direction, and strength of the
relationship between hair color and party voting. Consider Table 12-2.

The first question we need to answer is whether a relationship
between hair color and presidential vote does, in fact, exist. In other
words, do the votes of blondes differ from the votes of brunettes? To
answer that question, we need to calculate the percentage of people in
each column who voted a particular way because each column contains
people with the same hair color. Of 500 blondes, 300 or 60 percent voted
Republican; 200 or 40 percent voted Democratic. Of 1,000 brunettes, 400
or 40 percent voted Republican; 600 or 60 percent voted Democratic.

Table 12-2 Relationship Between Hair Color and Vote: A More Complex Crosstabulation

Dependent Variable: Vote	Independent Variable: Hair Color		
	Blonde	*Brunette*	*Total*
a.			
Republican	300	400	700
Democrat	200	600	800
Total	500	1,000	1,500
b.			
Republican	60%	40%	47%
Democrat	40	60	53
Total	100	100	100

Source: Hypothetical data.

Table 12-2 (b) with the column percentages shows at a glance that blondes do vote more Republican than brunettes do. Not all blondes vote Republican and not all brunettes vote Democratic, but the two groups defined by their values on the independent variable do differ. Consequently, we can conclude that there is a relationship—in this sample— between hair color and party vote.

Table 12-3 is a crosstab that shows no relationship between the independent and dependent variables. The cases in all the categories of the independent variable behaved the same on the dependent variable. And the percentage of cases with a particular value of the dependent variable is the same for every category of the independent variable: an

Table 12-3 A Crosstabulation Showing No Relationship between Hair Color and Vote: Column Percentages

Dependent Variable: Vote	Independent Variable: Hair Color			
	Blonde	*Brunette*	*Total*	*(n)*
Republican	47%	47%	47%	(700)
Democrat	53	53	53	(800)
Total	100	100	100	
(n)	(500)	(1,000)		(1,500)

Source: Hypothetical data.

equal proportion of blondes and brunettes voted Republican. Consequently, the hypothesis that hair color affects voting behavior would not be confirmed by this evidence.

The categories of the independent variable may be either the rows or columns in a crosstab. The convention is to place the independent variable across the top of a crosstab, thereby creating the categories of the independent variable in the columns of the table. However, to fit a crosstab on one page, it sometimes will be constructed with the variable with more categories down the side of the table. It really does not matter whether a crosstab is constructed with the independent variable across the top or down the side. Once that choice is made, however, the percentages in the table must be calculated for the values of the independent variable in order to test the existence of a relationship.

Table 12-4, for example, presents exactly the same information as Table 12-3 only the independent variable is down the side of the table rather than across the top. Therefore, the row rather than the column percentages indicate the lack of a relationship between hair color and vote.

After determining whether a relationship exists between the independent and dependent variables, a researcher should investigate its direction. The direction of a relationship shows which values of the independent variable are associated with which values of the dependent variable. The direction of the relationship presented in Tables 12-1 and 12-2 is that blondes, not brunettes, are more apt to vote Republican. Had we gotten different results, the direction of the relationship between hair color and party vote might have been different, with brunettes being more apt to vote Republican.

Table 12-5 displays hypothetical relationships between party identification and attitudes toward military spending. In Table 12-5 (a), the

Table 12-4　A Crosstabulation Showing No Relationship between Hair Color and Vote: Row Percentages

Independent Variable: Hair Color	Dependent Variable: Vote			
	Republican	Democrat	Total	(n)
Blonde	47%	53%	100%	(500)
Brunette	47%	53%	100%	(1,000)
Total	47%	53%	100%	
(n)	(700)	(800)		(1,500)

Source: Hypothetical data.

Table 12-5 Negative and Positive Relationships between Party Identification and Attitude toward Military Spending

Dependent Variable: Attitude toward Military Spending	Independent Variable: Party Identification				
	Democrats	Independents	Republicans	Total	(n)
a.					
Increase	20%	40%	60%	40%	(240)
Remain same	50	40	30	40	(240)
Decrease	30	20	10	20	(120)
Total	100	100	100	100	
(n)	(200)	(200)	(200)		(600)
b.					
Increase	60%	40%	20%	40%	(240)
Remain same	30	40	50	40	(240)
Decrease	10	20	30	20	(120)
Total	100	100	100	100	
(n)	(200)	(200)	(200)		(600)

Source: Hypothetical data.

Republicans are more apt to favor increased military spending; in Table 12-5 (b), the Democrats are more apt to favor increased military spending. In both cases there is a relationship between the two variables, but the direction of the relationship differs. Since the direction of the relationship yields important information for understanding the association between the two variables, its assessment is often a crucial part of testing a hypothesis.

When low values of one variable are associated with low values of another, a *positive relationship* exists between the variables; for example, "the more education one has, the higher one's political interest." When low values of one variable are associated with high values of another, a *negative relationship* exists between the two variables; for example, "the higher one's income, the less liberal one is."

Most computer programs print crosstabs with low values to the left and top of the table and high values to the right and bottom. Therefore, if the top left and bottom right corners are filled with higher values, it indicates a positive relationship (as was the case in Table 12-5 (b) since 60 percent and 30 percent are higher than 20 percent and 10 percent). But if the top right and lower left corners of a table are filled with higher values, a negative relationship is generally indicated (as was the case in Table 12-5 (a)). The direction of the relationship does not tell us how significant or important the relationship is, but it does tell us the nature of the relationship and it helps us test a hypothesis in which the direction has been proposed.

The *meaning* of a positive or negative relationship, however, cannot be determined without referring to how a crosstab is constructed. The meaning of the relationship in Table 12-6 is identical to the meaning of the relationship in Table 12-5 (b). The only difference is in how the values of the independent variable are displayed. Therefore, a crosstab must be inspected before the meaning of the direction of the relationship can be interpreted.

The strength of a relationship refers to how different the observed values of the dependent variable are in the categories of the independent variable. If blondes are voting much differently from brunettes, then we can say that there is a strong relationship between the two variables. If they are voting only a little bit differently, a weak relationship exists.

The strongest relationship possible between two variables is one in which the value of the dependent variable for every case in one category of the independent variable differs from that of every case in another category of the independent variable. We call such a relationship a *perfect relationship* because the dependent variable is perfectly associated with the independent variable; that is, there are no exceptions to the pattern. A perfect relationship between the independent and dependent variables enables a researcher to predict accurately a case's value on the dependent variable if the value on the independent variable is known. A perfect relationship for the hair color-vote example is illustrated in Table

Table 12-6   Relationship between Party Identification and Attitude toward Military Spending: Different Table Construction

Dependent Variable: Attitude toward Military Spending	Independent Variable: Party Identification				
	Republicans	Independents	Democrats	Total	(n)
a.					
Increase	20%	40%	60%	40%	(240)
Remain same	50	40	30	40	(240)
Decrease	30	20	10	20	(120)
Total	100	100	100	100	
(n)	(200)	(200)	(200)		(600)

Source: Hypothetical data.

Table 12-7 Perfect Relationship between Hair Color and Vote

Dependent Variable: *Vote*	*Independent Variable: Hair Color* *Blonde*	*Brunette*	*Total*	*(n)*
Republican	100%	0%	33%	(500)
Democrat	0	100	67	(1,000)
Total	100	100	100	
(n)	(500)	(1,000)		(1,500)

Source: Hypothetical data.

12-7. Either a perfect positive or a perfect negative relationship between variables may exist since the direction and the strength of a relationship are two different properties.

A weak relationship would be one in which the differences in the observed values of the dependent variable for different categories of the independent variable are slight. In fact, the weakest relationship is one in which the distribution is identical for all categories of the independent variable—in other words, one in which a relationship does not exist. Table 12-3 is an example.

In reality, the strength of most relationships falls somewhere in between perfect and nonexistent relationships. How strong a relationship is may be judged from how much the column percentages in a crosstab differ as one looks across the rows (when the independent variable has been placed across the top of the table and column percentages have been calculated). In Table 12-2 (b), for example, there is a 20 percent difference in the column percentages across the rows. In Table 12-8, however, there is a 70 percent difference in the column percentages. The

Table 12-8 A Strong but Imperfect Relationship between Hair Color and Vote

Dependent Variable: *Vote*	*Independent Variable: Hair Color* *Blonde*	*Brunette*	*Total*	*(n)*
Republican	80%	10%	33%	(500)
Democrat	20	90	67	(1,000)
Total	100	100	100	
(n)	(500)	(1,000)		(1,500)

Source: Hypothetical data.

relationship in Table 12-8, then, is much stronger than the one in Table 12-2 (b) since the difference more closely approximates the 100 percent difference in the perfect relationship shown in Table 12-7. Essentially, the larger the differences across the rows, the stronger the relationship.

The statistical significance of a relationship indicates whether the observed relationship could have occurred by chance alone. The determination of statistical significance requires the calculation of a statistic called *chi-square*, which will be discussed later in this chapter. The stronger a relationship is, the more likely it is to be statistically significant. Hence, a strong relationship is especially desirable. Moreover, the larger the number of cases in a crosstab, the more likely an observed relationship is to be statistically significant. Consequently, large samples are more likely to yield statistically significant results than are small samples.

Example of a Crosstab Analysis

So far we have illustrated crosstabulation exclusively with hypothetical data. Let us take a look now at an example of an actual observed relationship between a nominal and ordinal level measure.

Raymond Wolfinger and Steven Rosenstone, in their analysis of why people vote, use crosstab analysis to test their hypothesis that the more education one has, the more likely one is to vote.[1] Table 12-9 shows that this relationship between education and voter turnout exists, that the direction is *as hypothesized*, and that the strength of the relationship is fairly strong. This is a good example of a crosstab with the independent variable down the side because it has so many categories. In this case,

Table 12-9   Relationship between Education and Voter Turnout (in percent)

| Independent Variable: Education | Dependent Variable: Turnout | | | |
	Voted	*Did Not Vote*	*Total*	*Percent of Total*
0-4 years	38	62	100	4
5-7 years	49	51	100	6
8 years	59	41	100	10
9-11 years	55	45	100	16
12 years	69	31	100	38
1-3 years college	79	21	100	14
4 years college	86	14	100	7
5+ years college	91	9	100	4

Source: Raymond E. Wolfinger and Steven J. Rosenstone, *Who Votes?* p. 17. Copyright © 1980 by Yale University. Reprinted with permission.

then, the table is percentaged across the rows, and comparisons are made down the columns.

Measures of Association

So far we have measured the relationship between two variables by inspecting a crosstabulation percentaged on the categories of the independent variable. However, if a researcher's analysis involves many crosstabs or crosstabs that are so large that a way of summarizing the information is needed, *measures of association* may be used. These measures summarize efficiently the existence, direction, strength, and statistical significance of the relationship between two variables in a crosstab.

Measures of association take the number of observations in each of the cells and combine them arithmetically to produce a summary measure of the distribution of cases. Some of these measures indicate the direction and strength of a relationship and can vary from −1 to +1. The closer the value is to 0, the weaker the relationship; the closer the value is to ±1 the stronger the relationship. The direction of the relationship is indicated by the sign + or − that precedes the statistic.

The particular measure of association that is used to summarize a crosstab depends on the level of measurement of the variables and the intent of the researcher. When both variables in a crosstab are ordinal level measures, the most frequently used measures of association are *Kendall's tau, Somer's d,* and *Goodman and Kruskal's gamma*—named after the people who developed them. Most computer programs will calculate at least these statistics for any crosstab and print the value out for the researcher's use. Tau, d, and gamma are similar, but not identical in the way they summarize the contents of a crosstab. Each of them uses pairs of cases in the crosstab and measures whether those pairs are concordant, discordant, or tied.

Let us take the relationship between education and political interest. In Table 12-10 we have placed six cases in a crosstab so that we can illustrate the identification of concordant, discordant and tied pairs. A *concordant pair* is a pair of cases in which one case is higher on both variables than the other case. The pair of observation 1 and observation 2 is concordant because 2 is higher on both education and interest than 1 is. A *discordant pair* is one in which one case is lower on one of the variables but higher on the other variable. The pair of observation 3 and observation 4 is discordant because 4 is higher on education than 3 but lower than 3 on political interest. Therefore, this pair violates the expectation that as education increases, so does political interest. A *tied pair* is a pair in which both observations are tied on at least one of the variables. The pair consisting of observations 1 and 5 is tied because both observations have the same value on education.

Table 12-10   Relationship between Education and Political Interest:
Concordant, Discordant, and Tied Pairs

Dependent Variable: Political Interest	Independent Variable: Education		
	Low	*Medium*	*High*
Low	1		4
Medium		2	
High	5	3	6

	Type		
	Concordant	*Discordant*	*Tied*
	1, 2	3, 4	1, 5
	1, 6	2, 4	1, 4
	1, 3	2, 5	2, 3
	2, 6	4, 5	3, 5
			3, 6
			4, 6
			5, 6

Source: Hypothetical data.

Tau, d, and gamma all use this evaluation of pairs to summarize the relationship in the crosstab. The basic comparison that is made is between the number of concordant and discordant pairs. If both types of pairs are equally numerous, the statistic will be 0, indicating no relationship. If concordant pairs are more numerous, there will be a positive statistic; if discordant pairs are more numerous, there will be a negative statistic. The degree to which one type of pair is more frequent than the other will result in the size of the statistic, which is indicative of the strength of the relationship. Hence if only the main diagonal is filled with observations, all of the pairs would be concordant, and the statistic would be +1—a perfect, positive relationship. If only the minor diagonal is filled with observations, all of the pairs would be discordant, and the statistic would be −1—a perfect, negative relationship.

The formulas for tau, d, and gamma are as follows:

$$\text{tau } b = \frac{P - Q}{\sqrt{(P + Q + T_2)(P + Q + T_1)}}$$

$$\text{tau } c = \frac{P - Q}{1/2(N)^2\,[(m - 1)/m]}$$

Asymmetric D $= \dfrac{P - Q}{P + Q + T_1}$ (row variable is dependent)

$= \dfrac{P - Q}{P + Q + T_2}$ (column variable is dependent)

Symmetric D $= \dfrac{P - Q}{P + Q + (T_1 + T_2)/2}$

Gamma $= \dfrac{P - Q}{P + Q}$

Where

$P =$ number of concordant pairs
$Q =$ number of discordant pairs
$T_1 =$ number of ties on row variables
$T_2 =$ number of ties on column variables
$m =$ the smaller of the number of rows and columns
$n =$ number of cases

For all of these measures, the numerator in the equation is simply the comparison of the number of concordant and discordant pairs $(P - Q)$. The denominators differ, however, with the equation for gamma ignoring ties altogether, and the equations for the others taking ties into consideration in many different ways. Tau b is suitable for square tables (that is, tables with the same number of rows and columns); tau c is suitable for nonsquare tables, and Somer's D has both a symmetric and an asymmetric version, depending on which variable in the crosstab is dependent.[2]

We can illustrate the calculation of these statistics by using the data in Table 12-11. The number of concordant pairs may be found by multiplying the number of cases in each cell by the number in each cell below and to the right, and summing the result:

$$60(100 + 80 + 50 + 100) + 30(50 + 100)$$
$$+ 50(80 + 100) + 100(100) = 43{,}300$$

The number of discordant pairs may be calculated by multiplying the number of cases in each cell by the number in each cell above and to the right and summing the result:

$$30(50 + 20) + 10(50 + 20 + 100 + 80)$$
$$+ 100(20) + 50(20 + 80) = 11{,}600$$

The number of ties for the row variable may be found by multiplying the number of cases in each cell by the number of cases in the other cells in that row, and summing the result:

$$60(50 + 20) + 50(20) + 30(100 + 80)$$
$$+ 100(80) + 10(50 + 100) + 50(100) = 25,100$$

The number of ties for the column variable is the number of cases in each cell multiplied by the number of cases in the other cells in that column, added together:

$$60(30 + 10) + 30(10) + 50(100 + 50)$$
$$+ 100(50) + 20(80 + 100) + 80(100) = 26,800$$

Once these calculations are completed, each of the measures of association can be calculated as follows:

$$\text{tau b} = \frac{43,300 - 11,600}{\sqrt{(43,300 + 11,600 + 26,800)(43,300 + 11,600 + 25,100)}}$$

$$= \frac{31,700}{80,846} = +.39$$

$$\text{tau c} = \frac{43,300 - 11,600}{1/2\ (500)^2\ [(3 - 1)/3]} = \frac{31,700}{83,333} = +.38$$

$$\text{Asymmetric D} = \frac{43,300 - 11,600}{43,300 + 11,600 + 25,100}$$

$$= \frac{31,700}{80,000} = +.40 \qquad (12.2)$$

$$\text{Symmetric D} = \frac{43,300 - 11,600}{43,300 + 11,600 + (25,100 + 26,800)/2}$$

$$= \frac{31,700}{80,850} = +.40$$

$$\text{gamma} = \frac{43,300 - 11,600}{43,300 + 11,600} = \frac{31,700}{54,900} = +.58$$

Table 12-11   Relationship between Education and Political Interest: Calculating Measures of Association

Dependent Variable:	*Independent Variable: Education*			
Political Interest	*Low*	*Medium*	*High*	*Total*
Low	60	50	20	130
Medium	30	100	80	210
High	10	50	100	160
	100	200	200	500

Source: Hypothetical data.

Tau, d, and gamma will generally take on similar but not identical values for any given crosstab. They will all have a value of 0 when there is no relationship between the two variables, and they will all have the same sign for a given relationship. Values of gamma, however, are generally higher than the other statistics and may yield a misleading overestimation of the strength of a relationship. When a researcher is uncertain about the properties of the three measures of association, tau is probably the safest measure to use.

When one or both of the variables in a crosstab is a nominal level measure, tau, d, and gamma may not be used because the identification of concordant and discordant pairs requires that the variables possess an ordering of values (one value higher than another). Hence a different measure of association, called *Goodman and Kruskal's lambda,* is generally used.

Lambda is designed to indicate whether the values of one variable tend to cluster with certain values of the other variable so that knowing a case's value for the independent variable would help one predict that case's value for the dependent variable.

The formula for lambda is

$$\text{Lambda} = \frac{L - M}{L} \qquad (12.3)$$

where L is the number of mistakes one would make in predicting the values of the dependent variable without taking the independent variable into consideration, and M is the number of mistakes one would make in predicting values of the dependent variable when the independent variable is taken into consideration. The best prediction for values of the dependent variable without knowing the value of the independent variable is the modal value for the dependent variable. The best

Table 12-12   Relationship between Race and 1984 Democratic
Primary Votes: Predicting without the Help of an
Independent Variable

Dependent Variable: 1984 Democratic Primary Vote	Independent Variable: Race				
	White	Black	Hispanic	Oriental	Total
Mondale					410
Hart					295
Jackson					295
Total	600	300	50	50	1,000

Source: Hypothetical data.

prediction for values of the dependent variable when taking the independent variable into consideration is the modal value for each category of the independent variable. Let us consider an example of how these calculations are performed.

Suppose we are interested in the relationship between race and primary votes for the 1984 Democratic presidential candidates. Table 12-12 shows a hypothetical crosstabulation of this relationship without any cases inside the cells. Our best prediction of how particular people voted, based only on the information in Table 12-12, would be that the cases in every category of race voted for Mondale since that is the most numerous (or modal) value on the dependent variable. Such a prediction would yield 410 correct predictions and 590 errors, not a very impresssive performance.

Now suppose we know something about the relationship between race and 1984 primary votes as shown in Table 12-13 (a). The primary votes of the voters in each category of race can be predicted based on how the observations are distributed or clustered within the table. We would predict that each racial group voted for the modal value in that category: all white voters would vote for Mondale, all Black voters for Jackson, all Hispanic voters for Jackson, and all Oriental voters for Mondale. This prediction would be correct in 551 of the cases (300 + 201 + 25 + 25) and incorrect in 449 of the cases. We have improved our prediction from 410 correct predictions to 551. Consequently, lambda would be

$$\Lambda = \frac{590 - 449}{590} = \frac{141}{590} = .24$$

The extent of this improvement in prediction is dependent upon the extent to which the cases in each category of the independent variable

Table 12-13 1984 Democratic Primary Votes: Predicting with the Help of an Independent Variable

Dependent Variable: 1984 Democratic Primary Vote	Independent Variable: Race					
	White	Black	Hispanic	Oriental	Total	(n)
a.						
Mondale	50%	23%	30%	50%	41.0%	(410)
Hart	40	10	20	30	29.5	(295)
Jackson	10	67	50	20	29.5	(295)
Total	100	100	100	100	100.0	
(n)	(600)	(300)	(50)	(50)		(1,000)
b.						
Mondale	100%	0%	0%	0%	60.0%	(600)
Hart	0	0	100	100	100.0	(100)
Jackson	0	100	0	0	30.0	(300)
Total	100	100	100	100	100.0	
(n)	(600)	(300)	(50)	(50)		(1,000)
c.						
Mondale	90%	80%	70%	60%	84.5%	(845)
Hart	5	0	10	40	5.5	(55)
Jackson	5	20	20	0	10.0	(100)
Total	100	100	100	100	100.0	
(n)	(600)	(300)	(50)	(50)		(1,000)

Source: Hypothetical data.

cluster within particular categories of the dependent variable. It is this improvement on the original prediction that lambda is designed to measure. If all of the cases clustered within only one category of the dependent variable for each category of the independent variable, as in Table 12-13 (b), our prediction would be perfect and lambda would be 1. Since nominal measures do not have an ordering, we cannot speak of positive or negative relationships, and lambda therefore has no sign. The direction of the relationship in this case is simply which category of the dependent variable goes with which category of the independent variable.

Although lambda is the generally preferred measure of association for relationships involving nominal level measures, it yields a misleading result in two situations. First, if the best prediction (mode) for each category of the independent variable is the same as the overall mode of the dependent variable, lambda will always be 0, even if the column percentages for the categories differ markedly across the rows, as in Table 12-13 (c). Hence inspection of the column percentages would seem to indicate a relationship between two variables even though lambda indicates no relationship. Second, whenever there are more categories for the dependent variable than there are for the independent variable, lambda cannot take on a value of 1.0, even if the cases are clustered as much as the marginals permit. As both cases show, the result of any measure of association should not be taken at face value without inspecting the distribution of the observed values upon which that measure is based.

Statistical Significance

Whether a relationship is statistically significant—that is, whether it is the result of systematic factors rather than just chance—usually cannot be determined by inspecting a crosstab; instead, a statistic called chi-square (χ^2) must be calculated. Chi-square measures whether the observed relationship in the crosstab differs significantly from the relationship we might have observed by chance alone between the two variables.

Table 12-14 presents a crosstab exhibiting the relationship between sex and attitudes toward nuclear power plants. Table 12-15, an *expected values table,* will include the number of cases that we would expect in each cell if there were no relationship between the two variables. This table has the same marginals as Table 12-14, but the cell entries will probably be different. The expected values in each cell are calculated from the marginals in Table 12-14.

Table 12-14 Relationship between Sex and Attitudes toward Nuclear Power Plants: Observed Table, Observations

Dependent Variable: Attitudes toward Nuclear Power Plants	Independent Variable: Sex					
	Male		Female		Total	(n)
Open more plants	Cell a:	200	Cell d:	100	60%	(300)
Retain status quo	Cell b:	100	Cell e:	200	30%	(300)
Close plants	Cell c:	100	Cell f:	300	40%	(400)
Total		40%		60%	100%	
(n)		(400)		(600)		(1,000)

Source: Hypothetical data.

Table 12-15 Relationship between Sex and Attitudes toward Nuclear Power Plants: Expected Values Table, Marginals Only

Dependent Variable: Attitudes toward Nuclear Power Plants	Independent Variable: Sex			
	Male	Female	Total	(n)
Open more plants			30%	(300)
Retain status quo			30%	(300)
Close plants			40%	(400)
Total	40%	60%	100%	
(n)	(400)	(600)		(1,000)

Source: Hypothetical data.

Recall that no relationship is present in a crosstab when the column percentages are identical across the rows and when the column percentages are identical to the marginal percentages at the far righthand side of the table. If there were no relationship in Table 12-15, 30 percent of both males and females would be in favor of opening more plants, 30 percent of both males and females would be in favor of retaining the status quo, and 40 percent of both males and females would be in favor of closing plants. The distribution of cases in the crosstab, then, would look like Table 12-16.

In general, the expected number of cases in each cell may be calculated by multiplying the marginals for each cell together and dividing by the total sample size. Hence the expected values in Table 12-16 would be:

$$\text{Cell a: } (300)(400)/1000 = 120$$
$$\text{Cell b: } (300)(400)/1000 = 120$$
$$\text{Cell c: } (400)(400)/1000 = 160$$
$$\text{Cell d: } (300)(600)/1000 = 180$$
$$\text{Cell e: } (300)(600)/1000 = 180$$
$$\text{Cell f: } (400)(600)/1000 = 240$$

The next step is to calculate how much difference there is between the observed table (Table 12-14) and the expected values table with cell frequencies (Table 12-16). This will tell us how far the observed relationship is from the expected distribution if there were no relationship between the two variables. To do this, subtract the number of cases in each cell of Table 12-16 from the number of cases in the corresponding cell of Table 12-14, square the difference, and then divide the difference by the number of cases in that cell in Table 12-16. These calculations

Table 12-16   Relationship between Sex and Attitudes toward Nuclear
Power Plants: Expected Values Table, Cell Frequencies

Dependent Variable Attitudes toward Nuclear Power Plants	Independent Variable: Sex			
	Male	Female	Total	(n)
Open more plants	Cell a: 120	Cell d: 180	30%	(300)
Retain status quo	Cell b: 120	Cell e: 180	30%	(300)
Close plants	Cell c: 160	Cell f: 240	40%	(400)
Total	40%	60%	100%	
(n)	(400)	(600)		(1,000)

Source: Hypothetical data.

should be done separately for each cell in the two tables and then summed across all the cells to yield the chi-square value. The formula for chi-square, then, is

$$\chi^2 = \frac{(O - E)^2}{E}$$

For Table 12-14 and Table 12-16, the calculations would look like this:

Cell	Observed Value	Expected Value	Difference	(Difference)²	(Difference)² Expected Value
a	200	120	80	6400	53.33
b	100	120	−20	400	3.33
c	100	160	−60	3600	22.50
d	100	180	−80	6400	35.56
e	200	180	20	400	2.22
f	300	240	60	3600	15.00
				Sum	131.94

The value of chi-square in this example is 131.94. To determine if the relationship is statistically significant, we must calculate a number called the *degrees of freedom,* which is the number of columns in a table minus one (C − 1) times the number of rows in a table minus one (R − 1) or in this case (2 − 1) (3 − 1) or 2. Then we must look up the value of our chi-square on a chi-square table to determine whether it is high enough to indicate a statistically significant relationship. For a given value of chi-square and degrees of freedom, the chi-square table will indicate the probability that a χ^2 value of at least that magnitude would have been observed if there were no relationship between the two variables (or, in other words, if the *null hypothesis* were true). The lower this probability the better; to reject the null hypothesis the probability of the null hypothesis being true generally must be less than .01. The value of chi-square in our example, 131.94, is well above the criterion value, 9.21, and therefore the relationship is statistically significant at the .01 level.

Researchers generally want their chi-square value to be large so that they can reject the null hypothesis. Large values of chi-square result when the observed and expected tables are quite different and when the sample size upon which the tables are based is large. A weak relationship among a large sample may attain statistical significance while a strong relationship within a small sample may not. In other words, statistical significance is not the same as strength or substantive significance, and chi-square values should not be used as a measure of substantive importance. Rather, chi-square values tell us the probability that an observed relationship could have occurred by chance.

Difference of Means Test and Analysis of Variance

Crosstabulation is the appropriate analysis technique when both variables are nominal or ordinal level measures. When the independent variable is nominal or ordinal and the dependent variable is interval or ratio, however, a crosstab would have far too many columns or rows to permit a straightforward and meaningful analysis. Therefore, two similar analysis techniques—the *difference of means test* and *analysis of variance*—are used.

Both of these techniques help test the researcher's hypothesis that the dependent variable, which is measured at the interval or ratio level, is related to the independent variable. First the cases are divided into categories based on the values of the independent variable. Then, if the values of the dependent variable are 1) less varied within each category of the independent variable than they were before *and* 2) quite different in general for different values of the independent variable, a relationship exists.

A simple example will illustrate this point. Suppose we have hypothesized that there is a relationship between sex and the amount of money contributed to political campaigns. And suppose that we measure these two variables for a sample of 10 people and receive the following results:

Sex	Money Contributed (in thousands of dollars)	Sex	Money Contributed (in thousands of dollars)
Male	10	Male	15
Female	8	Male	20
Female	5	Female	2
Male	10	Female	5
Female	10	Male	15

Now if we ignore the independent variable, we can see that the mean amount of money for all 10 observations is 10 (thousand dollars) and that the variation around that mean looks like this:

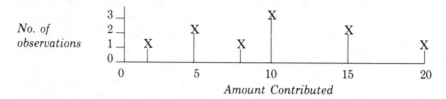

It is this variation (the actual variance is 26.8) that we are trying to explain.

Now let us consider whether the independent variable helps us account for this variation. The independent variable is clearly a nominal level measure. If we divide the cases into two groups based on this measure, we find that the original variation is distributed across the two groups in the following way:

Males	*Females*
10	2
10	5
15	5
15	8
20	10
Total = 70	Total = 30
$\overline{X}$ = 14	$\overline{X}$ = 6
s^2 = 14	s^2 = 7.6

The average amount of money contributed by the two groups is quite different, and the variation in the amount contributed is much less within both groups than it was originally. In other words, the independent variable has been helpful in grouping the observations into categories that are different from each other on the dependent variable and that contain observations that are similar to each other. The analysis has revealed a pattern in the data and has reduced the amount of unexplained variation.

This is the basic logic of both analysis techniques. We begin with a certain amount of unexplained variance in the dependent variable. We use the measurement of the independent variable to divide the cases into analysis groups and then determine if the groups created are dissimilar from each other and more homogeneous than the original data were. The difference of means test involves comparing the means of the groups created with the independent variable to see if the difference is statistically significant. The analysis of variance involves comparing the variance in each of the analysis groups with the total variance in the dependent variable to see how much variance has been explained by the independent variable.

Edward Tufte's study of automobile inspection policy and traffic fatality rates contains a good example of analyzing the relationships between a nominal and a ratio level measure.[3] Recall that Tufte was interested in whether states with mandatory auto inspections experienced lower auto fatality rates. His initial test of this hypothesis was to measure the relationship between auto inspection policy (a nominal level independent variable with only two categories) and auto fatality rates (a ratio level dependent variable).

Tufte began with a distribution of 50 observed values on the dependent variable, motor-vehicle deaths per 100,000 people. These observed values had a mean value of 29.8 deaths per 100,000 and a variance of 60.55. He then divided the cases (states) into two categories: states with and states without mandatory automobile inspections. This resulted in mean death rates of 26.1 for the 18 states with inspections (with a variance of 66.07) and 31.9 for the 32 states without inspections (with a variance of 45.46). Consequently, the two analysis groups defined by the values of the independent variable differed somewhat. Furthermore, visual inspection of the distributions within the two categories suggested that the variation within each group was less than it was for the whole set of observations. (See Figure 1-1.) Initially, then, it appears that dividing the cases into the two analysis groups was worthwhile and that there is a relationship between the two variables.

Since the number of cases analyzed is not usually as small as it was in Tufte's case, visual inspection of the distribution of cases in the analysis groups is not usually adequate. Furthermore, more precise measures of the direction, strength, and statistical significance of the relationships would be desirable. Therefore, both the difference of means test and the analysis of variance have been developed to provide a more precise measure of relationships between variables of this type.

The initial step in the difference of means test and the analysis of variance is to calculate the mean and variance for the cases on the dependent variable. This variance is called the *total variance*. The cases are then divided into two or more groups based on the independent variable and the mean and variance for each group are calculated. If the means of the groups are quite different, and the possibility that the difference in the means has occurred because of chance can be eliminated, then a relationship between the two variables is indicated by the difference of means test.

One can get an idea of the direction and strength of the relationship revealed by these procedures by noting which group (or groups) has the higher mean and by comparing the variances of the analysis groups with the total variance for all the observations. In Tufte's case, the direction of the relationship is that those states with mandatory auto inspections have fewer traffic fatalities, and the strength of the relationship is indicated by the variation left in the categories of the independent variable. However, a more precise measure of the relationship is given by an analysis of variance and a correlation called *eta-squared*.

Eta-squared is similar to lambda for a crosstabulation. It represents the amount of reduction that has occurred in the total variance as a result of dividing the cases into groups based on the independent variable. To calculate eta-squared, take the total variance, subtract from it a weighted sum of the variances left in the analysis groups (the *unexplained variance*), and divide this difference by the total variance. The numerator of this ratio is the *explained variance,* and the higher this number, the stronger the relationship:

$$E^2 = \frac{\text{total SS} - \text{unexplained SS}}{\text{total SS}} = \frac{\text{explained SS}}{\text{total}} \qquad (12.6)$$

Where SS = sum of squares.

In the sex-money example, the total variance was 26.8. The unexplained variance left after the cases were divided into males and females was an average of the two variances left (14 and 7.60 weighted by the number of cases in each group):

$$[5(14) + 5(7.6)]/10 = (70 + 38)/10 = 108/10 = 10.8$$

The unexplained variance is then subtracted from the total variance to get the explained variance, and the result is divided by the total variance:

$$\frac{26.8 - 10.8}{26.8} = \frac{16.0}{26.8} = .60 \qquad (12.8)$$

This value of eta-squared means that 60 percent of the variance in the dependent variable has been explained by the independent variable, indicating a fairly strong relationship.

In Tufte's analysis of auto inspection policy the total variance with which he began was 60.55. The unexplained variance left after the states were divided into categories was

$$\frac{(45.56)(32) + (66.07)(18)}{50} = 52.94 \qquad (12.9)$$

The explained variance, as a proportion of the total variance, was

$$\frac{60.55 - 52.94}{60.55} = .13 \qquad (12.10)$$

Eta-squared was .13, indicating a weak relationship, with 13 percent of the variance in the dependent variable explained by the independent variable. Remember that the closer eta-squared is to 0 the weaker the relationship, and the closer it is to 1 the stronger the relationship.

Both a difference of means test and an analysis of variance allow us to assess the direction and strength of a relationship between a nominal or ordinal level independent variable and an interval or ratio level dependent variable. The relative means for the analysis groups tell us the direction of the relationship, while the eta-squared, derived from the comparison of the explained and unexplained variance, tells us the strength of the relationship. In an analysis of variance, the strength of the relationship is indicated by the amount of variance left in the dependent variable when the cases are divided into groups based on the independent variable.

The statistical significance of a relationship also may be determined with a difference of means test and an analysis of variance. The test involves determining when the difference in the means on the dependent variable for the analysis groups could have occurred by chance. The larger the difference in means relative to the variances involved and the larger the sample size, the greater the chance that a given difference will be statistically significant.

Statistical significance may be calculated with a statistic called the *F ratio*. Like chi-square for a crosstab, the F ratio indicates the probability of the null hypothesis being true. The F ratio must be greater than a particular criterion level to show a statistically significant relationship between the independent and dependent variables. The criterion level depends upon the degrees of freedom (calculated from the sample size and the number of analysis groups) and the probability of rejecting the null hypothesis. Once the F-ratio is calculated, then the result may be compared with an F-ratio table to decide whether to accept or reject the null hypothesis in the population.[4]

Regression and Correlation Analysis

When both the independent and dependent variables are interval or ratio level measures, regression and correlation analysis are the standard techniques for measuring relationships and testing hypotheses. Both procedures are similar to crosstabulation, the difference of means test, and analysis of variance; although the terms regression and correlation may seem imposing, the analyses are really quite easy to understand.

Regression Analysis

To illustrate the technique of regression analysis, we will test the hypothesis that there is a positive relationship between income and the number of times people personally contact public officials. We will

Table 12-17   Relationship between Income and Contacts with Public
Officials: A Regression Analysis

Case	Independent Variable: Income	Dependent Variable: Number of Contacts
a	$ 3,000	0
b	15,000	3
c	42,000	3
d	22,000	2
e	10,000	1
f	85,000	7
g	30,000	4
h	70,000	6
i	100,000	4
j	55,000	6

Source: Hypothetical data.

consider just the first 10 cases in a sample of 500 people. The values on
the independent and dependent variables for these 10 cases are presented
in Table 12-17.

The first step is to display all of the cases in the sample so that we
can see each case's values on both the independent and dependent
variables. In crosstabulation, this is done by putting each case into its
proper category or cell in a table. In regression analysis, a graph called a
scattergram is drawn and each case is placed at the point that corresponds to the value of the independent and dependent variables for that
case.

The first 10 cases in our example are presented in Figure 12-1. The
values of the independent variable are placed along the bottom of the
graph on the *X-axis,* and the values of the dependent variable are placed
along the side of the graph on the *Y-axis.* Each case is then placed at the
point that corresponds to the intersection of that case's values on the
independent (X-axis) and dependent (Y-axis) variables and a line is
drawn through the points to show the overall pattern of the data. This *regression line* is usually calculated for you by a computer program in a
way that *minimizes* the vertical distances between the data points and
the line drawn. This line will be the best *linear* representation of the
relationship between the two variables.

Any straight line may be represented by the *regression equation*

$$Y = bX + a$$

Where

    Y = any case's value on the dependent variable

    X = any case's value on the independent variable

    a = the *Y-intercept* or the place at which the line crosses the Y-axis

    b = the *slope* of the line across the graph

As the regression equation indicates, there are two unknowns, a and b. From the observed values, b may be calculated directly:

$$b = \frac{N\Sigma XY - (\Sigma X)(\Sigma Y)}{N\Sigma X^2 - (\Sigma X)^2} \tag{12.12}$$

Where

    X = the observed values of the independent variable

    Y = the observed values of the dependent variable

    Σ = summation

Once b has been calculated, then it is a relatively simple step to calculate a, since

$$a = \bar{Y} - b\bar{X}$$

After b and a have both been determined, the regression line that minimizes the squared distances between observed and predicted values of Y may be drawn. Computer programs designed to perform regression analysis accomplish these calculations quickly and accurately.

Figure 12-1   Scattergram of Relationship between Income and Political Contacts

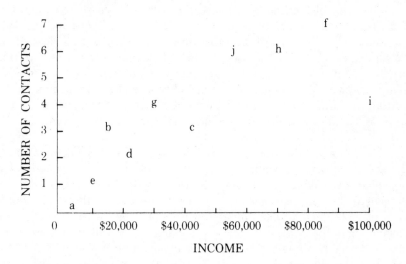

Source: Hypothetical data.

Figure 12-2   Regression Line for Relationship between Income and Political Contacts

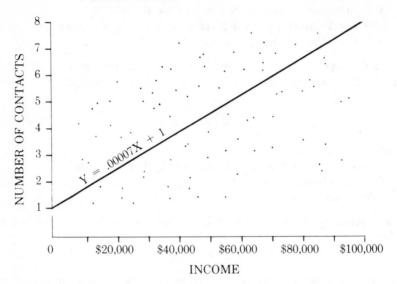

Let us suppose that after we have graphed all 500 data points testing the relationship between income and contacts with public officials, we end up with the *regression line* shown in Figure 12-2 and a regression equation of Y = .00007X + 1. What does this tell us about the relationship between the two variables and the hypothesis linking the two?

The slope of the line (also called the *regression coefficient)* and the Y-intercept tell us the nature of the relationship between the two variables. The Y-intercept tells us what the value of the dependent variable should be when the value of the independent variable is 0. In this case, a Y-intercept of 1 tells us that when a person's income (the independent variable) is 0, that person is likely to have contacted a public official one time (that is, the dependent variable at that point on the graph is 1). This is the place at which the regression line crosses the Y-axis.

The slope of the line tells us how much the dependent variable changes when the independent variable changes or how much change will take place in values of Y for every change in X of 1 unit. In this case, the slope of .00007 tells us that for every change in X of $1, there is a change in Y of .00007. Or if we compare two people—one with $15,000 more income than the other—the expected value of Y will be different by (.00007 x 15,000) or 1.05. Therefore, we expect a difference of $15,000 in income to be associated with a difference of about one personal contact with a public official. The slope shows how responsive, in a mathematical sense, the dependent variable is to changes in the independent variable.

Finally, the sign of the slope tells us the direction of the relationship. A *positive sign* indicates a positive relationship: as the values of one of the variables increase, the values of the other variable increase. A *negative sign* indicates a negative relationship: as the values of one of the variables increase, the values of the other variable decrease. Because most graphs are drawn with the lowest values for both variables at the bottom and left-hand side, a positive relationship is usually represented by a line that rises from lower left to upper right, and a negative relationship is represented by a line that falls from upper left to lower right.

The regression equation contains a lot of useful information. It gives the expected value of the dependent variable for any value of the independent variable and the general relationship between the two variables. In this case we could substitute any value of X (income) into the equation and calculate the expected value of Y (number of personal contacts with public officials). For example, someone who made $40,000 would have contacted a public official 3.8 times—(.00007 x 40,000) + 1.

The regression coefficient is not a good measure of the strength of the relationship between interval level measures because it is dependent upon the units in which the variables are measured. The regression coefficient in the income-political contacts example looks very small: .00007. But it is a small number because the independent variable is measured in terms of dollars, and most of the observed values of income were in the thousands of dollars range. If we measured income in thousands of dollars instead of dollars, the regression equation would change to $Y = .07X + 1$. This change in the regression coefficient does not mean that the relationship is any stronger; it means only that the units of measurement have changed. Although the regression coefficient indicates how much change in the dependent variable is generally associated with change in the independent variable, it does not indicate how strong that association is. *Correlation analysis,* discussed in the next section, measures the strength of the relationships between the independent and dependent variables.

A good example of the use of regression analysis may be found in a recent investigation of the performance of the 15 regional governments in Italy.[5] The researchers were interested in explaining why some of the Italian governments performed their governmental duties better than others did. First they devised a measure of institutional performance (the dependent variable) for each of the 15 governments based on 8 indicators of legislative activity, bureaucratic efficiency, programmatic innovation, and governmental stability. Then they measured the relationships between this measure and a number of possible explanations for governmental performance. One of the researchers' hypotheses was that performance would depend on socioeconomic development. Using per capita income, literacy, nonagricultural employment, and television and automobile ownership as measures of socioeconomic development, they graphed the relationship between development and performance, shown in Figure 12-3.

Clearly, a positive relationship exists between socioeconomic development and institutional performance. Although there are a few cases distant from the regression line, the best approximation of the data appears to be a straight line.

Figure 12-3 Regression Line for Relationship between Socioeconomic Development and Institutional Performance of Italian Regional Governments

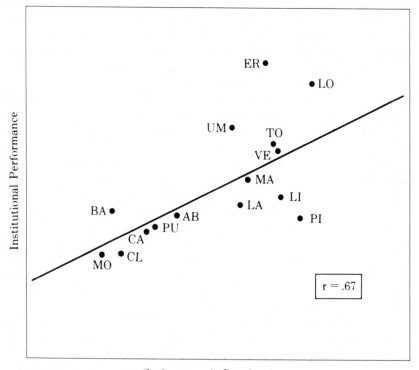

Socioeconomic Development

Key: AB = Abruzzo, BA = Basilicata, CA = Campania, CL = Calabria, ER = Emilia-Romagna, LA = Lazio, LI = Liguria, LO = Lombardia, MA = Marche, MO = Molise, PI = Piemonte, PU = Puglia, TO = Toscana, UM = Umbria, VE = Veneto.

Source: Robert D. Putnam et al., "Explaining Institutional Success: The Case of Italian Regional Government," *American Political Science Review* 77 (March 1983): 64. Reprinted with permission.

Since the researchers provide neither the regression equation that corresponds to the regression line nor the units of the measures along the axes, it is impossible to tell what the exact mathematical relationship is between the measure of socioeconomic development and institutional performance. This is probably because the measures are indices consisting of many different individual attributes; consequently, they lack a straightforward, intuitive meaning. Although the researchers have uncovered a fairly strong, positive relationship between development and performance, this does not necessarily mean that one is the cause of the other. Much more analysis is necessary before a causal relationship could be established.

Another good example of the use of regression analysis is Ted Robert Gurr's research concerning why some nations exhibit more domestic violence and turmoil than others do.[6] He hypothesized that there is a relationship between the size of a country's internal security force and the amount of civil strife. Figure 12-4 indicates that a relationship exists (the data approximate a straight line), that the relationship is positive (as the size of the coercive forces increases, so does the magnitude of civil

Figure 12-4   Regression Line for Relationship between Coercive Force Size and Magnitude of Civil Strife in 21 Western Communities

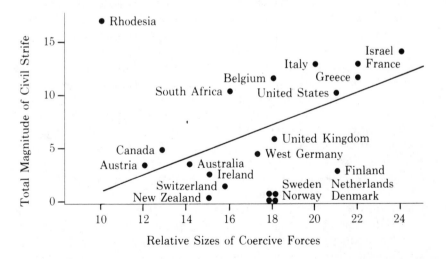

Source: Ted Robert Gurr, "A Comparative Study of Civil Strife," in Hugh Davis Graham and Ted Robert Gurr, eds., *Violence in America: Historical and Comparative Perspectives, A Report to the National Commission on the Causes and Prevention of Violence* (Washington, D.C.: U.S. Government Printing Office, 1969), 477.

strife), and that the relationship is fairly strong (most of the data points are fairly close to the regression line).

Again remember that the discovery of a positive relationship between the size of coercive forces and the magnitude of civil strife does not necessarily mean that one is causing the other. As Gurr himself concludes:

> The correspondence of force size and levels of strife does not necessarily imply a simple causal connection between the two. The military establishment is relatively large in most Western countries because of cold-war tension, not because of the threat of internal disorder. Nonetheless, the investment of large portions of national budgets in armaments; military conscription policies; and involvement in foreign conflict have directly generated widespread popular opposition in the United States and France in the past decade, and may have provided a similar though less dramatic impetus to public protest in other Western nations.[7]

Correlation Analysis

A straight line can be drawn through almost any set of data points, and as long as the slope of the line drawn is not 0, we can say that there is a relationship between the independent and dependent variables. However, that does not necessarily mean that the line is a close approximation of the data points or that the relationship is a statistically significant one. It may be that the line drawn is the best one possible, but that the data points are so scattered that no line would come close to very many of them. The test of the strength of a relationship is how close the data points are to the regression line that is drawn. The further away from the line the data points are, the weaker the relationship. The closer to the line the data points are, the stronger the relationship. If all of the data points are right on the regression line, then there is a perfect linear relationship between the two variables.

With hundreds of data points it is often difficult to tell visually exactly how close the regression line is to the points and how strong the relationship is between the variables. Consequently, there is a statistic, called the *Pearson product-moment correlation* (r), that may be calculated for any regression line. It tells you at a glance how good the fit is between the data points and the line. This correlation varies from 0 for no relationship to ±1 for a perfect relationship. It is calculated from the vertical distances between each of the data points and the regression line.

The product-moment correlation is very similar to eta-squared. It is based on the variance in the dependent variable (*total variance*) that we are trying to explain. We attempt to explain as much of the variance as possible by drawing a regression line through the points and approximating the values of the dependent variable from the values of the independent variable. The squared vertical distances from the data points to this line represent the variance in the dependent variable that is not accounted for by the regression line. The sum of these squared distances for all the data points is the *unexplained variance*.

The *square* of the product-moment correlation (r^2) shows exactly how much variance has been explained by the independent variable. Therefore, r^2 is exactly analogous to eta-squared; the closer it is to $+1$, the stronger the relationship.

$$r = \sqrt{\frac{1 - \text{unexplained variance}}{\text{total variance}}} \quad \text{or} \quad \sqrt{\frac{1 - \sum_{i=1}^{N} (Y_i - Y_p)^2}{\sum_{i=1}^{N} (Y_i - \bar{Y})^2}}$$

(12.14)

$$r^2 = \frac{1 - \text{unexplained variance}}{\text{total variance}} \quad \text{or} \quad \frac{1 - \sum_{i=1}^{N} (Y_i - Y_p)^2}{\sum_{i=1}^{N} (Y_i - \bar{Y})^2}$$

Where
  Y_i = actual observations
  Y_p = predicted observations

It is also possible to calculate r directly from the observed data:

$$r = \frac{N\Sigma XY - (\Sigma X)(\Sigma Y)}{[N\Sigma X^2 - (\Sigma X)^2][N\Sigma Y^2 - (\Sigma Y)^2]}$$

(12.15)

As we mentioned earlier, the slope of a regression line and the correlation coefficient for a regression line indicate two quite different things. The slope shows how much change in the dependent variable is associated with change in the independent variable; the correlation coefficient shows how much variance in the dependent variable is explained with the independent variable. It is quite possible to have a steep slope but a low correlation, indicating that the dependent variable changes a lot for every unit change in the independent variable but that the regression line does not approximate the data very well. It is also possible to have a very small slope but a very high correlation, indicating that the dependent variable does not change very much for every unit change in the independent variable but that the regression line is a good representation of the data.

Whether or not one expects a large slope is heavily dependent upon the variables involved and the units of measurement being used; almost always, however, researchers hope that the correlation is high; that is, that the regression line shows a close fit with the data points.

Figure 12-5 illustrates six different types of analytical results using regression and correlation analysis: a weak and positive relationship with a small slope (a), a weak and positive relationship with a large slope (b), a weak and negative relationship with a large slope (c), a strong and positive relationship with a small slope (d), a strong and negative relationship with a large slope (e), and no relationship between the

Figure 12-5   Six Different Types of Regression and Correlation Results

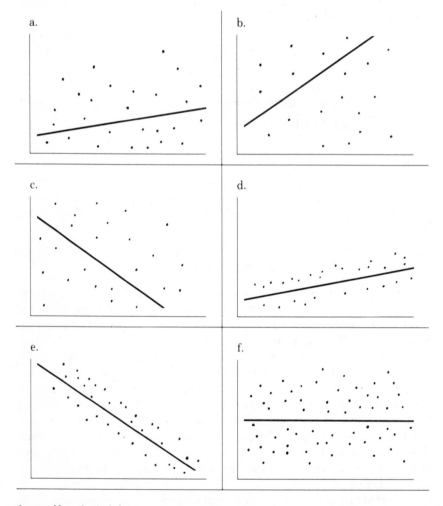

Source: Hypothetical data.

independent and dependent variables (f). In this last example, the value of the dependent variable is the same no matter what the value is of the independent variable.

The correlation coefficient also may be used to indicate the statistical significance of the observed relationship. Once the coefficient has been calculated, it can be checked against the appropriate table to determine if it is above or below the criterion level of statistical significance. This criterion level is dependent upon the size of the sample from which the data are drawn, and it indicates the probability of the null hypothesis being true. Again remember that statistical significance is not the same as substantive importance; very weak relationships observed in very large samples readily attain statistical significance.

Researchers often use correlation analysis to determine the strength of the relationships among many different variables. They are less concerned with the mathematical function associating independent and dependent variables than with how much variance in a dependent variable is explained by a number of independent variables. The results of a correlation analysis are often used to eliminate some variables from an analysis so that those most useful in accounting for the dependent variable can be studied more easily. A *correlation matrix* shows relationships *among* variables, whereas a scattergram only shows each individual relationship.

Gurr constructed a correlation matrix to test the relationship between a number of variables—such as economic deprivation, coercive force size, past strife levels, and system legitimacy—and civil strife. The matrix, presented in Table 12-18, shows the strength of the relationships among the independent variables, among the different measures of the dependent variable, and between the independent and dependent variables. Gurr then used this initial test of his hypothesis to guide him in the search for a more parsimonious explanatory model of civil strife, by eliminating from further analysis those variables weakly related to civil strife.

Another example of correlational analysis may be found in John McConahay's analysis of attitudes toward busing. As noted in Chapter 1, McConahay was interested in the relationships between a person's personal involvement in busing, racial attitudes, and attitudes toward busing.

His initial analysis of these relationships involved calculating the product-moment correlation between a number of independent variables and the dependent variable (attitudes toward busing). The correlations, reported in Table 12-19, led McConahay to an initial conclusion that it is racial attitudes rather than personal involvement that are associated with attitudes toward busing.

Table 12-18 Correlation Matrix Showing the Correlates of Civil Strife [a]

Variable [b]	1	2	3	4	5	6	7	8	9	10	11	12	13	14
1 Economic deprivation (+)		48	83	-02	-17	-16	-36	-09	26	32	34	31	25	44
2 Political deprivation (+)			88	08	-18	03	-37	-20	33	27	44	18	30	38
3 Short-term deprivation (+)				04	-20	-07	-42	-17	34	34	46	28	32	48
4 Persisting deprivation (+)					-04	-21	-14	-37	-04	17	29	26	27	36
5 Legitimacy (−)						25	48	02	-05	-15	-29	-23	-29	-37
6 Coercive force size (±)							53	27	31	04	-23	-11	-01	-14
7 Coercive potential (−)								41	-14	-37	-44	-39	-35	-51
8 Institutionalization (−)									-19	-40	-35	-23	-26	-33
9 Past strife levels (+)										41	24	16	30	30
10 Facilitation (+)											42	57	30	67
11 Magnitude of conspiracy												30	32	59
12 Magnitude of internal war													17	79
13 Magnitude of turmoil														61
14 Total magnitude of strife														

Source: Ted Gurr, "A Causal Model of Civil Strife: A Comparative Analysis Using New Indices," *American Political Science Review* 2 (December 1968): 1117. Reprinted with permission.

[a] Product moment correlation coefficients, multiplied by 100. Underlined r's are significant, for n = 114, at the .01 level. Correlations between 18 and 23, inclusive, are significant at the .05 level.

[b] The proposed relationships between the independent variables, nos. 1 to 10, and the strife measures are shown in parentheses, the ± for coercive force size signifying a proposed curvilinear relationship. Examination of the r's between the independent and dependent variables, in the box, shows that all are in the predicted direction with the anticipated exception of coercive force size, and that all but one are significant at the .05 level.

Table 12-19 Relationship between Self-Interest Measures, Racial
Attitudes, and Attitudes toward Busing: Product-
Moment Correlations

Independent Variable	Correlation
Parents of school-age children	.12[a]
Parents of public-school children	.10[b]
Parents of bused children	.03
Homeowner	.09[b]
Relatives in area	.04
Lived in area long time	.09[b]
Happy with neighborhood	−.06[c]
Intent to stay in area	−.01
Self Interest Index	.11[a]
Modern racism	.51[a]
Old-fashioned racism	.36[a]
Affect for blacks	−.15[a]

[a] $p \leq .001$
[b] $p \leq .01$
[c] $p \leq .05$

Source: John B. McConahay, "Self-Interest versus Racial Attitudes as Correlates of Anti-Busing Attitudes in Louisville: Is It the Buses or the Blacks?" *Journal of Politics* 44 (August 1982): 711. Reprinted with permission.

Other Issues

Before concluding our discussion of correlation and regression analysis, we will address two remaining issues. First, the information contained in a regression analysis may help a researcher analyze variation in the dependent variable. Recall that the regression equation indicates the expected value of the dependent variable for each case, given that case's value on the independent variable. The difference between this expected value and the actual observed value is called the *residual* (the variation left over), and it measures how well the regression line fits the data points. Residuals also may be used to explain why the cases did not take on the value for the dependent variable that was predicted from the regression line. The researcher might be able to identify a second independent variable that could account for a portion of the unexplained variance left by the first independent variable. (We examine this procedure in more detail in Chapter 13.)

In our example of the relationship between income and personal contacts with public officials, consider the case of a person who earned $80,000 and made three contacts. According to the regression equation describing the relationship between income and personal contacts, we would expect such a person to have made 6.6 contacts. Consequently, this person made 3.3 fewer contacts than expected; -3.3 is the residual of this case. This residual might stimulate our curiosity. Why did this particular person contact public officials so many fewer times than his income alone would have predicted? This question might lead us to analyze all of those who contacted public officials fewer times than expected and to develop a hypothesis that would explain this discrepancy. In this way residuals may be used to extend a researcher's analysis and provide a more complete understanding of the phenomenon under investigation. Residual scores may themselves become dependent variables in hypotheses designed to explain the amount of discrepancy between the expected and observed values for some dependent variable.

The second issue we need to address is the deceptive simplicity of linear regression. A computer can draw a straight line through almost any set of data points, yielding a regression equation purporting to capture the relationship between two variables. However, some data points may be better described by a parabola, sine curve, U-curve, or J-curve, than by a straight line. If a researcher fails to consider these other possibilities without first inspecting the graph of the data points and has a computer calculate only the best-fitting straight line, a more representative characterization of the relationship may never be discovered.

An actual example of a curvilinear relationship may be found in Wolfinger and Rosenstone's study of voter turnout. They hypothesized a relationship between age and voter turnout.[8] A scattergram of this relationship indicated that there was, indeed, a relationship, but that it was a curvilinear rather than a linear one, as Figure 12-6 shows. It is the middle-aged who vote the most frequently, and the young and old alike who vote the least frequently. Therefore, a straight line would not have been the best approximation of the relationship between age and turnout.

Like regression analysis, correlational analysis can disguise strong, nonlinear relationships. All the correlation coefficient indicates is the fit between the data points and the best-fitting straight line. Drawing a straight line through a set of data points better represented with a curve will often result in a very low product-moment correlation, perhaps leading the researcher to ignore a nonlinear relationship. Had the researcher checked the scattergram upon which the correlation coefficient was calculated, it would have become evident that a curvilinear relationship was a better representation of the data points. Researchers are well advised, therefore, to inspect the scattergrams corresponding to every regression equation and product-moment correlation that they calculate.

Figure 12-6 A Curvilinear Relationship between Age and Vote Turnout in 1972

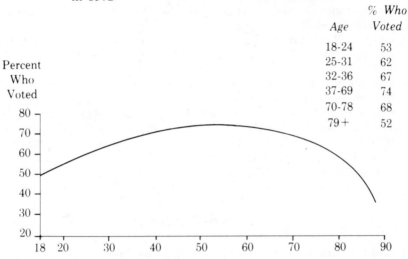

Age	% Who Voted
18-24	53
25-31	62
32-36	67
37-69	74
70-78	68
79+	52

Source: Raymond E. Wolfinger and Steven J. Rosenstone, *Who Votes?* p. 38. Copyright ©1980 by Yale University. Reprinted with permission.

Conclusion

In this chapter we have shown how to measure the existence, direction, strength, and statistical significance of relationships between two variables. The particular techniques used—crosstabulation, difference of means test, analysis of variance, regression analysis, and correlation analysis—depend, in part, on the levels of measurement—nominal, ordinal, interval, or ratio—of the independent and dependent variables. Just because a relationship is present, however, does not mean that a cause of the dependent variable has been discovered, as Chapter 13 will explain in more detail.

Notes

1. Raymond E. Wolfinger and Steven J. Rosenstone, *Who Votes?* (New Haven, Conn.: Yale University Press, 1980).
2. For further information about the calculation of each of these statistics, see Hubert M. Blalock, Jr., *Social Statistics,* rev. 2d ed. (New York: McGraw-Hill, 1979).

3. Edward R. Tufte, *Data Analysis for Politics and Policy* (Englewood Cliffs, N.J.: Prentice-Hall, 1974).
4. A more complete discussion of the calculation of the F ratio may be found in Blalock, *Social Statistics,* chap. 16.
5. Robert D. Putnam et al., "Explaining Institutional Success: The Case of Italian Regional Government," *American Political Science Review* 77 (March 1983): 55-74.
6. Ted Robert Gurr, "A Comparative Study of Civil Strife," in Hugh Davis Graham and Ted Robert Gurr, eds., *Violence in America: Historical and Comparative Perspecives* (New York: New American Library, 1969). See also Ted Gurr, "A Causal Model of Civil Strife: A Comparative Analysis Using New Indices," *American Political Science Review* 2 (December 1968): 1104-24.
7. Gurr, "A Comparative Study," 580-81.
8. Wolfinger and Rosenstone, *Who Votes?*

Terms Introduced

Analysis of variance. A technique for measuring the relationship between one nominal or ordinal level variable and one interval or ratio level variable.

Chi-square. A measure used with crosstabulation to determine if a relationship is statistically significant.

Correlation matrix. A table showing the correlations (usually Pearson product-moment correlations) among a number of variables.

Crosstabulation. A technique for measuring the relationship between nominal and ordinal level measures.

Degrees of freedom. A measure used in conjunction with chi-square and other measures to determine if a relationship is statistically significant.

Difference of means test. A technique for measuring the relationship between one nominal or ordinal level variable and one interval or ratio level variable.

Direction of a relationship. An indication of which values of the dependent variable are associated with which values of the independent variable.

Eta-squared. A measure of association used with the analysis of variance that indicates the proportion of the variance in the dependent variable explained by the variance in the independent variable.

Explained variance. That portion of the variation in a dependent variable that is accounted for by the variation in the independent variable(s).

F ratio. A measure used with the analysis of variance to determine if a relationship is statistically significant.

Goodman and Kruskal's gamma. A measure of association between ordinal level variables.

Goodman and Kruskal's lambda. A measure of association between one nominal or ordinal level variable and one nominal level variable.

Kendall's tau. A measure of association between ordinal level variables.

Measures of association. Statistics that summarize the relationship between two variables.

Negative relationship. When high values of one variable are associated with low values of another variable.

Pearson product-moment correlation. The statistic computed from a regression analysis that indicates the strength of the relationship between two interval or ratio level variables.

Positive relationship. When high values of one variable are associated with high values of another variable.

Regression. A technique for measuring the relationship between two interval or ratio level variables.

Regression coefficient. Another name for the slope of a regression equation.

Regression equation. The mathematical formula describing the relationship between two interval or ratio level variables.

Relationship. When the values of one variable covary with or are dependent upon the values of another variable.

Residual. In a regression analysis, the difference between the observed and predicted values of Y (the dependent variable).

Scattergram. A technique for displaying graphically the relationship between two interval or ratio level variables.

Slope. The part of a regression equation that shows how much change in the value of Y (the dependent variable) corresponds to a 1-unit change in the value of X (the independent variable).

Somer's d. A measure of association between ordinal level variables.

Statistical significance. An indication of whether an observed relationship could have occurred by chance.

Strength of a relationship. An indication of how consistently the values of a dependent variable are associated with the values of an independent variable.

Total variance. The variation in a dependent variable that a researcher is attempting to account for.

Unexplained variance. That portion of the variation in a dependent variable that is not accounted for by the variation in the independent variable(s).

Y-intercept. The value of Y (the dependent variable) in a regression equation when the value of X (the independent variable) is 0.

Exercises

1. A researcher interested in the relationship between city size and mass transit systems takes a random sample of 100 cities of varying sizes and finds that 20 of the small cities have transit systems, and 30 do not; 12 of the mid-size cities have transit systems, and 18 do not; 8 of the large cities have transit systems, and 12 do not.

Construct a crosstabulation showing the relationship between the independent and dependent variables. Place the independent variable across the top of the table and calculate the percentages in the correct way. What do the table percentages indicate about the relationship between city size and mass transit systems?

2. Senator Blowchill, Democrat from Massachusetts, has charged that the Reagan administration is directing more federal funds to the Sunbelt states than to those in the Frostbelt. Senator Dryheat, Republican from Arizona, disagrees and challenges Senator Blowchill to prove his claim. So Senator Blowchill tells his research assistant to select randomly 10 states and analyze the relationship between the region and amount of federal funds spent. The research assistant produces the following crosstabulation and then hands it to you, a summer intern, for your interpretation. What would you say about the relationship in the table? Be sure to discuss the statistical significance, direction, and strength of the observed relationship.

	Sunbelt States	Frostbelt States
State has received an above average amount of federal funds	3	2
State has received a below average amount of federal funds	1	4

3. Suppose you conducted a sample survey of 100 respondents and produced the following crosstabulation showing the relationship between religion and attitudes toward abortion. With 95 percent certainty, is there a relationship between the two variables? Is the relationship weak, moderate, or strong? What is the direction of the relationship? Which of the following correlation coefficients is correct for this crosstabulation: +.8, −.2, +.2, −.6? How would you express verbally the results of this crosstabulation?

	Catholic	Protestant
Oppose right to have an abortion	36	44
Favor right to have an abortion	4	16

4. What does the following crosstabulation of the relationship between education and ideology tell you about the strength, direction, and statistical significance of the relationship?

EDUCATION

	Low	*Medium*	*High*	
Liberal	20	50	80	150
Moderate	40	80	80	200
Conservative	40	70	40	250
	100	200	200	

Which of the following correlation coefficients is the most likely: $+.20$, $-.70$, $+.10$, $-.25$? How would you express verbally the meaning of this relationship?

5. Suppose you want to know if there is a relationship between the unemployment rate in cities and the number of robberies that occur within the city limits. You take a random sample of cities and plot the unemployment rates and number of robberies as shown in Figure 12-7. Answer the following questions about the graph and the regression line drawn to best approximate the data.

   a. What is the strength and direction of the relationship between the two variables? How do you know this? What does it mean?

   b. If the unemployment rate in a given city increases by 1 percent, about how many additional robberies would occur?

   c. If there is no unemployment in a city, how many robberies would you expect to occur?

   d. What other factors might make a city experience more robberies or fewer robberies than you would expect based on the unemployment rate alone?

6. You observe that there is a statistically significant relationship between the amount of television Americans watch and the number of violent crimes Americans commit. Therefore, you conclude that watching television causes Americans to commit violent crimes. What is wrong with your conclusion?

Figure 12-7   Regression Line for the Relationship between
Unemployment and Robberies

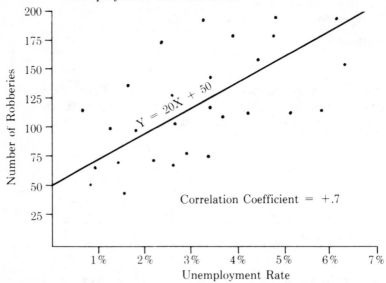

Source: Hypothetical data.

Suggested Readings

Blalock, Hubert M. *Social Statistics.* 2d ed. New York: McGraw-Hill, 1972.

Elifson, Kirk W., Richard P. Runyon, and Audrey Haber. *Fundamentals of Social Statistics.* Reading, Mass.: Addison-Wesley, 1982.

Healey, Joseph F. *Statistics: A Tool for Social Research.* Belmont, Calif.: Wadsworth, 1984.

Mueller, John, Karl Schuessler, and Herbert Costner. *Statistical Reasoning in Sociology.* 2d ed. Boston: Houghton Mifflin, 1970.

Nie, Norman H., et al. *SPSS.* 2d ed. New York: McGraw-Hill, 1975.

Phillips, John L. *Statistical Thinking.* San Francisco: W. H. Freeman, 1973.

Watson, George, and Dickinson McGraw. *Statistical Inquiry.* New York: John Wiley & Sons, 1980.

13. Searching for Complete Explanations and Causal Knowledge: Multivariate Data Analysis

Introduction

Chapter 12 discussed how to measure the existence, strength, direction, and statistical significance of a relationship between one independent variable and a dependent variable using various data analysis techniques. Measuring a single relationship between two variables is a fairly straightforward procedure. Most political science research, however, involves the measurement of many variables and the testing of several hypotheses involving more than two variables. As a result, *multivariate data analysis* techniques are required.

Each of the political scientists whose research we have discussed used multivariate data analysis to investigate the relationships between a number of independent variables and the dependent variable of interest. Gary Jacobson, for example, found that the variation in votes received by candidates for the U.S. Congress could be explained in a number of ways. Although he was most interested in the impact of candidate spending on electoral outcomes, he also considered the relationships between the distribution of the vote and the challenger's party, the challenger's prior political experience, the number of years the incumbent had held office, the challenger's district party strength, and whether the candidates ran in a primary election. Only by considering the relations among these variables could Jacobson reach some firm conclusions about campaign spending and its effect on the vote for congressional candidates.[1]

Ted Gurr also used a number of independent variables to explain the dependent variable of interest to him: crossnational variation in civil strife. Although his major independent variable was relative deprivation, he also tested the relationships between civil strife and legitimacy (the amount of popular support for and acceptance of the decisions made by the regime); coercive potential (the ability of the regime to punish those participating in civil strife); institutionalization ("the extent to which societal structures beyond the primary level are broad in scope, command substantial resources and/or personnel, and are stable and persisting"); and facilitation (the existence of social and environmental conditions that would encourage or enhance civil strife).[2] Gurr used all of these independent variables to account for levels of civil strife since he believed that each one would have some impact on the dependent variable. He measured the individual relationships between each of the independent variables and civil strife, and he also measured the relationships between all of the independent variables combined and civil strife. Persistent deprivation did have an impact on the magnitude of civil strife, he concluded, even when other possible explanations were taken into account.

Finally, to explain peoples' attitudes toward busing, David Sears, Carl Hensler, and Leslie Speer relied on more than one independent variable. They used three measures of self-interest (whether busing is happening or being proposed in the respondent's area, whether the respondent has children in public schools, and the racial composition of the neighborhood schools), two measures of symbolic attitudes (an eight-item scale of racial intolerance and a liberal-conservative self-identification question), and three measures of demographic characteristics (age, years of education, and region).[3] John McConahay, in turn, used eight measures of the respondent's "self-interest" regarding busing (such as whether the respondent had children, had children attending public schools, had children who were being bused, owned his or her own home, and planned to move out of the neighborhood soon); three measures of each respondent's racial attitudes (what the author called modern racial attitudes, old-fashioned racial attitudes, and feelings for blacks); and a host of other variables thought to be related to attitudes toward busing (such as measures of a respondent's education, income, sex, and union membership).[4] In both of these studies the relationship between *each* independent variable and attitudes toward busing was measured, and the relationships between *all* of the independent variables simultaneously and busing attitudes were observed. McConahay as well as Sears, Hensler, and Speer concluded that racial attitudes had a much greater impact on attitudes toward busing than did indicators of "self-interest."

There are essentially two reasons for measuring relationships involving more than two variables: to provide more complete explanations for political phenomena and to gain *causal knowledge*. For most political phenomena more than one independent variable is needed to explain the variation in the observed values of the dependent variable or to predict particular observed values of the dependent variable. Interesting political behavior is usually so complex that researchers need to rely on a number of concepts to explain it adequately.

Moreover, if a researcher is interested in acquiring *causal knowledge,* a number of possible explanations for the phenomenon of interest must be tested. Simply because an independent variable exhibits a strong relationship to a dependent variable does not mean that it caused it to occur. Both the independent and dependent variables might be caused by a third variable, which could create the appearance of a relationship between the first two and lead to an erroneous conclusion about the effect of the independent variable on the dependent variable. The possibility that a third variable is the real cause of both the independent and dependent variables must be considered in making causal claims. Only by eliminating this possibility can a researcher achieve some confidence that a relationship between an independent and dependent variable is a causal one.

In Tufte's study of automobile fatalities, a relationship between the existence of mandatory automobile inspections and a lower auto fatality rate was observed.[5] This does not necessarily mean, however, that inspections cause a decline in auto fatality rates. There may be another phenomenon related to inspections and auto deaths that is causing the relationship between the two. Tufte discovered a strong, inverse relationship between population density and auto fatality rates, and he also discovered that those states with mandatory inspections tend to be more densely populated. Therefore, until population density was eliminated as a possible cause of the relationship between inspections and auto fatalities, he could not make a causal claim about the observed bivariate relationship.

Similarly, Jacobson could not conclude that campaign spending caused an increase in the votes received by congressional candidates until he had evaluated other possibilities. For example, partisan strength in a district might cause both campaign spending and the vote distribution and therefore be the real cause of the relationship between spending and votes received. Although disconfirming this possibility still did not permit Jacobson to conclude with certainty that challenger spending increases votes, it did allow him to be somewhat more confident that the relationship is a causal one.

In this chapter we will explain how political scientists use multivariate data analysis techniques to *control for* the effects of a third variable. This means that the impact of other variables is removed or taken into account when observing the relationship between an independent and dependent variable. Generally, the impact of a third variable may be controlled either experimentally or statistically. Experimental control is introduced by assigning the participants in an experiment to different groups and controlling each group's exposure to the experimental stimulus. Statistical control, the procedure used more frequently by political scientists, involves measuring each observation's values on the control variables and using these measures to make comparisons between observations.

Multivariate Crosstabulation

How to display and measure the relationship between two nominal or ordinal level variables was explained in Chapter 12. The joint distribution of observations on the two variables is displayed in a crosstab table, and the researcher looks for different values of the dependent variable across the different categories of the independent variable. The extent to which the cases in the different categories of the independent variable exhibit different values on the dependent variable indicates the strength and direction of the relationship.

Suppose, for example, that we have hypothesized a relationship between attitudes toward government spending and presidential voting. Our hypothesis is that "the more in favor of decreasing government spending a person is, the more likely she is to vote Republican." Table 13-1 seems to confirm the hypothesis.

At this point, a researcher might ask, "Can I improve upon my explanation of presidential voting by including another independent variable?" Thirty-six percent of those who favored decreased spending voted contrary to the hypothesis, as did 46 percent of those in favor of maintaining or increasing spending levels. Perhaps it would be possible to provide an explanation for those voters' behaviors and hence improve the understanding of presidential voting behavior.

A second question a researcher might ask is "Does this analysis mean that attitudes toward government spending *caused* people to vote Republican?" Or, put another way, "Would people still have voted

Table 13-1   Relationship between Attitudes toward Government Spending and Presidential Vote

Dependent Variable: Presidential Vote	Independent Variable: Attitudes toward Government Spending		
	Decrease Spending	Keep Spending the Same or Increase It	(n)
Republican	64%	46%	(555)
Democratic	36	54	(445)
Total	100	100	
(n)	(550)	(450)	(1,000)

Source: Hypothetical data.

Republican even if they had had different attitudes toward government spending?" These two questions acknowledge the possibility that the observed relationship may not be a causal one, and they imply that an additional explanation of presidential voting should be considered.

A likely second independent variable for presidential voting might be income. Those people with higher incomes might be more in favor of decreased government spending because they feel they benefit little from most government programs. Those with higher incomes might also be more apt to vote Republican because they perceive the GOP to be the party that favors government policies that benefit the affluent. Therefore, income might influence both attitudes toward government spending *and* presidential voting and thus could create the appearance of a relationship between the two.

To consider the impact of income we need to control for it and then observe the resulting relationship between government spending attitudes and presidential vote. In crosstab analysis we control for a third variable by holding it constant; that is, by grouping the observations into categories of the third variable and then observing the original relationship within each of these categories. This has the effect of removing the impact of the variation in the third variable since we observe the original relationship within each group of identical or similar observations on the third variable. In this case we can observe the relationship between government spending attitudes and presidential vote separately among those with low, medium, and high incomes.

Table 13-2 shows what might happen were we to control for income. Within each of the categories of income there is no relationship between government spending attitudes and presidential voting. Regardless of their attitudes on spending, 80 percent of respondents with high incomes voted Republican, 60 percent with medium incomes voted Republican, and 30 percent with low incomes voted Republican. Once the variation in income was removed by grouping those with similar incomes together, the relationship between government spending attitudes and presidential voting disappeared.

What does this reveal about the original relationship between government spending attitudes and presidential voting? First, there is clearly a relationship between income and attitudes toward spending. Eighty-three percent of those with high incomes favored cutting spending while only 57 percent of those with medium incomes and 29 percent of those with low incomes did. Therefore, those who favored reducing spending were also more likely to be wealthy; they differed from those opposed to spending cuts not only on their attitudes toward spending but also on their incomes. In other words, the two groups with different spending attitudes differ in other ways.

Table 13-2   Relationship between Attitudes toward Government
Spending and Presidential Vote: Controlling for Income

	Independent Variable: Attitudes toward Government Spending		
Dependent Variable: Presidential Vote	*Decrease Spending*	*Keep Spending the Same or Increase It*	*(n)*
High income			
Republican	80%	80%	(240)
Democratic	20	20	(60)
Total	100	100	
(n)	(250)	(50)	(300)
Medium income			
Republican	60%	60%	(210)
Democratic	40	40	(140)
Total	100	100	
(n)	(200)	(150)	(350)
Low income			
Republican	30%	30%	(105)
Democratic	70	70	(245)
Total	100	100	
(n)	(100)	(250)	(350)

Source: Hypothetical data.

Second, it is also clear that income is related to presidential voting.
Eighty percent of the wealthy voted Republican, while only 60 percent of
middle-income respondents and 30 percent of low-income respondents
did. Consequently, income is a possible alternative explanation for the
variation in presidential voting.

Third, when we control for income by grouping those with similar
incomes together and observing the relationship between spending attitudes and presidential voting within each group, the original relationship
disappears. This indicates that the only reason for the original relationship was because of the variation in income. The original relationship was
spurious, that is, it was due entirely to a third variable. Therefore,
government spending attitudes cannot be a cause of presidential voting
because spending attitudes had no effect on voting above and beyond the
effect of income. Respondents did not vote the way they did because of
their different attitudes toward government spending.

This does not mean that there is no relationship between spending attitudes and presidential voting; we observed such a relationship in Table 13-1. It does, mean, however, that the original relationship occurred because of the variables' relationships with a third variable, income. It also means that the original relationship was not a causal one; spending attitudes cannot possibly be a cause of presidential voting because within income groups they make no difference whatever. The only reason for the relationship between spending attitudes and presidential voting is because of the effect of income differences.

Given the relationships between each pair of variables in this model, how do we know whether it is spending attitudes or income that has a larger impact on presidential voting and has causal priority? We have already seen that the relationship between spending attitudes and presidential voting disappears when we control for income. Now what happens if we observe the relationship between income and presidential voting while controlling for spending attitudes? Table 13-3 contains the answer.

The relationship between income and presidential voting persists after controlling for spending attitudes. In fact, the relationship is identical in both control groups to the original, "uncontrolled" relationship; controlling for spending attitudes does not alter the relationship one bit. This suggests that, *of the two independent variables,* income is by far

Table 13-3 Relationship between Income and Presidential Vote: Controlling for Government Spending Attitudes

Dependent Variable: Presidential Vote	Independent Variable: Income			
	High	Medium	Low	(n)
Favor spending reduction				
Republican	80%	60%	30%	350
Democratic	20	40	70	200
Total	100	100	100	
(n)	(250)	(200)	(100)	(550)
Keep spending same or increase it				
Republican	80%	60%	30%	205
Democratic	20	40	70	245
Total	100	100	100	
(n)	(50)	(150)	(250)	(450)

Source: Hypothetical data.

Figure 13-1 Impact of Income on the Relationship between Government
Spending Attitudes and Presidential Voting

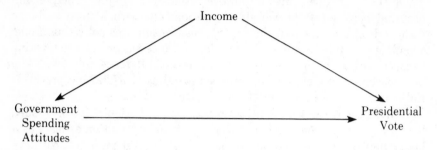

more important in accounting for variations in the presidential vote.
Income is also more likely than attitudes toward government spending to
have causal priority since a person's attitudes toward government spending are more likely to be caused by their income than vice-versa. Since it
is difficult to imagine that a person's income could be altered by attitudes
of this type, it is more plausible that spending attitudes are dependent
upon income, as Figure 13-1 illustrates.

A good example of an actual multivariate crosstabulation analysis
may be found in Raymond Wolfinger and Steven Rosenstone's study of
voter turnout.[6] They observed a positive relationship between education
and turnout (the higher the education, the higher the turnout) and a
curvilinear relationship between age and turnout (the older a person, up
to an age of about 70, the higher the turnout; after 70, turnout declined).
However, since there is also a relationship between age and education
(older people tend to have fewer years of formal education since they
grew up at a time when high school and college educations were rarer),
the researchers wondered whether it was more age, or education, or both,
that affected turnout. In other words, they were interested in testing the
three-variable model presented in Figure 13-2.

Figure 13-2 Impact of Age on the Relationship between Education and
Turnout

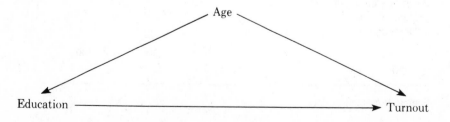

The last column on the righthand side of Table 13-4 shows the bivariate relationship between education and turnout; the bottom row shows the bivariate relationship between age and turnout. The relationship between education and turnout, controlling for age, may be observed by looking *down* each column of the table. Since each column contains observations grouped by age, age is being *held constant* (or nearly so). Turnout levels generally increase as one looks down each column. Thus the relationship to education persists after controlling for age. The relationship between age and turnout, controlling for education, may be observed by looking *across* each row. Since each row contains observations grouped by education, education is being *held constant* (or nearly so). Turnout levels increase, up to age 70, and then decrease in each row. Thus the relationship to age persists after controlling for education.

In this case, then, the relationship between education and turnout is not spurious. Both independent variables exhibit relationships with turnout independent of the other. Therefore, education and age account for more of the variation in turnout than would be the case with one variable alone.

When a researcher controls for a third variable, five general situations can arise. First, the original relationship may disappear entirely, indicating that it was spurious. This was the case with the government spending attitudes and presidential vote example. Second, the original relationship may decline somewhat but not completely disappear, indicating that it was partly spurious. That is, some but not all of the original relationship may be accounted for with the control variable. Third, the original relationship may remain *unchanged*, indicating that the third

Table 13-4 Relationship between Age, Education, and Turnout, 1972

| | | | *Age* | | | | |
Education	18-24	25-31	32-36	37-69	70-78	78+	Total
0-8 (grammar school)	14	26	36	56	58	44	52
9-12 (high school)	44	55	63	75	76	63	65
1-3 college	72	76	79	87	85	72	79
4 college	76	84	89	90	85	75	86
5+ college	85	86	91	93	94	80	91
Total	53	62	67	74	68	52	67

Source: Raymond E. Wolfinger and Steven J. Rosenstone, *Who Votes?* (New Haven, Conn.: Yale University Press, 1980), 47. Reprinted with permission.

Note: The entry in each cell is the percentage of people voting with the given combination of age and education. For example, 36 percent of people aged 32 to 36 who had not attended high school voted.

variable was not responsible for the original relationship. This suggests that the relationship between the independent and dependent variables may be causal, as in Wolfinger and Rosenstone's analysis of education, age, and voter turnout. Fourth, the original relationship may increase, indicating that the control variable was disguising or deflating the true relationship between the independent and dependent variables. Fifth, the controlled relationship may be different for different categories of the control variable. This is called a *specified relationship*. It indicates that the relationship between two variables is dependent upon the values of a third variable. For example, the relationship between residential mobility and turnout may be strong only when education is low. People with high education may vote no matter how geographically mobile they are, while for people of low education, mobility may interfere with voting. If the relationship between two variables differs significantly for different categories of a third, then we say that the third variable has specified the relationship.

Table 13-5 presents a useful summary of the possible results when a third variable is held constant. It displays the appropriate measures of association and statistical significance for the original, uncontrolled relationship between two variables. The same information for each category of the control variable is shown. Comparing the uncontrolled results with the controlled results indicates whether the relationship is spurious (a), partially spurious (b), unchanged (c), has increased (d), or has been specified (e).

Multivariate crosstabulation analysis, then, may be used to assess the impact of one or more control variables when those variables are measured at the nominal or ordinal level. Although this is a relatively straightforward and frequently used procedure, it has several disadvantages.

First, it is difficult to interpret the numerous crosstabs required when a researcher wishes to control for a large number of variables at once and the control variables have a large number of categories. Suppose, for example, that you wanted to observe the relationship between television news exposure and political knowledge while controlling for education (5 categories), newspaper exposure (4 categories) and political interest (3 categories). You would need to construct 60 different crosstabs to accomplish this very reasonable analytical objective!

Second, controlling by grouping similar cases together can rapidly deplete the sample size for each of the control situations, producing less accurate and statistically insignificant estimates of the relationships. Suppose that we had started out with a standard sample size of 1,500 respondents in our example of the relationship between television news exposure and political knowledge. By the time we had divided the sample

Table 13-5 Five Results When Controlling for a Third Variable

Uncontrolled Relationship	Measure of Association	Significance Level
a.	+.35	.001
Category 1	+.05	.07
Category 2	−.03	.14
Category 3	+.01	.10
b.	+.42	.001
Category 1	+.20	.01
Category 2	+.17	.05
Category 3	+.26	.001
c.	−.28	.01
Category 1	−.30	.05
Category 2	−.35	.01
Category 3	−.27	.05
d.	−.12	.08
Category 1	−.42	.001
Category 2	−.30	.01
Category 3	−.35	.001
e.	+.31	.001
Category 1	+.55	.001
Category 2	+.37	.01
Category 3	+.16	.05

Source: Hypothetical data.

into the 60 discrete control groups, each crosstab measuring the relationship between news exposure and political knowledge would have, on average, only 25 people in it. This would make it virtually impossible to observe a statistically significant relationship between news exposure and political knowledge.

Third, control groups in multivariate crosstabulation analysis often disregard some of the variation in one or more of the variables. For example, to control for income in our government spending attitude/ presidential vote example, we put all those with low incomes into one group. This grouping ignored what might be important variations in their precise income levels. Similarly, when Wolfinger and Rosenstone measured the combined effect of age and education on turnout, they combined people of different ages and educations into their control categories. This is often done because of the first two problems mentioned earlier—number of tables and sample size—but it has the unfortunate consequence of eliminating what might be consequential variations in the control variables.

Despite these three limitations, multivariate crosstabulation is used whenever the variables are measured at the nominal or ordinal level. It usually yields more insight into a researcher's hypothesis than would a simple bivariate crosstabulation alone. Multivariate crosstabulation helps explain the dependent variable and addresses the question of whether an observed relationship is a causal one.

Two-Way Analysis of Variance

Two-way analysis of variance may be used to assess the extent to which two or more independent variables measured at the nominal or ordinal level can explain the variance in a dependent variable measured at the interval or ratio level. The logic of this procedure is very similar to the one-way analysis of variance described in Chapter 12. Recall that in the one-way analysis of variance, we began with a certain amount of observed variance in the dependent variable. This variance may be calculated from the mean for this variable since it is measured at the appropriate level. Then we divided the observations into categories based on the measurement of the independent variable and measured the mean and variance within each of these categories. If the means for the categories were quite different and the variance within the categories was much less than the variance in the "ungrouped" dependent variable, then the categorization was judged successful in accounting for the dependent variable. The more different the means across categories and the smaller the variances within categories of the independent variable, the stronger the relationship between independent and dependent variables.

A two-way analysis of variance proceeds in a similar fashion. Again we begin with a certain amount of variance in the dependent variable. In this case, however, we have more than one independent variable with which to explain that variation. Consequently, the first step in measuring the impact of a control variable is to divide the observations into categories based on the values of the cases on each of the independent variables. The mean and variance on the dependent variable is then calculated for the cases in each of these categories.

For example, recall that Tufte hypothesized that those states with mandatory automobile inspections would have fewer auto fatalities than those without them. A one-way analysis of variance showed that there was a weak relationship between the two variables. To provide a more complete explanation of auto fatalities and to confirm his suspicion that inspection policy was an important cause of variations in auto fatalities,

Figure 13-3 Impact of State Population Density on the Relationship between State Inspection Policy and State Auto Fatality Rate

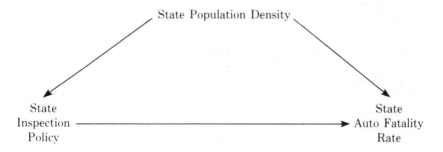

Tufte then considered the effect of another independent variable— population density— on auto fatalities. (See Figure 13-3.)

Tufte argued that the population density of a state has numerous effects on behavior related to auto fatalities—such as the speed at which cars are driven, the distances they are driven, and the proximity of medical services to crash victims. When he calculated the state-level relationship between population density and auto fatality rates, he discovered a fairly strong, negative relationship; that is, as the density of a state increases, the auto fatality rate decreases. Furthermore, he found that there is a relationship between population density and the existence of auto inspection policies; eight of the nine most densely populated states had mandatory inspections. Therefore, the relationship between auto inspections and auto fatality rates may be spurious. Population density may be a much more important explanation for auto deaths than the lack of inspection policies.

We can measure the impact of both population density and auto inspection policy on auto fatality rates by dividing the 50 observations (states) into categories based on their population density and on their inspection policies. If we then calculate the mean auto fatality rate and the variance around that rate for each of the categories, we can assess the impact of the independent variables, both individually and in combination.

Table 13-6 shows the mean and variance for each of the six categories of states created by the two independent variables. An inspection of the means for those categories shows that auto fatality rates for categories of states of differing population density are still quite different even after one has controlled for inspection policies (this can be

Table 13-6 Relationship between State Auto Inspection Policy
and State Auto Fatality Rates: Controlling for
Population Density

Auto Inspection Policy	Density Thin (<25 people/ square mile)	Medium (25-125 people/ square mile)	Thick (>125 people/ square mile)	Total
States without inspections	37.4	31.6	23.6	31.9
(n)	(10)	(16)	(6)	(32)
(s^2)	(47.0)	(11.5)	(29.5)	(31.9)
States with inspections	34.9	28.4	18.3	26.1
(n)	(3)	(9)	(6)	(18)
(s^2)	(77.6)	(33.6)	(23.1)	(26.1)
Total	36.8	30.5	21.0	29.8
(n)	(13)	(25)	(12)	(50)
(s^2)	(49.4)	(20.8)	(31.8)	(61.8)

Source: Edward R. Tufte, *Data Analysis for Politics and Policy*, copyright 1974, 23. Adapted by permission of Prentice-Hall, Inc., Englewood Cliffs, New Jersey.

Note: Entries are mean auto fatality rates for each group of states in each cell. Tufte eliminates Alaska in his analysis, but it is included here in the "thin, without inspections" cell.

seen by looking across the rows). In addition, the fatality rates for states with auto inspections continue to be less than for those without inspections, even when controlling for population density. The states without inspections have higher mean fatality rates by 2.5, 3.2, and 5.3 in each of the density categories, while the "uncontrolled" difference was 5.8. Therefore, although there has been some reduction in the relationship with auto inspections, the relationship has not disappeared entirely.

With the information contained in this table, a precise estimate of the impact of each independent variable on auto fatality rates can be calculated. A measure of the extent to which the two variables together account for the variation in auto fatality rates can also be calculated. In this case the relationship between population density and auto fatalities remains strong even when controlling for inspection policies, and the relationship between inspection policies and auto fatality rates is diminished and becomes modest when controlling for population density. The two variables combined account for a substantial portion (57 percent) of the variance in auto fatality rates across the 50 states.

Like multiple crosstabulation, two-way analysis of variance measures the relationship between one independent variable and a dependent variable while controlling for one or more other independent variables. Also like crosstabulation, it controls for a third variable by grouping together cases identical or similar on the control variable. The only major difference is that the dependent variable is measured at the interval or ratio level. Consequently, the variance is a mathematical one rather than one involving the distribution of cases across categories. For the specific mathematical calculations involved in the two-way analysis of variance, consult the readings at the end of this chapter.

Multiple Regression and Partial Correlation

So far we have described how to control for a third variable by grouping cases together that have identical or similar values on the control variable. Although this is an adequate procedure when the values of the control variable are discrete and homogeneous and is the only appropriate procedure when variables are measured at the nominal or ordinal level, control-by-grouping does cause two major problems: the proliferation of control groups in a complex multivariate model and the reduction in the sample size within each control group.

Fortunately, there is an alternative. When variables are measured at the interval or ratio level (and even sometimes when they are not), controlling may be done by *adjustment*. This is accomplished using the techniques of *multiple regression* and *partial correlation*. A partial correlation is a measure of the relationship between two variables after the effect of a third variable on both has been removed. Suppose, for example, that we are interested in the relationship between education and liberalism, controlling for age, where each of the variables is measured at the interval or ratio level. (See Figure 13-4.)

First, we would measure the relationship between age (the independent variable) and education (the dependent variable) using the regression equation described in Chapter 12. We could then calculate the residual value for each case on education. This would be the variance in education unexplained by age. Then, with a second regression equation, we could measure the relationship between age and the second dependent variable, liberalism, and calculate the residuals for this equation for each case. This is the variance in liberalism unexplained by age. Finally, we could use a third regression equation to calculate the relationship between the residuals from the first equation and the residuals from the second equation. This third equation would indicate the relationship between education and liberalism once the effects of age have been

Figure 13-4 Impact of Age on Relationship between Education and Liberalism

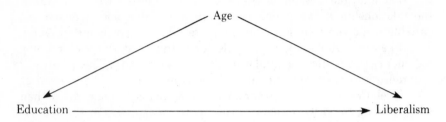

removed. The correlation associated with this final regression equation between the two sets of residuals is called a *partial correlation,* and it indicates the variance in the dependent variable explained by the independent variable once the effects of the control variable have been removed. The partial correlation must be squared to equal the actual "percent of variance explained."

Actually, there is a much simpler way to calculate the partial correlation coefficient:

$$r_{ij,k} = \frac{r_{ij} - (r_{ik})\,(r_{jk})}{\sqrt{1 - r^2_{ik}}\ \sqrt{1 - r^2_{jk}}}$$

Where

k = the control variable

i and j = the independent and dependent variables

and the correlation coefficients on the righthand side of the equation are calculated from the bivariate analysis involving i and j

Thus, if the correlation between age and education was +.38, the correlation between age and liberalism was +.20, and the correlation between education and liberalism was +.50, then the partial correlation coefficient between education and liberalism, while controlling for age, would be

$$r = \frac{+.50 - (+.38)(+.20)}{\sqrt{1 - .38^2}\ \sqrt{1 - .20^2}}$$

$$= \frac{+.50 - .076}{\sqrt{.8556}\ \sqrt{.96}}$$

$$= +.47$$

Partial correlations may be calculated for any number of control variables, as long as the sample size and variances permit. They are useful indicators of whether a relationship has persisted after controlling for one or more control variables. However, the partial correlation does not reveal very much about the mathematical relationship between an independent and dependent variable, after controlling for a control variable. For example, Jacobson did not want to know only how strong a relationship existed between campaign spending and votes received (after controlling for the partisan strength of a district); he also wanted to know how much money would have to be spent to receive a winning percentage of the vote.

A second multivariate data analysis technique, *multiple regression,* provides this type of information. Recall that regression analysis involves the display of data points in a two-dimensional space and the calculation of the line that best approximates the data points (a regression line). The algebraic equation corresponding to this best-fitting line describes the nature of the relationship between the independent and dependent variables, and the product-moment correlation coefficient indicates the strength and statistical significance of that relationship. This regression equation may be used to calculate the predicted value on Y (the dependent variable) for any value of X (the independent variable), and the residual or distance between the predicted and observed value of Y can be calculated for each observation.

Multiple regression does exactly the same thing, only the regression equation contains more than one variable, and the regression coefficient expresses the relationship between one independent variable and the dependent variable while controlling for all other variables in the equation. But control is done by adjusting the values of each case to take into account the effect of all the other variables rather than by grouping similar cases together.

The general form of a *linear multiple regression equation* is

$$Y = b_1 X_1 + b_2 X_2 + b_N X_N + a \qquad (13.3)$$

Here a indicates the Y-intercept or the value of Y when the values of all of the other variables are zero, and the b's indicate how much Y changes for a unit change in each of the independent variables, when the other variables are being held constant. Hence each b indicates the relationship between X and Y while controlling for all of the other independent variables simultaneously, and the expected value of Y may be calculated by substituting any values of the various independent variables into the equation.

The solution to the linear multiple regression equation is the mathematical relationship between the independent variables and the dependent variable. Usually by a computer, a and b are calculated to minimize the squared distances between each data point and its predicted Y-value. As a result, the multiple regression equation contains the same wealth of information that a bivariate regression equation does.

Remember, however, that it is difficult to judge the relative importance of the independent variables based on the multiple regression

Table 13-7 Multivariate Explanation of Vote for Congressional
Challengers: Multiple Regression Analysis, 1972-78

	Regression Coefficient	t Ratio[a]	Standardized Regression Coefficient (Beta)	
1972				
CV^b = a	20.7			
b_1 Challenger's expenditures	.112	9.42	.51	
b_2 Incumbent's expenditures	−.002	−.14	−.01	R^2 = .49
b_3 Challenger's party	−.47	−.61	−.03	
b_4 Challenger's district party strength	.299	6.94	.33	
1974[c]				
CV = a	15.6			
b_1 Challenger's expenditures	.121	10.45	.48	
b_2 Incumbent's expenditures	−.028	−2.34	−.11	R^2 = .65
b_3 Challenger's party	9.78	11.19	.42	
b_4 Challenger's district party strength	.351	7.75	.28	

(continued)

equation alone. The b's are calculated in tandem with the units of
measurement for each of the independent variables and are therefore
sensitive to how those variables are measured. One b may be much larger
than another b, not because the independent variable is more strongly
related to the dependent variable, but because the independent variable
is measured in much smaller units.

To assess the relative importance of a series of independent variables, the b's from a regression equation may be *standardized* to reflect
the mean and variance of each of the independent variables. When this is
done, the b's are converted into *standardized regression coefficients*—
also called *beta weights*—that indicate the relative importance of each
independent variable in explaining the variation in the dependent
variable, when controlling for all of the other variables in the equation.
Betas may vary from −1 to +1 so they indicate not only the direction of

Table 13-7

(continued)

		Regression Coefficient	t Ratio[a]	Standardized Regression Coefficient (Beta)	
1976[b]					
CV =	a	14.8			
	b_1 Challenger's expenditures	.074	9.57	.45	
	b_2 Incumbent's expenditures	−.003	−.27	−.01	$R^2 = .60$
	b_3 Challenger's party	.26	.32	.01	
	b_4 Challenger's district party strength	.441	10.84	.48	
1978[b]					
CV =	a	14.8			
	b_1 Challenger's expenditures	.063	11.10	.51	
	b_2 Incumbent's expenditures	−.002	−.35	−.02	$R^2 = .61$
	b_3 Challenger's party	−1.76	−2.15	−.08	
	b_4 Challenger's district party strength	.454	9.70	.42	

[a] A t ratio of at least 1.98 is necessary for a .05 level of significance, 2.58 for .01, and 3.35 for .001.
[b] CV is challenger's share of the vote.
[c] Variables are the same as those in the 1972 analysis.

Source: Gary C. Jacobson, *Money in Congressional Elections*, pp. 42, 235. Copyright © 1980 by Yale University. Reprinted with permission.

the controlled relationship with an independent variable but also the amount of variance in the dependent variable accounted for by each of the independent variables.

The statistical significance of a controlled relationship with an independent variable may also be derived from a multiple regression equation. The computer program that calculates a regression equation will print out the standard error of the regression coefficients. The usual test for a statement with 95 percent certainty is that the regression coefficient be at least twice its standard error. If the test is met, then the relationship is statistically significant. If it is not met, then the null hypothesis involving that relationship (controlling for the other independent variables in the equation) must be accepted.

The overall success of a multiple regression equation in accounting for the variation in the dependent variable is indicated with the multiple correlation coefficient (R) and its square (R^2). R^2 is the ratio of the explained variance in the dependent variable to the total variance in the dependent variable; hence it equals the proportion of the variance in the dependent variable that may be explained by the independent variables acting together in the multiple regression equation:

$$R^2 = \frac{\begin{matrix}\text{Sum of squares} \\ \text{for Y}\end{matrix} - \begin{matrix}\text{Sum of squares} \\ \text{for residuals}\end{matrix}}{\begin{matrix}\text{Sum of squares} \\ \text{for Y}\end{matrix}} = \frac{\begin{matrix}\text{Sum of squares} \\ \text{for regression}\end{matrix}}{\begin{matrix}\text{Sum of squares} \\ \text{for Y}\end{matrix}} = \frac{\begin{matrix}\text{Explained} \\ \text{variance in Y}\end{matrix}}{\begin{matrix}\text{Total variance} \\ \text{in Y}\end{matrix}} \quad (13.4)$$

R^2 itself can vary from 0 to 1.0, and it also has a corresponding significance test that indicates whether the entire regression equation permits a statistically significant explanation of the dependent variable.

Multiple regression is currently the preferred technique in political science for observing multivariate relationships. In fact, most of the political science researchers whose work we have been discussing used multiple regression. Gary Jacobson, for example, used this analytical tool to determine the relationships between campaign spending, partisan strength, the party of the challengers, and the vote for congressional challengers, shown in Table 13-7. He discovered that the strongest relationships are generally between challengers' expenditures and the vote, and between the challengers' district party strength and the vote, when controlling for the other variables. Incumbent spending and the challengers' party exhibit much weaker relationships to the distribution of the vote. Table 13-7 also shows that Jacobson's four-variable model generally explains over half of the variation in votes cast for challengers and that challengers have gained about 1 percent of the vote for every $5,000 to $10,000 spent (depending on the year).

Gurr used multiple regression to assess the impact of relative deprivation and other factors on crossnational measures of civil strife. The result of one of Gurr's multiple regression analyses intended to explain the variation in civil strife is shown in Table 13-8. Gurr's eight-variable equation explains 65 percent of the variation in strife, with persisting deprivation, short-term economic deprivation, social and political facilitation, and legitimacy contributing the most to the explana-

Table 13-8 Multivariate Explanation of Civil Strife: Multiple Regression Analysis

	Regression Coefficient	*Standardized Regression Coefficient (Beta)*
Total magnitude of strife = a	−3.11	
b_1 Economic deprivation, short-term	1.77	.24
b_2 Political deprivation, short-term	.66	.09[a]
b_3 Persisting deprivation	.271	.39
b_4 Coercive forces loyalty	.140	−.17
b_5 Institutionalization	.056	.07[a]
b_6 Past civil strife	.024	.04[a]
b_7 Facilitation	.481	.55
b_8 Legitimacy	−.184	−.26
$R^2 = .650$		

[a] Not significant at the .05 level.

Source: Ted Gurr, "A Causal Model of Civil Strife: A Comparative Analysis Using New Indices," *American Political Science Review* 2 (December 1968): 1119. Reprinted with permission.

tion. Because of the way the independent variables are measured in this case—with multimeasure scales and indices—the regression coefficients do not have a straightforward interpretation.

A final example of multiple regression analysis is McConahay's study of attitudes toward busing, shown in Table 13-9. The variable with the strongest relationship to busing attitudes is modern racial attitudes, followed at a considerable distance by family job status, parental status, and old-fashioned racial attitudes. In addition, this regression analysis is the least successful of the three examples presented here, explaining only 32 percent of the variation in attitudes toward busing.

Conclusion

As we have seen, multivariate data analysis helps researchers provide more complete explanations of political phenomena and produce causal knowledge. Observing the relationship between an independent and dependent variable while controlling for one or more control variables allows researchers to assess more precisely the effect attributable to each independent variable and to accumulate evidence in support of a causal

Table 13-9 Multivariate Explanation of Attitudes toward Busing: Multiple Regression Analysis

Predictors of Busing Attitudes	Standardized Regression Coefficient (Beta)
Self-Interest	
Parents	.11
Children in public school	−.06
Children being bused	.03
Homeowner	.07
Relatives in neighborhood	.00
Time lived in neighborhood	.02
Happy with neighborhood	−.02
Planning to stay in neighborhood	.01
Racial Attitudes	
Modern	.40[a]
Old-fashioned	.10[c]
Feelings for blacks	.07
Demographics and Other Attitudes	
Education	−.08
Family job status	−.11[b]
Union membership	.02
1975 income	−.01
Southern socialization	.08[c]
Sex	−.05
Political efficacy	.05
Authoritarianism	−.02
Life-style conservatism	−.01
$R^2 = .32$	

[a] Significant at .001 level.
[b] Significant at .01 level.
[c] Significant at .05 level.

Source: John B. McConahay, "Self-Interest versus Racial Attitudes as Correlates of Anti-Busing-Attitudes in Louisville: Is It the Buses or the Blacks?" *Journal of Politics* 44 (1982): 713. Reprinted with permission.

claim. Being able to observe simultaneously the relationship between a number of independent variables and a dependent variable also helps researchers construct more parsimonious and complete explanations for political phenomena.

Multivariate data analysis techniques vary in how they control for the control variable. Multivariate crosstabulation and two-way analysis of variance control by grouping similar observations; partial correlation and multiple regression control by adjustment. Both types of procedures have their advantages and limitations. Control by grouping can result in the proliferation of analysis tables, the reduction of the number of cases within categories to a hazardous level, and the elimination of some of the variance in the control variables. Control by adjustment, on the other hand, can disguise important specified relationships; that is, relationships that are not identical across the range of values observed in the control variables.

Notes

1. Gary C. Jacobson, *Money in Congressional Elections* (New Haven, Conn.: Yale University Press, 1980).
2. Ted Gurr, "A Causal Model of Civil Strife: A Comparative Analysis Using New Indices," *American Political Science Review* 2 (December 1968): 1104-24. The quote is on 1105.
3. David O. Sears, Carl P. Hensler, and Leslie K. Speer, "Whites' Opposition to 'Busing': Self-Interest or Symbolic Politics?" *American Political Science Review* 73 (June 1979): 369-84.
4. John B. McConahay, "Self-Interest versus Racial Attitudes as Correlates of Anti-Busing Attitudes in Louisville: Is It the Buses or the Blacks?" *Journal of Politics* 44 (1982): 692-720.
5. Edward R. Tufte, *Data Analysis for Politics and Policy* (Englewood Cliffs, N.J.: Prentice-Hall, 1974).
6. Raymond E. Wolfinger and Steven J. Rosenstone, *Who Votes?* (New Haven, Conn.: Yale University Press, 1980).

Terms Introduced

Analysis of variance. A technique for measuring the relationship between one nominal or ordinal level variable and one interval or ratio level variable.

Control by adjustment. A form of statistical control in which a mathematical adjustment is made to assess the impact of a third variable.

Control by grouping. A form of statistical control in which observations identical or similar for the control variable are grouped together.

Experimental control. Assessing the impact of a third variable by manipulating the exposure of experimental groups to experimental stimuli.

Multiple regression. A technique for measuring the mathematical relationships between more than one independent variable and a dependent variable, while controlling for all other independent variables in the equation.

Multivariate crosstabulation. A procedure by which crosstabulation is used to control for a third variable.

Multivariate data analysis. Data analysis techniques designed to test hypotheses involving more than two variables.

Partial correlation. A mathematical adjustment in the relationship between two variables, designed to control for the effect of a third.

Partly spurious relationship. A relationship between two variables caused partially by the impact of a third.

Specified relationship. A relationship between two variables that varies with the values of a third.

Spurious relationship. A relationship between two variables caused entirely by the impact of a third.

Statistical control. Assessing the impact of a third variable by comparing observations across the values of a control variable.

Two-way analysis of variance. An extension of the analysis of variance procedure to allow controlling for a third variable.

Suggested Readings

Anderson, T. W. *Introduction to Multivariate Statistical Analysis.* New York: John Wiley & Sons, 1958.

Blalock, Hubert M. *Causal Inference in Non-Experimental Research.* Chapel Hill: University of North Carolina Press, 1964.

_____. *Social Statistics,* 2d ed. New York: McGraw-Hill, 1972.

Draper, N. R. and H. Smith. *Applied Regression Analysis.* New York: John Wiley & Sons, 1966.

Kendall, M. G. and A. Stuart. *The Advanced Theory of Statistics.* Vol 2. Griffin: London, 1961, chap. 27.

Kerlinger, F. N. and E. Pedhazer. *Multiple Regression in Behavioral Research.* New York: Holt, Rinehart & Winston, 1973.

Overall, J. E. and C. Klett. *Applied Multivariate Analysis.* New York: McGraw-Hill, 1973.

Scheffe, H. A. *The Analysis of Variance.* New York: John Wiley & Sons, 1959.

14. The Research Report:
An Annotated Example

In the preceding chapters we have described important stages in the process of conducting a scientific investigation of political phenomena. In this chapter we will discuss the culmination of a research project: writing a research report. A complete and well-written research report that covers each component of the research process will contribute to the researcher's goal of creating transmissible, scientific knowledge.

This chapter examines how one researcher conducted and reported his research activities. We will evaluate how well he performed each component of the research process and how adequately he described and explained the choices he made during the investigation. To help you evaluate the report, the major components of the research process and some of the criteria by which they should be analyzed are presented here as a series of numbered questions. Refer to these questions while you read the article and jot the number of the question in the margin next to the section of the article in which the question is addressed. For easier reference, the sections of the article have been assigned letters and numbers.

1) Does the researcher clearly specify the main research question or problem? What is the "why" question?

2) Has the researcher demonstrated the value and significance of his own research question and indicated how his research findings will contribute to scientific knowledge about his topic?

3) Has the researcher proposed clear explanations for the political phenomena that interest him? What types of relationships are hypothesized? Does he discuss any alternative explanations?

4) Are the independent and dependent variables identified? If so, what are they? Has the author considered any alternative or control variables? If so, please identify them. Can you think of any that the researcher did not mention?

5) Are the hypotheses empirical, general, and plausible?

6) Are the concepts in the hypotheses clearly defined? Are the operational definitions given the variables valid and reasonable?

7) What method of data collection is used to make the necessary observations? Are the observations valid and reliable measurements?

8) Has the researcher made empirical observations about the units of analysis specified in the hypotheses?

9) If a sample is used, what type of sample is it? Does the type of sample seriously affect the conclusions that can be drawn from the research? Does the researcher discuss this?

10) What type of research design is used? Does the research design adequately test the hypothesized relationships? For example, if the researcher hypothesizes a causal relationship, does the research design permit the researcher to show a causal relationship?

11) Are the statistics that are used appropriate for the level of measurement of the variables?

12) Are the research findings presented and discussed clearly? Is the basis for deciding whether a hypothesis is supported or refuted specified clearly?

AMTRAK IN THE STATES

A   **Introduction**

1 In the concluding chapter of a thorough overview of the history of American railroading, John Stover observes, "Each generation in turn has felt that the existing form of rail transport presented difficulties requiring solutions or decisions." [1] The nature of the difficulties has varied over the years, as has the general response. The purpose of this analysis is to explain state responses to one of the most recent railroad problems, the decline of intercity rail passenger service.

2 State responses to this problem are significant in several respects. First, they indicate the willingness of state officials to intervene in and alter decisions made in the marketplace, albeit heavily regulated marketplace. [2] Second, recent research has found a substantial relationship between transportation policies (for highways) and economic growth. [3] Third, as we shall see, the survival of passenger rail service has potentially significant implications for the nation's energy consumption, environmental protection, and public safety.

3 State involvement in rail transportation is far from new. During the 1800s one of the major railroad problems was the total absence of rail service in many parts of the country. State governments responded to that problem through a variety of direct and indirect subsidy programs, including land grants, tax

David C. Nice, "Amtrak in the States," *Policy Studies Journal* (June 1983): 587-97. Reprinted with permission.

exemptions, bond guarantees, loans, purchases of railroad stock, and donations of cash and securities.⁴ State grants included roughly 49 million acres of land.⁵

4   With the growth of the railroads came a new set of problems, particularly abuses of customers and political corruption. Many areas had no developed mode of transportation except for a single railroad, a situation which opened the way for exorbitant rates. The wealth which the railroads generated and the ethics of some of the railroad magnates fostered ordinary bribery and more imaginative shenanigans. The states responded with a variety of railroad regulations in the late 1800s.⁶

5   One aspect of the "railroad problem" in recent years is the decline of rail passenger service. In 1944, passenger trains accounted for 31 percent of all intercity passenger miles and 75 percent of all intercity passenger miles on public carriers. By 1976 the respective shares were 0.7 percent and 5 percent.⁷ At the beginning of the Great Depression, the United States had approximately 20,000 passenger trains, a figure which had fallen below 500 by 1970.⁸ Consequently, total passenger miles covered by passenger trains in 1970 were lower than during the depths of the Depression,⁹ despite tremendous growth in travel by other transportation modes. Many areas now lack passenger train service entirely and most other areas have only limited service.

6   While the national government has taken the leading role in dealing with intercity passenger train service, the states also have an opportunity to become involved. They may induce Amtrak to provide additional service or continue services scheduled for termination if the states involved are willing to help pay for financial losses incurred on those routes.

B   The States Respond

1   In recent years a number of states have responded to the declining availability of rail passenger service in the same way that states responded to the lack of available rail service in the 1800s—by enacting subsidies.¹⁰ Most states have not chosen to subsidize intercity passenger service by Amtrak, but nine states have. What could account for the differences in state responses?

2   A variety of research has shown that state policy decisions in a number of fields are strongly influenced by historical-geographic, social, and economic forces.¹¹ An urban society creates problems and demands which are different from those of a rural society. A wealthy state can afford to support programs more generously than can a poor state. Ideological forces also shape state policy responses.¹² Conservative viewpoints discourage government intervention and expenditure, while liberal views have the opposite effect. Organizational influences may affect decisions by altering the perceptions and career incentives of bureaucrats.¹³

3   We must consider the possibility that a state's response to a new problem will be shaped by that state's general receptivity to new ideas and programs. Those states which are generally reluctant to do new things¹⁴ may not respond to a new problem due to sheer slowness overall rather than because of the particular issue involved. Prior policy decisions in related areas may affect current decisions, both by giving a sense of what officials have perceived as reasonable or important in the past and also because prior decisions and commitments may influence what

is politically feasible now. Intervention in one area in the past may facilitate involvement in a related area later.[15] Finally, interest group involvement may affect state responses, particularly in a field which is as heavily involved with interest group politics as is transportation.[16]

4   We have ample grounds to expect metropolitanization to encourage subsidization of Amtrak. Rural states tend to be more highway oriented and to devote more funds to highway programs,[17] a situation which should discourage rail subsidies. Railroads are believed to have relatively high fixed costs (though there is controversy on that point). If that is correct, then costs may be reduced through greater volumes of traffic.[18] Volume per mile of rail line is likely to be greatest when the population is relatively concentrated rather than dispersed across the countryside. As a result, subsidies will be most productive in terms of services in relatively urbanized states. Finally, the American railroad system has been designed primarily to link major metropolitan areas.[19] Overall, states which have more of their populations in metropolitan areas should be more likely to subsidize Amtrak.

5   The figures in Table 1 are entirely consistent with the hypothesis. Not a single state which was less than 60 percent metropolitan subsidized Amtrak (states which have no Amtrak service are omitted, but each which is within the 48 contiguous states is less than 60 percent urban). As states grow more metropolitan, the probability of subsidizing Amtrak rises to over 40 percent in the states which are 80 percent or more metropolitan.

6   Subsidy behavior is also likely to be affected by state wealth. Prior research has found that state-local expenditures are strongly influenced by the state economy.[20] A state which is hard-pressed to finance essential services is unlikely to be able to spare funds for intercity passenger rail service. Economic abundance, on the other hand, may encourage subsidization.

7   The evidence in Table 1 indicates that affluence does encourage subsidi-

Table 1

Percent of State's Population Living in Metropolitan Areas, 1976[a]

	80% or more	*60% to 79%*	*59% or less*
Subsidized[b]	6 (43%)	3 (21%)	0 (0%)
Not subsidized	8 (57%)	11 (79%)	16 (100%)

gamma = .79
tau$_c$ = .38

Per Capita Income, 1976

	Over $5,900	*Less than $5,900*
Subsidized	9 (33%)	0 (0%)
Not subsidized	18 (67%)	17 (100%)

gamma = 1.0
tau$_c$ = .32

[a] *Statistical Abstract*, 1978, 19.

[b] State subsidized Amtrak, 1980. *Amtrak National Train Timetables*, October 26, 1930 - January 31, 1981. Washington, D.C.: National Railroad Passenger Corporation, 1980. States not served by Amtrak are excluded.

zation of Amtrak. Not a single state with a per capita income less than $5,900 subsidized Amtrak, but a third of the states over that income level did.

8 Transportation policy is shaped by political ideology.[21] Where individualism, limited government, and private-sector decision making are prized, government efforts to alter the results of the market are likely to be frowned upon.[22] In general those views are associated with political conservatism; liberals are more likely to favor the use of governmental authority to change society.[23] Liberals might see passenger rail service as a desirable way to promote the public health and safety in view of the excellent safety record of passenger trains, particularly in contrast to automobiles.[24]

9 Table 2 indicates that state party ideology is clearly associated with subsidization of Amtrak. States with conservative Republican parties (categories 1-2) virtually never subsidize Amtrak, and states with conservative Democratic parties (categories 4-5) behave similarly. Of the states which have two conservative parties (Republican categories 1-2 and Democratic categories 4-5), not a single one subsidizes Amtrak (data not shown).

10 State transportation policies may also reflect the organizations which states have created to deal with transportation issues. Administrative arrangements are to some degree a function of political demands.[25] Dissatisfaction with the current state of affairs may lead to demands for the creation of new agencies.[26] The structure of administrative arrangements may also affect how agency officials perceive their jobs, set their agendas, and rank their priorities.[27] Agency officials tend to adopt the perspective of the agency they work in and to develop options and disseminate information which protects the agency's position.[28] When the dominant transportation agency is a highway department, transportation problems and solutions are very likely to be perceived in terms of roads and highways. A state department of transportation, by contrast, may encourge a broader perspective on transportation issues.

Table 2

Republican Party Ideology[a]

	1 − 2	*3 − 5*
Subsidized	1 (4%)	8 (38%)
Not subsidized	22 (96%)	13 (62%)

gamma = −.86
tau_c = .34

Democratic Party Ideology[b]

	1 − 3	*4 − 5*
Subsidized	8 (29%)	1 (6%)
Not subsidized	20 (71%)	15 (94%)

gamma = .71
tau_c = .21

[a] Eugene McGregor, "Uncertainty and National Nominating Coalitions," *Journal of Politics* 40 (1978): 1020-1021. Low scores indicate conservatism.
[b] Ibid., 1022-1023. Low scores indicate liberalism.

Table 3

State Had Department of Transportation as of 1977[a]

	Yes	No
Subsidized	9 (28%)	0 (6%)
Not subsidized	23 (72%)	12 (100%)

gamma $=$ 1.0

$\text{tau}_c = .22$

[a] *Book of the States*, 1978-79, p. 376.

11   As Table 3 indicates, administrative organization and subsidy behavior are indeed associated. States without a department of transportation were certain not to subsidize Amtrak. States with a department of transportation were moderately likely to subsidize.

12   Although state governments have subsidized railroads since the 1800s, financial aid to Amtrak is a comparatively recent activity. Prior research indicates that the states vary considerably in their inclinations toward adopting new ideas.[29] States may refrain from subsidizing Amtrak because they are slow to do new things.

13   Table 4 reveals that subsidy of Amtrak is clearly related to two measures of innovativeness. The first measure is the number of times a state is cited in the *1970 State Legislative Program* of the Advisory Commission on Intergovernmental Relations.[30] The measure gives a relatively recent perspective on state innovation and is strongly associated with Amtrak subsidization. Note that a majority of the most innovative states (4 or more citations) subsidize Amtrak but that only one of the 30 least innovative states does. Jack Walker's in-

Table 4

Innovation as Measured by 1970 ACIR Citations[a]

	4 or more	3 or fewer
Subsidized	8 (57%)	1 (3%)
Not subsidized	6 (43%)	29 (97%)

gamma $=$ .95

$\text{tau}_c = .47$

Innovation as Measured by Walker Index[b]

	.48 or higher	Less than .48
Subsidized	8 (50%)	1 (4%)
Not subsidized	8 (50%)	27 (96%)

gamma $=$ .93

$\text{tau}_c = .43$

[a] Jack Walker, "Innovation in State Politics," in Herbert Jacob and Kenneth Vines, eds., *Politics in the American States*, 2d ed. (Boston: Little, Brown, 1971), 379.
[b] Ibid., 358.

Table 5

	High Environmental Concern[a]		
	Yes	No	
Subsidized	7 (39%)	2 (8%)	gamma = .77
Not subsidized	11 (61%)	24 (92%)	tau_c = .30

[a] States were classified as having high environmental concern if they ranked in the top 15 in the nation in spending to control air (1961) or water (1962) pollution. Charles Jones, "Regulating the Environment," in Herbert Jacob and Kenneth Vines, eds., *Politics in the American States*, 3d ed. (Boston: Little, Brown, 1976), 400.

novation index, which is based on the speed with which states adopted innovations over a far longer time period, is also associated with Amtrak subsidies. Fully half of the most innovative states subsidize Amtrak, but only one of the 28 least innovative does.[31]

14   State subsidies of Amtrak may reflect a general concern for protecting the environment. Rail transportation requires much less land area to move a given number of passengers than does automobile transportation.[32] Trains are also more fuel efficient per passenger mile than airplanes or, to most observers, automobiles.[33] The greater fuel efficiency of rail travel in turn means less pollution than air or automobile travel.[34] Overall, then, we would expect states which have displayed more concern for the environment to be more likely to subsidize Amtrak.

15   Table 5 supports this hypothesis. A prior record of environmental concern is clearly associated with subsidization; high environmental concern states are almost five times as likely to subsidize Amtrak as are low environmental concern states.

16   Finally, support for Amtrak may reflect interest group pressure.[35] The National Association of Railroad Passengers was formed in the late 1960s to generate support for rail passenger service. Given the presumably limited salience of the issue for the general public, the existence of an organized voice may be crucial.

Table 6

Membership in National Association of Railroad Passengers Per Capita[a]

	Top 30	Bottom 20	
Subsidized	9 (33%)	0 (0%)	gamma = 1.0
Not subsidized	18 (67%)	17 (100%)	tau_c = .32

[a] Personal communication from Barry Williams, Assistant Director, National Association of Railroad Passengers, December 16, 1981. Membership figures are for November 1981.

17   The evidence in Table 6 supports the interest group hypothesis. Not a single state which ranks in the bottom 20 in NARP membership per capita subsidizes Amtrak, but a third of the states in the top 30 do.

C   A Multivariate Model

1   The preceding analysis shows that states which are metropolitan, wealthy, liberal, concerned for the environment, equipped with a department of transportation, and relatively well endowed with NARP members are likely to subsidize Amtrak. The analysis based on individual variables does not indicate their relative contributions, may include spurious relationships, and fails to explain the behavior of many states. A multivariate model could help overcome these problems, but most multivariate techniques are inappropriate for a dependent variable which is dichotomous and highly skewed.

2   A solution to this problem lies in simulation techniques, which have been used for such diverse purposes as analyzing municipal budgeting,[36] organizational behavior,[37] and congressional decision-making.[38] A decisional flow chart patterned after Kingdon's enables us to map out the influences on Amtrak subsidy decisions and to predict how states will respond to the issue. By specifying certain characteristics as preconditions for subsidy behavior, we can classify the states according to whether they meet each precondition.

3   An examination of Tables 1 through 6 indicates that several factors appear to be necessary but not sufficient conditions for subsidy of Amtrak. First, not a single state which is less than 60 percent metropolitan subsidizes Amtrak. Second, not a single state with per capita income less than $5,900 subsidizes Amtrak. Third, not a single state with two conservative parties subsidizes Amtrak. Fourth, no state without a Department of Transportation subsidizes. Finally, with one exception, states which are not relatively innovative decline to subsidize.[39]

4   These necessary but not sufficient conditions can be readily incorporated into a decisional flow chart which forms a model of the factors influencing state decisions to subsidize Amtrak (see Table 7). The ordering of the variables broadly follows Hofferbert's ordering of influences, with historic-geographic conditions (metropolitanization) preceding socio-economic factors (wealth), followed by institutional forces and elite behavior.[40] The resulting model correctly classifies 91 percent of all states which had Amtrak service as of November, 1980. The model also predicts that the four states of the continental 48 which lack Amtrak service will not subsidize Amtrak.[41]

5   The model indicates that 21 of the 35 states which do not subsidize Amtrak behave as they do because they are not sufficiently metropolitan and/or wealthy. Administrative and ideological factors exert comparatively modest influence, but innovativeness has considerable impact, particularly in view of the fact that the other four independent variables precede it in the model.

6   Overall, the model is quite successful in predicting subsidy behavior. Fully 97 percent of the states which are predicted not to subsidize Amtrak behave as predicted, and nearly three-fourths of the states predicted to subsidize fit the prediction.

Table 7

State Decisions to Subsidize Amtrak[a]

Step Number	Premise		Result	Accuracy	Cumulative Percentage[b]
1	Was state at least 60% metro, 1976?	no	Do not subsidize Amtrak (n=16)	100%	36%
	↓ yes				
2	Was per capita income over $5,900 in 1976?	no	Do not subsidize Amtrak (n=5)	100%	48%
	↓ yes				
3	Did state have a department of transportation, 1977?	no	Do not subsidize Amtrak (n=3)	100%	55%
	↓ yes				
4	Did state have at least one moderate or liberal party?[c]	no	Do not subsidize Amtrak (n=3)	100%	61%
	↓ yes				
5	Was state an innovator?[d]	no	Do not subsidize Amtrak (n=6)	83%	72%
	yes ↘		Subsidize Amtrak (n=11)	73%	91%

[a] The format of this table is taken from John Kingdon, *Congressmen's Voting Decisions,* 2d ed. (New York: Harper & Row, 1981), 244, 330.
[b] Percentage of cases correctly classified by this step and all preceding steps.
[c] Eugene McGregor, "Uncertainty and National Nominating Coalitions," *Journal of Politics* 40 (1978). Republican 3-5 or Democratic categories 1-3.
[d] Four or more citations in *1970 Legislative Program* of the ACIR. See Jack Walker, "Innovation in State Politics," in Herbert Jacobs and Kenneth Vines, eds., *Politics in the American States,* 2d ed. (Boston: Little, Brown, 1971), 379.

D   Conclusions

1 Historically, the American states have often sought to influence the production of goods and provision of services through regulation, licensing, tax policy, subsidies, and direct provision and production. A substantial portion of that effort has been directed toward various forms of transportation, from road building to creating special authorities to operate local airports. While the railroads were once the center of attention in state transportation policymaking, they have not been for many years. They have been crowded out by highways,

which have benefited from massive federal grants and the support of an impressive array of interest groups.[42]

2   As the railroads have fallen on hard times in some respects, service cutbacks have occurred in many areas. The termination of unprofitable activities may help the railroads' financial situation but may be traumatic for the communities affected. A major question facing the states is whether they should act to preserve a safe and fuel efficient form of transportation, both in terms of rural freight service[43] and in terms of intercity passenger service. If the trains are in trouble because they simply fail to meet current consumer needs and wants,[44] then subsidies will simply promote a lost cause and introduce distortions into the transportation system. If, on the other hand, the railroads are in trouble because of massive government subsidies to other forms of transportation and a long history of artificially low fuel prices, subsidies may help correct existing distortions and help lay the groundwork for a system which may grow increasingly necessary as fuel prices rise and petroleum products grow scarce.

3   The preceding analysis indicates that metropolitanization, affluence, and innovativeness play major roles in shaping state subsidy decisions. Ideological and administrative influences also play minor but discernible parts. A model based on these five factors predicts whether states will subsidize Amtrak with 91 percent accuracy.

E   Notes

1. John Stover, *American Railroads* (Chicago: University of Chicago Press, 1961).
2. One could argue that Amtrak, being a public corporation, is not affected by market forces, but the persistent concern over financial losses and limited ridership and the existence of private transportation competition place Amtrak in a marketplace environment.
3. Thomas Dye, "Taxing, Spending, and Economic Growth in the American States," *Journal of Politics* 42 (1980).
4. William Black and Jame Runke, *The States and Rural Rail Preservation* (Lexington, Ky.: Council of State Governments, 1975); and Roy Sampson and Martin Farris, *Domestic Transportation*, 4th ed. (Boston: Houghton-Mifflin, 1979).
5. Stover, *American Railroads.*
6. Daniel Grant and H. C. Nixon, *State and Local Government in America*, 3d ed. (Boston: Allyn and Bacon, 1975); and Stover, *American Railroads.*
7. Donald Harper, *Transportation in America* (Englewood Cliffs, N.J.: Prentice-Hall, 1978); and *Transportation Facts and Trends*, 13th ed. (Washington, D.C.: Transportation Association of America, 1977).
8. Carl Chelf, *Public Policymaking in America* (Santa Monica, Calif.: Goodyear, 1981); and Inez Morris and David Morris, *North America by Rail* (Indianapolis, Ind.: Bobbs-Merrill, 1977).
9. George Hilton, *Amtrak* (Washington, D.C.: American Enterprise Institute, 1980).
10. As of fall 1980 these states were California, Illinois, Maryland, Michigan, Minnesota, Missouri, New York, Oregon, and Pennsylvania. *Amtrak National Train Timetables*, October 26, 1980 - January 31, 1981.
11. Richard Dawson and James Robinson, "Interparty Competition, Economic Variables, and Welfare Policies in the American States," *Journal of Politics* 25 (1963);

and Thomas Dye, *Politics, Economics, and the Public* (Chicago: Rand McNally, 1966).

12. Edward Jennings, "Competition, Constituencies, and Welfare Policies in American States," *American Political Science Review* 73 (1979); and David Nice, "Party Ideology and Policy Outcomes in the American States," *Social Science Quarterly* 63 (1982).

13. Harold Seidman, *Politics, Position, and Power*, 2d ed. (New York: Oxford University Press, 1975); and George Edwards and Ira Sharkansky, *The Policy Predicament* (San Francisco: Freeman, 1978).

14. Jack Walker, "Innovation in State Politics," in Herbert Jacob and Kenneth Vines, eds., *Politics in the American States*, 2d ed. (Boston: Little, Brown, 1971).

15. Jack Walker, "Setting the Agenda in the U.S. Senate: A Theory of Problem Selection," *British Journal of Political Science* 7 (1977).

16. David Berman, *State and Local Politics* (Boston: Holbrook, 1975); and David Hapgood, "The Highwaymen," in Charles Peters and James Fallows, eds., *Inside the System*, 3d ed. (New York: Praeger, 1976).

17. Dye, *Politics, Economics, and the Public;* and Thomas Dye, *Politics in States and Communities*, 4th ed. (Englewood Cliffs, N.J.: Prentice-Hall, 1981).

18. Harper, *Transportation.*

19. John Harrigan, *Politics and Policy in States and Communities* (Boston: Little, Brown, 1980).

20. Dye, *Politics, Economics, and the Public.*

21. Frank Colcord, "Urban Transportation and Political Ideology: Sweden and the United States," in Alan Altshuler, ed., *Current Issues in Transportation Policy* (Lexington, Mass.: Lexington Books, 1979).

22. Ibid.; and Herbert Simon, Donald Smithburg, and Victor Thompson, *Public Administration* (New York: Knopf, 1950).

23. Lyman Sargent, *Contemporary Political Ideologies*, 5th ed. (Homewood, Ill.: Dorsey, 1981). For analysis of the impact of party coalitions and ideology on state policy making, see Jennings, "Competition," and Nice, "Party Ideology."

24. Hilton, *Amtrak;* and Morris and Morris, *North America by Rail.*

25. Peter Woll, *American Bureaucracy*, 2d ed. (New York: W. W. Norton, 1977).

26. Simon, Smithburg, and Thompson, *Public Administration.*

27. Seidman, *Politics.*

28. Edwards and Sharkansky, *The Policy Predicament.*

29. Jack Walker, "The Diffusion of Innovations among the American States," *American Political Science Review* 63 (1969); and Walker, "Innovation."

30. Walker, "Innovation."

31. Ibid.

32. Dye, *Politics, Economics, and the Public;* and Morris and Morris, *North America by Rail.*

33. The cited figures vary on the latter point. See Harper, *Transportation;* Hilton, *Amtrak;* Morris and Morris, *North America by Rail;* and *National Transportation Statistics* (Washington, D.C.: U.S. Department of Transportation, 1980).

34. Harper, *Transportation;* and Morris and Morris, *North America by Rail.*

35. Recent works on the role of interest groups in state policy making include John Hutcheson and George Taylor, "Religious Variables, Political System Characteristics and Policy Outputs in the American States," *American Journal of Political Science* 17 (1973); Lester Salamon and John Siegfried, "Economic Power and Political Influence: The Impact of Industry Structure on Public Policy," *American Political Science Review* 71 (1977); and Ronald Weber and William Shaffer,

"Public Opinion and American State Policy-Making," *Midwest Journal of Political Science* 16 (1972).

36. John Crecine, *Government Problem Solving* (Chicago: Rand McNally, 1969).

37. Richard Cyert and James March, *A Behavioral Theory of the Firm* (Englewood Cliffs, N.J.: Prentice-Hall, 1963).

38. John Kingdon, *Congressmen's Voting Decisions,* 2d ed. (New York: Harper & Row, 1981).

39. While high membership in NARP also appears to be a precondition, that variable's influence is largely a function of metropolitanization and wealth.

40. Richard Hofferbert, *The Study of Public Policy* (Indianapolis, Ind.: Boss-Merrill, 1974).

41. If the four states of the continental 48 which lack Amtrak service are included in the model, all four are predicted not to subsidize by the first stage. The model's accuracy is then 92 percent. A two-variable model based on the ACIR innovation measure (Walker, "Innovation") and Republican Party ideology (McGregor, "Uncertainty") has a comparable degree of predictive accuracy but has less theoretical appeal due to its omission of social and economic influences.

42. Hapgood, "The Highwaymen."

43. Black and Runke, *The States.*

44. Hilton, *Amtrak.*

Now that you have read this example of a research report and noted if and where the author has addressed the 12 research questions, compare your findings with ours. The letters and numbers after each question refer to where in the article the question under discussion is addressed.

1) *Does the researcher clearly specify the main research question or problem? What is the "why" question?* (A-1, B-1)

The research question is clearly specified. It is: What accounts for differences in state responses to the decline of intercity rail passenger service? Rephrased in the form of a "why" question it becomes: Why do some states subsidize rail passenger service while other states do not?

2) *Has the researcher demonstrated the value and significance of his own research question and indicated how his research findings will contribute to scientific knowledge about his topic?* (A, B)

Yes, this is done in the introduction. Nice presents three reasons why his research question is significant. First, the proper role of government in shaping economic activities is an important public policy issue. State subsidies for Amtrak service may be considered government intervention in the marketplace. Thus, to the extent that Nice's research provides knowledge about the conditions under which states engage in marketplace intervention, it contributes to our understanding of this issue. Second, state economic growth has been found to be related to highway transportation policies. Presumably other state transportation policies also will affect economic growth and, therefore, they are important to study. Third, passenger rail service may be a desirable transportation option to preserve for energy, environmental, and safety reasons. These reasons are not discussed in-depth, however, nor does Nice refer the reader to other discussions of these topics in the literature.

One other reason for the significance of knowledge about Amtrak subsidies emerges from the introduction: states have been involved in the regulation of railroads for some time. Thus subsidizing Amtrak may be seen as another chapter in railroad-state relations. Finally, a major contribution of Nice's research is implied rather than explicitly stated. In trying to explain state Amtrak subsidies, he tests the utility of factors that have been used by others to explain differences in state policy responses. Thus he is adding to our understanding of differences in state policy responses and to the identification of general explanations for these differences.

3) *Has the researcher proposed clear explanations for the political phenomena that interest him?* (B-2,3) *What types of relationships are hypothesized?* (B-4,6,8,10,12,14,16) (C-3,4) *Does he discuss any alternative explanations?*

In this article the researcher is interested in explaining state responses to the declining availability of rail passenger service. Some states have responded with subsidies, others have not. Nice proposes that the difference in response may be explained by differences among the states in urbanization, wealth, political ideology, innovativeness, environmental concern, interest group pressure, and the organization of state transportation agencies. The researcher does not discuss any alternative explanations to these seven.

All the hypotheses are directional. Directional hypotheses require ordinal or interval level measures. All the variables are either ordinal level variables or can be treated as such. (A nominal level variable with only two categories—that is, subsidized, not subsidized—can be treated as an ordinal level variable.) In each hypothesis a higher level of subsidization is associated with a higher level of an independent variable. The seven hypotheses advanced by the researcher are as follows:

1. States which have more of their populations in metropolitan areas should be more likely to subsidize Amtrak. (B-4)
2. Economic abundance ... may encourage subsidization. (B-6)
3. Transportation policy is shaped by political ideology. Where individualism, limited government, and private-sector decision making are prized, government efforts to alter the results of the market are likely to be frowned upon. (B-8)
4. State transportation policies may ... reflect the organizations which states have created to deal with transportation issues. ... A state department of transportation ... may encourage a broader perspective on transportation issues. (B-10)

5. States may refrain from subsidizing Amtrak because they are slow to do new things. (B-12).

6. We would expect states which have displayed more concern for the environment to be more likely to subsidize Amtrak. (B-14).

7. Support for Amtrak may reflect interest group pressure. (B-16)

The hypothesized relationships are also causal. Each of the independent variables is suggested as a cause of subsidies or lack of subsidies. In section C, the researcher argues that several of the variables are necessary conditions or preconditions for subsidy behavior.

4) *Are the independent and dependent variables identified? If so, what are they? Has the author considered any alternative or control variables? If so, please identify them. Can you think of any that the researcher did not mention?* (B) (C-1,2,3)

The dependent variable, whether or not a state subsidizes Amtrak passenger rail service, is clearly identified. Seven independent variables that measure three types of forces thought to influence state policy decisions (historical-geographic forces, social and economic forces, and institutional forces and elite behavior) are also clearly identified. Each one of these seven variables is suggested as an alternative, independent variable.

For statistical reasons mentioned in paragraph C-1, Nice does not introduce any control variables into his analysis. Thus he is unable to check for spurious relationships. It is also highly probable that several of the characteristics of states overlap or coincide (for example, metropolitan population and per capita income, and innovation and Transportation Department organization). This makes it difficult to determine the effect of an independent variable. Because Nice does not use any control variables, he is unable to isolate and measure precisely the effect of only one independent variable.

5. *Are the hypotheses empirical, general, and plausible?* (B)

The hypotheses are empirical. Each hypothesis relates a characteristic of states to the subsidization of Amtrak, and each concept can be measured empirically. The hypotheses can be objectively evaluated based on the data.

Reasons are given to support the plausibility of each hypothesis. For example, the hypothesis relating environmental concern and subsidization is justified on the grounds that rail transportation involves less land, consumes less fuel, and results in less air pollution than automobile transportation does—factors presumably of concern to environmentalists. (B-14) The hypotheses are also sufficiently general. They suggest relationships that may be tested for many states rather than one or a few. The hypotheses might also be adapted to explain the variation in a variety of state government activities, hence extending the application of the research beyond subsidies for Amtrak service.

6) *Are the concepts in the hypotheses clearly defined? Are the operational definitions to the variables valid and reasonable?* (B)

The meanings of the concepts Nice is using in his hypotheses are quite clear from the start, and they become clearer as they are given operational definitions. For several of the independent variables, however, serious questions remain unanswered concerning the adequacy of the operational definitions.

The operational definition of *urbanization*—percent of a state's population living in metropolitan areas in 1976—is reasonable since it is metropolitan areas that are linked by rail service. Other possible definitions of urbanization would tend to include quite small urban areas unlikely to be oriented toward rail transportation.

The operational definition of *state wealth*—per capita income in 1976—is also probably an appropriate measure of a state's financial resources. However, wealth, the concept used in the hypothesis, and income are not the same thing. A state may possess a lot of wealth (for example, in the form of land and commercial property that could be taxed by the state government) and yet not have an unusually high level of per capita income. Whether or not per capita income is a good indication of state wealth, then, is an issue that the researcher should have addressed.

Defining the *political ideology* of a state by the ideology of the two major parties also presents some difficulties. First of all, since the operational definition is taken from the work of another researcher, it is impossible to know how it is measured. Is it party leaders, or public officials, or rank-and-file identifiers whose ideology has been measured? Second, it is not clear that the best way to assess a state's political ideology is by observing the ideology of the two major parties separately. Perhaps we should be concerned only with the ideology of the party that has been dominant in state government over the last few years, or perhaps we should consider the effect of the combined ideologies of both parties rather than of each major party separately. (Nice mentions the latter possibility in passing in B-9.)

Nice's operational definition of *state transportation organization* is also problematic. The only thing the operational definition relies upon is the name of the state department charged with administering transportation policy. The names given to such agencies probably do indicate something about the programmatic concerns and intentions of the agency, but they also may disguise the realities of policy salience and development. As Nice himself points out, it may not be only the existence but also the structure of state administrative arrangements that have an impact on state public policy. One would have hoped for a more informative operational definition of state transportation organization.

The operational definitions used for *environmental concern* and *interest group pressure* in the states are also questionable. The top 15 states in the nation in spending to control air and water pollution are defined as having high environmental concern. This operational definition does not take into account the degree of severity of pollution in a state and the financial capability of states to address pollution problems. One would expect larger, wealthier, more industrialized states to spend more on pollution control than smaller, poorer, or less industrialized states, even though the latter may be exerting a proportionately larger effort to reduce pollution.

Similarly, membership in the National Association of Railroad Passengers is not the only way to measure interest group pressure for Amtrak subsidies. Other operational definitions might involve measurement of the organization's efforts to influence state policy decisions. The size of a group, even if accurately judged, does not necessarily indicate how active or influential that group is.

Finally, the operational definition for *innovation* is impossible to evaluate from this article alone since it depends on the research of another political scientist. This serves several purposes. First, it provides a check on the operational definitions of concepts used by others; that is, if Nice did not find support for his hypotheses using these definitions, he might have questioned the validity of the measures as well as the accuracy of his hypotheses. Second, by using previously employed measures, Nice's research findings may be more easily compared with other work that used these same measures. Third, less effort is required to collect the data to test his hypotheses since the original data collection and classification of states was done by others. To evaluate the adequacy of the operational definition, however, the reader would have to consult the articles cited in this research report.

7) *What method of data collection is used to make the necessary observations?* (B) *Are the observations valid and reliable measurements?* (B)

Nice relies primarily on published documents to measure his variables. He uses published data from the National Railroad Passenger Corporation to measure the dependent variable. Measures of the independent variables come from government documents (the *Statistical Abstract of the United States* and *National Transportation Statistics*), the published work of other political scientists, and, in the case of interest group membership, from personal communication with an individual from the National Association of Railroad Passengers (NARP).

Nice does not discuss potential measurement problems such as the possibility that the NARP overestimates its membership or that Census Bureau data underestimate the numbers of poor people and people living in urban areas because of difficulties in locating these people. Nor does Nice provide any evidence pertaining to the reliability and validity of the measurements used. At a minimum, it is possible that some of the observations are out of date. This is one drawback to relying on published data. By the time data are published, circumstances may have changed. For example, a state's per capita income may have dropped from above $5,900 in 1976 to below $5,900 in 1977 or 1978. Per capita income in these years may have more influence on Amtrak subsidization in 1980 than per capita income in 1976.

Another measurement decision that is never justified by Nice is the classification of a number of the independent variables into only two or three categories. The measures of urbanization, income, ideology, innovation, environmental concern, and interest group activity are all numerical measures that take on more than two values initially. Ordinarily, researchers are reluctant to sacrifice information by reducing the level of measurement of their measures. Nice, however, routinely turns his measures into ordinal ones, without explaining the decision to divide the measures into the categories selected.

  8) *Has the researcher made empirical observations about the units of analysis specified in the hypotheses?* (B)

The researcher has obtained measures of his variables for *states*, which are his units of analysis. In several cases, observations were made for units that are not states (individuals, parties), but the information about these units was aggregated by state and therefore became characteristics or attributes of a state.

  9) *If a sample is used, what type of sample is it?* (B-5) *Does the type of sample seriously affect the conclusions that can be drawn from the research? Does the researcher discuss this?*

Nice does not use a sample. The population of interest is all states with Amtrak service, and all these states are included in the study. Although Nice refers to states in a general way, he makes it clear that states without Amtrak service are omitted from the study. It makes sense to exclude states without Amtrak service: they could hardly be expected to subsidize a nonexistent service. Inclusion of these states would make it more difficult to examine the relationship between other state characteristics and Amtrak subsidization.

  10) *What type of research design is used?* (B,C) *Does the research design adequately test the hypothesized relationships? For example, if the researcher hypothesizes a causal relationship, does the research design permit the researcher to show a causal relationship?*

The type of research design is cross-sectional. Nice does not manipulate any of the independent variables. Rather he uses attributes of states measured prior to measurement of the dependent variable to sort the states into various "treatment" groups (for example, 80 percent or more metropolitan, 60-79 percent metropolitan, 59 percent or less metropolitan). In other words, he relies on existing variation among the states with respect to the independent variables to establish treatment and control groups.

The cross-sectional research design does not permit Nice to show a causal relationship. Because he has no control over the assignment of states to treatment and control groups, the states he is comparing could be nonequivalent with respect to some other characteristic related to Amtrak subsidization. Furthermore, for one independent variable, membership in NARP, the time of measurement (1981) is after the time of measurement of the dependent variable (1980). Thus no causal argument can be made.

11) *Are the statistics that are used appropriate for the level of measurement of the variables?* (Table 1)

The statistics are appropriate for the level of measurement. In each case the dependent variable and independent variables are ordinal level measures or, in the case of a dichotomous nominal level variable, may be treated as such. Thus the dependent variable with two categories—subsidized and not subsidized—may be considered an ordinal measure of subsidization, and the independent variable, high environmental concern (with "yes" and "no" categories), may be considered an ordinal measure of environmental concern.

Contingency tables are an appropriate way to present the data. Nice uses gamma and tau as measures of association that are appropriate for grouped, ordinal data. The use of both kinds of statistics illustrates how different methods of calculating measures of association yield different values. Generally gamma values will be higher than the tau values, as shown in the tables.

12) *Are the research findings presented and discussed clearly? Is the basis for deciding whether a hypothesis is supported or refuted specified clearly?* (B, C)

The research findings are reported clearly. Note that the findings for each hypothesis are reported and summarized in tables *and* discussed in the text. Nice does not interpret the gamma and tau values, but this is not a serious omission because the strength of the relationships between the independent and dependent variables can be easily grasped by reading the contingency tables. These tables provide a clear basis for deciding whether to reject or accept a hypothesis.

Because of the limited number of cases (44 states) and the small number of states that subsidize Amtrak (9 states), Nice is unable to check for spurious relationships by introducing control variables or to ascertain the relative explanatory power of the independent variables. Thus the relationship shown in a contingency table may be the result of several factors in combination, rather than the single independent variable. For example, innovative states may also be wealthy states, thus the relationship between innovation and Amtrak subsidies could be due primarily to wealth.

Nice uses a model rather than multiple regression to examine the combined explanatory power of the independent variables. The model begins with those variables that have the least direct impact on public policy (historic-geographic) and ends with those factors thought to have the most direct and immediate impact on public policy (institutional forces and elite behavior). The model thus indicates how each variable contributes to the accurate prediction of whether a state subsidizes Amtrak. Using five factors, the model makes accurate predictions about subsidization for 91 percent of the states.

Nice describes the basis for calculating the percentages shown in Table 7 but the actual calculations themselves are not shown. This is common practice when the calculations or formulas are well-known. Often an author will refer the reader to a source that describes more fully the statistical procedures used in analysis. If desired, more information about calculations may be requested from an author.

Conclusion

A research report rarely answers all the questions that can be raised about a topic. But a well-written report, because it carefully explains how the researcher conducted each stage in the research process, makes it easier for other researchers to evaluate the research. It helps other investigators build upon it by varying the method of data collection, the operationalization of variables, or the research design.

The model developed by Nice does not predict successfully the behavior of all of the states in his study. You may be interested in trying to explain the behavior of the states that did not fit the model's predictions. One method of investigation would be to read published accounts of state legislative and executive activities and pronouncements concerning Amtrak subsidies. Another would be to interview key individuals involved in a subsidy decision. You may find that a determining factor was the political ideology of the dominant party in a state legislature; Nice measures only if there is at least one moderate or liberal party in the state. Or perhaps the political ideology of a state as indicated by Nice's measure taken in 1978 or earlier had changed in 1979. Therefore, his measure would not have been a valid measure of political ideology at the time subsidy decisions were made. Thus you could identify and measure new independent variables or modify existing independent variables.

Another research direction would be to measure the subsidy behavior of states for a year other than 1980. Perhaps in 1981 or 1982 more states subsidized Amtrak than in 1980. By replicating Nice's research for different years, you could test the general applicability of the model.

By now you should understand how scientific knowledge about politics is acquired. You should know how to formulate a testable hypothesis, choose valid and reliable measures for the concepts that you relate in the hypothesis, develop a research design, conduct a literature review, and make empirical observations. You also should be able to analyze data using appropriate univariate, bivariate, and multivariate statistics. Finally, you should be able to evaluate most research reports as well as write a research report yourself.

We encourage you to try to think up research questions of your own. Some of these may be feasible projects for a one- or two-semester course. You will learn much more about the research process by doing research than by just reading about it. We wish you success.

Exercises

1. Choose one of the following research articles or one assigned to you by your instructor and see if you can answer the series of questions on pages 335-36 on your own.

Alan S. Zuckerman and Darrell M. West, "The Political Bases of Citizen Contacting: A Cross-National Analysis," *American Political Science Review* 79 (March 1985): 117-31.

Michael J. Robinson, "Public Affairs Television and the Growth of Political Malaise: The Case of 'The Selling of the Pentagon,'" *American Political Science Review* 70 (June 1976): 409-32.

Marc Howard Ross, "Political Alienation, Participation, and Ethnicity: An African Case," *American Journal of Political Science* 19 (May 1975): 291-311.

Michael E. Hilton, "The Impact of Recent Changes in California Drinking-Driving Laws on Fatal Accident Levels during the First Post-intervention Year: An Interrupted Time Series Analysis," *Law & Society Review* 18 (1984): 605-28.

2. Using the article assigned in Exercise 1, describe how you would build upon the research and mount a related investigation of your own.

Index

Ross, Marc Howard - 226, 244*n*, 245*n*, 247, 354
Routing respondents - 169
RRT. *See* Randomized response technique
Rubin, Herbert J. - 85
Running records - 198-99
  bibliographical data - 202
  campaign spending - 200-201
  congressional voting - 199
  crime statistics - 200
  defined - 221
  election returns - 199
  vs. episodic records - 202-203
  foreign affairs - 202
  government policy - 199
  judicial decisions - 199
  mass media materials - 201
  speeches - 201
Runyon, Richard P. - 264*n*, 266, 310
Rusk, Jerrold G. - 85

Saliency - 167-68
Salmon, Charles T. - 186*n*
Sample, defined - 137, 154
Sample bias - 139, 154
Sample size - 150, 151, 152*n*, 215
Sample statistic - 149, 154
Sampling - 135-36
  basis of - 137-39
  error in - 150-51, 152*n*, 154
  information gained from - 148-49
  types of - 139-48
Sampling distribution - 260-61
Sampling error - 150-51, 152*n*, 154
Sampling frame - 137-39, 154, 207
Sampling interval - 141-42, 154
Sampling unit - 139, 154
Scales - 79-81
Scammon, Richard M. - 62
Scattergram - 292, 304, 307
Schacter, Stanley - 245*n*
Schafer, Marianne - 187*n*
Scheffe, H. A. - 334
Schewe, Charles D. - 185*n*
School busing, sample study of - 9-11
Schuessler, Karl - 310
Schuman, Howard - 186*n*, 189
Scientific knowledge - 1
  acquisition of - 19-22, 33
  characteristics of - 13-19
Scientific law - 19
Sears, David O. - 9-10, 12*n*, 34, 59, 62, 82*n*, 115*n*, 135, 312, 333*n*
Segal, Morley - 221
Selection, as factor affecting internal validity of experimental research - 91, 117
Self-interest model - 9-10
Semistructured interview - 181

Sense of civic competence. *See* Political efficacy
Sensitive questions - 174, 176. *See also* Randomized response techniques
Seymour, Daniel T. - 184*n*
Shaffir, William B. - 245*n*, 246*n*, 247
Shapiro, Robert Y. - 57
Sharp, Laure M. - 184*n*
Sheatsley, Paul - 186*n*
Sheehan, Margaret A. - 210-14, 220*n*
Shimizu, Iris - 187*n*
Shively, W. Phillips - 12*n*, 55*n*, 58, 219*n*, 221
Shosteck, Herschel - 185*n*
Shotland, R. Lance - 225, 244*n*
Shupe, Anson D., Jr. - 233, 245*n*
Shurtleff, Nathaniel B. - 219*n*
Sieber, Joan E. - 245*n*, 247
Sigelman, Lee - 167, 184*n*
Simon, Julian L. - 58
Simple post-test design - 93-94
Simple random samples - 140-41, 150, 152*n*, 154
Singer, Eleanor - 186*n*
Single-sided question - 165, 189
Slope, 294-95, 299-300, 307
Smead, Raymond J. - 187*n*
Smith, Barbara - 85
Smith, H. - 334
Snowball sampling - 148, 153*n*, 154
Social science research
  defining concepts for - 37-43
  formulating hypotheses - 43-54
  proposing explanations in - 33-37
  sample projects in - 3-11
  specifying the question in - 31-33
Social Register - 202
Solomon four-group design - 100-102
Somer's d - 277-81, 307
Specified relationship - 320, 334
Spector, Paul E. - 115*n*, 119
Speeches given by politicians, information on - 201
Speer, Leslie K. - 9-10, 12*n*, 34, 59, 62, 82*n*, 115*n*, 135, 312, 333*n*
Split-halves method - 65-66, 83
Spurious relationship - 319-20, 334
Standard deviation - 258-60, 262, 265
Standard error - 261-62
Standard normal distributions - 262-63
Standardized regression coefficients - 328-29
Stanley, Julian C. - 115*n*, 119
Statistical Abstract of the United States - 198-200
Statistical control - 313-14, 334
Statistical explanation - 18
Statistical regression - 90, 117

~~~~~~~~~

~~~~~~~~~~

DISCHARGED

MAR 2 0 1991
DISCHARGED